AF798857

Exploring the Basic Income Guarantee

Series Editor
Karl Widerquist, Georgetown University in Qatar, Doha, Qatar

Basic income is one of the most innovative, powerful, straightforward, and controversial proposals for addressing poverty and growing inequalities. A Basic Income Guarantee (BIG) is designed to be an unconditional, government-insured guarantee that all citizens will have enough income to meet their basic needs. The concept of basic, or guaranteed, income is a form of social provision and this series examines the arguments for and against it from an interdisciplinary perspective with special focus on the economic and social factors. By systematically connecting abstract philosophical debates over competing principles of BIG to the empirical analysis of concrete policy proposals, this series contributes to the fields of economics, politics, social policy, and philosophy and establishes a theoretical framework for interdisciplinary research. It will bring together international and national scholars and activists to provide a comparative look at the main efforts to date to pass unconditional BIG legislation across regions of the globe and will identify commonalities and differences across countries drawing lessons for advancing social policies in general and BIG policies in particular.

Tijs Laenen

The Popularity of Basic Income

Evidence from the Polls

palgrave
macmillan

Tijs Laenen
KU Leuven
Leuven, Belgium

Tilburg University
Tilburg, The Netherlands

ISSN 2662-3803 ISSN 2662-3811 (electronic)
Exploring the Basic Income Guarantee
ISBN 978-3-031-29351-1 ISBN 978-3-031-29352-8 (eBook)
https://doi.org/10.1007/978-3-031-29352-8

© The Editor(s) (if applicable) and The Author(s), under exclusive license to Springer Nature Switzerland AG 2023
This work is subject to copyright. All rights are solely and exclusively licensed by the Publisher, whether the whole or part of the material is concerned, specifically the rights of translation, reprinting, reuse of illustrations, recitation, broadcasting, reproduction on microfilms or in any other physical way, and transmission or information storage and retrieval, electronic adaptation, computer software, or by similar or dissimilar methodology now known or hereafter developed.
The use of general descriptive names, registered names, trademarks, service marks, etc. in this publication does not imply, even in the absence of a specific statement, that such names are exempt from the relevant protective laws and regulations and therefore free for general use.
The publisher, the authors, and the editors are safe to assume that the advice and information in this book are believed to be true and accurate at the date of publication. Neither the publisher nor the authors or the editors give a warranty, expressed or implied, with respect to the material contained herein or for any errors or omissions that may have been made. The publisher remains neutral with regard to jurisdictional claims in published maps and institutional affiliations.

This Palgrave Macmillan imprint is published by the registered company Springer Nature Switzerland AG
The registered company address is: Gewerbestrasse 11, 6330 Cham, Switzerland

Preface

Basic income is increasingly seen as a very promising cure for some of today's and tomorrow's societal ills, including the persistent problem of poverty, the accelerating trend towards greater income inequality and the imminent threat of mass unemployment. In light of all this, it is often assumed that the idea of basic income is rapidly growing in popularity; not only among academics, activists and politicians, but also among the general public. Although this may appear intuitive and reasonable, the fact of the matter is that our current understanding of popular support for basic income is far from perfect. It is true that recent years have seen a major upsurge in public opinion polls and scientific studies investigating the popularity of basic income. However, these are very much scattered, like trees in a forest, preventing us from seeing the full picture.

Over recent years, I have been involved in a number of initiatives that have aimed to put the pieces together. This all started in 2019 in Belgium, when I hosted an international seminar on public attitudes towards basic income. As the first of its type, the seminar brought together an international group of researchers from different academic disciplines to facilitate the exchange of theoretical ideas and empirical findings, and to explore promising paths for future cooperation. One of these paths resulted in a special issue on the social legitimacy of basic income, published by the Journal of International and Comparative Social Policy a year after the seminar. The main takeaway from both the seminar and the special issue was that popular support for basic income should be studied from a cross-national perspective (as it seems to vary across countries), as well as from a multidimensional perspective (as it also seems to depend on the design characteristics of basic income). Nevertheless, it also became evident that research into the popularity of basic income was—and still is—in its infancy and that much more work needed to be done to gain a better understanding of the subject.

That is where this book steps in. Inspired by the previous work, the book provides the most up-to-date and fine-grained picture of popular support for basic income currently available. It tries to be as comprehensive as possible, but at the same time acknowledges that the evidence presented is not exhaustive and that new evidence will undoubtedly appear after the book has been published. Nevertheless, the book tells you as much as it currently can about the popularity of basic income. In doing so, it is an invaluable source of information for all those who aspire to introduce some sort of basic income in the future. Although public opinion is certainly not the only—and perhaps not even the most important—factor determining the political feasibility of basic income, there can be little doubt that it does play at least some part in taking it from a fictional policy idea to factual policy implementation.

The book should not, however, be seen as an act of activism, unlike many other books on basic income. I am neither in favour of nor against basic income per se. This allows me to study its popularity with an open mind, without having a preconceived point to prove. Although this may seem obvious to the majority of neutral readers, those who are to some degree acquainted with the basic income debate know that the ferocity with which both advocates and opponents defend their—often ideologically oriented—positions often gets in the way of an honest and unbiased discussion. The goal of this book is clearly not to settle the debate and decide whether basic income is, all things considered, a good or a bad idea. Instead, the book's central aim is much more modest than that: to describe how popular basic income is among the general public, using empirical evidence from public opinion polls, and to reflect on the implications thereof for the political feasibility of implementing a basic income in a real-world policy setting.

Leuven, Belgium Tijs Laenen

Acknowledgements

I want to thank everyone who has, in their own unique way, contributed to the making of this book. First, this includes the members of the self-composed advisory committee: Jurgen De Wispelaere, Femke Roosma, Yannick Vanderborght and Wim Van Lancker. Thank you for taking the time to provide expert feedback on the content of the book. Second, I want to thank Marie-Laure Mulayi and Cyrille Francisco for helping me conduct the Basic Income in Belgium Survey, which is used throughout the book. Third, credit is due to Joe Chrisp, Erwin Gielens and Isabelle Stadelmann-Steffen, for openly sharing their survey data with me. Fourth, I want to express my gratitude to Romy Geschiere and Sarah Puijk for the preliminary data analyses they carried out within the framework of their student traineeship under my supervision. Fifth, I would like to thank Richard Bowles and Anne Lee for their thorough language revision. Sixth, I am grateful to Karl Widerquist, the editor of the Guaranteed Basic Income Series, for encouraging me to submit a book proposal. Seventh, I want to thank all staff members of Palgrave Macmillan who helped me through the publishing process. Last, I want to give recognition to the two funding agencies that made the research reported in this book possible: the European Union's Horizon 2020 Research and Innovation Programme (grant number 101023631) and the Belgian Federal Science Policy (grant number B2/191/P3/BABEL).

Praise for *The Popularity of Basic Income*

"Basic income is caught in a policy paradox: the more people support the proposal, the less certain we are that what they favour is really the idea of giving each individual member of a polity an unconditional regular income. Getting a proper handle on the complex reality underlying popular support for the "simple idea" of basic income requires taking a really deep dive into the existing survey evidence as well as the systematic collection and analysis of new data using a diverse range of innovative methods. *The Popularity of Basic Income* does exactly that – and much more! Tijs Laenen has written an insightful and important book that not only tells the reader what to make of the recent surge in popular support for basic income, but also how it affects the prospect of basic income becoming policy reality in our near future. A must-read for anyone taking basic income seriously!"

—Jurgen De Wispelaere, *Visiting Professor, Götz Werner Chair of Economic Policy & Constitutional Theory, University of Freiburg & Adjunct Professor, Faculty of Social Sciences, Tampere University*

"Basic income is increasingly described as an idea whose time has come. But ultimately in liberal democracies its political feasibility will depend, among other things, on the potential support of public opinion. For the very first time, a book examines this issue in a systematic, rigorous, and detailed way. Tijs Laenen, himself an expert in the design and conduct of opinion polls, offers us an invaluable overview of the popularity of basic income across the developed world. His book is an indispensable tool for those who have an interest in the future of basic income and, more generally, in the feasibility of social protection reforms."

—Yannick Vanderborght, *Professor of political science at University of Louvain, Belgium*

Contents

About the Author

Tijs Laenen is a social worker turned social scientist who is currently a Marie Sklodowska-Curie Postdoctoral Fellow at Tilburg University (the Netherlands) and coordinator of the Basic Income in Belgium project at KU Leuven (Belgium). He has previously published articles on popular support for basic income in academic journals, including the Journal of European Public Policy, the International Journal of Social Welfare, the Journal of International and Comparative Social Policy and Acta Politica. Tijs has also written and edited several other books on popular welfare attitudes, including the monograph 'Welfare Deservingness and Welfare Policy. Popular Deservingness Opinions and their Interaction with Welfare State Policies'. For more information about Tijs and his publications, visit www.tijslaenen.com.

Country Abbreviations

AT	Austria
AU	Australia
BE	Belgium
BG	Bulgaria
CA	Canada
CH	Switzerland
CZ	Czech Republic
DE	Germany
DK	Denmark
EE	Estonia
ES	Spain
FI	Finland
FR	France
GR	Greece
HU	Hungary
IE	Ireland
IL	Israel
IS	Iceland
IT	Italy
JP	Japan
KR	South Korea
LT	Lithuania
LU	Luxembourg
MX	Mexico
NL	Netherlands
NO	Norway

NZ	New Zealand
PH	Philippines
PL	Poland
PT	Portugal
RO	Romania
RU	Russia
SE	Sweden
SI	Slovenia
UK	United Kingdom
US	United States

List of Figures

List of Tables

CHAPTER 1

Introduction: How Popular Is Basic Income?

This book is all about finding out how popular basic income is. At first sight, this may seem a very simple question. However, as will become abundantly clear throughout the book, the answer to it proves to be extremely complex. This complexity starts from the fact that the two core concepts embedded in the question—'basic income' and 'popularity'—are not as easy to define as one would intuitively think. Most of the introduction therefore attempts to clarify what these two concepts are actually taken to mean in this book.

With regard to the concept of 'basic income', I will start by discussing the most commonly used definition of what a basic income is: a periodic cash payment unconditionally delivered to all on an individual basis, without any means test or work requirement. Throughout the book, this will be referred to as the 'ideal-typical' version of basic income. History has taught us, however, that a great many differently designed variants of the ideal-typical basic income exist. It is mainly the existence of those other variants that adds complexity to the seemingly simple question of how popular a basic income is, as it is not the popularity of only one type that is the object of study, but rather that of a huge variety of different forms.

Turning to concept of 'popularity', I will explain that this refers to the degree of support there is for the introduction of a basic income among the *general* public. I will argue that there are several interrelated reasons

© The Author(s), under exclusive license to Springer Nature Switzerland AG 2023

T. Laenen, *The Popularity of Basic Income*, Exploring the Basic Income Guarantee, https://doi.org/10.1007/978-3-031-29352-8_1

that studying popular support for basic income is important. The most significant of these is arguably the fact that public opinion constitutes a crucial factor in determining the political feasibility of implementing a basic income scheme in the real world. After establishing *why* studying the popularity of basic income is important, it will be clarified *how* this is accomplished in the book. As the book's subtitle suggests, the popularity of basic income is mainly scrutinized with the help of 'evidence from the polls', referring to public opinion surveys conducted among large samples of the general population in different countries and over different years.

1.1 Basic Income: From a Disarmingly Simple Idea to a Deceptively Simple One

To this day, basic income is very often presented as a disarmingly simple idea (Van Parijs, 2004): 'just give everyone a sum of money on a regular basis, with no questions asked whatsoever'. Could things be any simpler than that? However, at the same time as the basic income debate progresses, it is increasingly acknowledged that things are nowhere near as simple as they seem. First of all, the ideal-typical definition of basic income is remarkably silent about several crucial policy design features, including—among other things—the level and financing of basic income. How generous should it be, and who will end up paying for it? In addition, a glance at both distant and recent policy proposals, pilots and experiments shows that a wide variety of differently designed basic income types exist, which often deviate—albeit in differing degrees—from their ideal-typical counterpart; two well-known examples being a participation income (Atkinson, 1996) and a negative income tax (Friedman, 1962). These types of schemes are often labelled as 'cousins' of basic income. Accordingly, basic income is perhaps better thought of as a family of policies, consisting of the ideal-typical version (its *mater familias*), alongside many different breeds that share some family resemblance with the ideal type, but at the same time have unique features distinguishing them (Martinelli, 2017).

In the following, I first describe the ideal-typical version of basic income as defined by the leading Basic Income Earth Network (BIEN), and point out exactly what is missing from or what is unclear in that definition. After that, a brief overview of basic income's history is provided, in order to demonstrate that there has in fact always been a huge variety of differently designed types. To create some kind of order in the relatively chaotic history of basic income, I continue with a summary of the policy design dimensions that can differ between variants. All this should make very clear why basic income is a *deceptively* simple idea rather than a *disarmingly* simple one. As we will see later on, this observation will also have some very important ramifications for public opinion about basic income.

1.1.1 The Ideal-Typical Basic Income

At least from a layperson's perspective, there seems to be a remarkable degree of agreement about what a basic income is. Around the globe, advocates and activists have rallied around one particular definition, articulated by BIEN—the most prominent international network involved in the promotion of basic income. Their widely accepted definition was heavily influenced by the work of one of the network's co-founders, Philippe Van Parijs (2004), and states that basic income is 'a periodic cash payment unconditionally delivered to all on an individual basis, without means test or work requirement'. Five core characteristics of basic income are recognized in this definition. The first one is that it is paid periodically at regular intervals, in contrast to a one-off payment scheme such as a basic endowment (one of basic income's many cousins) (Ackerman & Alstott, 1999). The second defining characteristic is that basic income is paid in cash rather than in kind; the latter being the case for universal basic services, yet another of the 'cousins' (Gough, 2019). The third characteristic is that basic income is paid to individuals rather than to households, as has been proposed by some basic income advocates (Sanzo & Pinilla, 2004). The fourth core characteristic of the ideal-typical basic income is its universality, meaning that it will be paid to all, without means testing. The fifth characteristic is that basic income is granted unconditionally, without any requirement to work or to demonstrate a willingness to work.

Although the BIEN definition seems as clear as day, it leaves out a number of very important issues concerning policy design. First, it remains unclear what the 'to all' stipulation in the definition actually means. Assuming first that basic income is supposed to be implemented nationally—as suggested in most proposals—does 'all' then refer to all *citizens* or to all *residents* of a country? If the latter is intended, does it refer to everyone who resides in the country or only to those who do so legally? In addition, what about newly arrived migrants? Will there be any residency requirements that need to be fulfilled before the right to a basic income is granted, and if so, can and will those requirements be equal for different types of migrants? In the context of the European Union (EU), for example, it seems somewhat difficult to imagine a national basic income scheme that excludes EU nationals coming from other Member States, as that would probably violate the legal framework of equal rights set within the EU, as well as the spirit of free movement of labour on which the union was founded. The 'to all' stipulation in the BIEN definition could thus equally refer to all citizens or residents of a broader supranational entity, as is the case in proposals for a Europe-wide (Van Parijs & Vanderborght, 2001) or even a worldwide (Pogge, 2001) basic income. At the other end of the spectrum, basic income could also be implemented locally, in specific regions within countries. Different states within the United States (US), for example, could decide to roll out their own version of basic income, as is currently the case in the state of Alaska (Widerquist & Howard, 2012).

Second, BIEN's definition of the ideal-typical basic income does not specify the level at which it should be set. Given the global character of the organization, this makes perfect sense: it is extremely difficult to settle on a fixed, uniform amount across richer and poorer countries alike. Nevertheless, in the accompanying commentary, BIEN does state that the level of basic income should be 'stable in size and frequency and high enough to be, in combination with other social services, part of a policy strategy to eliminate material poverty and enable the social and cultural participation of every individual'. This fits well with most other basic income proposals, which tend to envision an amount somewhere around an agreed-on level of subsistence, so that it covers *basic* needs and provides *basic* income security to all. A basic income could, however, just as well be higher or lower than the subsistence level (Van Parijs, 2004). In fact, although such uniformity is often assumed by basic income advocates, the BIEN definition does not even seem to insist that the benefit amount be equal for all. Instead, it leaves open the possibility that the level of basic income is allowed to vary between individuals with different characteristics—such as their age, place of residence or even their financial means or work history—as long as 'everyone gets something' (De Wispelaere & Stirton, 2004).

Third, exactly what basic income would or would not replace in the existing welfare state is left unspecified. The above-mentioned extract from the BIEN commentary suggests that 'other social services' are to be kept in place, but it is unclear what is actually meant by that. Does this refer exclusively to in-kind services such as healthcare, childcare and education, or does it also include cash transfers such as child benefits, unemployment insurance and old-age pensions? How a basic income could be integrated in an existing system has been a major topic of dispute ever since people started to consider its concrete implementation in any given context. At one extreme, a basic income does not replace a single welfare provision, but should instead be seen as an additional, complementary layer on top of the system already in place. Most advocates nevertheless realize that this is probably unaffordable and perhaps even undesirable, and thus suggest scaling back at least some of the existing provisions. However, they disagree massively about which specific provisions should be replaced, and the stringency with which this ought to happen. While most seem to agree that basic income should supplement rather than substitute in-kind services, there is substantial disagreement about the fate of cash transfers after the implementation of a basic income (Van Parijs, 2004). According to some (mostly left-wing liberals), existing cash benefits should generally remain in place, so that they can provide top-ups for those who are faced with particular social risks such as illness or disability. Others (mostly right-wing conservatives) are much stricter about this, arguing for the elimination of most other cash transfers, as everyone would already receive a basic income and thus enjoy the basic security that comes with it (Murray, 2008). A few even dare to take this a step further by pleading for the total abolishment of in-kind services as well, given that basic income would allow everyone—not just the rich—to pay for these services privately. Such an all-abolishing basic income, located right at the other extreme of the integration debate, is a dream for some but a nightmare for many others.

Fourth, nothing is mentioned in the BIEN definition about the financing of basic income, which is nevertheless a hugely important factor. Many believe that basic income can—at least partially—be 'self-financed' in several ways. The most evident mechanism is to use some of the funds designated for the cash transfers that basic income is intended to replace. This involves both the actual payments of the transfers and the administrative costs necessary to make those payments—which would, in most accounts, be much lower in the case of a cheap and simple-to-administer basic income. Less obvious is perhaps the idea that basic income would mainly finance itself because of its (predicted) positive effects on labour market participation and productivity rates (Van Parijs &

Vanderborght, 2017). However, even with the spread of basic income experiments, this claim presently remains highly speculative. It therefore seems more reasonable that basic income would have to be funded by raising additional revenue. In the bulk of concrete proposals, basic income would be to some extent funded by (an increase in) personal income taxes, of a progressive, proportional or even regressive type (Widerquist et al., 2013). However, countless other funding mechanisms have been proposed, often in addition to income taxation. These include consumption taxes, wealth taxes, climate taxes, revenue from natural resources and money creation (Van Parijs & Vanderborght, 2017).

The key takeaway from all this, is not that all these specific policy design features should be included in the ideal-typical definition of basic income, as they are very likely to be context-specific. A basic income in Belgium, for example, would look very different from one in Belize in terms of its coverage, level, integration and financing. Instead, the key point is that the ideal-typical definition does nothing more than sketch out the very broad contours within which concrete policy proposals can take shape, making basic income a deceptively simple idea, rather than a disarmingly simple one.

1.1.2 The History of the Basic Income Family

One of the best ways to further illustrate the fact that basic income is a deceptively simple idea rather than a disarmingly simple one is to outline its historical development. The history of basic income, as it tends to be told even by the basic income community itself (see, for example, Cunliffe & Erreygers, 2004; Torry, 2021), is actually far more accurately described as a history of differently designed *varieties* of basic income. Some see these as end-of-the-road variations that are considered desirable and/or feasible in their own right, sometimes even more so than the ideal-typical basic income. Others regard them instead as middle-of-the-road stepping stones, the main purpose of which is to help achieve the ultimate goal of introducing the ‘real deal’—that is, the ideal-typical version of basic income—through the back door (Van Parijs & Vanderborght, 2017). Which of the two perspectives is most common is difficult to gauge, but the fact of the matter is that there has always been a huge variety in the types of basic income that have been proposed and piloted throughout history.

Most writings trace the origins of basic income back centuries, to 1795, when the British-American philosopher Thomas Paine advocated something that many consider to be the first-ever basic income proposal. A closer look at Paine's plans, however, reveals that he in fact suggested two varieties of something that would probably not be classified as a basic income according to contemporary standards. His first proposal was more akin to a basic *endowment* than a basic *income*, as it entailed a one-off payment to be paid as people reached adulthood. Paine's second proposal argued for something that we now know as a basic *pension*: a regular cash benefit paid only to the elderly and the disabled. Because both schemes were meant to compensate for the unequal division of an 'equal birthright in natural resources', they were to be funded by some sort of land tax (Cunliffe & Erreygers, 2004: xiv). Shortly after, and partly in response to Paine, a type of basic income was also proposed by the British revolutionary, Thomas Spence. His suggestion, which has been paid far less attention in the basic income literature, was also inspired by the idea that every individual has a fundamental right to society's natural resources (King & Marangos, 2006). Spence argued that all land inherently belongs to the community and should therefore be rented for use. The proceeds thereof were then to be paid as a quarterly dividend, to be divided 'fairly and equally among all the living souls in the parish, whether male or female; married or single; legitimate or illegitimate; from a day old to the extremest age; making no distinction between the families of the farmers and merchants [...] and the families of poor labourers [...], but giving to the head of every family a full and equal share for every name under his roof' (Spence, 1797 in Cunliffe & Erreygers, 2004: 87). Although Spence's scheme seems to meet most of the core characteristics of the ideal-typical basic income, the final part of the quote makes it clear that the payment would probably not have been strictly individual, as promoted by most of today's basic income advocates. Instead, the money would have gone to the 'head of the family', which in those days almost certainly meant it would have been paid to the male breadwinner of the household, who could have then spent it as he wished. This implies that there would have been little assurance that 'every name under the roof' was in fact given his or her fair share of the basic income payment.

In the years after Paine and Spence had published their proposals, many others—often independently of each other—recommended that some type of basic income could be implemented. Right after the turn of the eighteenth into the nineteenth century, the French philosopher Charles

Fourier came up with his so-called 'social minimum': a scheme that some contemporary commentators have designated as an early version of basic income. A closer look at Fourier's social minimum, however, reveals that it was in fact far removed from the ideal-typical basic income, given that it was to be delivered in kind (so not in cash) and restricted to the poor (so not universal). The fact that the social minimum was to be free of work requirements, and thus unconditional, does not seem enough to categorize it as a real basic income (Cunliffe & Erreygers, 2001). Fourier did nevertheless inspire others, such as the relatively unknown Belgian thinker, Joseph Charlier, who proposed something he called a 'territorial dividend'. This was a cash benefit to be paid on a regular basis to every 'indigenous' resident of Belgium, and was to be financed by so-called 'real estate' taxes on land and buildings (Cunliffe & Erreygers, 2001). Although Charlier's proposal seems to tick most of the boxes for an ideal-typical basic income, its universality was severely constrained by the fact that all 'foreigners living in Belgium, and their descendants born in the country until the third generation, cannot participate in the territorial dividends, except in the cases of full naturalization or of reciprocity with their countries of origin, and on condition that the descendants have shown their willingness to be part of the nation' (Charlier, 1894 in Cunliffe & Erreygers, 2001). Thus, even after having obtained Belgian nationality, benefit access would still have been conditional on a willingness-to-integrate requirement for first-generation up to third-generation migrants, making the scheme both less universal and more conditional than most modern-day basic income proposals. However, Charlier's assumption, or better yet his aspiration, was that the dividend would ultimately be calculated globally, thereby making the criterion of nationality obsolete. In that sense, Charlier was perhaps the first to propose some kind of global rather than national basic income scheme.

After the likes of Fourier and especially Charlier had suggested schemes in continental Europe, the focal point of the basic income idea seems to have shifted towards Britain, at least in the first half of the twentieth century. At the end of World War I in 1918, Dennis Milner and his wife Evelyn Mabel (1918), both Quakers, were probably the first to propose a genuinely modern basic income. Their proposal, known as the 'state bonus scheme', can be considered modern in the sense that it was the first not to rely on any 'natural rights to natural resources' arguments and accompanying land taxes (Van Trier, 2018). Instead, they saw the state bonus as a way to ensure that every citizen—rich or poor, working or not—shared in the fruits of the economic progress being made by industrialized Britain at the time. More specifically, Milner and Mabel proposed to pay a flat-rate amount to each citizen on a regular basis out of the revenue from personal income taxes. Although the state bonus scheme never garnered sufficient political support to be implemented, it did influence subsequent proposals made in Britain. Two of these proposals are especially worth mentioning here. The first was from the hand of G. D. H. Cole (1935: 159), who dreamt of a fully planned economy in which there would be 'direct payments from the State to every citizen as a "social dividend"—a recognition of each citizen's claim as a consumer to share in the common heritage of productive power'. According to Cole, the dividend should be equal for all adults, large enough to cover basic necessities and cumulative with wages from labour so as to preserve work incentives. Although Cole was somewhat vague about the precise financing of the social dividend, he seems to imply that interest from capital investments would be completely abolished and replaced by 'new methods of collective provision for the accumulation of capital' (Cole, 1935: 158). In a way, Cole's proposal can therefore be seen as the first to hint at funding basic income—at least partially—through some type of capital gains tax. About ten years later, during World War II, the second noteworthy proposal was published by Lady Juliet Rhys Williams (1943), in response to the famous Beveridge report that was to shape British social policy in the decades to follow. As an alternative to the plans of Lord Beveridge, she proposed the introduction of a regular universal payment to all on an individual basis. Importantly, however, Lady Williams added that these payments should be made 'conditional on willingness to work (for men and single women), or the provision of care (for married women and mothers), to enforce the reciprocity principle' (Miller et al., 2019: 137). It is that conditionality which actually brings the proposal much closer to what we know today as a participation income, distinguishing it from the ideal-typical, *unconditional* basic income.

As is well-known, it was nevertheless Lord Beveridge's plan that eventually won, leading to the institutionalization of various social insurance schemes covering specific social risks, such as sickness and unemployment. Lady William's proposal for a universal payment to all was thereby consigned to the dustbin of history, as have so many basic income proposals been. Nevertheless, there is no denying that the events of the two world wars had sparked widespread recognition of universal suffering, which many felt should be met with universal coverage. This realization surely accommodated the spread of categorical universal schemes aimed at the non-working-age population, most notably children and elderly people. The first universal child allowance was introduced in 1932 in France, but other countries soon followed suit, including Belgium, Germany and Sweden. The first universal pension system came into being in New Zealand in 1937, and was shortly after added to by the Nordic countries (Denmark, Finland and Sweden) and the Netherlands in the 1940s and 1950s. Although such universal schemes are usually left out of tales of the history of basic income (see Van Parijs & Vanderborght, 2017 for an exception), they deserve a place there because they share some important family resemblance with the ideal-typical version. Universal pensions and child allowances are very similar to basic income in the sense that they grant benefit access on the basis of citizenship or residency, rather than work history (as social *insurance* schemes do) or financial means (as social *assistance* schemes do). This is why they are often considered as promising stepping stone policies, paving the way for the introduction of a fully fledged basic income for all. Occasionally, there have also been suggestions to treat basic pensions and child allowances as end products in their own right, instead of merely stopovers.

In the 1960s and 1970s, basic income was mainly discussed in the US, albeit under the name of a negative income tax (NIT). This all began when two very prominent economists—who were both to become Nobel Prize winners some time later—proposed their version of an NIT: Milton Friedman (1962) and James Tobin (1966). Although the specifics of their proposals varied, they were both convinced that an NIT would contribute much more to solving the persistent problem of poverty than did the messy mix of welfare programmes introduced under President Lyndon B. Johnson's famous 'war on poverty'. In simple terms, an NIT provides a direct cash payment in the form of a tax credit to all those whose income does not reach a predefined level, without any attached work-related requirements. The fact that an NIT would be unconditional in the sense of being obligation-free is *the* main reason why so many consider it as part of the broader basic income family. At the end of the day, an NIT nevertheless remains a selective policy that excludes people with an income above a certain threshold. How far an NIT is removed from a basic income then depends on the level at which that threshold is set: the higher the level, the more income categories are included, and the closer we get to the ideal-typical, *universal* basic income. Most NIT proposals, however, opt for a relatively low income threshold, so that only the poor can benefit from it. This was also what the two main candidates in the 1972 US presidential campaign (George McGovern for the Democrats and Richard Nixon for the Republicans) had in mind when they included their own versions of an NIT in their electoral programmes (Van Parijs & Vanderborght, 2017). McGovern's plan was to pay a sum of $1000 a year to each American, which would then be partially clawed back through the tax system so that it would ultimately benefit mostly low-income families. However, his 'demogrant' proposal was considered highly unrealistic at the time and was never really taken seriously. This stands in stark contrast to Nixon's proposal, called the 'Family Assistance Plan' (FAP), which was taken into serious consideration by Congress and almost made it into legislation, were it not for concerns by the Democrats that the value of the cash payment was too low, as well as for Republican worries that the programme would sap work incentives (Caputo, 2012). To this day, many commentators continue to argue that the discussion of Nixon's FAP in the US Congress is the closest that any industrialized nation has come to implementing a basic income (Widerquist & Sheahan, 2012). A more detailed look at the programme, however, shows that it was in fact very different from the ideal-typical basic income as we know it today. One important qualification is that the FAP was restricted (as the name already suggests) to poor *families*, leaving childless people to fend for themselves. On top of that, notwithstanding a few exceptions, people had to prove they were willing to work in order to receive the cash payment. This shows that the FAP was anything but a universal and unconditional basic income, which was also exactly how Nixon wanted it to be:

> This national floor under incomes for working or dependent families is not a 'guaranteed income'. Under the guaranteed income proposal, everyone would be assured a minimum income, regardless of how much he was capable of earning, regardless of what his need was, regardless of whether or not he was willing to work. Now, during the presidential campaign last year, I opposed such a plan. I oppose it now and I will continue to oppose it, and this is the reason: A guaranteed income would undermine the incentive to work; the family assistance plan that I propose increases the incentive to work. A guaranteed income establishes a right without any responsibilities; family assistance recognizes a need and establishes a responsibility. It provides help to those in need and, in turn, requires that those who receive help work to the extent of their capabilities. (Quote

taken from Richard Nixon's address to the nation on August 8, 1969; reported in Caputo, 2012: 269)

The 1960s and 1970s were also a period during which there were several scientific experiments investigating the effects of an NIT—four in the US and one in Canada (Widerquist, 2018). Although some see these as the first series of *basic income* experiments, it has to be said that all the programmes being tested were not universal because they were targeted at low-income households only. So too was the only programme similar to basic income that was actually introduced in the US in that period: the Earned Income Tax Credit (EITC). Originally enacted in 1975 and gradually expanded in the subsequent decades, the EITC is a type of NIT that is paid out as a yearly tax credit to workers whose earned income falls below a threshold determined by the federal government (Leff et al., 2019). The fact that the EITC is restricted only to low-income *workers* surely takes it even further away from the ideal-typical basic income. As some nevertheless believe, the programme may well be the most viable road to a fully fledged basic income in the US, as it could easily be 'expanded into a negative income tax by removing the link to earnings, and could then be further expanded into a basic income' (Shafarman, 2004: 205).

It can, however, also be argued that the US already has a basic income scheme in place, albeit not a nationwide one. Since 1982, every legal resident of the state of Alaska has received a uniform cash payment each year from the Permanent Fund Dividend (PFD), which is financed by the state's oil revenue (Widerquist & Howard, 2012). By doing this, the programme meets all the core characteristics of the ideal-typical basic income: it is paid periodically, in cash, to every resident and without a means test or a work requirement. Regardless of this, many refuse to categorize it as such, for three main reasons. The first is that the amount of the PFD is often considered as too low for it to be labelled as a genuine basic income, given that it does not come anywhere near the subsistence level needed to guarantee a decent standard of living. Alaska's PFD is, in other words, closer to a 'partial' basic income (which is so low that it is unlikely to replace existing social benefits) than it is to a 'full' basic income—which provides a higher level of payment and could therefore be seen as a substitute for other benefits. The second reason is that the amount varies too much from year to year. Although nothing in the ideal-typical definition says that the amount should always be the same, this is implicitly assumed by most basic income advocates (De Wispelaere, 2015). Third, one could say that the PFD is only equal for all because it was implemented regionally in the state of Alaska, rather than nationally across the US. The programme's main policy champion, Governor Jay Hammond, originally wanted to make the benefit level proportional to the length of legal residence, rather than paying it as a flat-rate amount, as in most other basic income proposals. He indeed strongly believed that higher amounts should be paid to people who had lived in Alaska for a longer period of time. He was, however, held back by the US Supreme Court, which regarded the proposal as an act of unjust discrimination against fellow Americans moving to Alaska from other states (Grog & Erickson, 2012).

After the NIT proposals and experiments in the US, the basic income debate went relatively silent in the 1980s and 1990s, at least for the broader audience. Behind the scenes, a movement was nevertheless steadily growing, and beginning to study basic income in greater detail and advocate it with greater passion than ever before. This movement culminated in 1986, with the establishment of the Basic Income European Network (BIEN), which later turned into the Basic Income Earth Network (in 2006), as the basic income debate went global. As mentioned earlier, BIEN's definition of basic income is without doubt still the most widely accepted, which is why it was labelled as the ideal-typical version. However, this does not mean that there has been full unanimity since BIEN issued its definition. Throughout the 1990s, proposals continued to be made for different types of basic income, often inspired by—and responding to—the standard definition provided by BIEN. Just a few examples are mentioned here to illustrate the continued diversity within the broader basic income family. The first was from the hand of Nobel Prize winner James Meade (1990), who envisioned that in his ideal society—called 'Agathotopia'—all existing social benefits would be replaced by a single basic income scheme providing generous cash payments to all Agathotopians, with no strings attached. Unlike many other basic income advocates, Meade was also relatively specific about how to finance this basic income:

> The reliance on pollution tax (whose incentive effects are socially desirable) rather than on taxes, such as the income tax (whose disincentive effects on work and enterprise are undesirable), enabled a given level of real Basic Income to be maintained at a markedly lower social cost. [...] Another

> form of tax employed by the Agathotopians to finance a really adequate Basic Income is the imposition of a special surcharge on the first slice of every citizen's income other than the Basic Income itself. This is a form of levy which in effect withdraws part of the Basic Income as a citizen's other income increases, a levy which is additional to the ordinary current rate of tax on income. (Meade, 1990 in Widerquist et al., 2013: 202)

Interestingly, Meade's second funding mechanism implies that the basic income itself ought to be taxed and thus, in effect, decrease as earnings increase. This stands in stark contrast to most other proposals, which see basic income as a non-withdrawable benefit that has to come *on top of* any earnings from other sources. This principle of accumulation is the main reason why, many argue, basic income would strengthen rather than weaken work incentives (Van Parijs & Vanderborght, 2017). By making basic income taxable, Meade set a limit to the extent to which it could be accumulated with other earnings. This discussion is less important with regard to the second example of a policy proposal that is similar to, but at the same time different from, the ideal-typical basic income: the basic endowment. Although it has a rich history of its own, going way back to Thomas Paine (Cunliffe & Erreygers, 2004), the most elaborate proposal for a basic endowment probably came from Bruce Ackerman and Anne Alstott (1999). They suggested the introduction of a so-called 'stakeholder grant'—a lump sum disbursed to citizens (and *only* citizens) when they reach adulthood. It is often argued that the only real difference between this and the ideal-typical basic income is that the stakeholder grant would not be paid periodically, but only once in a lifetime (Van Parijs & Vanderborght, 2017). There are, however, other differences. The most important one is arguably the fact that in contrast to the ideal-typical basic income, a stakeholder grant is not always fully unconditional. This is because—at least in the Ackerman and Alstott plan—there are two very specific requirements citizens would have to meet before they could receive any money: to graduate from secondary school and to have a spotless criminal record.

Adding some ingredient of conditionality to the recipe of basic income was also the intention of the two final examples of basic income proposals made in the 1990s. The most well-known of these is arguably the participation income suggested by Anthony Atkinson (1996). He proposed instituting a universal cash payment granted to all citizens, on the condition that they engage in labour or other socially appreciated activities such as caregiving, studying or volunteering. How far such a participation income is removed from the ideal-typical, *unconditional* basic income eventually depends on the combination of three factors: (1) the range of activities a society labels as 'participation', (2) the distance of those activities to paid work and (3) the strictness with which participation is enforced in everyday policy practice. A similar taste for imposing conditionality can be found in our last illustrative example: the sabbatical grant, proposed by Claus Offe and Johan de Deken (1999). This type of grant is similar to a basic income, except for the fact that it is conditional on prior employment and is limited in duration. The aim is to prevent people 'living off' state benefits for a prolonged period of time, leading to welfare dependency. Instead, a sabbatical grant would 'allow people to leave the workforce temporarily for any reason whether they were unemployed, couldn't find good enough work, wanted to take care of an infant or a sick relative, or even if they simply wanted to take some time off. But people would have to return to the labor force eventually' (Widerquist et al., 2013: xviii).

These and other types of basic income proposals were commonplace throughout the 1990s and continued to be so in the early 2000s. At the end of the day though, they were all just that: *proposals*. None of them were ever actually translated into legislation. This all changed in 2004, when Brazilian President Lula Da Silva ratified an official basic income law for the first time ever (Coêlho, 2012). After years of struggle, the policy's most prominent advocate, Senator Eduardo Suplicy, finally saw his dream fulfilled when Brazil enacted a law stipulating that every Brazilian would be periodically granted a universal and unconditional cash payment. The basic income as it was written in the law, however, never made it to policy implementation, mainly because of one particular clause stating that the basic income had to comply with Brazil's overall economic policy, which policymakers to this day continue to argue it does not. Instead, Brazil has taken the road of the *Bolsa Familia* as its main anti-poverty programme—a policy that some regard as a stepping stone towards the ideal-typical basic income, but that is at the moment quite far removed from it, for two main reasons. The first is that the *Bolsa Familia* is not universal, but targeted at low-income families only. The second reason is that it is not obligation-free but conditional on children's school attendance. This brings it closer to being a 'conditional cash transfer' (CCT), a type of policy that has been making headway for some time now in much of Latin America. Taken together, it seems that Brazil is the only country in the world where basic income is formally written into the law, but has become 'lost in legislation' along the way (De Wispelaere, 2015).

Perhaps one of the key reasons why basic income was never really implemented in Brazil has to do with the sizeable uncertainty over the effects it would produce. At the time, little was known about the impact a basic income would have on crucial policy outcomes such as poverty, income inequality, employment, productivity and many others. A real turning point in this regard was the launch of the first experimental pilot project with an actual basic income—rather than a negative income tax—conducted in Namibia between 2008 and 2009 (Haarmann et al., 2019). During that period, all permanent residents below the age of 60 living in two specific villages, Otijvero and Omitara, received a relatively small but universal and unconditional cash transfer each month. Importantly, this excluded people who moved to the village *after* the pilot had started. While this choice was of course important for the credibility of the experiment itself (as there would otherwise have been an overlap between the treatment and control group), it was probably to some extent also driven by fears that the basic income would attract people living in other parts of the country, who would not have moved to one of these villages in the absence of the pilot scheme. This resonates quite well with the widespread belief that a basic income—whether implemented locally or nationally—could work very much like a welfare magnet, attracting a substantial number of migrants (Scharpf, 2000). During the course of the Namibian pilot, there indeed proved to be a notable amount of inward migration, mostly by extended family members of the pilot participants (Haarmann et al., 2019). As a result, the basic income—which was supposed to be strictly aimed at individuals—unintentionally turned into a form of household-based basic income, shared among all members of the household, including those who were in fact not entitled to it.

Such a household-based basic income was introduced for real a few years later, by accident, in Iran. In 2011, the Iranian government decided to replace its long-standing price subsidies programme with a scheme paying out regular cash transfers to Iranian citizens (Karshenas & Tabatabai, 2019). Originally, the plan was to target these transfers at low-income households only, through the use of means testing. It quickly turned out, however, that there was great public resistance against the use of a means test, and even more importantly, that the administrative apparatus proved incapable of executing it. To deal with this, Iran switched to a universal scheme to which every household could apply on its own initiative, which—perhaps much to the government's surprise—they did to a massive extent. In some ways, Iran's version of basic income is very similar to the Alaskan PFD, given that both of them are financed mainly from oil revenue, albeit through somewhat different mechanisms, with Alaska using a sovereign wealth fund and Iran using the revenue accrued from the sharp increase in the price of domestically produced oil. There are nevertheless some important differences. The first is that, relatively speaking, the Iranian scheme provides somewhat higher amounts than the Alaskan one, bringing it closer to a full basic income. The second difference is that Iran does not pay the basic income to each *individual*—as Alaska does—but to the head of each *household*. It is mainly in this regard that the Iranian version of basic income deviates from the ideal type, which is strictly individual. The third difference is that Iran did not implement its basic income scheme regionally, in the way that Alaska did. Accordingly, Iran is now the only country in the world where some kind of basic income has been introduced on a nationwide basis.

Introducing a national basic income scheme was also the subject of a people's referendum held in Switzerland a few years later; regarded by many as another very important milestone in the history of basic income. More specifically, a group of activists managed to collect a sufficiently high number of signatures from Swiss citizens to make basic income the object of a legally binding popular vote. Although the proposal left many design features unspecified, such as its funding, it was clear from the campaign leading up to the referendum that the amount of basic income would be relatively generous, at around 2500 Swiss francs (CHF) per month. Other than that, voters were told that the basic income would be paid to each Swiss citizen, without a means test or work requirement, thereby conforming to all of the core characteristics of the ideal-typical basic income. Although the basic income proposal was rejected by a clear majority of the Swiss electorate in June 2016—some 77% voted against it (Colombo et al., 2016)—the popular initiative did attract a wave of media attention and sparked lively academic and political discussions around the globe. Especially in Europe, the Swiss referendum gave a major push to the basic income debate, leading to increased attention paid to the basic income experiments that would take place in the ensuing years in different European countries.

On closer inspection, however, all of the basic income schemes that were tested in the European experiments deviated significantly from the ideal-typical version. The 2017–2018 Finnish experiment, which has received most attention so far, was the first of its kind to be organized on a national scale (Kangas et al., 2021). It paid a randomly selected group of people a (relatively modest) basic income of €560 per month, which they could limitlessly accumulate with earnings from other sources. Importantly, however, the selected group were all *unemployed* people between the ages of 25 and 58, who were chosen because policymakers were primarily interested in the effects of basic income on labour market participation. Therefore, what the Finnish experiment actually piloted was a *categorically* universal scheme limited to a delineated target group, rather than a true universal basic income for all. A similar issue arises with the basic income experiments—otherwise known as the trust experiments—conducted in several municipalities in the Netherlands from 2017 to 2020 (van der Veen, 2019). There, the experiments were restricted to the recipients of means-tested social assistance, who were (1) exempted from the usual job-seeking obligations and (2) allowed to top up their social assistance benefit with earnings from other sources (albeit to a limited extent). The same applies to the B-Mincome experiment conducted in about the same period in one of the poorer areas of Barcelona, Spain (Bollain et al., 2019). In this case, the basic income under testing was also far from universal, as the experiment provided regular cash payments only to low-income households while relaxing the work requirements and the withdrawal rates they are commonly confronted with under the existing welfare system. Overall, the basic income schemes that were tested in the Dutch and the Spanish experiments thus deviated quite significantly from their ideal-typical counterpart, as they were not universal but selectively targeted at the poor and they did not take the individual but the household as the unit of entitlement.

While Europe—and by extension, the whole world—was still trying to make sense of the results that came out of the basic income experiments, almost every country was struck hard by a global pandemic from early 2020 onwards. Bringing economic and social life to a near standstill, COVID-19 caused a major upsurge in the appeal of basic income as a radical but required alternative to the welfare state. Around the globe, the call for basic income began to ring louder than ever before. While some argued that it was the right time to implement a basic income permanently, others were more cautious and pleaded for a temporary 'emergency' basic income to soften the widespread negative effects of the pandemic (De Wispelaere & Morales, 2021). In Europe, a cross-national group of basic income advocates saw the COVID-19 crisis as the perfect moment to launch a second European Citizen's Initiative (ECI) in 2020, years after a first attempt had been unsuccessful. This initiative, which pleads for the introduction of an unconditional basic income across the EU—without specifying in any detail what is actually meant by that—did not succeed in obtaining the necessary number of signatures. Nevertheless, this does illustrate that basic income seems to have gained momentum once again because of the COVID-19 pandemic.

It is extremely difficult to predict what the future has in store for basic income. However, it seems very likely that its future will continue on the same path as its past: as an 'exceedingly simple idea' with a 'surprisingly diverse pedigree' (Van Parijs, 2004: 7).

1.1.3 The Policy Design Dimensions of Basic Income

A glance at the rather chaotic history of basic income has taught us that there is a large assortment of differently designed varieties. To create some order out of that chaos, I distinguish 12 policy design dimensions on which concrete basic income schemes can vary. These are mostly taken from the work of De Wispelaere and Stirton (2004), and Philippe Van Parijs and Yannick Vanderborght (2017). These dimensions, depicted in Fig. 1.1, should be looked at as the building blocks that policymakers

BASIC INCOME		
Accumulation	Administration	Conditionality
Duration	Financing	Frequency
Generosity	Individuality	Integration
Modality	Uniformity	Universality

Fig. 1.1 The policy design dimensions of basic income

take with them to the drawing table when working out the blueprints for any basic income scheme. They are, in other words, the policy design dimensions that need to be taken into account before basic income can move from a fictional idea to factual implementation. In the following, I will briefly describe what the different design dimensions entail and will provide some examples of the huge number of concrete policy options available to policymakers within each dimension. I will return to most of the policy design dimensions in somewhat greater detail when discussing their relationship with public opinion in Chapter 3.

The first of the policy design dimensions (listed in alphabetical order), *accumulation*, refers to the extent to which basic income may be combined with earnings from other sources, such as work or capital investments. While most proposals argue for unlimited accumulation, there are some who oppose this and would rather see that at least some part of the basic income is withdrawn—mostly through taxes—as earnings rise above the level of basic income. Although most agree that any marginal tax rate higher than zero could be detrimental to work incentives, many regard setting a limit to the accumulation of basic income with other earnings as an effective way to directly reduce its costs (Meade, 1990).

The second design dimension, *administration*, often tends to be ignored in the literature (De Wispelaere, 2015). It concerns the crucial issue of how and by whom basic income will be administered. For example, will the administration be handled by state bureaucracies? If so, which ones will be involved? In the case of a negative income tax, administration would logically be entrusted to the tax authorities, whereas in the case of basic income, other administrative agencies are called for. Further, what role will the social partners, most notably the trade unions, play in the administration of a scheme that will in all probability no longer be conditional on work?

The third dimension, *conditionality*, has to do with the obligations attached to benefit receipt: how conditional will basic income be on the fulfilment of work-related or other activities? As discussed earlier, the ideal-typical version of basic income stipulates that there should be no conditions whatsoever. There are, however, plenty of other proposals deviating from that principle, demanding at least some form of conditionality in return for the receipt of the regular cash payments provided by basic income. The most prominent of these is arguably Anthony Atkinson's (1996) participation income, which is conditional on the fulfilment of some sort of socially appreciated activity, such as training, caring or volunteering. There are others, however, who suggest being stricter in imposing conditionality by making basic income accessible only after proving past employment or present job-seeking efforts (e.g. Offe & De Deken, 1999).

The fourth dimension, *duration*, refers to the period of time during which basic income can be received. Although the ideal-typical definition does not mention it, most commentators seem to agree that basic income is supposed to be a life-long entitlement, received from the cradle to the grave. However, many concrete proposals envision a temporary version of basic income, either because they want to limit the number of years for which it can be paid (Offe & De Deken, 1999), or because they restrict it to specific age groups (Torry, 2019). With regard to the latter, suggestions have frequently been made to limit basic income—at least initially—to under-aged children, to working-age adults or to pensioners. In any of these scenarios, the implication is that entitlement will cease to exist once people fall out of the respective age category, thereby making it de facto temporary.

The fifth dimension, *financing*, pertains to the various mechanisms that can be put in place to fund a basic income scheme. The bulk of proposals suggest personal income taxes as the main funding source. There is stronger disagreement, however, about the specific set-up of these taxes: should they be progressive (levying a higher tax share on higher earners), proportional (levying an equal tax share on everyone) or even regressive (levying a higher tax share on lower earners)? In addition, a large number of alternative funding mechanisms have been put forward by basic income advocates. Quite a few proponents propose a basic income financed by revenue from natural resources, as is done in Alaska and Iran (cf. supra). Other than that, it has been discussed that basic income could be financed from other types of taxes, including capital and climate taxes, or from other sources such as money creation (Van Parijs & Vanderborght, 2017). Lastly, many argue that if a basic income is to replace other welfare schemes, the money saved from that operation could be directly used to fund a basic income.

The sixth dimension, *frequency*, concerns the regularity of basic income payments. While the ideal-typical version requires basic income to be paid out on a regular basis, it does not actually specify what this means. Thus, if policymakers decide to implement a basic income, they will need to decide whether it should be paid weekly, monthly, yearly or even at another time interval. As we have seen above, however, there is one particular type of basic income that deviates from the principle of regularity: the basic endowment or stakeholder grant (e.g. Ackerman & Alstott, 1999). Under such an arrangement, the cash payment is provided only once in a lifetime.

The seventh dimension, *generosity*, refers to the level of basic income. Most proposals set the amount of basic income at or around the prevailing level of subsistence within the society in which it will be implemented (De Wispelaere & Stirton, 2004). Others suggest amounts that are either less generous or more generous. Advocates of a lower-than-subsistence version of basic income usually argue that its level should be relatively low—or at least lower than the minimum wage—because it would otherwise undermine the incentive to work. By contrast, proponents of a higher-than-subsistence version of basic income tend not to give much credence to the story of generous benefits being bad for work incentives. Instead, they often argue that a generous basic income is the most promising road to securing real freedom for all, because it will allow people to turn down so-called 'shitty jobs' characterized by very low wages and poor working conditions (see discussion in Van Parijs & Vanderborght, 2017).

The eighth dimension, *individuality*, concerns the unit at which basic income is targeted. In its ideal-typical version, basic income is strictly individual, as that supposedly guarantees the greatest degree of real freedom for all (Van Parijs, 2004). Some proposals, however, suggest taking the household instead of the individual as the primary unit of entitlement (Sanzo & Pinilla, 2004), for two main reasons. The first is administrative: some suggest it would be a great deal simpler to target households if many of the existing welfare schemes are already targeted at households. In that case, basic income can simply 'piggy-back' onto the administrative modus operandi of the current system (De Wispelaere, 2015). The second reason is financial: taking the household as the target unit is cheaper because it allows economies of scale to be taken into account. Multi-member households tend to have lower living costs than single-member households, as the former can buy home appliances together, share the rent or mortgage and so on. Accordingly, people living together require less money to fulfil their basic needs, which is why some proposals take the household as the unit of entitlement, so that the amount of basic income can be varied in line with the household size (De Wispelaere & Stirton, 2004).

The ninth dimension, *integration*, refers to the position basic income takes within the broader welfare system: will it supplement or substitute existing schemes? If the latter, which ones? According to the likes of Milton Friedman (1962) and Charles Murray (2008), the existing welfare system ought to be fully dismantled and replaced by a single cash payment, in the form of a negative income tax or basic income, respectively. At the opposite end of the spectrum, there is the view that the existing system should be kept (almost) entirely intact, which then involves adding basic income as an additional layer to the welfare provisions already in place. In reality, most proposals are situated somewhere in between these two extremes, replacing some existing schemes while keeping others (Van Parijs & Vanderborght, 2017).

The tenth dimension, *modality*, concerns the particular form taken by a basic income. The ideal-typical definition clearly stipulates that it should be provided as a cash transfer. Nevertheless, it has been suggested that basic needs can also be met—and possibly in an even better way—by so-called 'universal basic services', providing people with accessible and free in-kind support such as healthcare, education and childcare (see, for example, Gough, 2019). Although most argue that a universal basic income and universal basic services are supplements rather than substitutes, there are some who feel that it is generally a bad idea to provide people with cash, as there is always the risk of it being used for 'socially irresponsible' behaviour, such as drug and alcohol abuse. As a response, basic income could also be provided through a voucher system, lying somewhere in between a pure cash transfer and a pure in-kind service. Under such a proposal, everyone would be given vouchers that can only be used to purchase the goods and services required to fulfil basic necessities such as food, shelter and clothing.

The eleventh dimension, *uniformity*, relates to the way in which the benefit level is determined. Most proposals are based on a uniform amount, even though the ideal-typical definition of basic income does not require this. Accordingly, many other proposals allow the level of basic income to vary between people with different characteristics. Most of the time, these characteristics refer to people's needs, so that higher amounts are paid to those who have a greater need. This can refer to either financial needs or health needs, and usually boils down to giving a more-generous basic income to, respectively, people with a lower income or to those who are sick or disabled. Given the administrative complexity of assessing individual-level needs, however, many basic income advocates resort to group-level proxies of need. For example, it is sometimes suggested that amounts should be adjusted to the local cost of living, so that people residing in more-expensive regions (or countries) receive higher payments (De Wispelaere & Stirton, 2004). Another proposal is to increase the basic income in line with the size of the household, or alternatively the number of under-aged children in the household. People's needs can also be taken into account by setting different levels of basic income for different age groups (Torry, 2019). This usually means that children would be granted lower amounts than adults. Nevertheless, a distinction is also often made between the working-age and the old-age population within the adult group, with the former being granted lower amounts because they can still earn a living through paid employment.

The twelfth and last dimension, *universality*, refers more broadly to benefit access: who is entitled to and eligible for basic income? Most advocates argue that basic income should be universal, by which they usually mean that it is not selective, in two main ways. First, basic income is not *categorically* selective in the sense of being restricted to certain categories within the population—such as the old, the unemployed or children—as are most existing welfare provisions. Second, basic income is not *financially* selective in the sense that access is not limited to poor people through the application of some type of means test. At the same time, however, there are plenty of proposals that do envision a basic income that is selective in nature, by restricting it to certain groups (such as in a basic *pension*) or to poor people (for example, a negative income tax). Additionally, those who argue for a fully universal basic income tend to be somewhat vague about what that universality actually entails. It is indeed often left unspecified whether benefit access would be granted on the basis of citizenship or on the basis of residency, and whether there would be any requirements regarding the minimum length of citizenship or residency needed to qualify for basic income. These are, however, crucial issues to consider when designing a basic income scheme, especially in light of widespread concerns about potential welfare magnet effects on migrants (Scharpf, 2000).

1.2 The Popularity of Basic Income

Especially in recent years, it has often been said that basic income is rapidly growing in popularity. This usually refers to the vastly increased amount of attention and support from academics, activists and politicians across the world. This is *not*, however, how popularity is understood in this book. Instead, here the popularity of basic income is defined as the extent to which the general public—the man and woman in the street—supports its implementation in the country where they live. How much popular support is there for introducing basic income? To what extent does such support differ across countries and evolve over time? Also, to what extent do *specific* groups within the *general* public—such as trade unionists or different party electorates—endorse or oppose basic income? Before addressing these questions, the remainder of the introductory chapter does two things. First, it explains *why* it is important to know how popular basic income is. Second, it describes *how* the popularity of basic income is examined in this book.

1.2.1 The Importance of Studying the Popularity of Basic Income

There are at least three interrelated reasons why the popularity of basic income is a very important topic of study. The first concerns the basic income part of the topic. Despite its rich history, basic income has lived in the shadows for a very long time, regarded by many as a silly, utopian idea. Accordingly, it has lost battle after battle against its main competitors: social insurance, social assistance and universal but categorical schemes (Van Parijs & Vanderborght, 2017). It was not until recently, in the last two decades or so, that basic income grew considerably closer to mainstream thinking about welfare provision. Today, basic income is more than ever seen as a promising and realistic alternative to the welfare systems currently in place, mainly because it has the potential to mitigate some old but unresolved—as well as future—societal ills. Indeed, after years and years of conditional and selective welfare provision, we are still nowhere near to eradicating poverty, we have not been able to put an end to the persistent problem of income inequality and we continue to struggle with high levels of structural unemployment. On top of that, many of these ills are expected to worsen in the future due to the rapidly accelerating automation, digitalization and flexibilization of human labour. Whether basic income is the most effective and efficient way of dealing with these issues remains to be seen, and is a matter of scientific study. What matters here is that many commentators are adamant that it would be effective, which is why the political salience and relevance of basic income has skyrocketed in the last few years.

While the first reason makes clear why basic income is an exceptionally important topic to study *tout court*, the second and the third explain why it is imperative to know about its *popularity* among the general public. They nevertheless do so in different ways, because they relate to different types of feasibility. The second and probably most important reason that we should gain knowledge about the popularity of basic income starts from the old idea that public opinion is a crucial factor for the *political* feasibility of introducing a particular policy in a particular polity. A large body of literature argues that especially in democracies, policymakers are responsive to the public's wishes to some extent, either because they have electoral incentives to do so or because they feel it is their moral duty to respect the voice of the people (Brooks & Manza, 2006; Page & Shapiro, 1983). Accordingly, it has been widely recognized that public opinion constitutes a hugely important factor for the political feasibility of introducing a basic income scheme (De Wispelaere & Noguera, 2012). It seems indeed highly unlikely that politicians would take the risk of implementing a basic income without the active support—or at least silent approval—of the general public, as that could cost them (and the political party they are affiliated with) dearly in any future elections. This is probably why Malcolm Torry (2019: 529), the creator of the first *Palgrave International Handbook of Basic Income*, argued that 'the more that is known about public opinion about Basic Income, and particularly the more that is known about the detail of that opinion, the better informed will be the debate about the idea's political feasibility'.

Studying popular support for basic income allows us to expose the political constituencies that may be mobilized in favour of it or against it. If a public opinion poll conducted among a representative sample of the general public finds, for instance, that about 70% support the introduction of a basic income in their country, it could be argued that public acceptance is sufficiently large for basic income to be considered politically feasible. However, things tend to be somewhat more complex than that, in the sense that policy responsiveness not only works through across-the-board levels of support among the public at large (general responsiveness), but also through the levels of support found among specific groups within the general public (group-specific responsiveness) (Ezrow et al., 2010; Gilens, 2012). For politicians and their parties, it is all about keeping their current voting constituencies on board, while at the same time trying to attract important new ones. Most socialist parties, for example, will strive to implement policies that are in line with the demands of the working class, or even more specifically, of labour market insiders represented by organized trade unions. Thus, exploring the heterogeneity in public opinion towards basic income is absolutely crucial for exposing the potential political constituencies in favour of—or against—its introduction in a real-world policy setting.

It is nevertheless important to note that the claim here is certainly *not* that the political feasibility of basic income is single-handedly driven by public opinion, or that it is most decisively so. Other actors in the policymaking arena are just as important as the general public (and possibly even more important) in determining the political feasibility of a policy. The most influential actors are of course the protagonists of policymaking: the elected politicians themselves. Most of them will certainly have opinions of their own concerning basic income, and it seems unlikely that they would push hard for a policy they personally dislike (for whatever reason), just because it is liked by the public. Going beyond that, some politicians may actually favour the introduction of basic income and feel strengthened by public approval of it, but decide not to act on it because they are being held back by coalition partners with whom they have to co-operate, or by party leaders they rely on for political survival. In addition to politicians, there are of course plenty of other stakeholders whose opinions are important for the political feasibility of basic income. These include, to name but a few, policy administrators such as civil servants and social workers, and organized interest groups such as trade unions and employers' associations. All these actors play their part, in addition to public opinion, in determining the political feasibility of basic income, although they are not studied in great detail in this book. Wherever possible, however, the book does compare levels of support for basic income among relevant subgroups of the general public, including trade union members, public sector employees and the self-employed. It is nevertheless fully acknowledged here that the opinions of 'the base' could well differ from those at 'the top': trade unionists and self-employed people, for example, may think very differently about a basic income than their official representatives do, while the latter tend to have greater political power to influence the political feasibility of a policy.

Additionally, the political feasibility of basic income is also influenced by other types of feasibility, including administrative and financial aspects (Torry, 2016). No reasonable politician will want to push for a basic income scheme, no matter how popular it is, if that scheme proves to be administratively impractical and financially irresponsible. This brings us to the third reason for it being important to study the popularity of basic income: hostile public opinion can in the long run threaten its financial sustainability. There are at least two mechanisms through which this could happen. The first, overt mechanism concerns the occurrence of tax revolts, in which citizens openly express their deep-seated dissatisfaction with the taxes that are needed to finance a basic income, and demand that the government scales them down (Wilensky, 1975). If there is enough public pressure, governments may indeed do exactly that, thereby undercutting their financial capacity to continue funding a generous basic income. The second, covert mechanism involves the spread of tax fraud and tax evasion, which is likely to increase if and when citizens do not accept the policies they are obliged to pay taxes for. The proponents of basic income generally believe that it will be free from fraud—unlike social assistance and social insurance schemes, its selective and conditional counterparts (Van Parijs & Vanderborght, 2017). They tend to have a blind spot, however, for the serious threat that citizens will avoid paying taxes in order to maximize their personal gains from a basic income scheme. Every basic income scheme financed at least partly from (income) taxation will have net contributors, who pay more in taxes than they receive in benefits, and net beneficiaries, who receive more in benefits than they pay in taxes (Torry, 2016). However, basic income involves the fact that it is relatively easy for someone to turn from a net contributor into a net beneficiary, simply by lowering their market income. In that light, the real jackpot is won when people manage to earn a market income through undeclared work, as that income will not be taxed to fund the basic income but will nevertheless be topped up by it. As a result, there would no longer be a natural incentive under a basic income scheme to declare your work and income truthfully to the tax authorities. This is very different in social insurance systems for example, where access is conditional on legal employment and amounts are often earnings-related. In the absence of such a natural incentive, the tax system needed to fund a basic income would either have to be monitored with extreme rigour by state bureaucracies, or would have to rely on the goodwill and compliance of citizens. It seems obvious that the latter is much easier to achieve if most citizens support, rather than oppose, basic income itself.

1.2.2 How to Study Popular Support for Basic Income

This book brings together all the currently available, but scattered, information on the popularity of basic income among the general public. It mainly does so by presenting the results from a series of quantitative public opinion polls held in different years and different countries (see Table 1.1). With regard to the time dimension, however, it should be noted that most polls on basic income were conducted after 2015, in response to the rapidly growing political salience of the matter. Nevertheless, as there have been sporadic surveys since the first survey item on basic income in 1989, at least some picture has emerged of how public support for basic income has subsequently evolved. For the geographical dimension, it has to be stated that the debate on the popularity of basic income has not gone as global as the debate on basic income itself. The bulk of public opinion polls have been held in relatively rich and well-developed parts of the world—most notably Europe, North America, Japan and South Korea. Even though this reduces the country variation, the fact of the matter is that less-developed countries simply tend to lack the necessary resources and infrastructure needed to organize large-scale surveys among the general public.

The first polls on basic income go back to the late 1980s and early 1990s, when the International Social Survey Programme (ISSP) included an item examining respondents' agreement with the idea that 'government should provide everyone with a guaranteed basic income'. This item has, however, been widely criticized for not specifying what a basic income actually is. Given that a basic income has never been implemented anywhere—except for in Iran and Alaska, where it is not actually labelled as such—it simply cannot be taken for granted that everyone has a clear and similar understanding of the notion of basic income. Indeed, there are some opinion polls showing that most people are not very familiar with the term. For example, a survey conducted by Dalia Research in 2017 across various European countries shows only about 25% of the respondents stated that they 'fully understand' the concept of basic income. The remaining 75% either knew 'something' about basic income (40.6%), had heard 'only little' about it (24.1%), or had 'never' even heard of it (10.2%) (Delsen & Schilpzand, 2019). These findings are also corroborated by qualitative research asking people to describe what they think basic income is. For example, one recent study shows that Dutch citizens had limited prior knowledge of basic income, despite living in a country

Table 1.1 Overview of the public opinion polls analysed in the book

Year	*Survey*	*Countries*	*Chapter*
1989, 1994	International Social Survey Program (ISSP)—Social Inequality modules I & II	AU, AT, BG, CA, CZ, CH, DE (East), DE (West), IT, HU, NL, NZ, PH, PL, RU, SE, SI, UK, US	2
1995	Tisser Solidarity Survey	NL	2, 4
2000	Factorial survey experiment by Liebig and Mau (2004)	DE	3
2001	Eurobarometer 56.1	AT, BE, DE (East), DE (West), DK, ES, FI, FR, GR, IE, IT, LU, NO, PT, UK	2
2001	Opinion on Social Welfare Survey (reported in Le Clainche, 2004)	FR	2
2002	Gallup of Finland and TEMO Sweden (reported in Andersson & Kangas, 2004)	FI, SE	2, 3
2003	Ipsos MMI (reported in Bay & Pedersen, 2006)	NO	2, 3
2009	Questionnaire Survey on the Community Life and Welfare (reported in Takamatsu & Tachibanaki, 2014)	JP	2, 3
2015, 2017	Dalia Research	DE, FR, ES, IT, UK, PL (other countries N < 1000)	2, 4
2016	Conjoint experiment by Stadelmann-Steffen and Dermont (2019)	CH, FI	3
2017	Ipsos MORI (reported in Chrisp et al., 2020)	UK	2, 3, 4
2016/17	European Social Survey (ESS), Round 8	AT, BE, CH, CZ, DE, EE, ES, FI, FR, HU, IE, IL, IS, IT, LT, NL, NO, PL, PT, RU, SI, SE, UK	2
2017	Ipsos	BE, CA, DE, ES, FR, IT, MX, PL, SE, UK, US	2, 4
2017, 2018	German Socioeconomic Panel (SOEP) (reported in Adriaans et al., 2019)	DE	2
2018	Survey within the Finnish basic income experiment	FI	4

(continued)

Table 1.1 (continued)

Year	*Survey*	*Countries*	*Chapter*
2019	Survey experiment by Jordan et al. (2022)	US	4
2018, 2020	Populus	UK	2, 3, 4
2019	Survey on European Dreams for the Future of Europe	BE, CZ, DE, ES, FR, GR, HU, IT, NL, PL, PT, SE, RO, UK	2
2019	Conjoint experiment by Rincon (2021)	ES, FI	3
2019/20	Belgian National Elections Study (BNES)	BE	2
2020	Gallup Panel	US	2
2020	Pew Research Centre	US	2
2020	Survey by Richards and Steiger (2021)	US	4
2020	Survey by Nettle et al. (2021)	UK, US	2
2020	Yougov	DE, ES, FR, IT, PL, PT	3, 4
2021	Basic Income in Belgium (BABEL) Survey	BE	3, 4
2021	Basic Income in the Netherlands (BIN) Survey	NL	3
2021	Public Perception Survey on Basic Income	KR	4
2021	Survey experiment by Yeung (2022)	US	4
2021	Survey experiment by Thomas et al. (2023)	US	4

with a relatively rich history of discussions on the matter (Rossetti et al., 2020). It turns out that—at least initially—basic income was often misunderstood as being a minimum wage or minimum income protection. This demonstrates that asking about 'basic income' in a survey without specifying its details involves the risk that people interpret it as a means-tested social assistance scheme of the conditional type rather than as a universal and unconditional basic income (Chrisp et al., 2020).

To deal with people's unfamiliarity with basic income, surveys gradually started explaining what it entails—in greater or lesser detail—by stipulating some of its policy design features. This strategy should provide people with the information they need to indicate their level of support for the not-yet policy of basic income. In Round 8 of the European Social

Survey (ESS), for example, respondents were asked how they felt about the introduction of a basic income that is (a) paid to all individuals on a monthly basis, (b) sufficient to cover essential living costs and to guarantee everyone a minimum standard of living, (c) a substitute for many other social benefits, (d) equal for all, (e) granted irrespective of work status and other earnings, and (f) financed through taxes. Some critics continue to argue, however, that most people will still find it too difficult to articulate an informed opinion about a non-existing policy as complex as basic income. Usually, these critics rely on the so-called 'file-drawer model' of public opinion, which assumes that people have fixed preferences stored as 'files' in an imaginary drawer, which they then bring out when asked about them in a survey setting (Zaller, 1992). Accordingly, if people are unfamiliar with the notion of basic income, they are unlikely to have a file on the subject in their drawer, and are therefore unable to give an informed opinion about it in a survey. This is miles away, however, from the reality we tend to observe in qualitative in-depth interviews (Laenen et al., 2021; Rossetti et al., 2020). These usually demonstrate quite clearly that people who were at first unfamiliar with the concept of basic income are perfectly capable of understanding what it entails after it is explained to them. Accordingly, these studies also show that most people are indeed able to express their support for—or opposition to—the potential introduction of a basic income in the country they live in. This is also confirmed by the typically relatively low proportion of respondents choosing the 'don't know' answer option in quantitative surveys asking about basic income (see Chapter 2).

Regardless of the fact that people can and will state their support for, or opposition to, basic income in a public opinion poll, there are nevertheless those who argue that this means preciously little for its political feasibility. After all, is ticking a box on a survey questionnaire not a classic example of what Jurgen De Wispelaere (2015) has called 'cheap political support'? It is certainly true that the significance of survey answers should not be overstated. People who answer 'yes' to basic income in a survey are not all fierce advocates, eager to passionately promote its real-world implementation. Likewise, not all the people who say 'no' to basic income in a survey are fierce opponents, seeking to penalize every politician who even hints at the idea of implementing it. At the same time, however, the significance of survey responses to basic income should also not be understated. As explained above, a high level of popular support for basic income makes it considerably less risky for policy entrepreneurs to push for its introduction. It is nevertheless not enough to look exclusively at the *absolute* level of support for basic income. In each policymaking arena, basic income has to compete with other policies, including means-tested social assistance, contributory social insurance and many others. This makes it extremely important to also analyse the *relative* level of support for basic income in comparison with competing policy schemes (Rincon, 2021). If it turns out that basic income is popular, but less so than some of the alternatives, then this will be bad news for its political feasibility. After all, why would electorally motivated and responsive politicians opt for a policy scheme that is less popular than others—especially others that are already in force?

1.2.3 Outline of the Book

The remainder of the book is structured as follows. Chapter 2 starts off by analysing popular support for the ideal-typical version of basic income. It deals with both absolute and relative levels of support for the ideal type, and investigates how these have evolved over time and how they vary across countries. The chapter also scrutinizes how support for the ideal-typical basic income differs between individuals with different characteristics. More specifically, the focus is on people's social-structural position (for example, age and income) and their ideological orientations (such as political ideology and deservingness beliefs).

Chapter 3 broadens the scope by also investigating popular support for other, differently designed varieties of basic income that deviate in some way from the ideal-typical definition. Here, I examine which types of basic income are most (un)popular, in which contexts and for whom. The chapter's core argument is that popular support for basic income indeed depends on its policy design. To demonstrate this argument empirically, I mostly use data from newly conducted vignette experiments (Auspurg & Hinz, 2015) that asked respondents to rate fictional descriptions of concrete basic income schemes that randomly vary on the different policy design dimensions discussed earlier (see Fig. 1.1).

At the same time, it is acknowledged that support for basic income is not only affected by its policy design on the input side, but also by its policy outcomes on the output side. Chapter 4 therefore focuses on the reasons people have for supporting, or opposing, basic income. In doing so, it draws a rough distinction between *practical* and *principled* support, with the first referring to support (or opposition) based on arguments about the (promised/predicted) outcomes of basic income—such as its effects on poverty, income inequality and labour supply—and the second involving support (or opposition) based on arguments related to the expected normative virtues or vices of basic income—such as its capacity to ensure real freedom for all or its vulnerability to promoting laziness.

Lastly, Chapter 5 ties this all together by summarizing what we know about the popularity of basic income and discussing the main implications for its political feasibility. It also identifies remaining gaps in our knowledge and offers suggestions for future research.

References

Ackerman, B., & Alstott, A. (1999). *The Stakeholder Society*. Yale University Press.

Adriaans, J., Liebig, S., & Schupp, J. (2019). In Germany, Younger, Better Educated Persons, and Lower Income Groups Are More Likely to Be in Favor of Unconditional Basic Income. *DIW Weekly Report, 15*, 127–134.

Andersson, J. A., & Kangas, O. (2004). Popular Support for Basic Income in Sweden and Finland. In G. Standing (Ed.), *Promoting Income Security as a Right: Europe and North America* (pp. 285–298). Anthem Press.

Atkinson, A. (1996). The Case for a Participation Income. *The Political Quarterly, 67*(1), 67–70.

Auspurg, K., & Hinz, T. (2015). *Factorial Survey Experiments*. Sage.

Bay, A., & Pedersen, A. (2006). The Limits of Social Solidarity: Basic Income, Immigration and the Legitimacy of the Universal Welfare State. *Acta Sociologica, 49*(4), 419–436.

Bollain, J., Groot, L., Miller, A., Schmidt, E., Tahiraj, E., Verlaat, T., & Yi, G. (2019). A Variety of Experiments. In M. Torry (Ed.), *The Palgrave International Handbook of Basic Income* (pp. 407–435). Palgrave Macmillan.

Brooks, C., & Manza, J. (2006). *Why Welfare States Persist: The Importance of Public Opinion in Democracies*. Chicago University Press.

Caputo, R. (Ed.). (2012). *Basic Income Guarantee and Politics*. Palgrave Macmillan.

Chrisp, J., Pulkka, V. V., & Rincon, L. (2020). Snowballing or Wilting? What Affects Public Support for Varying Models of Basic Income? *Journal of International and Comparative Social Policy, 36*(3), 223–236.

Coêlho, D. B. (2012). Brazil: Basic Income—A New Model of Innovation Diffusion. In M. C. Murray & C. Pateman (Eds.), *Basic Income Worldwide. Horizons of Reform* (pp. 59–77). Palgrave Macmillan.

Cole, G. D. H. (1935). *Principles of Economic Planning*. Macmillan & Co.

Colombo, C., De Rocchi, T., Kurer, T., & Widmer, T. (2016, Juni). *Analyse der eidgenössichen Abstimmung vom 5.* GfS Bern.
Cunliffe, J., & Erreygers, G. (2001). The Enigmatic Legacy of Charles Fourier: Joseph Charlier and Basic Income. *History of Political Economy, 33*(3), 459–484.
Cunliffe, J., & Erreygers, G. (Eds.). (2004). *The Origins of Universal Grants. An Anthology of Historical Writings on Basic Capital and Basic Income.* Palgrave Macmillan.
Delsen, L., & Schilpzand, R. (2019). Individual Preferences for the Unconditional Basic Income in the European Union. In L. Delsen (Ed.), *Empirical Research on an Unconditional Basic Income in Europe* (pp. 29–60). Springer.
De Wispelaere, J. (2015). *An Income of One's Own? The Political Analysis of Universal Basic Income* (Unpublished doctoral dissertation). University of Tampere.
De Wispelaere, J., & Morales, L. (2021). Emergency Basic Income During the Pandemic. *Cambridge Quarterly of Healthcare Ethics, 30*, 248–254.
De Wispelaere, J., & Noguera, J. (2012). On the Political Feasibility of Universal Basic Income: An Analytic Framework. In R. Caputo (Ed.), *Basic Income Guarantee and Politics. International Experiences and Perspectives on Income Guarantee* (pp. 17–39). Palgrave Macmillan.
De Wispelaere, J., & Stirton, L. (2004). The Many Faces of Universal Basic Income. *The Political Quarterly, 75*(3), 266–274.
Ezrow, L., De Vries, C., Steenbergen, M., & Edwards, E. (2010). Mean Voter Representation and Partisan Constituency Representation: Do Parties Respond to the Mean Voter Position or to Their Supporters? *Party Politics, 17*(3), 275–301.
Friedman, M. (1962). *Capitalism and Freedom.* University of Chicago Press.
Gilens, M. (2012). *Affluence & Influence. Economic Inequality and Political Power in America.* Princeton University Press.
Gough, I. (2019). Universal Basic Services: A Theoretical and Moral Framework. *The Political Quarterly, 90*(3), 534–542.
Grog, C., & Erickson, G. (2012). The Improbable but True Story of How the Alaska Permanent Fund and the Alaska Permanent Fund Dividend Came to Be. In K. Widerquist & M. W. Howard (Eds.), *Alaska's Permanent Fund Dividend. Examining its Suitability as a Model* (pp. 15–39). Palgrave Macmillan.
Haarmann, C., Haarmann, D., & Nattrass, N. (2019). The Namibian Basic Income Grant Pilot. In M. Torry (Ed.), *The Palgrave International Handbook of Basic Income* (pp. 357–472). Palgrave Macmillan.
Jordan, S., Ferguson, G., & Haglin, K. (2022). Measuring and Framing Support for Universal Basic Income. *Social Policy & Administration, 56*(1), 138–147.

Kangas, O., Jauhiainen, S., Simanainen, M., & Ylikännö, M. (2021). *Experimenting with Unconditional Basic Income. Lessons from the Finnish BI Experiment 2017–2018*. Edward Elgar Publishing.

Karshenas, M., & Tabatabai, H. (2019). Basic Income by Default: Lessons from Iran's 'Cash Subsidy' Program. In M. Torry (Ed.), *The Palgrave International Handbook of Basic Income* (pp. 339–356). Palgrave Macmillan.

King, J. E., & Marangos, J. (2006). Two Arguments for Basic Income: Thomas Paine (1737–1809) and Thomas Spence (1750–1814). *History of Economic Ideas, 14*(1), 55–71.

Laenen, T., Mulayi, M. L., Francisco, C., & Van Lancker, W. (2021). *Basic Income in Belgium (BABEL) Survey Codebook V1*. Centre for Sociological Research, KU Leuven. https://osf.io/7ghfs/

Le Clainche, C. (2004). Public Support for Basic Income Schemes and a Universal Right to Health Care: What the French People Think. In G. Standing (Ed.), *Promoting Income Security as a Right: Europe and North America* (pp. 401–426). Anthem Press.

Leff, B., Percy, A., Story, M., & Szlinder, M. (2019). Alternatives to Basic Income. In M. Torry (Ed.), *The Palgrave International Handbook of Basic Income* (pp. 213–231). Palgrave Macmillan.

Liebig, S., & Mau, S. (2004). A Legitimate Guaranteed Minimum Income? In G. Standing (Ed.), *Promoting Income Security as a Right: Europe and North America* (pp. 207–228). Anthem Press.

Martinelli, L. (2017). *Assessing the Case for a Universal Basic Income in the UK* (IPR Policy Brief). University of Bath.

Meade, J. (1990). What Can We Learn from the Agathotopians? *Il Politico: rivista Italiana di scienze politiche, 55*, 5–16.

Miller, A., Yamamori, T., & Zelleke, A. (2019). The Gender Effects of a Basic Income. In M. Torry (Ed.), *The Palgrave International Handbook of Basic Income* (pp. 133–153). Palgrave Macmillan.

Milner, M., & Mabel, E. (1918). *Scheme for a State Bonus*. Simpkin, Marshall & Co.

Murray, C. (2008). Guaranteed Income as a Replacement for the Welfare State. *Basic Income Studies, 3*(2). https://doi.org/10.2202/1932-0183.1115 [online only]

Nettle, D., Johnson, E., Johnson, M., & Saxe, R. (2021). Why Has the COVID-19 Pandemic Increased Support for Universal Basic Income? *Humanities & Social Sciences Communications, 8*(1), 1–12.

Offe, C., & De Deken, J. (1999, November 5). *Work, Time, and Social Participation. Policy Options for Dealing with Labor Market Precariousness*. Paper Presented at the Workshop "Back to Full Employment? Employment Subsidies vs Sabbatical Grants", Brussels.

Page, B. I., & Shapiro, R. Y. (1983). Effects of Public Opinion on Policy. *American Political Science Review, 77*(1), 175–190.

Pogge, T. W. (2001). Eradicating Systemic Poverty: Brief for a Global Resources Dividend. *Journal of Human Development and Capabilities, 2*(1), 59–77.

Rhys Williams, J. (1943). *Something to Look Forward To. A Suggestion for a New Social Contract*. Macdonald & Co.

Richards, D. R., & Steiger, T. L. (2021). Value Orientations and Support for Guaranteed Income. *Social Science Quarterly, 102*(6), 2733–2751.

Rincon, L. (2021). *The Paradox of Universality: Preferences for Universal Basic Income in Finland and Spain* (Unpublished doctoral dissertation). Universitat de Barcelona.

Rossetti, F., Roosma, F., Laenen, T., & Abts, K. (2020). An Unconditional Basic Income? How Dutch Citizens Justify Their Opinions About a Basic Income and Work Conditionality. *Journal of International and Comparative Social Policy, 36*(3), 284–300.

Sanzo, L., & Pinilla, R. (2004). A Household Basic Income. In K. Widerquist, J. A. Noguera, Y. Vanderborght, & J. De Wispelaere (Eds.), *Basic Income: An Anthology of Contemporary Research*. Wiley Blackwell.

Scharpf, F. W. (2000). Basic Income and Social Europe. In R. van der Veen & L. Groot (Eds.), *Basic Income on the Agenda. Policy Objectives and Political Chances* (pp. 155–160). Amsterdam University Press.

Shafarman, S. (2004). Mobilizing Support for Basic Income. In G. Standing (Ed.), *Promoting Income Security as a Right: Europe and North America* (pp. 195–206). Anthem Press.

Stadelmann-Steffen, I., & Dermont, C. (2019). Citizens' Opinions About Basic Income Proposals Compared—A Conjoint Analysis of Finland and Switzerland. *Journal of Social Policy, 49*(2), 383–403.

Takamatsu, R., & Tachibanaki, T. (2014). What Needs to Be Considered When Introducing a New Welfare System: Who Supports Basic Income in Japan? In Y. Vanderborght & T. Yamamori (Eds.), *Basic Income in Japan. Prospects for a Radical Idea in a Transforming Welfare State* (pp. 197–218). Palgrave Macmillan.

Thomas, C. C., Walton, G. M., Reinhart, E. C., & Markus, H. R. (2023). Mitigating Welfare-Related Prejudice and Partisanship Among U.S. Conservatives with Moral Reframing of a Universal Basic Income Policy. *Journal of Experimental Social Psychology, 105*. https://doi.org/10.1016/j.jesp.2022.104424 [online only]

Tobin, J. (1966). The Case for an Income Guarantee. *The Public Interest, 4*, 31–41.

Torry, M. (2016). *The Feasibility of Citizen's Income*. Palgrave Macmillan.

Torry, M. (Ed.). (2019). *The Palgrave International Handbook of Basic Income*. Palgrave Macmillan.

Torry, M. (2021). *Basic Income: A History*. Edward Elgar Publishing.
van der Veen, R. (2019). Basic Income Experiments in the Netherlands? *Basic Income Studies, 14*(1). https://doi.org/10.1515/bis-2018-0023 [online only]
Van Parijs, P. (2004). Basic Income: A Simple and Powerful Idea for the Twenty-First Century. *Politics & Society, 32*(1), 7–39.
Van Parijs, P., & Vanderborght, Y. (2001). From Euro-Stipendium to Euro-Dividend. *Journal of European Social Policy, 11*(4), 342–346.
Van Parijs, P., & Vanderborght, Y. (2017). *A Radical Proposal for a Free Society and a Sane Economy*. Harvard University Press.
Van Trier, W. (2018, January 3–5). *Scheme for a State Bonus and the Early Roots of the Basic Income Idea in the UK*. Paper Presented at the HES Sponsored Session "Basic Income: The Past and the Present", AEA-ASSA Conference, Philadelphia.
Widerquist, K. (2018). *A Critical Analysis of Basic Income Experiments for Researchers, Policymakers, and Citizens*. Palgrave Macmillan.
Widerquist, K., & Howard, M. W. (Eds.). (2012). *Alaska's Permanent Fund Dividend. Examining its Suitability as a Model*. Palgrave Macmillan.
Widerquist, K., Noguera, J. A., Vanderborght, Y., & De Wispelaere, J. (Eds.). (2013). *Basic Income: An Anthology of Contemporary Research*. Wiley Blackwell.
Widerquist, K., & Sheahan, A. (2012). The United States: The Basic Income Guarantee—Past Experience, Current Proposals. In M. C. Murray & C. Pateman (Eds.), *Basic Income Worldwide. Horizons of Reform* (pp. 11–30). Palgrave Macmillan.
Wilensky, H. (1975). *The Welfare State and Equality: Structural and Ideological Roots of Public Expenditure*. University of California Press.
Yeung, E. S. (2022). Can Conservatives Be Persuaded? Framing Effects on Support for Universal Basic Income in the US. *Political Behavior*. https://doi.org/10.1007/s11109-022-09824-z [online first]
Zaller, J. R. (1992). *The Nature and Origins of Mass Opinion*. Cambridge University Press.

CHAPTER 2

Popular Support for the Ideal-Typical Basic Income

This chapter investigates popular support for the ideal-typical version of basic income, broadly defined as a periodic cash payment unconditionally delivered to everyone on an individual basis, without any means test or work requirement. Some claim that asking about the popularity of such a basic income is actually a rhetorical exercise: *of course* it will be popular among the general public. At least two reasons are often given to support this assumption. The first is that people will come to see and appreciate the positive outcomes a basic income produces after it has been implemented (Delsen & Schilpzand, 2019). The idea here is that most people will learn to love basic income after noting that it reduces poverty and income inequality, enhances work incentives, boosts employment rates, provides real freedom for all, and so on. In anticipation of that, so the argument usually goes, it is the job of advocates and activists to 'educate' the public, by informing them about the positive effects of basic income (Shafarman, 2004). However, this is a somewhat risky strategy for politicians seeking re-election. Beyond the existence of a few pilots and experiments, we are still very much in the dark about the specific policy outcomes a fully fledged basic income would produce were it to be introduced. These outcomes could, in reality, also prove to be mostly negative, thereby eroding rather than building popular support for basic income. In addition to that, the argument starts from a somewhat outdated, elitist view on public opinion—that it can easily be steered in any direction

© The Author(s), under exclusive license to Springer Nature Switzerland AG 2023

T. Laenen, *The Popularity of Basic Income*, Exploring the Basic Income Guarantee, https://doi.org/10.1007/978-3-031-29352-8_2

policy entrepreneurs see fit. However, it seems very doubtful that people, especially adults with a well-developed ideological outlook on life, can still be 'educated' so easily in the current day and age. Accordingly, it should not be taken for granted that people will come to love basic income simply because they are told that it will yield positive outcomes.

The second reason that it may be a rhetorical exercise to ask about basic income's popularity is rooted in the disarmingly simple idea that everyone will support it because it offers everyone 'free money' with no strings attached (Shafarman, 2004). Who in their right mind would oppose having a cash payment deposited regularly into their bank account? However, similar to the notion of basic income itself, this line of reasoning is in fact *deceptively* rather than *disarmingly* simple. It will seldom be the case that everybody wins under a basic income scheme, as the cash being paid out to all will of course also have to be paid for by someone. It tends to be true that there is no such thing as a free lunch, as so eloquently argued by Milton Friedman, one of the most prominent promoters of a negative income tax. Most basic income schemes will have to be financed by some sort of taxation—be it income, consumption, ecological, wealth or some other type—and will therefore foster not only net beneficiaries, but also net contributors. From a self-interest perspective, it follows that while the former are likely to support the introduction of a basic income, because they will gain more income than they lose, the latter are bound to oppose it, because they will lose more income than they gain. This type of argument has been widely used in the past to explain why means-tested welfare programmes are supposed to be unpopular: they split the population into two groups—poor beneficiaries versus better-off benefactors—and thereby reduce support among the second group that loses out financially (Laenen & Gugushvili, 2021). However, this issue is rarely raised when it comes to universal basic income, which may be just as vulnerable as means-tested programmes to the threat of fierce opposition from the net contributors. After all, it will not take long for political opponents of basic income to make these people aware of the fact that they have more to lose from basic income than they stand to gain from it.

Even if people are unaware of—or indifferent about—their personal gains and losses from a basic income scheme, there is yet another important qualification to the simple story that basic income will generate its own support base because everyone loves to receive 'free money'. That is, basic income will also go to *other* people, who may be considered undeserving of it. Many commentators indeed argue that the ideal-typical version of basic income is likely to generate widespread opposition from the general public because a substantial proportion of its recipients are generally regarded as unworthy of government aid (Steensland, 2008). Due to its universality, basic income will be paid to those who are not really in need of it as well as those who are. The main concern here is that it would be unfair to waste scarce public resources on better-off people from the middle and upper classes who are perfectly capable of living comfortably without a basic income. Further, due to its unconditional nature, basic income will also be granted to those who contribute little to the society in which it is introduced. The main worry here is that it would be unfair to give a regular cash handout to able-bodied people who are not working and perhaps have no intention of doing so in the near future. Some even go as far as saying that most workers would quickly start to feel exploited by non-workers under a basic income scheme, and therefore come to oppose it (Delsen, 2019).

Combined with the argument that basic income is likely to trigger opposition from its net contributors, the deservingness argument leads to the exact opposite prediction to the one we started out with, in that basic income will be *unpopular* among the general public. It is a matter for empirical research, however, to find out which of these opposing predictions is closest to the truth. Therefore, in the remainder of this chapter, I first piece together all the available information from public opinion polls on basic income, conducted in different years and different countries. This allows an assessment of the overall, across-the-board level of popular support for basic income, and to see how it has evolved over time and how it varies between countries. Additionally, I will explore how support for basic income varies among individuals with different characteristics. As the discussion above already suggests, it is highly unlikely that all the groups within a particular society will feel exactly the same about introducing a basic income. Instead, individual differences in social-structural position and ideological orientations are likely to lead to diverging opinions on the matter (Roosma & van Oorschot, 2020). Taken together, the evidence presented in this chapter offers the most complete picture to date of popular support for the ideal-typical version of basic income.

2.1 Across the Board

2.1.1 The First Opinion Polls on Basic Income

To the best of my knowledge, the first methodologically sound public opinion poll on basic income dates back to the late 1980s, when the International Social Survey Programme (ISSP) included an item on basic income in its first Social Inequality module. More specifically, the item asked people from nine different countries to indicate their agreement or disagreement with the statement that 'government should provide everyone with a guaranteed basic income'. As shown in Fig. 2.1, about half of the respondents thought that their government should indeed do so. There is, however, considerable cross-national variation in the results, with support ranging from a high of 79.4% in Hungary to a low of 21.3% in the US—the latter being a clear outlier. Importantly, however, the ISSP item fails to explain what it actually means by a 'guaranteed basic income', as it lacks details about the design characteristics of the policy. For example, it is unclear from the description that basic income is supposed to be fully universal (paid to rich and poor alike) and fully unconditional (paid to those who work and to those who do not). Accordingly, it seems plausible that people did not have the ideal-typical basic income in mind when responding to the ISSP question. They could just as well have been thinking about other types of basic income—such as a participation income—or even about some of basic income's selective and conditional counterparts—such as means-tested social assistance.

There are nevertheless several valid reasons for discussing the ISSP item in a chapter about the popularity of the ideal-typical version of basic income. First, the item is sometimes presented *as if* it measures public opinion about the ideal type. This is mostly done by committed advocates of basic income, who see the relatively high levels of support found in most countries as strong evidence that the ideal-typical basic income is in fact very popular among the public, making the policy also politically feasible. As I will show later on, however, there seems to be a significant fall in popular support for the ideal-typical version of basic income when its design details are laid out to people more clearly. Second, the item was repeated verbatim in the subsequent round of the ISSP in 1994, as well as in the Eurobarometer in 2001, and it remains the only item that can be directly compared over time in different countries. Third, the item is interesting because it can be compared with another one included in the ISSP (and the Eurobarometer), gauging support for one of basic income's

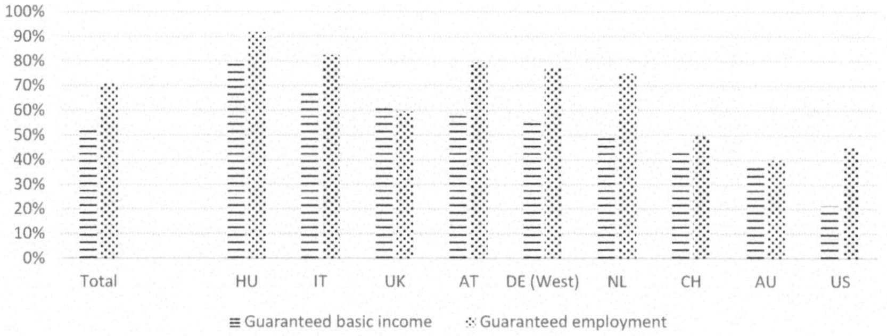

Fig. 2.1 Support for guaranteed basic income and guaranteed employment, 1989 (*Source* ISSP [1989]. Question wording: 'The government should provide everyone with a guaranteed basic income' and 'The government should provide a job for everyone who wants one'. The graph shows the percentage of respondents agreeing [strongly] with these statements)

policy competitors: guaranteed employment. There are indeed some who argue that it would be better to provide everyone with a paid job—with the state acting as an employer of last resort—than to give everyone an unconditional cash payment (Leff et al., 2019). This makes it relevant to find out how popular a guaranteed basic income is, *relative* to guaranteed employment.

Data from the 1989 ISSP, shown in Fig. 2.1, demonstrates that a guaranteed *income* programme is less popular than a guaranteed *employment* equivalent. In each participating country, the general public seems to prefer the government to provide jobs rather than cash (although the difference is negligible in Australia). Even in the US, where support for basic income was lowest, almost 45% of respondents supported guaranteed employment. These findings suggest that basic income clearly loses out to guaranteed employment in terms of public opinion. A few years later, however, when the ISSP repeated these question items in 1994 (see Fig. 2.2), this gap became significantly smaller: support for basic income appears to have caught up with support for guaranteed employment. In Hungary, West Germany and the Netherlands, for example, basic income became about equally as popular as guaranteed employment. This is the case for many other countries, especially Eastern and Central European ones. In the United Kingdom (UK) and Australia, basic income actually became the more popular policy of the two; as is also the case for Canada

Fig. 2.2 Support for guaranteed basic income and guaranteed employment, 1994 (*Source* ISSP [1994]. Question wording: see Fig. 2.1. The graph shows the percentage of respondents agreeing [strongly] with the statements. DE-E = former East Germany. DE-W = former West Germany)

and New Zealand. By contrast, in the US—the only other Anglo-Saxon country in the sample—basic income remained less popular than guaranteed employment in 1994 (Italy also shows a similar degree of stability over time). In Austria and Sweden, there appears to be also less support for basic income than for guaranteed employment in 1994.

In 2001, the same items were repeated again in a survey conducted in a selection of EU Member States (see Fig. 2.3). The general pattern here is that support for basic income and guaranteed employment is just about equal at a very high level: almost eight out of ten believe that government should provide both things. In most countries, the level of support for the two policies is very close, except for Finland and Norway, where basic income is more popular, and Germany (East and West) and Portugal, where guaranteed employment is more popular.

Taken together, the findings from the ISSP and the Eurobarometer teach us three general lessons about popular support for (an unspecified) basic income. First, there proves to be considerable cross-national variation: basic income is more popular in some countries than it is in others. This variation is explored in greater detail below, when discussing the findings from cross-national surveys that provide a definition of basic income. Second, support for basic income varies over time, but the precise trajectory differs between countries. While support for basic income grew stronger in some countries—such as Italy, where it rose

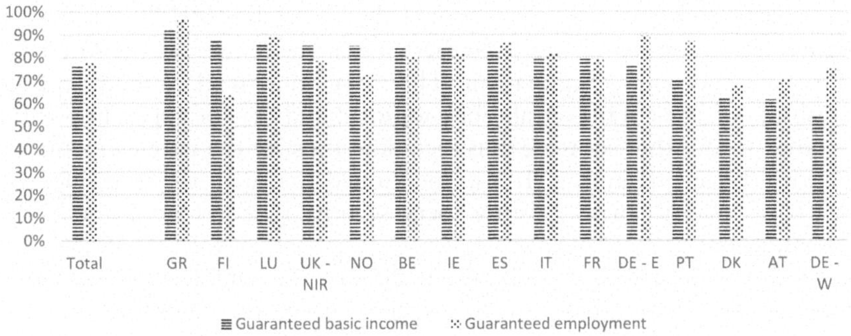

Fig. 2.3 Support for guaranteed basic income and guaranteed employment, 2001 (*Source* Eurobarometer 56.1 [2001]. Question wording: see Fig. 2.1. The graph shows the percentage of respondents agreeing [strongly] with the statements. UK-NIR = Northern Ireland. DE-E = former East Germany. DE-W = former West Germany)

about 10 percentage points between 1989 and 2001—it remained relatively stable in others—including West Germany, where support stayed at around 50% for the entire decade. Third, in most countries, basic income is not more popular than guaranteed employment, one of its policy competitors. Although levels of support for the two policies seem to have converged over the years, there are very few countries (except Australia, Canada and New Zealand) in which the general public prefers a guaranteed income to guaranteed employment. In most other countries, either guaranteed employment is more popular, or the two policies are about evenly matched in terms of popularity.

2.1.2 Polls with More-Detailed Definitions of Basic Income

As mentioned above, the earliest survey items on basic income probably portray an imprecise picture of its popularity, as they do not specify what a basic income scheme entails, leaving it up to respondents to figure out the design details for themselves. Accordingly, it is difficult to tell whether people actually had the ideal-typical version of basic income in mind when responding to these items. To gain a better understanding of the popularity of the ideal-typical basic income in particular, it is better to rely on surveys that provide some kind of explanation of what basic income is.

The first to do so—at least to my knowledge—was the 1995 TISSER Solidarity Survey conducted in the Netherlands at the request of the Ministry of Social Affairs and Employment. The survey described basic income as a cash benefit that is universal, unconditional and may be topped up with earnings from other sources; thus including most of the core elements of the ideal-typical definition. It also mentioned that with the introduction of a basic income, many existing social security schemes would be likely to disappear.

As shown in Fig. 2.4, only about 20% of the Dutch supported the implementation of a basic income scheme as it was described. This is

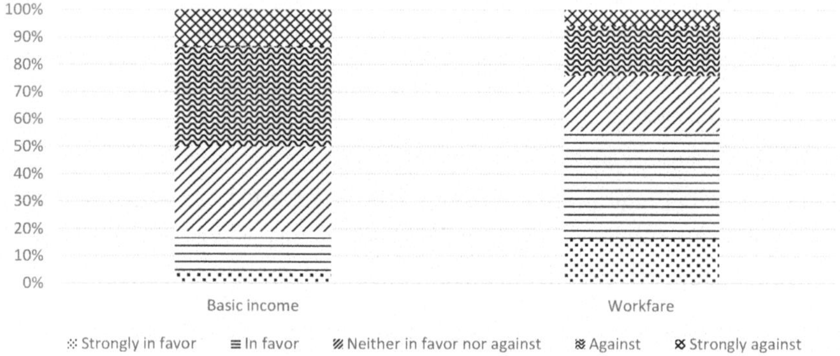

Fig. 2.4 Support for basic income and workfare in the Netherlands, 1995 (*Source* TISSER Solidarity Survey [1995]. Question wording: 'In the newspapers and on television, there is talk of the implementation of a basic income. This means that in the future all Dutch people, workers and nonworkers, will receive a fixed amount from the government, which is just enough to get by. Those who work complement this amount with a salary. Those who do not work are not obliged to search for paid work. Because of the basic income many of the existing social security schemes will become obsolete. Are you in favor or against the introduction of such a basic income?' and 'Another possibility is that all Dutch adults younger than 65 are forced to work. Someone who is unemployed or disabled and cannot find a job on their own will get a job from the government in which he or she performs work that is useful for society. In return, he or she receives the minimum wage. People who refuse the job offer do not get any benefits from the government. Only severely sick people are not forced to work. Are you in favor or against the introduction of such a system of compulsory work for everyone who can?')

much lower than the relatively high level of support (78.5%) that was found in the Netherlands just one year before, with the ISSP item that did not define basic income (see Fig. 2.2). Although it could be that support for basic income drastically shifted in a very short time, it seems more plausible that support was lower in the TISSER survey because it gave more information about the design of the proposed scheme. More specifically, the item placed relatively strong emphasis on the fact that basic income is fully unconditional, by stating: 'those who do not work are not obliged to search for paid work'. As we will see later on, it seems likely that it was this manifest mention of the absence of any work-related obligation that drove public opposition to basic income. Indeed, the same survey also shows a much higher level of support for the polar opposite of basic income in terms of conditionality: workfare. That is, about 56% of the Dutch population considered it a good idea to implement a workfare scheme paying minimum wage benefits to able-bodied people of working age, on the strict condition of them being willing to accept societally useful work provided by the government.

Since the 1995 TISSER survey, there have been many other public opinion polls that have described—in more or less detail—what a basic income is, before asking people whether or not they are in favour of its introduction in their country of residence. Most of these surveys were conducted in recent years, following the vast increase in public and political attention paid to basic income. There were in fact very few polls between 1995 and 2015; not coincidentally the year before the Swiss referendum on basic income was held. However, three exceptions are worth discussing here. The first is the Opinion on Social Welfare Survey, conducted in France in 2001 (Le Clainche, 2004), the second involves surveys conducted in Finland and Sweden in 2002 (Andersson & Kangas, 2004) and Norway in 2003 (Bay & Pedersen, 2006), and the third is the Survey on the Community Life and Welfare conducted in Japan in 2009 (Takamatsu & Tachibanaki, 2014). Let us first discuss the French survey, which described basic income as a cash payment of about €305 per month provided to all by the state in order to achieve greater income redistribution and to stimulate employment. The survey then asked people whether they considered the introduction of a basic income as morally acceptable and as economically viable. As shown in Fig. 2.5, about 38% of the French population responded that basic income was morally acceptable to them, while 49% said it was not and 13% had no firm opinion on the matter. Even fewer people deemed basic income to be economically viable

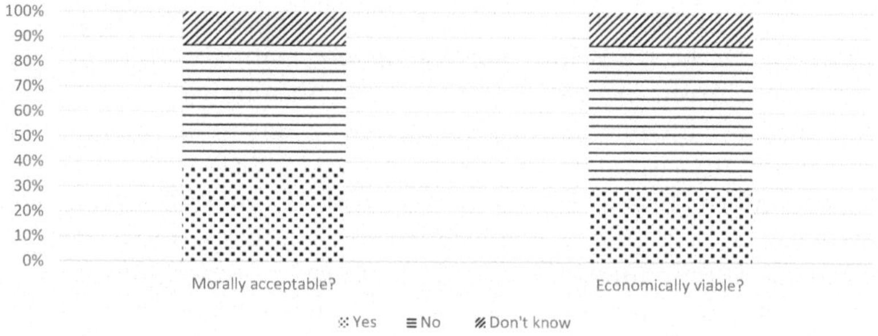

Fig. 2.5 Support for basic income in France, 2001 (*Source* Direction de la Recherche, des Etudes, de l'Evaluation et des Statistiques, Opinion on Social Welfare Survey [2001], reported in Le Clainche (2004). Question wording: 'Basic income is a principle of income redistribution within society. It aims at replacing a certain number of social minima in order to encourage the resumption of employment. It would consist of giving to each person, via the State, a basic income of about 2,000 francs per month, whatever the other sources of income. What would you say about this?')

(29.8%). Only 18.3% of those who had an opinion on the matter felt that basic income was both morally acceptable and economically viable, while 26.1% thought the exact opposite.

Around the same period as the French survey, relevant data was being gathered in three Nordic countries: Finland and Sweden in 2002 and Norway in 2003 (see Fig. 2.6). All three surveys used the same, relatively short, definition of basic income, describing it as a 'system that would automatically guarantee a certain basic income to all permanent residents'. Support for basic income proved to be higher than in France and the Netherlands a few years earlier, especially in Finland (76%) and Norway (66%), although less so in Sweden (43%). The lower level of support in Sweden is consistent with data from the ISSP and the Eurobarometer (see Figs. 2.2 and 2.3), but is somewhat difficult to explain, as it could be driven by many factors. Some of these refer to the economic, demographic and institutional characteristics of Sweden (when the survey was held), such as its relatively low level of unemployment, its relatively large immigrant population and its relatively generous welfare state, respectively (Andersson & Kangas, 2004; Bay & Pedersen, 2006). With only three countries to compare, however, such explanations remain somewhat speculative for the time being. Nevertheless, as shown below, in particular

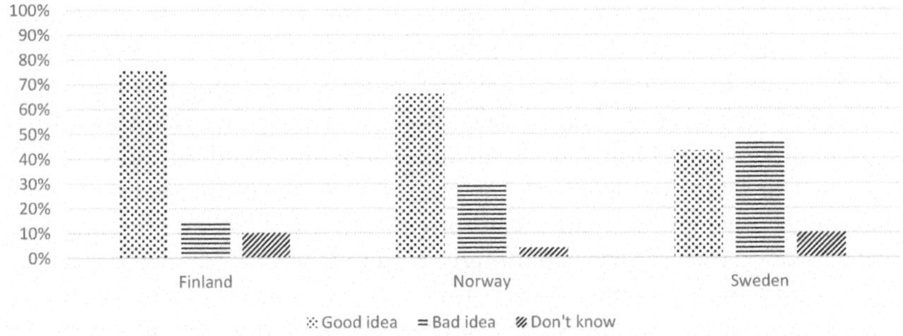

Fig. 2.6 Support for basic income in Finland, Norway and Sweden, 2002–2003 (*Source* Andersson and Kangas [2004] and Bay and Pedersen [2006]. Question wording: 'What do you think about a system that would automatically guarantee a certain basic income to all permanent residents?')

the latter explanation—referring to characteristics of the existing welfare state—will prove to be an important factor driving cross-national variation in popular support for basic income across Europe.

After the Nordic surveys in the early 2000s, there was a long period during which no new information on public opinion about basic income was collected. Only one other poll was held, in Japan in 2009, asking people to indicate their support for the idea that the government would provide 'a minimum living expense to all citizens regardless of their income, assets, or their employment situation'. At the time, 28.5% agreed with the implementation of such a basic income in Japan, while 36% disagreed and 35.5% were neutral about it (see Takamatsu & Tachibanaki, 2014).

Research into the popularity of basic income subsequently stalled, until the run-up to the Swiss referendum, which rekindled interest in the topic and sparked a series of new public opinion polls, conducted both nationally and cross-nationally. Before discussing these, it is worth looking at the results of the referendum itself, which is perhaps the most direct measurement of popular support for basic income currently available to us. On 5 June 2016, the Swiss were given the opportunity to cast their vote on the possible inclusion of a new article in the constitution that would guarantee the right to a basic income, loosely defined as a scheme that would provide a monthly cash payment to all Swiss adult residents, without any means test or work requirement. Although the amount was left unspecified in the policy proposal, it was clear from the campaign that the initiators of the referendum had a relatively generous basic income in mind, at around €2330 per month, reflecting the high cost of living in Switzerland. Additionally, because many other design features of basic income (including its financing, integration and administration) were unclear from the proposal, the referendum was more about a somewhat vague policy idea than a carefully constructed policy scheme. The idea was nevertheless overwhelmingly rejected, with 77% of the participants voting 'no' and only 23% voting 'yes' (Colombo et al., 2016). It is clear from these numbers that the Swiss population did not support the real-life introduction of an ideal-typical version of basic income. It should nevertheless be noted that referenda rarely reflect the opinions of the entire population eligible to vote in them, as a result of non-participation. Indeed, in the referendum on basic income, only about 47% of the eligible population participated, which is quite common in Switzerland. Also, and importantly, voter turnout was disproportionally higher among those who—as we will see below—demonstrate relatively stronger opposition to basic income, such as high-income earners and older people. This could mean that the referendum underestimated the actual level of popular support for basic income in Switzerland. At the same time, it also indicates that many of those who might have supported the idea of basic income in a survey did not take the trouble to go out and vote for it in a referendum—a clear case of 'cheap' political support (De Wispelaere, 2015).

2.1.3 *The Rise of Cross-National Polls on Basic Income*

Before, during and after the Swiss referendum, a series of new public opinion polls on basic income emerged. The first of these was conducted in 2015 by Dalia Research, among 10,000 Europeans living in 28 EU countries. It is important to note, however, that although the Dalia survey was cross-national in scope, the number of respondents is too small in most countries to draw reliable cross-national comparisons. Therefore, only those countries with a minimum of 1000 respondents will be compared here, including France, Germany, Italy, Poland, Spain and the UK. The survey described basic income as 'an income unconditionally paid by the government to every individual regardless of whether they work and irrespective of any other sources of income', and that also 'replaces other social security payments and is high enough to cover

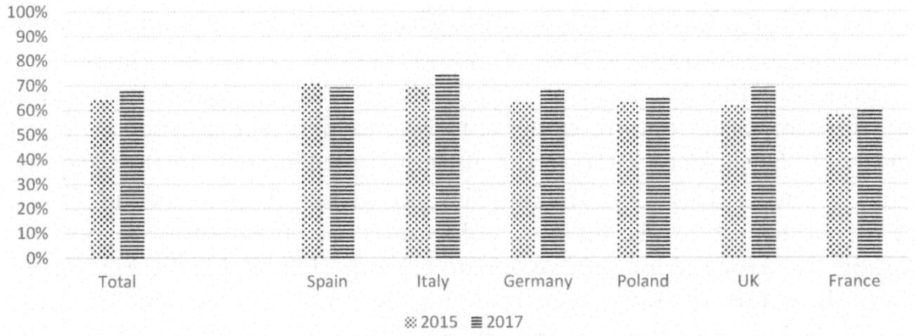

Fig. 2.7 Support for basic income in Europe, 2015–2017 (*Source* Dalia Research [2015, 2017]. Question wording: 'A basic income is an income unconditionally paid by the government to every individual regardless of whether they work and irrespective of any other sources of income. It replaces other social security payments and is high enough to cover all basic needs (food, housing, etc.). If there would be a referendum on introducing a basic income today, how would you vote?' The graph shows the percentage of respondents saying they would vote in favour of basic income in a referendum)

all basic needs (food, housing, etc.)'. Respondents were then asked how they would vote if this basic income was the subject of a referendum held in their country. In 2015, 64% of the 10,000 interviewed Europeans responded that they would vote in favour of basic income. That number rose a little to 68% in 2017, when the question was repeated.

As shown in Fig. 2.7, there is relatively little cross-national variation in the Dalia survey, with the highest level of support at 75% in Italy (in 2017) and the lowest at 58% in France (in 2015). There also seems to be a relatively high degree of stability between 2015 and 2017, with the largest shifts being an increase of 7 and 5 percentage points in the UK and Italy, respectively. In the 2017 survey, it was also asked at what point a basic income should be introduced. Most respondents (48%) stated it should only be after successful experiments had been completed, either in their own country or in others. This seems to indicate that for many people, support for basic income depends (at least in part) on the outcomes the policy produces—a point to which I will return in Chapter 4. By contrast, the remaining half of the Dalia respondents did not feel the need to wait for the results of experiments: while 31% suggested that basic income should be introduced as soon as possible, 13% stated it should not be realized anytime soon and 8% that it should never be implemented.

Soon after the first Dalia survey, another cross-national survey with a question on basic income came out: Round 8 of the European Social Survey (ESS), held in 2016–2017 among approximately 44,000 respondents living in 23 different countries. To date, many continue to see the ESS question as *the* most reliable source of information on popular support for basic income, for two main reasons. The first is the exceptionally high quality of this purely academically driven survey, which invests a great deal of time and resources in data quality assessment. It is a well-known fact that the ESS sets very high standards throughout the survey process, from the initial design stage to the delivery of the final data. Most importantly, its sampling method is probability-based, meaning that respondents are randomly selected from national registers to avoid self-selection bias. Combined with the fact that the ESS also has outstanding procedures with regard to non-response and weighting, the probability-based sampling guarantees that the people who are interviewed are as representative of the respective national population as is possible. The second reason that the ESS question on basic income is so highly regarded has to do with the level of detail in which it describes the policy. Unlike many other surveys, the ESS provides a relatively precise description of basic income, as being a cash benefit that is (a) paid to all individuals on a monthly basis, (b) sufficient to cover essential living costs and to guarantee everyone a minimum standard of living, (c) a substitute for many other social benefits, (d) equal for all, (e) granted irrespective of work status and other earnings and (f) financed through taxes. After reading the description—which comes very close to the ideal-typical definition—people are asked to indicate whether they are in favour or against the implementation of a basic income in their country.

As shown in Fig. 2.8, about 55% of all those interviewed in the ESS supported the introduction of basic income. However, there is considerable cross-national variation. The greatest levels of support—above 65%—are observed for Central and Eastern Europe (Lithuania, Russia, Hungary and Slovenia), and Israel. The lowest levels of support—below 45%—are found in Switzerland, Sweden and Norway. The relative position of the Nordic countries—including Iceland, though not so much Finland—seems notably surprising at first sight. Some have argued that these countries in fact have the most suitable institutional framework to introduce a universal basic income, as a logical extension of the already

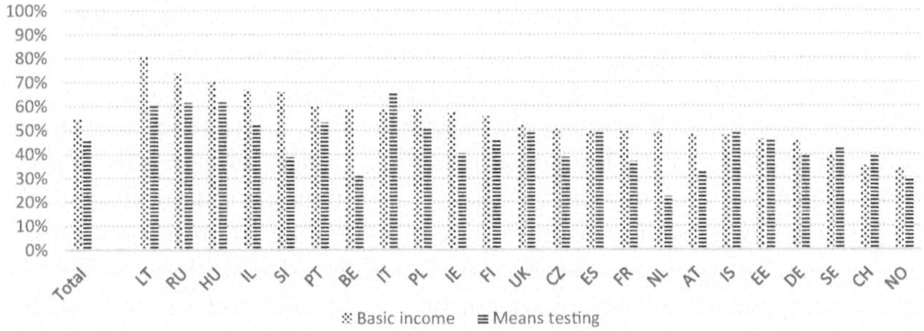

Fig. 2.8 Support for basic income and fully means-tested welfare in Europe, 2016 (*Source* ESS [2016/2017]. Question wording: 'Some countries are currently talking about introducing a basic income scheme. In a moment, I will ask you whether you are against or in favour of this scheme. First, I will give you some more details. A basic income scheme would include all of the following: (1) The government pays everyone a monthly income to cover essential living costs, (2) It replaces many other social benefits, (3) The purpose is to guarantee everyone a minimum standard of living, (4) Everyone receives the same amount regardless of whether or not they are working, (5) People also keep the money they earn from work or other sources, (6) This scheme is paid for by taxes. Overall, would you be against or in favour of having this scheme in [country]?'; and 'In the next 10 years the government may change the way it provides social benefits and services in response to changing economic and social circumstances. Would you be against or in favour of the government providing social benefits and services only for people with the lowest incomes, while people with middle and higher incomes are responsible for themselves?' The graph shows the percentage of respondents stating they are [strongly] in favour of these policies)

very universal welfare provisions currently in place there (Bay & Pedersen, 2006). It turns out, however, that this relatively favourable institutional background is precisely what drives public opposition to basic income. Studies using the ESS data clearly show that support for basic income is lower in countries with greater levels of social spending relative to their GDP (as also shown in panel A in Fig. 2.9). Some suggest this relationship exists because people living in high-spending countries are happier with the current welfare system and thus see less need for a radical reform (Lee, 2018). Relatedly, it could also be that the relationship exists because a higher degree of social spending reduces the demand for basic income, by cushioning some of the societal needs that a basic income is supposed to address (Roosma & van Oorschot, 2020). Indeed, panels B and C in Fig. 2.9 show that support for basic income is somewhat lower in countries where fewer people are at risk of poverty and where there is less income inequality. Of course, the opposite also holds true: support is higher in countries with less social spending, which tend to have higher levels of poverty and income inequality. It seems likely that the people living in the low-spending countries are more willing to push for a reform towards basic income because they are less satisfied with the workings of the existing welfare provisions. According to Parolin and Siöland (2020: 12), this results in a demand-capacity paradox in which 'the countries with the greatest demand for a universal basic income are those which possess the least institutional capacity to implement a generous, unconditional and universal cash assistance programme'.

Figure 2.9 indicates that there are some factors that can help explain the relatively large cross-national variation in popular support for basic income found in the ESS. In addition, the figure reveals two other things. First, it shows that the institutional welfare setting is not the only contextual driver of people's opinions about basic income. The general level of economic development—measured by the GDP per capita—also seems to matter, as reflected by the fact that there is less support for basic income in comparatively wealthier countries (see panel D). However, there is no significant relationship with a number of other contextual factors that have been hinted at in the literature on basic income, such as a country's unemployment rate (Lee, 2018) or the proportion of the population that is foreign-born (Bay & Pedersen, 2006) (which are not shown here). Second, Fig. 2.9 clearly indicates that the relationship between support for basic income and the different contextual factors is far from perfect. There are always some countries deviating from the general trend as depicted by the dotted line. One would, for example, expect to see a higher level of support for basic income in Estonia given its low social spending, and a lower level in Ireland given its high GDP per capita. This shows that there are no universal, law-like generalizations allowing us to predict how popular basic income will be in different countries. Instead, it seems more plausible that such support is driven by a combination of factors that is unique to each individual country. The results presented here nevertheless offer some valuable clues as to which factors are worth considering when exploring the popularity of basic income in different countries.

Despite the large cross-national variation in the ESS, it is often argued that the data generally—and perhaps unexpectedly—reveals fairly high

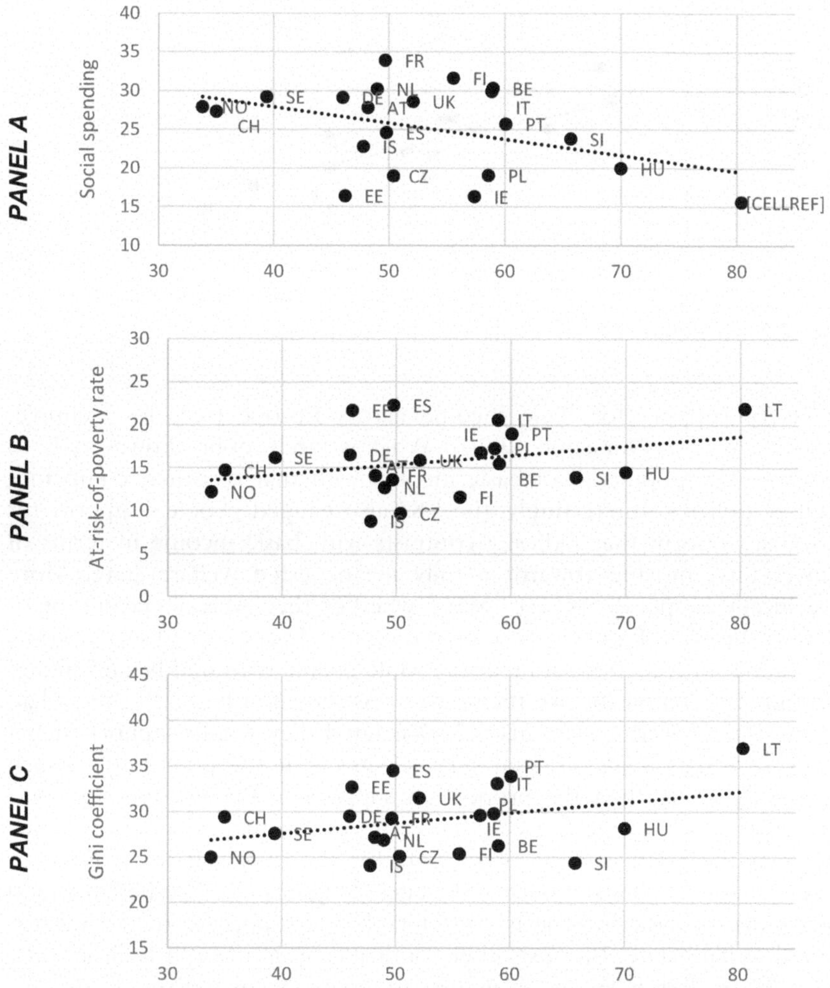

Fig. 2.9 Cross-national variation in support for basic income in Europe (*Source* ESS [2016/2017] and Eurostat [2016]. The horizontal axis presents the proportion of respondents agreeing with the introduction of baic income in their country. The vertical axis presents the respective country indicators: social spending as a percentage of GDP, the GDP per capita in Purchasing Power Standards [PPS], the Gini coefficient of equivalized disposable income, and the at-risk-of-poverty rate, with 60% of the median equivalized income taken as the cut-off point. Israel and Russia are dropped from the analyses because of missing data)

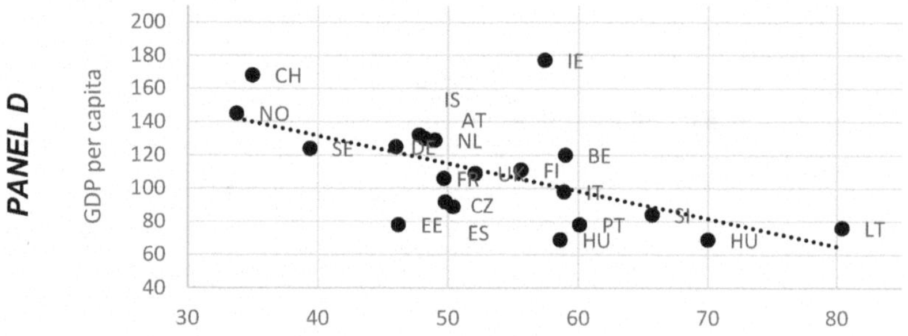

Fig. 2.9 (continued)

levels of support for basic income across Europe (see, for example, Roosma & van Oorschot, 2020). What is rarely done, however, is to compare the popularity of basic income with that of other, competing welfare policies. Interestingly, the ESS also gauged people's support for a welfare reform that radically contrasts with basic income in terms of universality, moving towards a fully means-tested welfare state. More specifically, respondents were asked whether they were in favour of or against the idea of 'government providing social benefits and services only for people with the lowest incomes, while people with middle and higher incomes are responsible for themselves'. As shown in Fig. 2.8, almost half of the interviewed Europeans (45.4%) stated they would support such a residual welfare state targeted very selectively at the poor only—which is slightly lower than the proportion supporting the introduction of a universal basic income (54.7%). There is again some cross-national variation in the relative levels of support for the two welfare reforms. In some countries—most notably Slovenia, Belgium, the Netherlands and Lithuania—a basic income is considerably more popular than a means-tested welfare state. In most other countries, by contrast, it is either on a par with or slightly less popular than complete means testing.

Although this observation already suggests that the popularity of basic income might have been somewhat overestimated in the past, it is worth taking a closer look at how people *combine* their opinions concerning the two opposing welfare reforms. That is, people can either support both reforms, support one of the two but not the other, or oppose both of them. As shown in Fig. 2.10, it seems that Europeans are about equally divided between the four opinion categories, with the exception of a

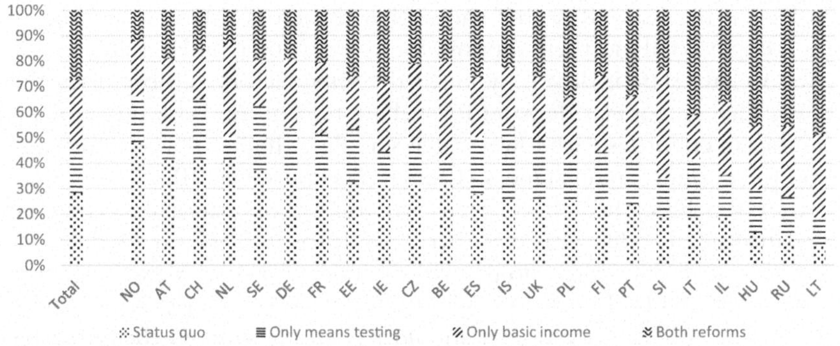

Fig. 2.10 Combined support for basic income and fully means-tested welfare (*Source* ESS [2016/2017]. Question wording: see Fig. 2.8. The graph shows the percentage of respondents agreeing with the respective reform options)

radical reform towards a fully means-tested welfare state (but not a basic income). This option is supported by only 17%, compared with a little over 25% for the other categories. Importantly, the fact that about half of the supporters of basic income simultaneously support a completely means-tested welfare state indeed indicates that the popularity of basic income is overestimated when only looking at absolute, rather than relative, levels of support (see also Rincon, 2021). After all, people who endorse a reform towards a *universal* basic income but at the same time favour a move towards a *selective* welfare state are arguably less passionate about it than those who support only a basic income.

There is, however, again a great deal of cross-national variation. In some countries—most notably Norway, Austria, Switzerland and the Netherlands—the status quo is clearly the most favoured alternative. This stands in stark contrast to a number of other countries—for example, Lithuania, Russia, Hungary and Italy—in which the largest group supports a radical drift away from the status quo, but does not seem to care whether reform is towards a basic income or an entirely means-tested welfare state. In other countries—such as Belgium, Finland and Slovenia—there is a clear preference for a radical reform towards a basic income. Only in Iceland is the most popular reform option a shift towards completely means-tested welfare provision. Nevertheless, the difference between the categories is very small there. This brings Iceland closer to the situation in Spain and the UK, where the population is also highly divided on the issue. Research shows that this cross-national variation in how people combine their support for basic income and a fully means-tested welfare state is driven by much the same factors as those discussed above. That is, popular demand for welfare reform—in both directions—is higher in countries with lower social spending, higher poverty rates and poorer economic circumstances (Laenen & Gugushvili, 2022).

After the ESS, there have been two more cross-national surveys on basic income. The first was carried out by Ipsos in 2017, in 11 different countries, including three non-European ones: Canada, Mexico and the US (see Fig. 2.11). It asked people to indicate their (dis)agreement with the statement that 'government should pay all residents in their country a basic income in the form of free and unconditional money in addition to any income received from elsewhere'. Although the description is short, it includes most of the design characteristics of the ideal-typical basic income, such as its universality and unconditionality. For some of the European countries—including Germany, Poland and Sweden—the level of support found in the Ipsos survey is quite similar to the level observed in the ESS. For most others, by contrast, support is considerably lower. This is presumably due to the fact that the Ipsos survey allowed people to indicate the more neutral opinion of 'neither agree nor disagree', which the ESS did not. In particular in France (46%), Spain (45%) and the UK (38%), a relatively large proportion of the respondents opted for this in-between position.

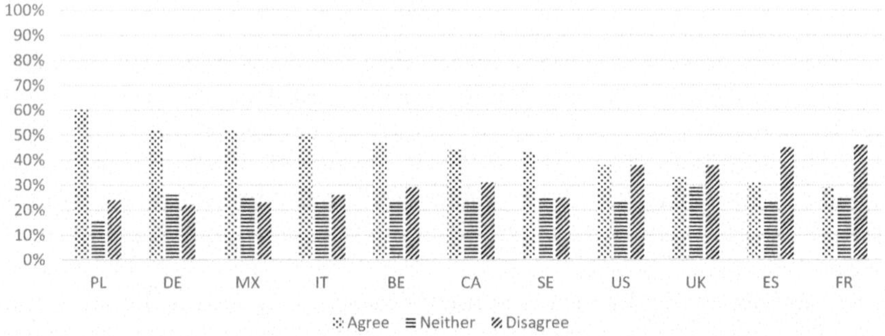

Fig. 2.11 Support for basic income in Europe, Canada, Mexico and the US, 2017 (*Source* Ipsos [2017]. Question wording: 'The government should pay all residents in [country] a basic income in the form of free and unconditional money in addition to any income received from elsewhere')

With regard to the non-European countries participating in the Ipsos survey, we see that support for basic income is highest in Mexico (52%), followed by Canada (44%) and the US (38%). In the latter, support seems to have remained relatively stable at around 40%, as demonstrated by two national surveys conducted a few years later. One of these was held in 2020 by the Pew Research Centre and showed that about 45% of the US population endorsed—either strongly or somewhat strongly—the idea that the federal government would provide 'a guaranteed income, sometimes called a "Universal Basic Income", of about $1000 a month for all adult citizens, whether or not they work'. In a similar vein, a 2020 Gallup survey commissioned by the Boston Northeastern University found that 43% of the US population showed support for a 'universal basic income program as a way to help people who lose their jobs because of advances in artificial intelligence'. The same question was also asked in Canada and the UK, where the level of support was 75% and 77%, respectively. The fact that these levels of support are much higher than they were in the Ipsos survey may again have to do with the lack of a neutral response option, but could also be driven by the fact that the Gallup survey insinuates that a basic income offers a potential solution to the problems associated with increasing automation and digitalization—a point that seems convincing to a large number of British and Canadian people, but not many Americans. This cross-national variation in the types of arguments used to support or oppose basic income is discussed in greater detail in Chapter 4.

The second cross-national survey coming after the ESS was the Survey on European Dreams for the Future of Europe, conducted in 2019 in 14 different countries. It asked Europeans whether they agreed or disagreed with the statement that 'each citizen, including those in work, should receive a guaranteed income from the state without work requirement'. Again, the description is short but conveys the core characteristics of the ideal-typical basic income. As shown in Fig. 2.12, some 46% of the respondents claimed to support basic income—which is similar to (albeit somewhat lower than) the overall level of support found in the ESS. Interestingly, however, the relative position of some of the participating countries appears very different in this instance. At one extreme, Portugal now shows the lowest level of support (at 35%), whereas it was among the most supportive countries in the ESS, at 60%. At the other extreme, Germany now appears at the top of the ranking with a support level of 62%, while it was among the least supportive countries in the ESS, with

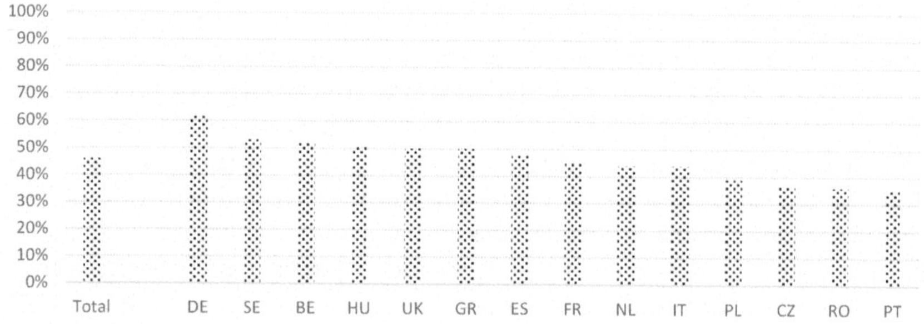

Fig. 2.12 Support for basic income in Europe, 2019 (*Source* Survey on European Dreams for the Future of Europe [2019], commissioned by the Foundation for European Progressive Studies and Policy Solutions. Question wording: 'Do you agree or disagree that each citizen, including those in work, should receive a guaranteed income from the state without work requirement?')

a level of 46%. It is nevertheless difficult to tell why exactly these differences exist. On the one hand, it could indicate that support for basic income had genuinely shifted in different directions in these countries. On the other hand, it could also be that these differences are simply the result of the fact that different questions were put to different people. More generally, it can indeed be said that because different polls present different questions to different samples, direct (over-time) comparisons are impeded, and it should not be surprising that they spawn diverging results. Nevertheless, this should not be seen as a purely methodological matter. Instead, it implies that how a basic income is described and framed also has an impact on its popularity—a point I will return to in Chapter 4.

2.1.4 *Polls About Changes over Time in Support for Basic Income*

In addition to the cross-national surveys, recent years have also seen an increase in national surveys on basic income, as a response to both national debates and international developments such as the Swiss referendum and the COVID-19 pandemic. Some of these surveys—conducted in Canada, the UK and the US—were briefly discussed above. There are, of course, several others. Considering all of these would take this book too far, however, especially since most of the countries where they were conducted have already been covered in the discussion of the cross-national surveys. Instead, the specific focus here is on two countries where it is to some extent possible to track how support for basic income has evolved over time: Germany and the UK.

In Germany, there is the comparatively unique situation that the ESS question on basic income has been repeated multiple times after it was initially included in 2016 (Adriaans et al., 2019). As shown in Fig. 2.13, a follow-up survey held in 2018 among the same sample of respondents as the 2016 ESS demonstrates that the level of support for basic income remained very stable—in fact almost identical—between the two time points, at around 45%. When the ESS question was also repeated in two waves of the German Socioeconomic Panel (SOEP), a longitudinal survey of approximately 2,000 people per wave, support for basic income grew slightly to 56% in 2017, but went back down to 51% in 2018. Overall, it thus seems that the popularity of basic income was relatively stable in Germany between 2016 and 2018. The gap in support between former East Germany and former West Germany also remained stable. As was already shown by the 1994 ISSP (see Fig. 2.2), Germans living in the eastern part of the country are generally more in favour of basic income than their counterparts living in the western part. This is, however, not specific to basic income, as other research has consistently shown that East Germans are stronger supporters of basically any type of welfare provision, presumably because of their communist heritage and because they generally still face greater economic hardship than West

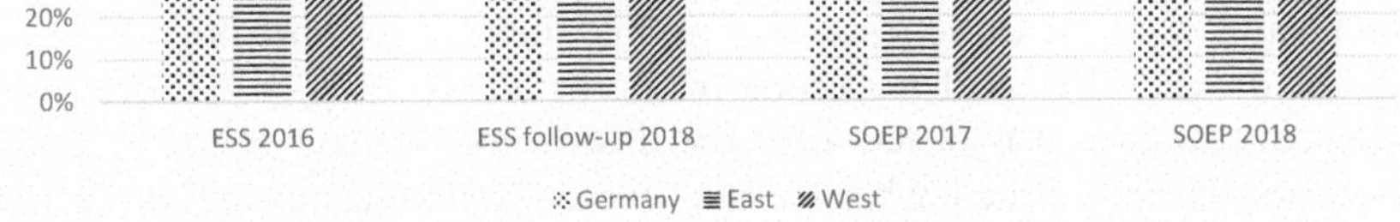

Fig. 2.13 Support for basic income in Germany, 2016–2018 (*Source* European Social Survey [ESS], Socioeconomic Panel [SOEP]. Question wording: see Fig. 2.8. The graph shows the percentage of respondents saying they are [strongly] in favour of introducing a basic income in their country)

Germans do (Alesina & Fuchs-Schündeln, 2005). The important thing to remember here is that popular support for basic income can also vary across regions *within* countries, depending on their economic and cultural characteristics.

The UK is the second country where a comparison over time is possible. However, in Germany the same question was repeated several times whereas in the UK different polls asked somewhat different questions about basic income. By piecing together these different polls, it is nevertheless possible to form some idea of how the popularity of basic income evolved between 2017 and 2020. In 2017, an Ipsos MORI survey (see Chrisp et al., 2020) gave its respondents a fairly detailed description of basic income, as being a scheme that provides 'a regular income paid in cash to every individual adult in the UK, regardless of their working status and income from other sources'. The survey further emphasized some of the design characteristics of the ideal-typical version of basic income, by mentioning that it would be universal (paid to all), unconditional (paid without a requirement to work) and paid to individuals (rather than to households). It then added that the level of basic income would be set 'roughly at the amount the UK government judged to be necessary to cover basic needs, e.g. food and clothing (but not housing costs)'. The results show that 48% of the respondents supported the introduction of basic income in the UK—only just below the 52% found in the ESS in 2016.

After the Ipsos MORI survey, two other polls on basic income were conducted by Populus in the UK, in 2018 and 2020. In both years, the same description of basic income was given, stating that it would provide 'everyone in society with a minimum level of cash to meet basic needs' and would replace many of the existing cash benefits (see Fig. 2.14). In 2018, people were asked whether they supported the idea of basic income 'in principle', which 41% stated that they did. All others either opposed the idea (17%), chose the neutral option of 'neither support nor oppose' (25%), or said they had no opinion on the matter (16%). In 2020, a different question was posed after the description of basic income. This time people were asked whether they would welcome testing the idea of basic income in their local area. About half (46%) of the respondents expressed support for a local pilot scheme: slightly higher than the proportion in 2018 that supported basic income *in principle*. Although the two Populus surveys are difficult to compare because of the two-year time gap between them, these results seem to indicate that people are more supportive of basic income after it has been successfully tried and tested.

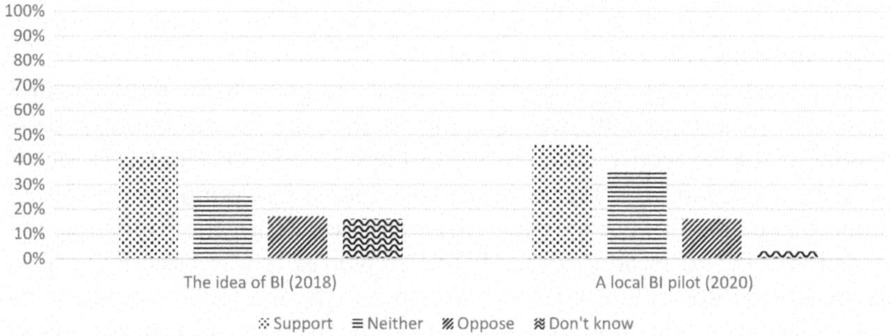

Fig. 2.14 Support for basic income in the UK, 2018–2020 (*Source* Populus [2018, 2020], commissioned by the Royal Society for Arts, Manufactures and Commerce. Question wording: 'In recent years, a range of people and organisations in the UK and elsewhere have called for a "Universal Basic Income" to be considered as an alternative to the current way in which cash entitlements such as tax credits, Jobseeker's Allowance and child benefit are paid. At its most simple, a "Universal Basic Income" would replace cash entitlements and benefits. Instead it would provide everyone in society with a minimum level of cash to meet basic needs. Every citizen would receive it and then pay tax as they earn. Which of the following statements best fits your view?' 'I support/oppose this idea in principle' [in 2018], and 'I support/oppose testing this idea in my local area' [in 2020])

This is a point to which I will return in Chapter 4, when discussing the distinction between *practical* and *principled* support for basic income.

Generally, these trends over time suggest that popular support for basic income is relatively stable, at least over the short-term span of a few years. Nevertheless, there is one particular study by Nettle and colleagues (2021) that seems to indicate that support for basic income has increased in response to the health and economic crisis induced by the COVID-19 pandemic (see also Weisstanner, 2022). In this study, British and American respondents were asked about their opinion towards 'a social security system where every citizen is paid a modest guaranteed income every month, just enough to cover basic necessities. The payment is the same for everyone. The payment is not conditional on what other earnings the person has and they do not have to do anything in particular to receive it'. The peculiarity of the survey was that respondents were asked to indicate their support twice—once with 'normal' times in mind and once using 'pandemic' times as a frame of reference. As it turned out, support for basic income was substantially higher for pandemic times than for normal times, and this was the case in both the UK and the US. Indeed, the average level of support in the two countries grew from 64.2 to 80.3 on a scale from 0 to 100, where 0 means that the introduction of basic income in the respective country is considered a bad idea and 100 means it is seen as a good idea. Furthermore, this increase in popularity persisted (albeit less evidently) even six months after the start of the pandemic and proved specific to basic income. In other words, it was basic income in particular that grew in popularity, compared with targeted and conditional social assistance. This finding was seen by the authors as confirmation of their assumption that the pandemic increased support for basic income specifically, rather than support for welfare provision more generally.

There is, however, one very important caveat to the study by Nettle and colleagues: The respondents were asked to retrospectively rate how they supported basic income before the pandemic, *as if* it had never happened. This was then compared with the support they showed for the policy in times of the pandemic. Although the authors recognize that a longitudinal experiment with a pre-pandemic and a peri-pandemic measurement would have been more suited for the task, they seem to assume that their study actually underestimates the opinion shift in favour of basic income: 'If respondents' normal-times responses were contaminated by their current high level of support due to the ongoing pandemic, then the true opinion shift they have undergone in the last six months or so may be larger than our study implies' (Nettle et al., 2021: 11). This conclusion is called into question in the research by Van Hootegem and Laenen (2022), relying on a natural experiment to compare popular support for basic income before and during the pandemic using data from the Belgian National Election Study. Although their results also indicate that support for basic income has risen somewhat because of the pandemic, the authors formulate three important nuances. First, they argue that the increase is most likely short-lived, as the level of support drops down again when the number of COVID-related hospitalizations decreases. Second, it turns out that the increase in support is only observable for groups who felt relatively deprived and for those living in the more deprived region of Wallonia. Their respective counterparts, that is, those without feelings of deprivation and those living in the more wealthy region of Flanders either did not change their opinion or became *less* supportive of basic income during the pandemic. Third, it is suggested that the increase in support might not have been specific to basic income, as it turns out that there are in fact some more-restrictive variants of basic income—rather than the fully universal and unconditional ideal type—that were given greater support during than before the pandemic. I will return to this issue (and the data) in greater detail in Chapter 3, where popular support for a wider variety of differently designed types of basic income is evaluated.

Summary Box 2.1 Across-The-Board Support for the Ideal-Typical Basic Income

Overall, the discussion of all the different opinion polls makes clear that the ideal-typical basic income is not inherently *popular* or inherently *unpopular*. Instead, it is shown that:

- There is usually large cross-national variation in support for basic income. This variation often—although certainly not always—follows the prevailing levels of social spending and economic wealth; with support being greater in poorer, lower-spending countries. In addition, support also seems to vary between different regions within a country, as was the case, for example, in the eastern and western part of Germany.
- Support for basic income seems to shift over time, as it varies between surveys conducted in different years. However, it should be noted that most of these are difficult to compare over time, because they put different questions to different people. The few surveys that do allow over-time comparisons show relative stability over the short term, even though there is some evidence that support for basic income increased somewhat in response to the COVID-19 pandemic.
- Basic income is not notably more popular than some of its policy competitors, including guaranteed employment (Figs. 2.1–2.3), workfare (Fig. 2.4) and means-tested welfare provision (Fig. 2.8). Relatively speaking, basic income is thus certainly not always the most preferred option.

There are also several intersections between these three sources of variation. This mainly occurs when absolute levels of support for basic income evolve differently in different countries—for example, stability in some countries but large fluctuations in others—and when relative levels of support differ between countries or years—for instance basic income being at the top of the priority list in some contexts but at the bottom in others.

2.2 Individual Differences

So far, this chapter has focused on across-the-board levels of support for basic income among the population at large, and how these vary across space and time. It seems very likely, however, that important differences exist between groups of individuals *within* the general public. It has indeed long been recognized that popular attitudes towards welfare state policies—including basic income—are driven by two main factors: people's social-structural position in society and their ideological outlook on it (van Oorschot et al., 2022).

With regard to social-structural characteristics, such as age, gender and income, the usual assumption is that they influence welfare attitudes through self-interest: the more a person stands to gain from a given welfare policy, the more he or she is likely to endorse it. There are two sides to this, however, that need to be considered in tandem. On the one hand, people may support a welfare policy because they think they will be on the receiving end of it, and oppose it when they come to the realization that they will not. On the other hand, people may also favour a given policy because they do not have to pay for it, and contest it when they do. Taking both sides of the self-interest argument into account is always important, but especially so in the case of basic income. Indeed, one of the unique features of the ideal-typical basic income is that everyone benefits from it because it is both universal and unconditional. Additionally, although it is not part of the ideal-typical definition, most advocates propose flat-rate payments, meaning that everyone is given exactly the same amount. From this perspective, it therefore seems that everyone would be likely to support basic income, simply because they all benefit from it. Yet, there are two important caveats to this argument. The first is that some people need a basic income more than others do and will hence support it more. More specifically, it seems plausible that support will be greater among those who occupy relatively precarious positions in society, as they would rely more strongly on a basic income for their survival (Roosma & van Oorschot, 2020). The second caveat is that support for basic income will probably be lower among those who carry the greatest burden of financing it. Although a great deal would depend on the specific funding mechanisms put in place, it will in many cases be those in the *least* precarious positions who will be required to contribute most; for example, if basic income is paid for by (progressive) income taxes, as is often suggested (Van Parijs & Vanderborght, 2017). Taken together, the self-interest argument thus predicts that support for basic income is greatest among those who stand to gain most, because they benefit more than they contribute, and lowest among those who stand to lose most, because they contribute more than they benefit. Who those people are, is explored in greater detail below.

Regardless of the arguments above, it is very unlikely that support for basic income is based solely on rational cost–benefit calculations. Indeed, decades of research show that people's attitudes towards different welfare provisions are also shaped by their broader ideological outlook on society (van Oorschot et al., 2022). In this book, these attitudes refer more specifically to political views and allegiances, as well as to normative beliefs about the welfare state and its clientele. With regard to the first, it seems safe to assume that support for basic income is at least partly shaped by political ideology. Left-wing liberals are unlikely to have the same opinion on the matter as right-wing conservatives, given their vastly diverging views on economic issues such as income redistribution, and cultural issues such as immigration (Schwander & Vlandas, 2020). However, for reasons explained in greater detail below, it should not be taken for granted that basic income will naturally be more popular among left-wing constituencies, as one could intuitively expect. Many of them, for example trade unionists, have very good reasons to oppose the introduction of a basic income scheme (Vanderborght, 2006). Likewise, one could argue that many right-wing voters could well be more supportive of basic income than they are of most traditional, existing welfare provisions—perhaps because they see it as a tool to reduce state bureaucracy (Murray, 2008).

Next to political ideology per se, people presumably also take their normative beliefs about the current welfare state into account when thinking about basic income (Roosma & van Oorschot, 2020). One could argue that basic income will not be seen as very desirable by those who think the prevailing system performs reasonably well. If people believe that the welfare state as we know it succeeds in reaching its central social goals—such as alleviating poverty—they will probably feel less inclined to support a radical reform towards a new system that has hitherto not been tried and proven. Likewise, support for basic income will probably decrease the more people think that the welfare state lacks unwanted side-effects, such as damaging the economy, and operates in a procedurally fair and effective way, for example with low rates of benefit abuse. Conversely, negative evaluations of the current welfare system may increase support for a radical reform towards basic income. In addition to such performance evaluations, it seems likely that support for basic income will also be influenced by popular perceptions regarding the deservingness of the groups currently targeted by the welfare state, such as the elderly or the unemployed. Some people may consider these target groups as undeserving of social welfare, for example because they perceive them as financially well-off and thus not in *need*, or as lazy and thus in *control* of their neediness (Laenen, 2020). Accordingly, such negative deservingness perceptions are bound to lower support for the ideal-typical basic income, given that it would be paid to *everyone* on a universal basis with no strings attached—including those who are seen as undeserving of it (Liebig & Mau, 2004).

In the following, I use data from the 2016/2017 European Social Survey (ESS) to empirically explore these individual differences in support for basic income. Although many other opinion polls could be used for this purpose, there are three main reasons for selecting the ESS in particular. First, methodologically speaking it is the most reliable source of information on popular support for the ideal-typical basic income, thanks to the rich level of detail in the question wording and the fact that the probability-based sampling guarantees representativeness. Second, the ESS includes information on a broad range of relevant individual characteristics that can be linked to support for basic income in light of the discussion above. More specifically, these are age, gender, household composition, education, income, labour market status, trade union membership, political ideology, welfare performance evaluations and welfare deservingness perceptions. Third, the fact that the ESS data was collected in multiple countries makes it possible to uncover possible cross-national variation in the relationship between these individual characteristics and support for basic income—an issue that will prove to be very important.

2.2.1 Age

With regard to age, the most intuitive expectation is that younger people will be more supportive of the ideal-typical basic income than older people will, for two main reasons. First, young people usually have more to gain from a basic income than their older counterparts, because they are more vulnerable on the labour market and are less protected by existing welfare states. In many countries, it is more difficult for young people to find jobs due to a lack of work experience; in turn, this is reflected in disproportionally higher unemployment rates among the young. Even when young people do find work, it is often under insecure, volatile employment contracts paying lower wages (that tend to increase with seniority). Further, if young people (temporarily) lose their income from employment after encountering a social risk—such as unemployment or sickness—they very often receive lower social insurance benefits than their older counterparts, as these payments tend to be linked to prior earnings. Many argue that it is the accumulation of these risks and disadvantages that makes young people particularly supportive of basic income (Roosma & van Oorschot, 2020). Older people, by contrast, generally do not experience the same levels of job and income insecurity, especially if they have reached the official retirement age and are in receipt of an old-age pension. In that case, opposition is expected to be even stronger, as retired people may fear that the introduction of a basic income scheme will replace the existing pension system, potentially making them worse-off (Yang et al., 2020). Given the risk-averse nature of the human psyche, it seems likely that many pensioners will see basic income as a potential threat to their acquired standard of living. Second, young people may also be more likely to support basic income because they are generally more progressive, with a greater openness towards radical reforms of the existing welfare system. Older people, by contrast, are known to be more conservative, leaning towards the preservation of the status quo. This should make them more strongly opposed to the introduction of basic income.

As shown in Fig. 2.15, the data from the ESS confirms the majority of the expectations regarding age differences in support for basic income. In most countries, the youngest age category (between 15 and 30 years of age) is clearly the most supportive and the oldest category (over 60) is the least in favour. In Switzerland, Sweden and Iceland, the gap between the two age groups actually exceeds 15 percentage points. Nevertheless, there are exceptions to the general pattern. In some countries, such as Finland, Ireland and Slovenia, the youngest category supports basic income to about the same degree as the middle category, aged between 30 and 60. Nevertheless, the youngest group is almost always more supportive than the oldest group—with the exception of Lithuania, where the difference between the two is negligible. Other countries deviate from the general pattern insofar as the middle category is equally as supportive or more

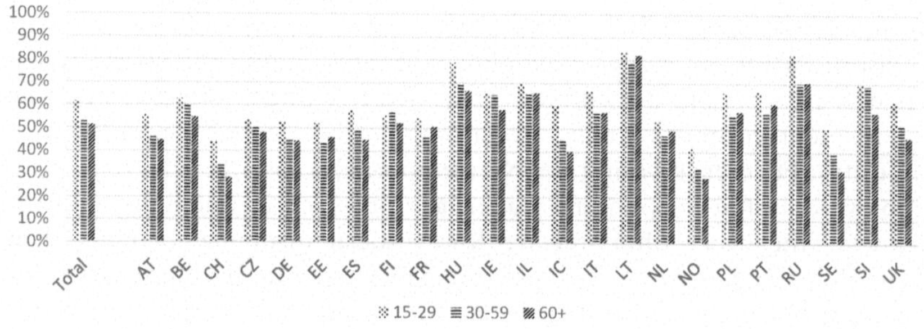

Fig. 2.15 Support for basic income by age (*Source* ESS [2016/2017]. The graph presents the percentage of respondents in favour of introducing a basic income within the respective age categories)

supportive than the oldest category—as is the case, for example, in Italy and Russia, and in France and Portugal, respectively.

Notwithstanding these exceptions, the evidence clearly indicates that basic income is most popular among the young, a trend that has also been consistently observed in other studies. Some suggest this gives 'some hope to basic income advocates who present the proposal as a social system of the future' (Roosma & van Oorschot, 2020: 14–15). After all, so the argument goes, if young people support basic income, then future generations will be more open to the idea of introducing the policy, making it much more likely that politicians will introduce it. There are, however, two very important nuances to this optimistic prognosis. The first is that the age differences should be interpreted in relative terms. Young people are certainly more supportive of basic income than their older counterparts, but this does not imply that basic income always receives support from an overwhelming majority of the young. This is clearly not the case in Norway and Switzerland, where a slight majority of young people actually oppose basic income. It is also not the case in a host of other countries—such as Germany and Sweden—where about half of the youngest age group supports basic income, but the other half opposes it. Having said that, even when a clear majority of the young would favour basic income, we still cannot know for certain whether this will lead to greater levels of support among future generations. In fact, it could well be that what we are observing here is not a cohort effect but a life-cycle effect, in which support for basic income among young people will reduce as they grow older. Building on the idea that our living conditions often become more secure and our values turn more conservative as we get older, this seems a plausible expectation. The life-cycle hypothesis certainly cannot be ruled out at this point, given the lack of longitudinal data allowing us to track people's support for basic income over time.

2.2.2 *Gender*

With regard to gender, it is generally assumed that women are more likely to support the ideal-typical basic income than men (Roosma & van Oorschot, 2020). Most of the time, this is based on the idea that women have comparatively more to gain from its introduction, in at least three respects. First, in many countries women continue to face greater disadvantages on the labour market, as illustrated, for example, by persistent gender pay gaps. With a basic income, many women would instantly obtain greater income security than they currently have. Second, despite their highly increased labour market participation, informal care—for young children or dependent elderly relatives for example—still falls disproportionally on the shoulders of women, leading to more and longer career breaks. Many argue that the status of such care work will vastly improve under a basic income scheme, as caregivers will receive the same payments as workers. Third, because of these two issues, women are in turn more often financially dependent on others, particularly on their (male) spouse or partner. It is claimed that an ideal-typical basic income would significantly increase women's financial autonomy, as it is universally and unconditionally granted to *individuals* rather than *households*. According to some, however, gender differences in support for basic income are also driven by the fundamentally different values held by men and women, in addition to their diverging self-interest considerations. It has indeed long been argued that most women are more supportive of welfare provision because from early childhood onwards, they have been socialized to be more caring and compassionate towards others than most men have (Gilligan, 1982). Accordingly, this should spill over into higher levels of support for basic income among women.

Contrary to expectations, Fig. 2.16 shows that there is barely any gender gap in support for basic income. In most countries, the opinions of men and women are very similar, and there is only a difference of more than 5 percentage points in a few countries. Moreover, these differences do not always point in the direction of women being most supportive

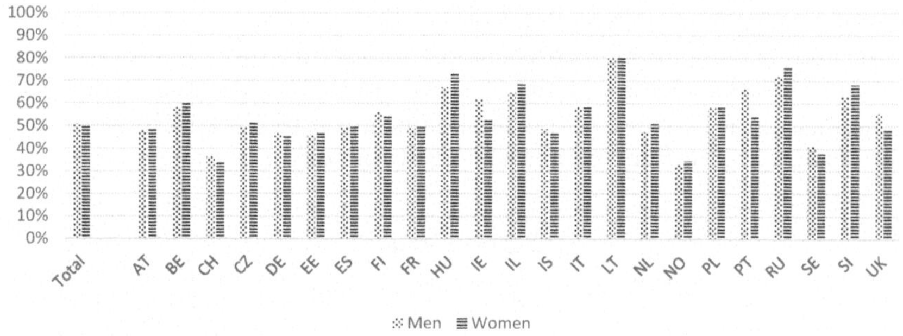

Fig. 2.16 Support for basic income by gender (*Source* ESS [2016/2017]. The graph presents the percentage of respondents in favour of introducing a basic income within the respective gender categories)

of basic income, as one would expect. This is only the case in Hungary and Slovenia. In other countries—most notably Ireland, Portugal and the UK—the opposite is in fact observed, with women being slightly *less* supportive of basic income than men. There are at least two explanations that could account for these unexpected gender differences. The first assumes that only some women have a greater self-interest in basic income while others do not, which should then lower the overall level of support among women. It seems plausible, for example, that women with (young) children have more to gain from a basic income than those who are childless, as they will have more and longer employment gaps. This applies less to men, who tend to have shorter career breaks due to fatherhood. This explanation is nevertheless not confirmed by the data, as women with children (54.9% in the full sample) are about as equally supportive of basic income as their childless counterparts (55%), as are mothers compared with fathers (52.9%). By contrast, the second explanation is that we were possibly incorrect to assume that basic income is of greater personal interest to women than it is to men. Indeed, feminist scholars have warned that a basic income could actually take us back to the male breadwinner model, in which men go out to work and women stay at home to care for the children and do domestic work (Robeyns, 2000). They have also reminded us of the fact that many of the existing gender inequalities—such as the persistent wage gap—will not be solved overnight by a basic income. It could indeed be that many women are aware of these issues, and therefore oppose basic income more strongly than one would expect.

2.2.3 Household Composition

With regard to household composition, it seems likely that support for the ideal-typical basic income will be greater among larger households, as they stand to gain more than smaller ones (Van Parijs & Vanderborght, 2017). If a basic income is on a strict individual basis, as in most proposals, each member of the household will receive a regular cash amount adding to the total household budget. In addition to having more income, larger households also tend to have somewhat lower living costs, because they are able to benefit from 'economies of scale'. This is one of the main reasons that many existing welfare arrangements—especially means-tested social assistance—take the household rather than the individual as their unit of entitlement. From this perspective, one would expect support for basic income to be higher among multi-person households than among single-person households. However, as shown in Fig. 2.17, this pattern is only apparent in a few countries, Norway and Slovenia in particular. In many others—most notably Sweden, Israel and Finland—it is actually single-person households that are most supportive of basic income. All in all, however, the size of the household as such does not seem to make a

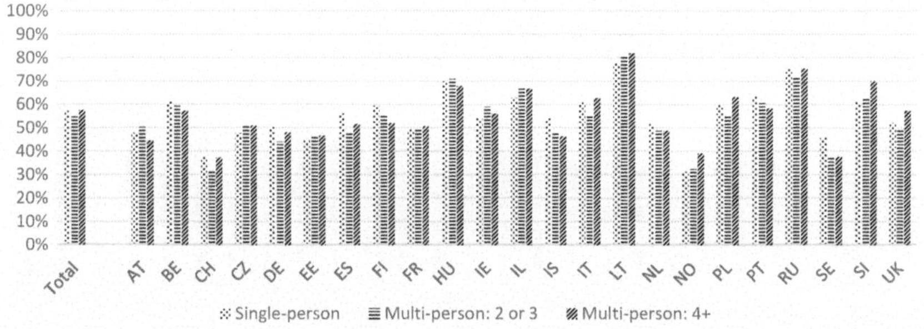

Fig. 2.17 Support for basic income by household size (*Source* ESS [2016/2017]. Question wording: 'Including yourself, how many people–including children–live here regularly as members of this household?' The graph presents the percentage of respondents in favour of introducing a basic income within the respective household categories)

major difference: support for basic income often is very similar among single-person households, smaller multi-person households (of two or three members) and larger multi-person households.

Next to the simple size of the household, support for basic income could also be influenced by the composition of households. In particular, it seems plausible that the presence of dependent children will increase support, as a basic income would provide greater income security during periods in which parents reduce their working hours (or stop working altogether) to care for their children (Roosma & van Oorschot, 2020). In addition, the ESS question seems to imply that children would also receive a basic income, by stating that 'everyone receives the same amount regardless of whether or not they are working'. Although we cannot be fully confident that respondents interpreted this as including children, nothing in the question suggests they would be excluded. In fact, whether people have children living in the household or not proves to have little bearing on their support for basic income. As demonstrated by Fig. 2.18, the difference in support between those who have children and those who do not is very small in most countries. When there is a (small) difference, it is almost always the people who have children that are somewhat *less* supportive of basic income—notably apparent in Austria, France and Sweden. This is an observation that clearly goes against expectations and is somewhat difficult to make sense of. One plausible explanation is that parents are concerned a basic income would replace existing child

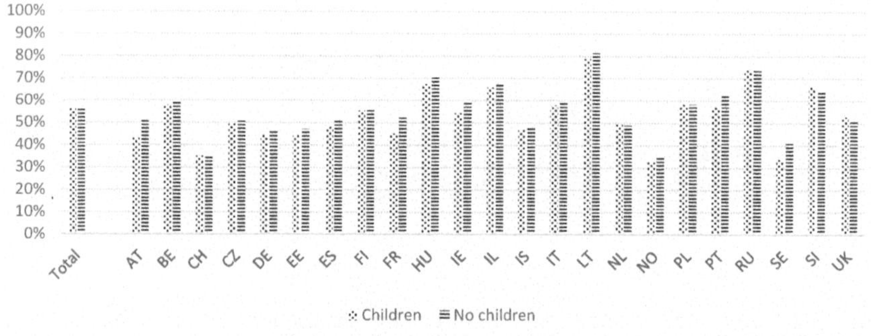

Fig. 2.18 Support for basic income by the presence of children in the household (*Source* ESS [2016/2017]. The graph presents the percentage of respondents in favour of introducing a basic income within the respective household categories)

allowances, which already provide greater income security to their family and could well be higher than the amount paid to children under a basic income scheme. As the ESS item does not specify the exact amount, risk-averse parents may thus decide to reject basic income and the uncertainty that comes with it.

2.2.4 Education

With regard to education, one would expect—from a self-interest perspective at least—that people with a lower level of education will be greater supporters of basic income than their higher-educated counterparts. The former are, after all, in a much more vulnerable position in most of today's knowledge-based economies, in which the risk of unemployment is known to increase with lower levels of education. Low-skilled workers are also more vulnerable to the threat of technological unemployment, because they often have routine jobs that are particularly exposed to potential automation (Busemeyer & Sahm, 2022). Additionally, the lower educated are more likely to be trapped in precarious labour market situations—such as zero-hour contracts or platform work—that tend to provide less job security, worse working conditions, lower wages and less income stability. Taking all this into account, it seems very reasonable to expect that support for basic income will be greater among the lower educated than among the higher educated (Roosma & van Oorschot, 2020).

Things are less clear, however, from the perspective of ideological beliefs. Lower-educated people are very often *working-class* people, who have traditionally been the main constituencies of left-wing parties striving for greater economic redistribution and egalitarianism. From this point of view, it seems plausible that the lower educated are also more likely to support basic income out of ideological considerations. At the same time, however, many lower-educated, working-class people have shifted to the right of the political spectrum in recent decades, voting for conservative and nationalist parties. At the same time this has been unfolding, the political left—especially Green parties and to some extent also social-democratic parties—has been attracting mostly higher-educated people (Dolezal, 2010; Rennwald, 2020). This shift in voting behaviour is usually attributed to the fact that the higher educated are culturally (rather than economically) more left-wing than the lower educated, meaning that among other things, they exhibit greater openness to migration, are less

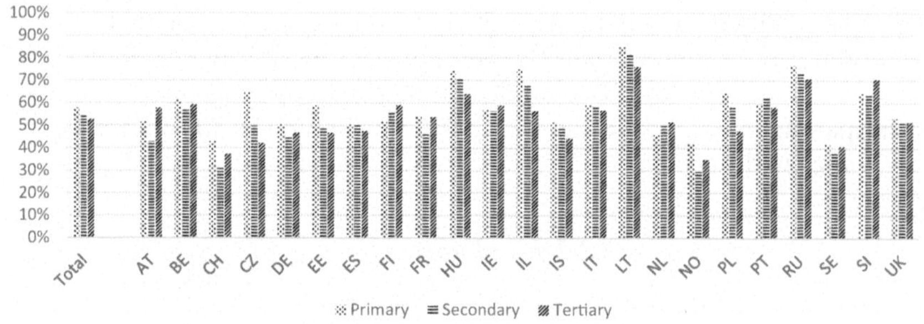

Fig. 2.19 Support for basic income by highest attained level of education (*Source* ESS [2016/2017]. The graph presents the percentage of respondents in favour of introducing a basic income within the respective educational levels, which are based on the International Standard Classification of Education)

authoritarian, care more about gender equality and are more strongly oriented towards post-materialist values (ESS ERIC, 2021). These ideological orientations, which are often acquired through formal education, could well make the higher educated more supportive of a universal and unconditional basic income compared with their lower-educated counterparts.

As shown in Fig. 2.19, the overall results suggest that support for basic income decreases in line with higher levels of education. Those with tertiary education, who have obtained a bachelor's or master's degree (52.6%), are somewhat less supportive than those who only went to secondary (54.2%) or primary (57.5%) school. It thus seems that the lower educated are indeed more inclined to support the introduction of a basic income, presumably because they have a greater (perceived) self-interest in it. On closer inspection, however, it turns out that this general pattern is only found in a relatively limited number of countries: most notably the Czech Republic, Estonia, Hungary, Israel, Lithuania and Poland. In other countries—Finland, the Netherlands and Slovenia in particular—the opposite is true, with support for basic income *increasing* with higher levels of education. This finding seems to suggest that, at least in these countries, ideological orientations make the higher educated more inclined to endorse basic income. Yet in other countries, especially France and Norway, it is the medium educated (with secondary education) that are least supportive. In the remaining countries, the gaps between the different levels of education are very small, indicating that education is not an important determinant of support for basic income. Thus, all things considered, it seems safe to conclude that there is no simple one-size-fits-all explanation for any link between education level and support for basic income. Instead, there proves to be a great deal of cross-national variation in this relationship.

2.2.5 *Income*

With regard to income, the story is relatively straightforward, at least when basic income is largely financed by income taxes (as it is in most proposals, including the one described in the ESS). In that case, it seems logical that support will be greatest among people on a low income, as they are likely to be net beneficiaries of a tax-financed basic income (Torry, 2019). Especially under a progressive tax system, which most European countries have in place, those at the bottom of the income ladder will receive more money from a basic income than they have to pay in taxes, thereby putting them in a situation in which the benefits clearly outweigh the costs. This is completely different for people on a high income, who are most likely to be net contributors to a basic income scheme, paying more than they would receive (De Wispelaere, 2015). Accordingly, one would expect those on higher incomes to be particularly opposed to the introduction of a basic income. It is less clear, however, what position those in the middle of the income ladder (mostly the middle class) will take. Depending on their exact income, some may be net contributors while others may be net beneficiaries. However, in most cases they will come probably close to the point of breakeven, neither profiting nor losing. Although this makes it hard to predict how supportive people from the middle income category are of basic income, it seems reasonable to expect that they will find themselves in the middle of the support scale, endorsing it more than those on higher incomes but less than those with lower incomes.

Figure 2.20 clearly demonstrates that in the majority of countries, people on a high income are indeed the most opposed to basic income, while their low-income counterparts are the most supportive of it—a finding that makes perfect sense from the perspective of self-interest. There are nevertheless a few countries where the opposite is found. In the Czech Republic, Hungary and Slovenia in particular, it turns out that the highest income category is in fact the most supportive of basic income. As expected, the middle income category tends to be in-between the two

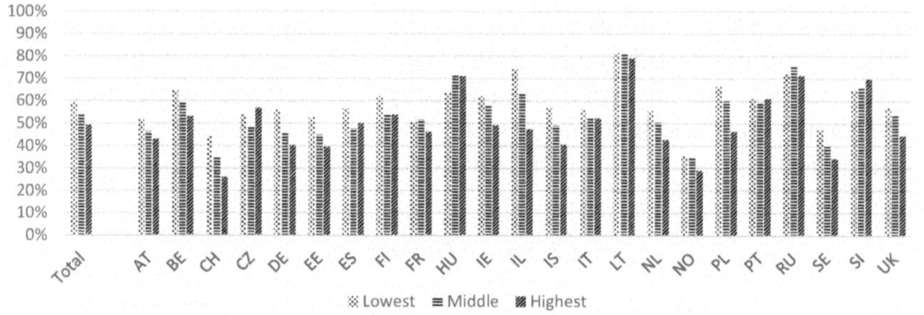

Fig. 2.20 Support for basic income by household income (*Source* ESS [2016/2017]. The graph presents the percentage of respondents in favour of introducing a basic income within the respective income categories, which are based on self-reported estimates of the total household income, from all sources and after tax and compulsory deductions. The following categories were created: 'lowest' = income deciles 1 through 3, 'middle' = deciles 4 through 7, and 'highest' = deciles 8 through 10)

others. In some countries, such as Lithuania, Portugal and Russia, the level of support is very similar between the different income categories. It is important to note, however, that the income variable in the ESS has a large number of missing values: about 20% of the full sample did not provide an answer to the relevant question. There are good reasons to believe that many of the non-responders have either extremely low or extremely high incomes, which could lead to underestimating the actual income differences in support for basic income. To deal with this, I also use a subjective indicator of income that asks people whether they are 'living comfortably', 'coping' or 'finding it (very) difficult' on their present household income. Again, the expectation is that support for basic income will be highest among those who claim to struggle financially and lowest among those who do not. Figure 2.21 illustrates that this is indeed the case, and it is also true for those countries in which people on a low income were previously shown to be less supportive than their high-income counterparts. Additionally, differences in support are larger in most countries when using the subjective indicator of income, suggesting that income differences are indeed underestimated in Fig. 2.20. It also means that support for basic income depends much more on people's subjective perceptions of their income than it does on the actual income they have at their disposal.

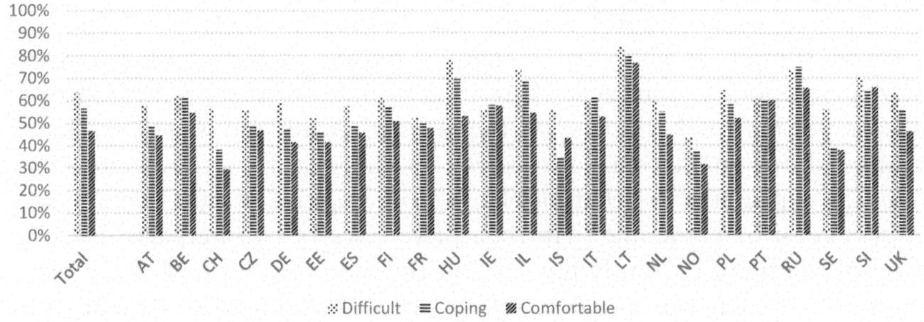

Fig. 2.21 Support for basic income by subjective income (*Source* ESS [2016/2017]. The graph presents the percentage of respondents in favour of introducing a basic income within the respective income categories. These are based on a question asking people whether they are either [1] 'living comfortably', [2] 'coping' or [3] finding it 'difficult'/'very difficult' on their present household income)

2.2.6 Labour Market Status

With regard to labour market status, we should expect to see that greater vulnerability on the labour market increases support for basic income, as already noted several times above. Accordingly, the most basic hypothesis states that there is a clear gap in support between, on the one hand, those who are in paid work, and on the other, those who are not. However, sub-group differences are also likely to exist within these broad categories. Within the group of non-workers, an important distinction needs to be drawn between the working-age population—consisting mainly of sick or disabled people, the unemployed, students, carers and homemakers—and the elderly population above the official retirement age. As shown above, the elderly are not very supportive of basic income. By contrast, non-workers of working age—especially those who do not receive any welfare benefits, or only low-level and highly conditional benefits—are more likely to be fierce advocates of a basic income that would cushion their labour market vulnerability and increase their income security (Vlandas, 2021).

Within the working population, it also seems reasonable to expect significant sub-group differences, for example in terms of education or wages, and the job as well as the income security (or insecurity) linked to these factors (see the two previous sections). Additionally, one would expect the type of employment contract and the sector of employment to influence support for basic income (Vlandas, 2021). For the first of these, support is likely to be greater among workers with part-time and/or temporary contracts than it is among workers with full-time and/or permanent contracts, as the former group tends to experience greater labour market precariousness. With regard to the sector, one plausible expectation is that public sector employees are generally less supportive of basic income than their private sector counterparts, because many of them are currently involved in the administration of the welfare schemes that such a proposal could replace and also tend to benefit from more-stable employment. Lastly, the position of self-employed workers is more difficult to predict. Although the self-employed have traditionally shown somewhat greater opposition to generous welfare benefits, they could actually be more supportive in the case of basic income, given that this policy would provide them with better coverage and protection than they have in most existing welfare systems. In addition, the greater income security that comes with a basic income is also claimed to boost risk taking and entrepreneurship, which may be particularly appealing to self-employed people (Van Parijs & Vanderborght, 2017).

Starting with the crude distinction between workers and non-workers, Fig. 2.22 shows that basic income is generally less popular among those who are in paid work, especially for Estonia, Poland and Portugal. In most other countries, the difference is very small, which seems to indicate that being in paid work or not has little impact on people's support for basic income. However, further analyses demonstrate that underneath the relatively similar levels of support among workers and non-workers, there are important sub-group differences within these broader categories. Among the non-working population, it turns out that the level of support for basic income is mainly driven down by pensioners. As shown in Fig. 2.23, they are considerably less supportive than non-working people of working age, and this pattern holds for all countries except Lithuania and Poland.

Within the working population, basic income is somewhat less popular among the self-employed than it is among employees. As shown in Fig. 2.24, this is especially the case in the Czech Republic, Italy and the UK. Only in Germany and France are the self-employed slightly more supportive of basic income (at least, compared with private sector employees). The difference between private and public sector employees is usually relatively small, but can be in either direction. In some countries, such as Estonia, Ireland and Poland, public employees are less supportive than their privately employed counterparts, possibly because

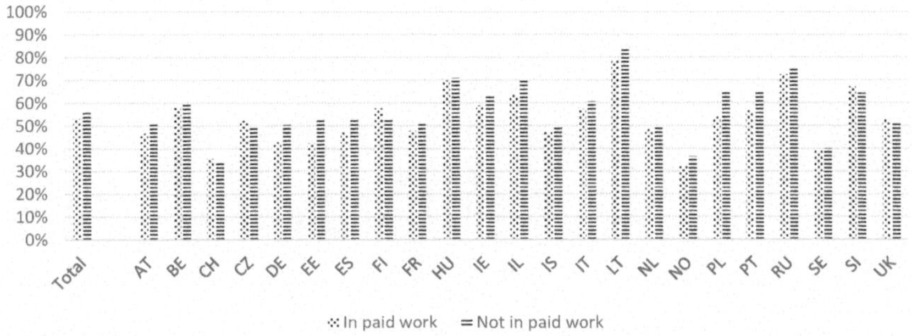

Fig. 2.22 Support for basic income by work status (*Source* ESS [2016/2017]. Question wording: 'Which of these descriptions best describes your situation (in the last seven days)?' Answer categories: [1] 'in paid work (or away temporarily) (employee, self-employed, working for your family business)', [2] 'in education', [3] 'unemployed and not actively looking for a job', [4] 'unemployed, wanting a job but not actively looking for a job', [5] 'permanently sick or disabled', [6] 'retired', [7] 'in community or military service' and [8] 'doing housework, looking after children or other persons'. The 'not in paid work' category comprises all of the answers except 'in paid work'. The graph presents the percentage of respondents in favour of introducing a basic income within the respective work status categories)

Fig. 2.23 Support for basic income by type of labour market inactivity (*Source* ESS [2016/2017]. Question wording: see Fig. 2.22. The 'working age' category comprises all of the answers except 'in paid work' and 'retired'. The graph presents the percentage of respondents in favour of introducing a basic income within the respective categories for labour market inactivity)

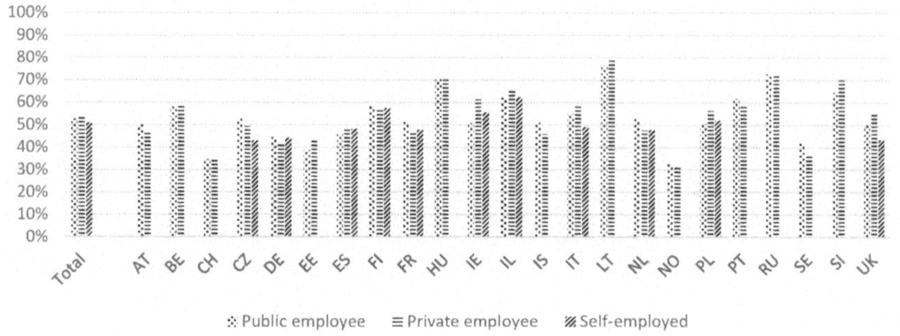

Fig. 2.24 Support for basic income by sector of employment (*Source* ESS [2016/2017]. Question wording: 'Which of the types of organization do you work for?' Answer categories: [1] 'Central or local government', [2] 'Other public sector (such as education and health)', [3] 'A state-owned enterprise', [4] 'A private firm', [5] 'Self-employed' and [6] 'Other'. The 'public employee' category consists of answers [1], [2] and [3]. The graph presents the percentage of respondents in favour of introducing a basic income within the respective employment sector categories. The percentage is not reported in case a category has fewer than 100 respondents in a country)

they fear losing their job if a basic income is introduced. In other countries, such as France, Israel and Sweden, the opposite is found. Although this seems to go against the self-interest of many public sector employees, it could well be that they are more supportive of basic income because they tend to have a stronger ideological allegiance towards the welfare state in general. It should be noted, however, that the ESS data does not allow us to meaningfully differentiate within these somewhat broad employment sectors. Some public employees (for example, social workers employed in social assistance agencies) should feel much more threatened by basic income than others (such as school teachers), because their jobs are more likely to be ended by it. In a similar vein, support for basic income may vary between private employees working in different sub-sectors. For example, some sectors (such as the food industry) are more susceptible to the automation of work tasks than others (such as the care sector), which could make workers employed in the former more supportive of basic income than those employed in the latter (Dermont & Weisstanner, 2020).

In addition to the sector of employment, it is also worth looking at the role played by the type of employment contract. As shown in Fig. 2.25, those working based on a fixed, short-term contract or even no contract at all tend to support basic income more than those with an open-ended, unlimited contract, presumably because they have less job and income security. This is especially the case in Austria, Sweden and Slovenia, where the gap exceeds 15 percentage points. In a host of other countries—such as Germany, Estonia and Hungary—the gap is also approximately 10 percentage points. This demonstrates that the type of employment contract—fixed versus open-ended—is an important driver of support for basic income in many countries, surpassing the importance of some of the other social-structural characteristics discussed above. This is, however, not the case in all countries—for example, Belgium, Israel and the UK—where the difference between the two types of employment contract is negligible.

Lastly, support for basic income could also be influenced by the type of employment contract in terms of working hours. Similar to the above argument, one would expect that workers with a part-time contract are more supportive of basic income than workers with a full-time contract. To test this, I use information about respondents' actual number of

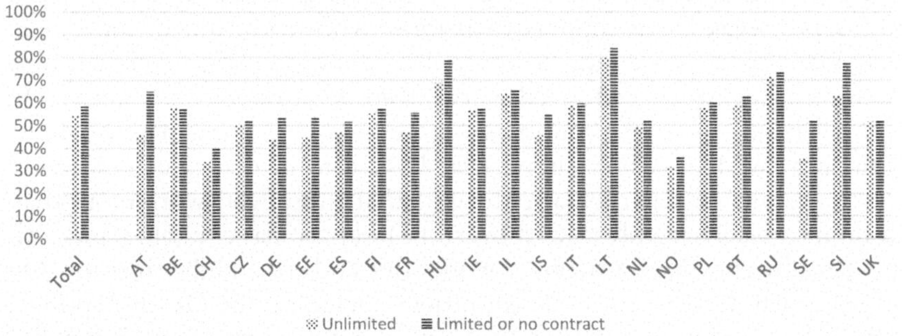

Fig. 2.25 Support for basic income by employment contract (*Source* ESS [2016/2017]. Question wording: 'Do you have a work contract of unlimited duration or limited duration, or do you have no contract?' The graph presents the percentage of respondents in favour of introducing a basic income within the respective contract type categories. The percentage is not reported in cases where a category has fewer than 100 respondents in a country)

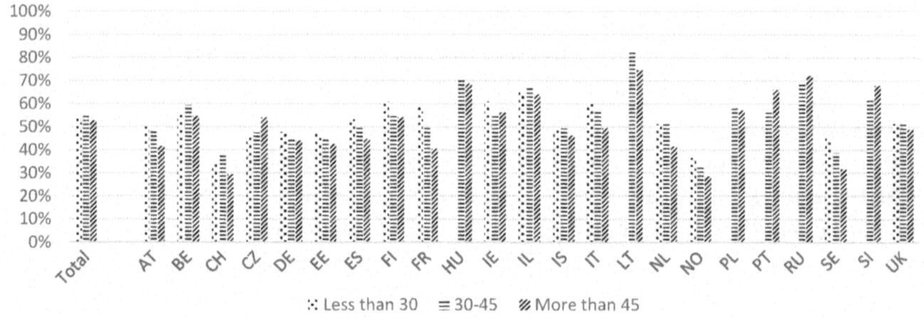

Fig. 2.26 Support for basic income by weekly working hours (*Source* ESS [2016/2017]. Question wording: 'Regardless of your basic or contracted hours, how many hours do you normally work a week (in your main job), including any paid or unpaid overtime?' The graph presents the percentage of respondents in favour of introducing a basic income within the respective categories for working hours. The percentage is not reported in cases where the category has fewer than 100 respondents in a country)

(rather than contracted) working hours, which may differ due to overtime, for example. Looking at the overall figures across countries (see Fig. 2.26), it seems that people's support for basic income is barely influenced by the number of hours they work: those who work fewer than 30 hours a week are as supportive as those who work (much) more than that. On closer inspection, however, there is again large cross-national variation, which is characterized by two somewhat opposing patterns. On the one hand, there are countries—most notably Austria, France, Italy, Spain and Sweden—where support for basic income decreases as working hours increase. It is particularly the case that those who work more than 45 hours a week (mainly due to overtime) oppose basic income, presumably because they have a stronger work ethic and/or a higher income. On the other hand, there are some countries—including the Czech Republic, Portugal and Slovenia—where those who work more than 45 hours a week are actually more supportive of basic income than those working 30 to 45 hours. This suggests that the relationship between the number of working hours and support for basic income may have a U-shaped pattern in these countries: support increases as people work more hours, but only up to a certain point, after which it begins to reduce again. In this scenario, people working more than full-time hours may see basic income as a way to reduce their working hours without incurring large financial losses.

2.2.7 Trade Union Membership

With regard to trade union membership, it is first worth looking at the position taken by the trade unions in the basic income debate, which seems to be ambiguous (Cigna, 2022; Vanderborght, 2006). There are indeed several reasons why trade unions are likely to support, or at least tacitly approve, the introduction of the ideal-typical basic income. Most importantly, it has been argued that a basic income would contribute to a valuable strike fund, allowing an increase in the collective bargaining power of workers and their unions. This, in turn, would lead to higher wages and better working conditions, forcing employers to get rid of so-called 'shitty jobs'. In addition to collective bargaining power, a basic income could also improve individual bargaining power and increase wages, by offering workers a genuine exit option to leave (or threaten to leave) their job with a safety net in place to cushion the accompanying loss of income. At the same time, however, this potential increase in individual bargaining power is often cited as an important reason for trade unions to oppose a basic income, as it could well weaken their power position. After all, if workers are able to negotiate directly with employers as a result of the security provided by a basic income, why would they still need a trade union to represent them? From this perspective, it seems to be in the unions' best interest to prevent this from happening.

Additionally, there are at least three other reasons for trade unions being likely to oppose basic income. First, there are genuine concerns that a basic income would incite a downward spiral in wages. Knowing that there is an income floor for all, employers could start lowering wages, thereby effectively demoting basic income to a wage subsidy. Relatedly, there are some concerns that a basic income would replace hard-fought minimum wage legislation. Second, trade unions may feel threatened by the prospect that basic income would stimulate self-employment and entrepreneurship on the one hand, and informal caregiving on the other. If that were to take place on a large scale, it could lead to a noticeable decrease in the number of wage labourers and thus also in the pool of potential trade union members—a trend that is bound to negatively affect the bargaining power of unions in the long run. Third, if a basic income is financed by income taxes—which is the case in most proposals—the probable increase in tax rates would fall predominantly on the shoulders of unionized workers, who tend to be labour market insiders with relatively secure and well-paid jobs. It seems highly likely that these insiders—as well as their representatives—would not be overly keen on imposing a higher tax burden on themselves in order to redistribute the money to labour market outsiders. While this clearly goes against their own self-interest, a basic income also clashes with moral beliefs that many unionized workers hold dear. Indeed, it seems safe to assume that most trade union members, being workers themselves, place great emphasis on the central role of paid employment in society, which they may think is threatened by an unconditional basic income. Driven by a strong work ethic, trade union members (and their official representatives) may see basic income as a form of exploitation of workers by non-workers. From this viewpoint, it is unfair to pay the same amount of money to everyone, knowing that workers are required to give up a significant part of their wages while non-workers contribute little in terms of taxes (Raes, 1988).

Although there will certainly be some degree of overlap, the positions taken by the trade union leadership could well differ from those of their rank-and-file members, because of diverging stakes. Trade union members of course have the organizations' interests to consider, as well as—and perhaps even more so—their own. For example, if unionized workers genuinely believe a basic income will succeed in boosting their *individual* bargaining power, leading to higher wages and better working conditions for themselves, they may be more willing to accept its introduction, even if it comes at the expense of the unions' *collective* bargaining power. This intertwinement of organizational and individual interests makes it somewhat difficult to predict how trade union members will react to a basic income from a self-interest perspective. From an ideological point of view, however, it seems more likely that basic income will be opposed by trade union members, given their strong adherence to the work ethic.

As shown in Fig. 2.27, the overall difference across countries between members (both current and past) and non-members of a trade union is very small. In many countries—Austria, Estonia and the UK for example—both groups seem to support basic income to a very similar extent. However, there are a number of countries in which trade union members are clearly less supportive of basic income, most notably Germany, Hungary, Ireland, Israel, Italy, Sweden and Slovenia. On the one hand, this lower level of support among trade unionists could be

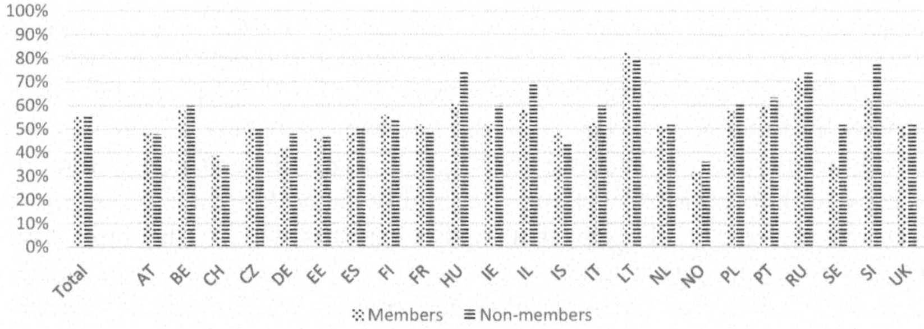

Fig. 2.27 Support for basic income by trade union membership (*Source* ESS [2016/2017]. Question wording: 'Are you or have you ever been a member of a trade union or similar organisation? If yes, is that currently or previously?' Answer categories: [1] 'Yes, currently', [2] 'Yes, previously' and [3] 'No'. The category 'members' consists of both [1] and [2], because the group of current members was too small in a number of countries. The graph presents the percentage of respondents in favour of introducing a basic income within the respective categories)

driven by the perception that basic income will worsen members' individual interests and/or the collective interests of the trade unions more generally. On the other hand, it may also reflect the fact that many unionized workers feel that the unconditional nature of basic income endangers the highly valued work ethic. Nevertheless, the ESS data does not seem to support the often made assumption that basic income will face outright opposition among the rank and file of the trade unions. In several countries—most notably Lithuania (82.1%), Russia (71.1%) and Slovenia (62.7%)—the majority of trade unionists express support for introducing a basic income. At the same time, there are nevertheless other countries—such as Norway (68.4%), Sweden (64.5%) and Switzerland (61.4%)—where basic income is opposed by the majority of trade union members.

2.2.8 *Political Ideology*

With regard to political ideology, the most obvious place to start is by examining differences between the 'left' and the 'right'. Many have argued that basic income is first and foremost a left-wing project, mainly because it promises to achieve a number of outcomes that left-wing parties and their constituencies have persistently pursued for decades: greater redistribution from rich to poor, strongly reduced levels of poverty, increased bargaining power for workers and so on (Chrisp & Martinelli, 2019; Schwander & Vlandas, 2020). If left-wingers believe a basic income does a better job of reaching these goals than the existing system of selective and conditional welfare, it is highly likely that they will support a reform towards it. This probably also explains why in the rare cases that basic income has received explicit political support, this has mostly come from left-wing (particularly Green) parties (Van Parijs & Vanderborght, 2017). From this perspective, it seems clear that basic income should be more popular among left-wingers than it is among their right-wing counterparts, whose political parties seem to be either opposed to, or indifferent about, the whole idea. While this stems to some extent from a long-rooted apathy concerning excessive economic redistribution, right-wing parties also often invoke cultural counter-arguments. Most importantly, they tend to loathe the idea that the universality of basic income may mean it would also be paid to migrants, thereby creating an unprecedented welfare magnet effect (Borjas, 1999). At the same time, there are nevertheless good reasons to believe that right-wing voters could be quite supportive of basic income. Some highly influential right-wing thinkers, such as Milton Friedman (1962) and Charles Murray (2008), have in fact proposed policies that are very similar to basic income in order to reduce state interference and welfare bureaucracy. In this view, the single payment provided by a basic income is a lesser evil than the complex web of existing welfare benefits and services that makes government far larger than it ought to be, controlling people's lives to the point of taking away their freedom. If the level of basic income is sufficiently low—as it is in most right-wing proposals—it could ultimately lead to the dismantling of the welfare state, thereby handing back the responsibility for welfare to the actors that were crowded out by the state: the family, the community and the market.

As shown in Fig. 2.28, support for basic income in most of the countries is clearly highest among those who identify as left wing, and lowest among those who see themselves as right wing. However, there are some countries in which the exact opposite is found. In Hungary, Lithuania, Poland and Russia in particular, basic income is indeed more popular among right-wingers than it is among left-wingers. People in the political centre, which are neither left nor right, are usually in between the

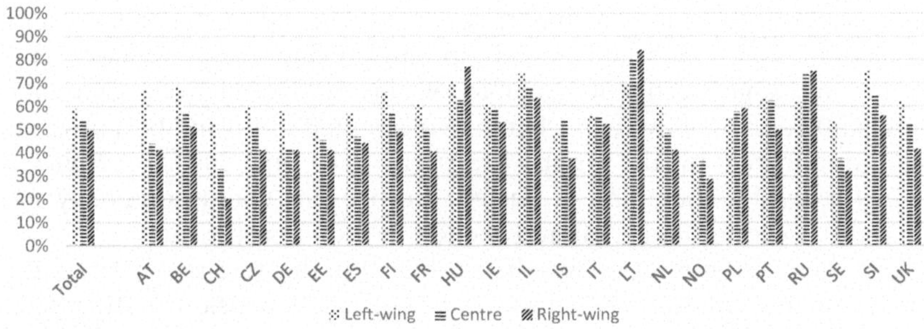

Fig. 2.28 Support for basic income by political orientation (*Source* ESS [2016/2017]. Question wording: 'In politics people sometimes talk of "left" and "right". Where would you place yourself on this scale, where 0 means the left and 10 means the right?' If the respondent's answer was between 0 and 3, they are placed in the category 'left-wing'. If the answer lies between 4 and 6 or between 7 and 10, respondents are placed in the 'centre' and 'right-wing' category, respectively. The graph presents the percentage of respondents in favour of introducing a basic income within the respective categories)

two extremes. With an eye on political coalition building, it is also interesting to see whether the centrists are closest to the left or the right. In that regard, the centre is clearly closer to the right in Austria, Belgium, Denmark, Lithuania, Russia, Spain and Sweden. The opposite pattern is observed in Ireland, Iceland, Norway and Portugal. In the remaining countries, the centrists are about as close to left-wingers as they are to right-wingers. Italy, in particular, stands out from the rest because the level of support for basic income is nearly identical across leftist, centrist and rightist groups, at around 50%.

It is increasingly recognized, however, that 'left' and 'right' can mean different things in different countries, complicating the use of left-right orientation in cross-national comparisons. In this regard, it is well-documented that the left-right axis has a very different meaning in Western and Eastern Europe, especially on its economic dimension (Tavits & Letki, 2009). In the East, left-wing parties have a history of implementing austerity and retrenchment policies that are traditionally associated with right-wing parties. These former communist parties mainly did so because they were under national and international pressure to prove that they took the transition from a planned to a market economy seriously. By contrast, the post-communist right-wing parties had greater leeway in reacting to popular demands for greater social protection, and eventually ended up introducing many welfare state expansions. One pertinent example of this is the relatively generous Family 500+ child allowance scheme implemented in Poland by a government dominated by the right-wing party 'Law and Justice' (*Prawo i Sprawiedliwość*). Therefore, in Eastern Europe one could potentially see the right as economically left and the left as economically right.

For these reasons, it is worth breaking up the traditional left-right divide into an economic dimension and a cultural dimension. With regard to the first, I look at the relationship between people's support for basic income and their egalitarian beliefs, measured as the acceptance of 'large income differences due to differences in individual talents and effort'. The assumption here is that people who accept these income differences are less supportive of economic redistribution and thus anti-egalitarian, while those who refute them are more supportive of such redistribution and thus pro-egalitarian. As Fig. 2.29 shows, we see that in most countries basic income is more popular among those who argue against large income differences. These pro-egalitarians are probably more supportive because they see basic income as a promising tool to close

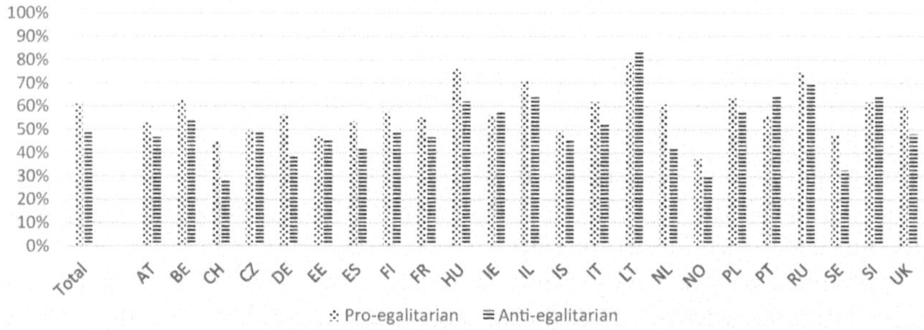

Fig. 2.29 Support for basic income by egalitarian beliefs (*Source* ESS [2016/2017]. Question wording: 'How much do you agree or disagree with the following statement: Large differences in people's incomes are acceptable to properly reward differences in talents and efforts'. The category 'pro-egalitarian' consists of all respondents who disagree with the statement. The 'anti-egalitarian' category consists of all those who agree with it. Those who answered 'neither agree nor disagree' are excluded from the analysis. The graph presents the percentage of respondents in favour of introducing a basic income within the respective categories)

the gap between society's rich and poor through redistribution. At the same time, there are some countries—most notably Portugal—in which basic income is actually more popular among those who tolerate large income differences, and some countries—such as the Czech Republic and Ireland—where there is barely any difference between anti-egalitarians and pro-egalitarians.

With regard to the cultural dimension of the left-right axis, it is interesting to look at how people's support for basic income is related to their stance towards migration, which is probably the most divisive cultural issue in modern politics. In this respect, one would expect that anti-migration attitudes would lower support for basic income, given that its universality makes the policy easily accessible for migrants, or even worse, could attract new migrants to the country (Vlandas, 2021). As shown in Fig. 2.30, support for basic income in most countries is indeed lower among those who agree with the statement that migrants make their country of residence 'a worse place to live', compared with those who think it makes the country 'a better place to live'. This supports prior research by Bay and Pedersen (2006) in Norway, in which they found a significant drop in support for basic income after people had

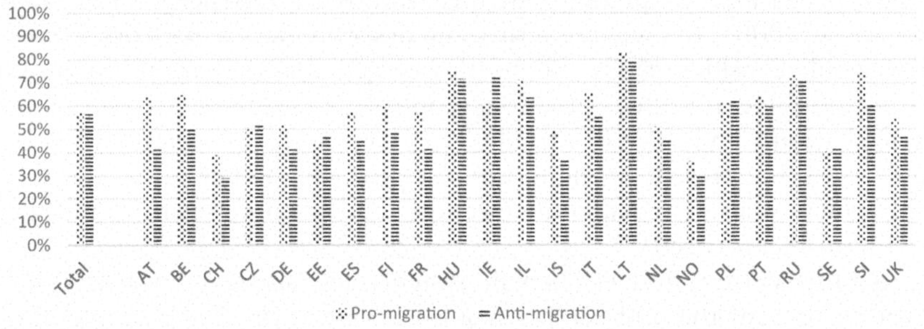

Fig. 2.30 Support for basic income by migration beliefs (*Source* ESS [2016/2017]. Question wording: 'Is [country] made a worse or better place to live by people coming to live here from other countries?' The 11-point answer scale ranged from 'worse place to live' [0] to 'better place to live' [10]. If a respondent's answer was between 0 and 4, they are placed in the category 'anti-migration'. If the answer lies between 6 and 10, respondents are placed in the 'pro-migration' category. Those on the mid-point of the scale are excluded from the analysis. The graph presents the percentage of respondents in favour of introducing a basic income within the respective categories)

been told that it would also be paid to migrants. It is also in tune with the well-established finding that anti-migration attitudes also tend to decrease support for most other types of welfare provision (see, for example, Garand et al., 2017). Nevertheless, there are a number of countries in which support for basic income is more-or-less equal between those with anti-migration attitudes and those with pro-migration attitudes. These are mostly Central and Eastern European Countries (the Czech Republic, Estonia, Lithuania, Poland and Russia), but also Sweden. Only in Israel do we observe the complete opposite of the general pattern, with support for basic income being higher (rather than lower) among those with anti-migration attitudes.

2.2.9 Welfare Deservingness Perceptions

With regard to welfare deservingness, the basic expectation is that support for a fully universal and unconditional basic income will be lower among those who think most current welfare recipients are undeserving of help (Roosma & van Oorschot, 2020). From the deservingness literature, we know that people generally apply five criteria—the so-called 'CARIN criteria'—to determine who should receive what from the welfare state: control, attitude, reciprocity, identity and need (Laenen, 2020; van Oorschot, 2000). In concrete terms, the deservingness framework argues that people consider others as more deserving if they: (1) are not personally responsible for their situation (control), (2) adhere to prevailing societal norms and values (attitude), (3) contribute to society, whether in the past, the present or the future (reciprocity), (4) belong to a group with which we can easily identify (identity) and (5) have financial and/or health problems (need).

In most current welfare benefit systems and services, measures are taken to prevent the undeserving from receiving them. For example, the conditionality embedded in social insurance schemes ensures that only those with a sufficiently long work record are included, thereby excluding labour market outsiders. Another relevant example involves means-tested social assistance schemes that are targeted at the poor only, thereby excluding all who are not in proven need. The issue with basic income, however, is that because it is paid to everyone with no strings attached whatsoever, it also goes to those groups that many perceive as being undeserving of government support. On the one hand, this includes people who do not work. If these people are jobless through their own fault—for example, because they are unwilling to work—many would consider them as being in control of their situation and thus undeserving of a basic income. Additionally, the jobless may also be blamed for making insufficient contributions to society through labour market participation and for having an immoral attitude that deviates from the dominant work ethic. On the other hand, a basic income also goes to people with middle and higher incomes, who are generally not considered to be in genuine need of government support. Accordingly, it seems only natural that many will wonder why the government should provide a regular income to both rich and poor, knowing that the rich can make do without while the poor really need it for their survival.

To explore the relationship between welfare deservingness and support for basic income, Figs. 2.31 and 2.32 show how support relates to popular perceptions of unemployed people's job-seeking efforts and material needs, respectively. For the former, we can see that support for basic income tends to be lower among those who think that most unemployed people are lazy because they 'do not really try to find a job'. This is most evident in Austria, the Czech Republic, Finland, Hungary and Poland, where the difference is larger than 10 percentage points. By contrast, in a number of other countries—such as Estonia, Ireland and Sweden—this support gap is relatively small. Only in Norway is support for basic income greater (though only marginally) among those who think most unemployed lack job-seeking efforts. Overall, these findings nevertheless confirm that at least in some countries, negative deservingness perceptions pertaining to the issues of control, reciprocity and attitude can and do lower popular support for basic income.

With regard to the second type of deservingness considerations, relating to the material needs of unemployed people, it can be seen that basic income is generally less popular among those who feel that the unemployed have a fairly good standard of living and are thus not in need. This gap is clearly widest in Austria, followed by countries such as the Czech Republic, Germany and Switzerland. However, in many other countries the difference is relatively small (see, for example, Lithuania, Spain and the UK). The results do nevertheless suggest that a perceived lack of material needs can drive down popular support for the introduction of a basic income, albeit more in some countries than in others.

Fig. 2.31 Support for basic income by perceptions of unemployed people's efforts (*Source* ESS [2016/2017]. Question wording: 'How much do you agree or disagree with the following statement about people in [country]: Most unemployed people do not really try to find a job'. The graph presents the percentage of respondents in favour of introducing a basic income within the respective categories)

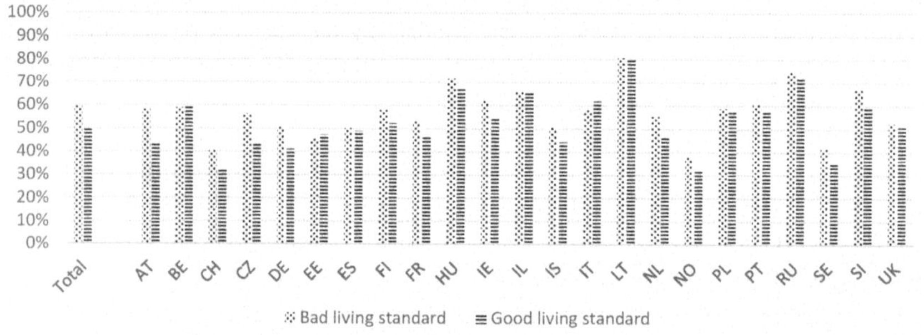

Fig. 2.32 Support for basic income by perceptions of unemployed people's needs (*Source* ESS [2016/2017]. Question wording: 'What do you think overall about the standard of living of people who are unemployed? Please tell me on a score of 0 to 10, where 0 means extremely bad and 10 means extremely good'. If a respondent's answer was between 0 and 5, they are placed in the category 'bad living standard'. If their answer lies between 6 and 10, respondents are placed in the 'good living standard' category. The graph presents the percentage of respondents in favour of introducing a basic income within the respective categories)

They also help us understand why basic income is less popular in high-spending countries (see Fig. 2.9), where the current welfare system is better equipped to maintain or even improve people's living standards.

2.2.10 *Welfare Performance Evaluations*

A basic expectation put forward in the literature with regard to welfare state performance is that support for basic income will be higher among those who feel disgruntled about the workings of the current system (Lee, 2018; Roosma & van Oorschot, 2020). If people are truly dissatisfied with the welfare state in its current form, they may be more open to accept a radical reform of it, including a move towards a fully universal and unconditional basic income. Conversely, the appetite for basic income as an alternative to the status quo is probably lower among those who think the existing welfare system is functioning well. Things are, however, likely to be more nuanced than that. In fact, whether people support a basic income as a radical alternative is most likely to depend on what specific aspects of the welfare state they are happy or unhappy with (Laenen & Gugushvili, 2022). In this regard, previous work distinguishes three different types of welfare state criticism: social, moral and economic (van Oorschot et al., 2012). For the first, it seems plausible that people who think the current system is not realizing its social goals—such as the reduction of poverty and income inequality—will be more supportive of a basic income scheme that promises to improve the lot of the poor. Especially when the failure to reach these goals is (partly) attributed to high levels of non-take up of social rights, we expect to see greater support for the introduction of a basic income scheme that would—due to its universality—virtually eliminate the problem of non-take up.

For the two other types of welfare state criticism, it seems more likely that support for basic income will be lower among those who see the current welfare system as dysfunctional. With regard to moral criticism, it indeed seems unlikely for basic income to be popular among those who feel that the existing system is plagued by fraud on the part of welfare claimants. Although a basic income is less prone to abuse (because everyone receives it), we should not expect strong endorsement from those who perceive most current welfare recipients as welfare frauds. In a similar vein, it seems equally unlikely that basic income will be endorsed by those who feel that the existing welfare state is too expensive and harmful for the economy, given that the implementation of a basic income

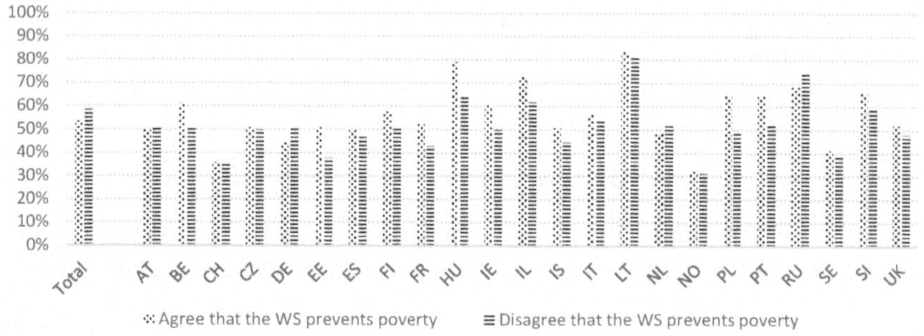

Fig. 2.33 Support for basic income by perceptions of the welfare state's effect on poverty (*Source* ESS [2016/2017]. Question wording: 'To what extent do you agree or disagree that social benefits and services in [country] prevent widespread poverty?' The graph presents the percentage of respondents in favour of introducing a basic income within the respective categories. 'WS' stands for 'welfare state')

is likely to increase the prevailing levels of taxation. Instead, negative perceptions of the welfare state's economic consequences could well lead to greater support for less costly policy alternatives, such as means-tested social assistance.

Starting with social criticism of the welfare state, the results are mixed. On the one hand, Fig. 2.33 shows that in most countries, basic income is more popular among those who think that the welfare state is already successful at preventing widespread poverty. This is especially the case in Belgium, Estonia, Hungary, Ireland, Israel, Poland and Portugal, where the difference is larger than 10 percentage points. One plausible explanation is that people who are satisfied with the poverty-reducing capabilities of the welfare state tend to see basic income as an *extension* rather than a *replacement* of the existing system, making it just one more instrument to be utilized in the ongoing fight against poverty. This interpretation clearly goes against the common expectation that basic income will receive greater support from those who are unhappy with the current system because it fails to reach the goal of poverty reduction—a pattern that is only found in some countries, most notably Germany and Russia. On the other hand, Fig. 2.34 shows that in almost every country, support for basic income is higher among those who agree with the statement that 'many people with very low incomes get less benefits than they are legally

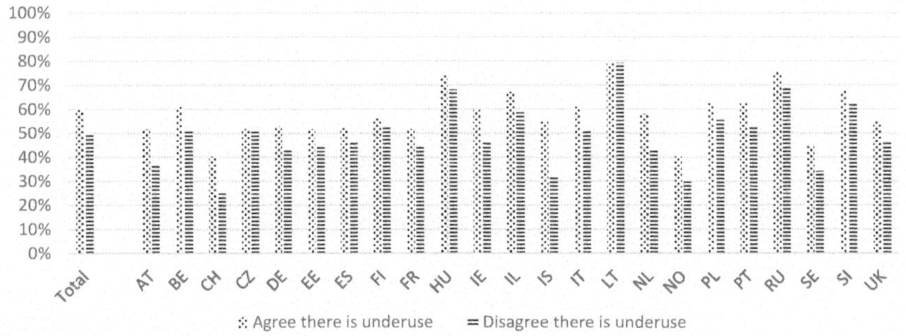

Fig. 2.34 Support for basic income by perceptions of underuse of social benefits (*Source* ESS [2016/2017]. Question wording: 'How much do you agree or disagree with the following statement about people in [country]: Many people with very low incomes get less benefits than they are legally entitled to'. The graph presents the percentage of respondents in favour of introducing a basic income within the respective categories)

entitled to'. In this view, basic income is clearly seen as a fertile solution to the problem of non-take up, which leaves low-income groups in particular under-protected. Basic income is much less attractive for people who think such underuse of social benefits only occurs sporadically.

For the other side of the coin—the overuse of social benefits—the opposite is found: in almost every country, support for basic income is lower among those who are dissatisfied with the current system, as indicated by their agreement with the statement that 'many people manage to obtain benefits and services to which they are not entitled' (see Fig. 2.35). The only exceptions to this general trend are Estonia, Ireland and Russia (where there are no differences between those who think such overuse is prevalent and those who do not), and Israel (where basic income is actually more popular among those who believe there is a great deal of fraud and abuse in the current system). Overall, however, the findings clearly indicate that moral criticism of the existing welfare system decreases (rather than increases) the popularity of basic income.

As shown in Fig. 2.36, a similar story applies to economic criticism of the welfare state. In most countries, support for basic income is lower among those who agree with the statement that 'the welfare state places too great a strain on the economy'. As noted above, this is presumably prompted by the pervasive idea that a basic income will require an increase

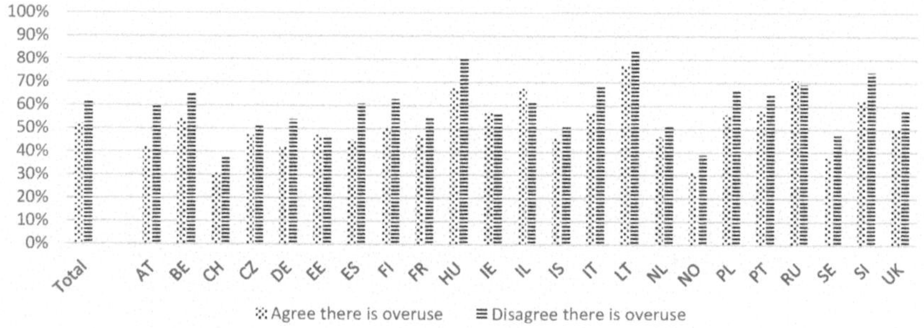

Fig. 2.35 Support for basic income by perceptions of overuse of social benefits (*Source* ESS [2016/2017]. Question wording: 'How much do you agree or disagree with the following statement about people in [country]: Many people manage to obtain benefits and services to which they are not entitled'. The graph presents the percentage of respondents in favour of introducing a basic income within the respective categories)

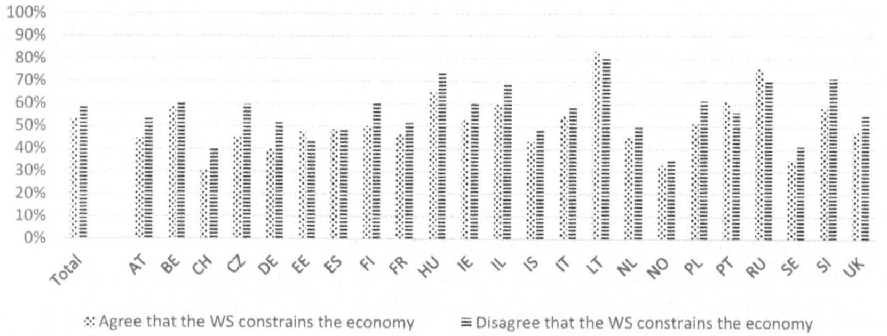

Fig. 2.36 Support for basic income by perceptions of the welfare state's economic effect (*Source* ESS [2016/2017]. Question wording: 'To what extent do you agree or disagree that social benefits and services in [country] place too great a strain on the economy?' The graph presents the percentage of respondents in favour of introducing a basic income within the respective categories. 'WS' stands for 'welfare state')

in taxes, thereby making the welfare state more costly and potentially worse for the economy than it was before. There are, however, a few countries that deviate from the general pattern. In Estonia, Lithuania, Portugal and Russia in particular, it turns out that basic income is actually more popular among those who think the existing welfare system is bad for the economy. Perhaps in these countries, citizens are more likely to think of basic income as a means to improve the economy, for example, by making flexible forms of work more attractive than they are in the existing welfare state.

Summary Box 2.2 Individual Differences in Support for the Ideal-Typical Basic Income

Overall, the data from the European Social Survey demonstrates the importance of looking at individual differences underlying across-the-board levels of support for basic income.

Some groups of people prove to be consistently and considerably more supportive of the ideal-typical basic income than others. From a social-structural perspective, these are younger people, those with a lower income (especially those who *perceive* they have a lower income) and those with precarious employment contracts; all of whom have a higher than average degree of self-interest in the introduction of basic income because they experience higher than average job and income insecurity. From an ideological perspective, basic income is more popular among those who identify themselves as politically left wing, have pro-egalitarian and pro-migration attitudes, think most current welfare recipients are deserving of help and positively evaluate the performance of the existing welfare system.

By contrast, a number of other individual characteristics do not seem to matter much for popular support for basic income, even though there are good theoretical grounds to assume that they would. In particular, these are gender, household composition, sector of employment and trade union membership.

Importantly, there are always some countries that prove exceptions to these general patterns. For example, although trade union membership is not an important factor in most countries, it clearly does matter in Hungary and Slovenia, where members are much less supportive of basic income compared with non-members. Likewise, while in most countries basic income receives greater support among low-income earners, this is clearly not the case in Portugal, where all income categories show equal levels of support.

These findings indicate that there usually is some degree of cross-national variation in the relationship between individual characteristics and support for basic income. For some characteristics, these differences are relatively large. A case in point is education: while in some countries—such as the Czech Republic and Poland—the popularity of basic income decreases as educational levels increase, it is actually the other way around in a host of other countries, including Finland and the Netherlands.

Taken together, the results show that there is almost never a simple, one-size-fits-all story to tell about the relationship between people's characteristics and their support for the ideal-typical basic income. Instead, this relationship very often varies between countries.

References

Adriaans, J., Liebig, S., & Schupp, J. (2019). In Germany, Younger, Better Educated Persons, and Lower Income Groups Are More Likely to Be in Favor of Unconditional Basic Income. *DIW Weekly Report, 15*, 127–134.

Alesina, A., & Fuchs-Schündeln, N. (2005). Goodbye Lenin (or Not?): The Effect of Communism on People's Preferences. *The American Economic Review, 97*(4), 1507–1528.

Andersson, J. A., & Kangas, O. (2004). Popular Support for Basic Income in Sweden and Finland. In G. Standing (Ed.), *Promoting Income Security as a Right: Europe and North America* (pp. 285–298). Anthem Press.

Bay, A., & Pedersen, A. (2006). The Limits of Social Solidarity: Basic Income, Immigration and the Legitimacy of the Universal Welfare State. *Acta Sociologica, 49*(4), 419–436.

Borjas, G. J. (1999). Immigration and Welfare Magnets. *Journal of Labor Economics, 17*(4), 607–637.

Busemeyer, M., & Sahm, A. (2022). Social Investment, Redistribution or Basic Income? Exploring the Association Between Automation Risk and Welfare State Attitudes in Europe. *Journal of Social Policy, 51*(4), 751–770.

Chrisp, J., & Martinelli, L. (2019). Neither Left Nor Right. In M. Torry (Ed.), *The Palgrave International Handbook of Basic Income* (pp. 477–492). Palgrave Macmillan.

Chrisp, J., Pulkka, V. V., & Rincon, L. (2020). Snowballing or Wilting? What Affects Public Support for Varying Models of Basic Income? *Journal of International and Comparative Social Policy, 36*(3), 223–236.

Cigna, L. M. (2022). Looking for a North Star? Ideological Justifications and Trade Unions' Preferences for a Universal Basic Income. *European Journal of Industrial Relations, 28*(2), 129–146.

Colombo, C., De Rocchi, T., Kurer, T., & Widmer, T. (2016, Juni). *Analyse der eidgenössichen Abstimmung vom 5.* GfS Bern.

Delsen, L. (2019). *Empirical Research on an Unconditional Basic Income in Europe*. Springer.

Delsen, L., & Schilpzand, R. (2019). Individual Preferences for the Unconditional Basic Income in the European Union. In L. Delsen (Ed.), *Empirical Research on an Unconditional Basic Income in Europe* (pp. 29–60). Springer.

Dermont, C., & Weisstanner, D. (2020). Automation and the Future of the Welfare State: Basic Income as a Response to Technological Change? *Political Research Exchange, 2*(1). https://doi.org/10.1080/2474736X.2020.1757387 [online first]

De Wispelaere, J. (2015). *An Income of One's Own? The Political Analysis of Universal Basic Income* (Unpublished doctoral dissertation). University of Tampere.

Dolezal, M. (2010). Exploring the Stabilization of a Political Force: The Social and Attitudinal Basis of Green Parties in the Age of Globalization. *West European Politics, 33*(3), 534–552.

ESS ERIC. (2021). *The Human Values Scale: Findings from the European Social Survey*. ESS ERIC.

Friedman, M. (1962). *Capitalism and Freedom*. University of Chicago Press.

Garand, J. C., Xu, P., & Davis, B. C. (2017). Immigration Attitudes and Support for the Welfare State in the American Mass Public. *American Journal of Political Science, 61*(1), 146–162.

Gilligan, C. (1982). *In a Different Voice: Psychological Theory and Women's Development*. Harvard University Press.

Laenen, T. (2020). *Welfare Deservingness and Welfare Policy. Popular Deservingness Opinions and their Interaction with Welfare State Policies*. Edward Elgar Publishing.

Laenen, T., & Gugushvili, G. (2021). Are Universal Welfare Policies Really More Popular Than Selective Ones? A Critical Discussion of Empirical Research. *International Journal of Sociology and Social Policy, 41*(9/10), 1134–1147.

Laenen, T., & Gugushvili, G. (2022). Welfare State Dissatisfaction and Support for Major Welfare Reform: Towards Means-Tested Welfare or Universal Basic Income? *International Journal of Social Welfare*. https://doi.org/10.1111/ijsw.12546 [onlinefirst]

Le Clainche, C. (2004). Public Support for Basic Income Schemes and a Universal Right to Health Care: What the French People Think. In G. Standing (Ed.), *Promoting Income Security as a Right: Europe and North America* (pp. 401–426). Anthem Press.

Lee, S. (2018). Attitudes Toward Universal Basic Income and Welfare State in Europe: A Research Note. *Basic Income Studies, 13*(1). https://doi.org/10.1515/bis-2018-0002 [online only]

Leff, B., Percy, A., Story, M., & Szlinder, M. (2019). Alternatives to Basic Income. In M. Torry (Ed.), *The Palgrave International Handbook of Basic Income* (pp. 213–231). Palgrave Macmillan.

Liebig, S., & Mau, S. (2004). A Legitimate Guaranteed Minimum Income? In G. Standing (Ed.), *Promoting Income Security as a Right: Europe and North America* (pp. 207–228). Anthem Press.
Murray, C. (2008). Guaranteed Income as a Replacement for the Welfare State. *Basic Income Studies, 3*(2). https://doi.org/10.2202/1932-0183.1115 [online only]
Nettle, D., Johnson, E., Johnson, M., & Saxe, R. (2021). Why Has the COVID-19 Pandemic Increased Support for Universal Basic Income? *Humanities & Social Sciences Communications, 8*(1), 1–12.
Parolin, Z., & Siöland, L. (2020). Support for a Universal Basic Income: A Demand–Capacity Paradox? *Journal of European Social Policy, 30*(1), 5–19.
Raes, K. (1988). Basic Income and Social Power. In A. G. Miller (Ed.), *Proceedings of the First International Conference on Basic Income, Louvain-la-Neuve, Belgium, 4–6 September 1986* (pp. 106–122). Basic Income European Network.
Rennwald, L. (2020). *Social Democratic Parties and the Working Class*. Springer Nature.
Rincon, L. (2021). *The Paradox of Universality: Preferences for Universal Basic Income in Finland and Spain* (Unpublished doctoral dissertation). Universitat de Barcelona.
Robeyns, I. (2000). Hush Money or Emancipation Fee? A Gender Analysis of Basic Income. In R. van der Veen & L. Groot (Eds.), *Basic Income on the Agenda. Policy Objectives and Political Chances* (pp. 121–136). Amsterdam University Press.
Roosma, F., & van Oorschot, W. (2020). Public Opinion on Basic Income: Mapping European Support for a Radical Alternative for Welfare Provision. *Journal of European Social Policy, 30*(2), 190–205.
Schwander, H., & Vlandas, T. (2020). The Left and Universal Basic Income: The Role of Ideology in Individual Support. *Journal of International and Comparative Social Policy, 36*(3), 237–268.
Shafarman, S. (2004). Mobilizing Support for Basic Income. In G. Standing (Ed.), *Promoting Income Security as a Right: Europe and North America* (pp. 195–206). Anthem Press.
Steensland, B. (2008). *The Failed Welfare Revolution. America's Struggle over Guaranteed Income Policy*. Princeton University Press.
Takamatsu, R., & Tachibanaki, T. (2014). What Needs to Be Considered When Introducing a New Welfare System: Who Supports Basic Income in Japan? In Y. Vanderborght & T. Yamamori (Eds.), *Basic Income in Japan. Prospects for a Radical Idea in a Transforming Welfare State* (pp. 197–218). Palgrave Macmillan.

Tavits, M., & Letki, N. (2009). When Left Is Right: Party Ideology and Policy in Post-Communist Europe. *American Political Science Review, 103*(4), 555–569.

Torry, M. (Ed.). (2019). *The Palgrave International Handbook of Basic Income.* Palgrave Macmillan.

Vanderborght, Y. (2006). Why Trade Unions Oppose Basic Income. *Basic Income Studies, 1*(1). https://doi.org/10.2202/1932-0183.1002 [online only]

Van Hootegem, A., & Laenen, T. (2022). A Wave of Support? A Natural Experiment on How the COVID-19 Pandemic Affected the Popularity of a Basic Income. *Acta Politica.* https://doi.org/10.1057/s41269-022-00260-9 [online first]

van Oorschot, W. (2000). Who Should Get What, and Why? On Deservingness Criteria and the Conditionality of Solidarity Among the Public. *Policy & Politics, 28*(1), 33–48.

van Oorschot, W., Laenen, T., Roosma, F., & Meuleman, B. (2022). Recent Advances in Understanding Welfare Attitudes in Europe. In K. Nelson, R. Nieuwenhuis, & M. Yerkes (Eds.), *Social Policy in Changing European Societies, Research Agendas for the 21st Century* (pp. 202–217). Edward Elgar Publishing.

van Oorschot, W., Reeskens, T., & Meuleman, B. (2012). Popular Perceptions of Welfare State Consequences: A Multilevel, Cross-National Analysis of 25 European Countries. *Journal of European Social Policy, 22*(2), 181–197.

Van Parijs, P., & Vanderborght, Y. (2017). *A Radical Proposal for a Free Society and a Sane Economy.* Harvard University Press.

Vlandas, T. (2021). The Political Economy of Individual-Level Support for the Basic Income in Europe. *Journal of European Social Policy, 31*(1), 62–77.

Weisstanner, D. (2022). COVID-19 and Welfare State Support: The Case of Universal Basic Income. *Policy & Society, 41*(1), 96–110.

Yang, J., Mohan, G., & Fukushi, K. (2020). An Analysis of the Factors Influencing Public Attitudes Toward Implementing Basic Income (BI) from an Individual Perspective: A Case Study of Hokuriku Region, Japan. *Societies, 10*(3). https://doi.org/10.3390/soc10030052 [online only]

CHAPTER 3

Popular Support for Differently Designed Varieties of Basic Income

In the previous chapter, attention was limited to the popularity of the ideal-typical version of basic income. This is broadly defined as a periodic cash payment, unconditionally delivered to all on an individual basis and without any means test or work requirement. As shown in Chapter 1, however, there have always been many different varieties and cognates of basic income that deviate—to differing degrees—from the broadly described ideal type. It is therefore equally important to assess popular support for a wider range of differently designed forms of basic income. To do so, I mainly rely on data from five survey experiments conducted in different European countries: Belgium, Finland, the Netherlands, Spain and Switzerland. More specifically, these are so-called 'vignette' or 'conjoint' experiments (Auspurg & Hinz, 2015), in which respondents are asked to rate randomly assigned basic income schemes that randomly vary on a number of policy design dimensions. Because of these experimental manipulations, vignette and conjoint experiments have high internal validity, making them particularly well suited for estimating (and comparing) the impact of different policy design characteristics of basic income on its popular support (Hainmueller et al., 2014). Where possible and relevant, the experimental data is complemented with information from traditional polls.

In the following, I first assess across-the-board levels of support for types of basic income with different policy designs. I start out

© The Author(s), under exclusive license to Springer Nature Switzerland AG 2023

T. Laenen, *The Popularity of Basic Income*, Exploring the Basic Income Guarantee, https://doi.org/10.1007/978-3-031-29352-8_3

by providing some background information and offer a few general observations on the five different survey experiments used. After that, I zoom in on the twelve different policy design dimensions distinguished in Chapter 1: accumulation, administration, conditionality, duration, financing, frequency, generosity, individuality, integration, modality, uniformity and universality. The chapter ends with an investigation of relevant individual differences in popular support for differently designed varieties of basic income.

3.1 Across the Board

Before delving into the specific policy design dimensions, I first discuss the five survey experiments considered in this chapter in a more general way.

The first experiment is a vignette experiment embedded in the Basic Income in Belgium (BABEL) Survey, which was held in Spring 2021 among 3000 respondents recruited online via the Bilendi panel (Laenen et al., 2021). Respondents were asked to indicate their support (on a scale from 0 to 100) for the introduction of a hypothetical basic income scheme, the characteristics of which randomly varied on the following five design dimensions: conditionality, financing, generosity, integration and universality (see Table A1.1 in Appendix 1 for the full question wording). The second experiment is a near-replication of the BABEL one, incorporated in the Basic Income in the Netherlands (BIN) Survey, conducted in late 2021 with a sample of approximately 1200 respondents (Gielens, 2022a). In addition to the vignette experiments, the BABEL Survey includes several questions related to basic income that will be discussed later. For now, it suffices to note two general observations that stand out from the marginal means reported in Fig. 3.1. The first of these is that overall support for basic income proves to be somewhat higher in the Netherlands than in Belgium. Averaged across all the vignettes, the mean level of support is 64.1 among Dutch respondents and 54.6 among their Belgian counterparts. Another general observation is that within Belgium, overall support is higher among French-speaking respondents (who tend to live in the region of Wallonia) than their Dutch-speaking counterparts (who mostly live in the region of Flanders). These differences are likely to be due to the vastly distinct economic and political realities in the two regions, with Wallonia lagging behind economically and having a much more left-wing-oriented political landscape than in Flanders. Taken

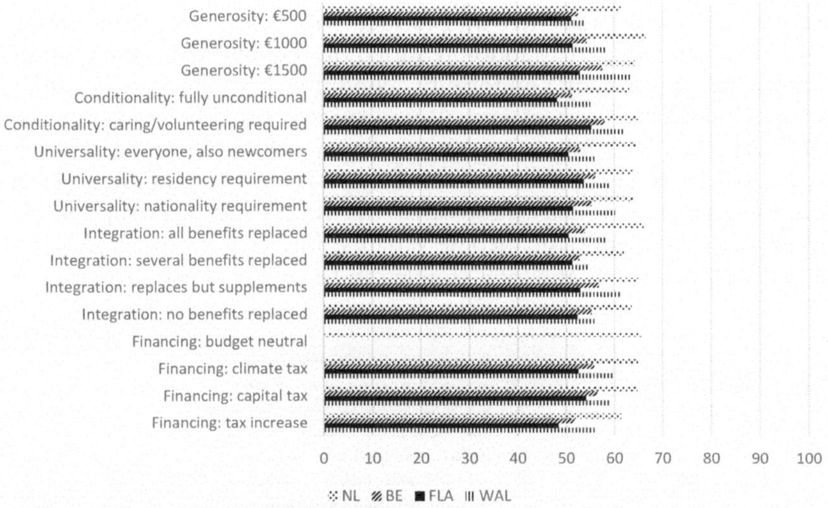

Fig. 3.1 Support for different basic income varieties in Belgium and the Netherlands, 2021 (*Source* BABEL Survey [2021] for Belgium and BIN Survey [2021] for the Netherlands. Question wording: 'Suppose the Belgian/Dutch government wants to introduce a basic income. This basic income would include the following characteristics: [...]. To what extent are you in favour of or against the introduction of this basic income in Belgium/the Netherlands?' The answer scale ranged from 'strongly against' [0] to 'strongly in favour' [100]. The graph presents the mean score for each level in the vignette experiment. For Belgium, the graph shows the mean scores for all respondents living in Belgium [BE], the Dutch-speaking respondents living in Flanders [FLA] and the French-speaking respondents living in Wallonia [WAL]. The 'Financing: budget neutral' condition was only presented in the BIN Survey)

together, these first observations already suggest that support for differently designed varieties of basic income varies both between countries and across regions within a country—as does support for the ideal-typical version (see Chapter 2).

The third experiment is another vignette experiment that was incorporated in the Belgian National Election Study (BNES), a large and representative survey held among approximately 1650 adult respondents who were eligible to vote in the federal elections of May 2019 (Abts, Swyngedouw, et al., 2021). Respondents were asked to rate (on a scale from 0 to 10 that was then transformed to a scale from 0 to 100) a basic income scheme that randomly varied on the following policy design dimensions: universality, uniformity, conditionality, integration within the broader welfare system and accumulation with other earnings (see Table A1.2 for the full question wordings). Although some of these dimensions were also part of the BABEL/BIN Survey, different policy options were shown. This means that the BNES measures support for a very different set of basic income variants. Interestingly, because of the COVID-19 pandemic, the total sample can be split into two sub-samples:

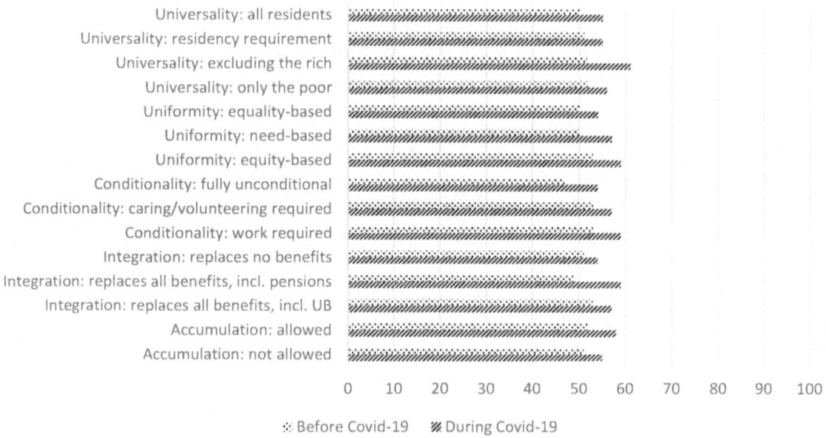

Fig. 3.2 Support for different basic income varieties in Belgium, 2019/2020 (*Source* BNES [2019/2020]. Question wording: 'In some countries there is a debate about whether or not to introduce a basic income. In a moment, I will ask you to what extent you are in favour of or against this basic income. First I will give you some more information on what we understand by a basic income. [...] To what extent are you in favour of or against the introduction of this basic income in Belgium?' The answer scale ranged from 'very strongly against' [0] to 'very strongly in favour' [10]. This was converted to a scale from 0 to 100. The graph represents the mean score for each level in the vignette experiment among all respondents interviewed before the start of the COVID-19 pandemic and all respondents interviewed during the pandemic. 'UB' stands for unemployment benefits. It should be noted that the vignettes mentioned that basic income is paid for by taxes)

one interviewed before the outbreak of the pandemic and the associated economic crisis (between December 2019 and March 2020, when the Belgian government announced the first general lockdown) and one interviewed during the pandemic (between June and November 2020). What seemed an unforeseen and unfortunate delay to the fieldwork at the time now actually offers a unique opportunity to uncover—in a sort of natural experiment—how the COVID-19 crisis affected support for different forms of basic income.

As shown by the marginal means in Fig. 3.2, it seems that basic income was generally more popular during than before the COVID-19 pandemic, possibly due to an overall increase in risk exposure and income insecurity in the midst of what was both a health and an economic crisis. This is confirmed by prior research that asked respondents (from the UK and the US) to indicate their support for basic income retrospectively, as if the

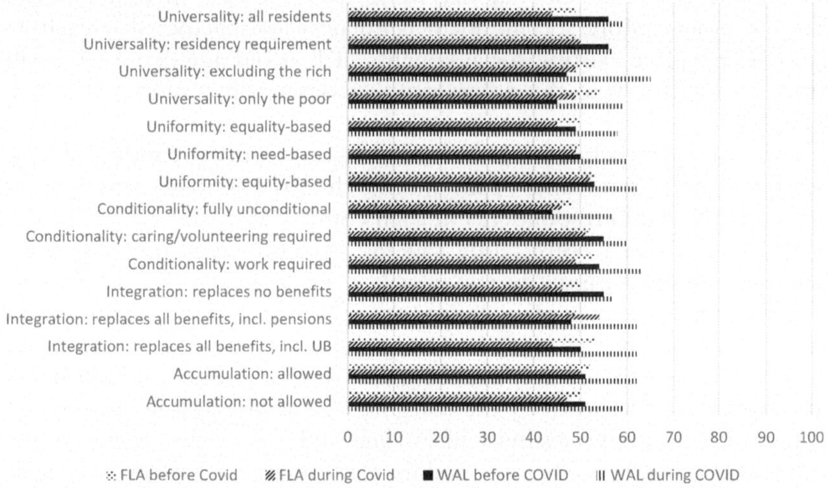

Fig. 3.3 Support for different basic income varieties in Flanders and Wallonia, 2019/2020 (*Source* BNES [2019/2020]. Question wording: see Fig. 3.2. The graph represents the mean score for each level in the vignette experiment among all Dutch-speaking [FLA] and French-speaking [WAL] respondents interviewed before the start of the COVID-19 pandemic and during the pandemic. 'UB' stands for unemployment benefits. It should be noted that the vignettes mentioned that basic income is paid for by taxes)

pandemic had never happened (Nettle et al., 2021). As Van Hootegem and Laenen (2022) have pointed out, three important nuances should nevertheless be made in this regard. First, the increase in support for basic income only applies to people living in the more-deprived region of Wallonia (see Fig. 3.3) or to those who believe their group was relatively deprived. Among their 'non-deprived' counterparts, support either remained stable or decreased somewhat, leading to greater polarization. Second, the authors suggest that the increase in support (even among the deprived) may not be long term, as it seems to closely follow the number of COVID-19-related hospitalizations—which is taken as a proxy for the societal insecurities brought about by the pandemic. This could mean that support for basic income will swiftly decrease again after the pandemic, when the economy starts to recover. It could also indicate that people are mostly supportive of a temporary, emergency basic income paid out only in a time of crisis (De Wispelaere & Morales, 2021). Third, the increase in popularity is (especially in Wallonia) larger for some basic income varieties than for others. More specifically, it is greatest for schemes that exclude the rich or replace existing social benefits such as old-age pensions. I will return to the trends in the different policy design dimensions in further detail below.

The fourth experiment is a conjoint experiment conducted (by Netquest) in Finland and Spain in March 2019 among a sample of approximately 1000 respondents in each country (Rincon, 2021). In the experiment, which I consistently call the 'Rincon experiment', respondents were asked to indicate (on a scale from 0 to 10) their likelihood of voting for a number of basic income proposals that randomly varied on the following policy design dimensions: universality, conditionality, individuality, generosity and financing (see Table A1.3 for the full question wordings). As shown by the marginal means in Fig. 3.4, the level of support was overall very similar in Finland and Spain (the precise means could unfortunately not be obtained for this experiment). However, there are important country differences with regard to popular support for specific types of basic income. These are discussed below.

The fifth experiment, which I label as the 'Stadelmann-Steffen and Dermont experiment', is another conjoint experiment carried out in June 2016 in Switzerland (closely after the basic income referendum) and in December 2016 in Finland (closely after the basic income experiment) among a sample of approximately 1000 respondents in each country (Stadelmann-Steffen & Dermont, 2020). The participants were asked to

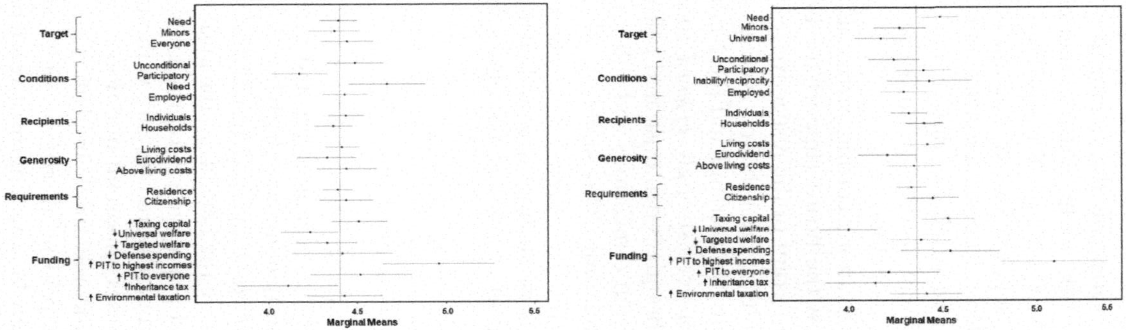

Fig. 3.4 Support for different basic income varieties in Finland and Spain, 2019 (*Source* Rincon [2021: 58, 85]. Question wording: 'Please read the two income benefit proposals carefully and rate each policy according to how likely you are to vote in favour of it. Note that 0 is not at all, and 10 means definitely voting in favour of it.' The graph represents the mean score for each [collapsed; see Table A1.3] level in the conjoint experiment in Finland [left] and Spain [right])

indicate (on a scale from 0 to 100%) their likelihood of approving specific basic income proposals as if these were the subject of a people's referendum. The proposals randomly varied on the following policy design dimensions: financing, generosity (for adults and for children), integration and universality (see Table A1.4 for question wordings). As shown by the marginal means in Fig. 3.5, support for basic income is consistently higher in Finland than in Switzerland. In both countries, but especially in Finland, people also seem to make relatively few distinctions between the different basic income varieties presented to them, notwithstanding some notable exceptions that I will discuss below.

Lastly, one other general observation, cutting across all five survey experiments, is that overall, across-the-board support for basic income tends to be much closer to the mid-point of the respective response scales than to either end of it. These results suggest that on average, the respondents from Belgium, Finland, Spain, Switzerland and the Netherlands are not very strongly *supportive* of or very strongly *opposed* to any specific type of basic income proposal, although as demonstrated below, there are many differences across policy design dimensions and sub-groups within the population that are highly relevant. This stands in sharp contrast to the findings from studies investigating support for traditional welfare policies (such as old-age pensions or unemployment benefits) that are generally much closer to the 'support end' of the response scale (Laenen, 2020).

3.1.1 Universality

Let us first discuss one of *the* core design dimensions of basic income—its universality. This broadly refers to benefit access and can be broken down into two sub-dimensions: entitlement and eligibility. With regard to the former, every basic income proposal has to determine which primary target population is entitled to receive the benefit. In the ideal-typical definition, the description of the target population is kept notably vague, as it only states that basic income will be delivered 'to all', without specifying who the 'all' are. This vagueness raises important questions of entitlement that require answers before basic income can be implemented in practice. First of all, is basic income to be paid to all *citizens* or to all *residents*, and if the latter, should there then be any length of residency requirements before access can be granted? Also, should basic income operate nationally (as in most proposals), or regionally within/across countries

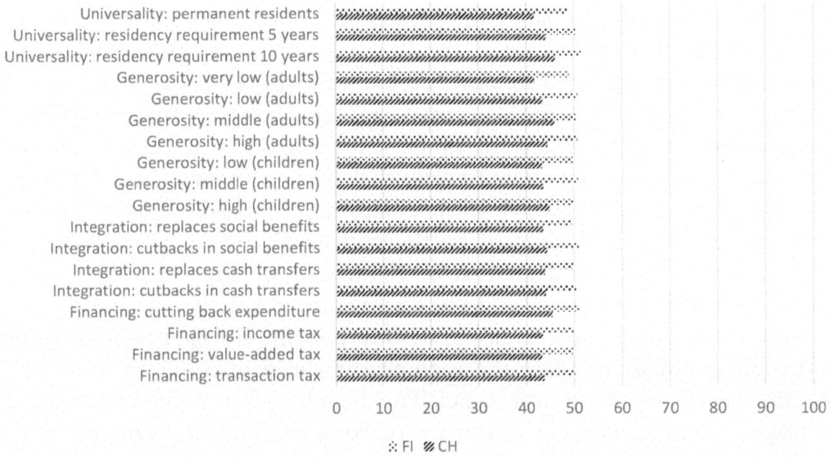

Fig. 3.5 Support for different basic income varieties in Finland and Switzerland, 2016 (*Source* Stadelmann-Steffen and Dermont [2020]. Question wording CH: 'Basically, an unconditional basic income can be designed very differently and be associated with different objectives. In the following, we present two variants which differ in various respects. [...] Regardless of which variant you prefer, how likely is it that you would agree to these variants in a referendum?' Question wording FI: 'There are many ways to implement an unconditional basic income. [...] Regardless of which option you prefer: if a binding referendum on this issue were held in Finland, how likely is it that you would vote in favour of these systems?' The answer scale ranged from 'definitely refuse' [0] to 'definitely accept' [100]. The graph shows the mean scores for each level in the conjoint experiment among respondents living in Finland [FI] and Switzerland [CH]. Please note that the specified amounts were different in the two countries [see Table A1.3] because of the different currencies and cost of living standards)

(as in proposals for a Eurodividend, for example: Van Parijs & Vanderborght, 2001)? The second sub-dimension of universality concerns the eligibility criteria that determine who will receive basic income within the primary target population. Although the ideal-typical definition clearly states that basic income is 'without means test', there have been more than a few proposals and experiments in which access to a basic income is made dependent on people's financial means. This can take the shape of a targeted basic income that either includes only the poor or excludes only the rich, depending on the level at which the threshold for the means test is set (see, for example, Spies-Butcher et al., 2020). Alternatively, it can also take the shape of a negative income tax, which only allocates cash to those below a pre-defined income level (Friedman, 1962).

There are arguably some who may suggest that these types of welfare schemes have no place in a book on basic income, because they are means tested and thus not universal. I argue that there are nevertheless at least two good reasons why they deserve a place here. First of all, such means-tested schemes do not have to be the end goal (although some do see them as such), but can also serve as important stepping stones towards a fully universal basic income. One could start out with a targeted basic income or negative income tax that only benefits lower-income groups and then gradually increase the income threshold in order to make the scheme more universal over time. The benefit of such an incremental strategy is that it allows the impact of basic income in terms of work incentives, wages, poverty and many other important policy outcomes to be carefully and patiently tested, without having to go 'all out' from day one. Second, some also see a selectively designed variety of basic income as an improvement on current means-tested social assistance schemes, which tend to be highly conditional (see the next design dimension). Accordingly, even though they are not the 'real deal', targeted types of basic income may be considered a step in the right direction, towards a less controlling and less punitive welfare system.

In terms of public opinion, clear expectations can be formulated with regard to the sub-dimension of entitlement. Prior survey research has consistently shown that people are generally unwilling to grant newly-arrived migrants access to 'their' welfare state provisions (Careja & Harris, 2022). Indeed, data from the 2016–2017 ESS shows that only 9.6% of the respondents feel that immigrants should be given rights to social benefits and services immediately on their arrival in the host country. At the same time, there is nevertheless equally low support for the idea that migrants should never have the right to these benefits and services (9.1%). Instead, most people are situated somewhere in between these two extremes: while 42.1% feel that immigrants should be granted access to welfare 'after having worked and paid taxes for at least a year', 29.6% think this should happen 'once they have become a citizen' and 9.6% 'after a year, whether they have worked or not'. From a self-interest perspective, it has been argued that this so-called 'welfare chauvinism' (Andersen & Bjørklund, 1990) is mostly driven by the fear of (especially low-skilled) people in the host country that newly-arrived migrants will create unwanted competition for scarce welfare benefits and services. From a more ideological point of view, it is also known that migrants are generally seen as less deserving of welfare by the general public, mainly because they have yet to contribute to the host society and because their diverging cultural, linguistic and religious backgrounds tend to make them 'different from us' (van Oorschot, 2008). In addition to such perceptions of threat and deservingness, people in the host country may worry that a universal basic income, granted to all residents with no requirements whatsoever, could attract migrants even further, acting as a form of 'welfare magnet' (Borjas, 1999). For these reasons, I expect to find higher levels of support for basic income varieties that either restrict access to citizens only or impose residency requirements in order to exclude newly-arrived migrants.

These expectations are partly rejected and at the same time partly confirmed by the findings from the above-described survey experiments. On the one hand, the BNES experiment (see Fig. 3.2) shows that there is no notable difference in support for a basic income for all residents compared with one that is only paid to people who have been living in Belgium for a particular (unspecified) number of years. In a similar vein, both the BABEL and the BIN experiments (see Fig. 3.1) demonstrate that there are approximately equal levels of support for basic income varieties with a citizenship or a residency requirement in Belgium and the Netherlands, respectively. This is also the case in Finland, as observed in the Rincon experiment (see Fig. 3.4). On the other hand, the Spanish respondents in the same experiment show slightly greater support for the somewhat stricter requirement of citizenship rather than residency as a 'ticket' to receive basic income payments. Likewise, there is a slightly higher level of support for basic income proposals that set residency requirements compared with ones that involve universal payments to all (permanent) residents in the Stadelmann-Steffen and Dermont experiment conducted in Finland and Switzerland (see Fig. 3.5). Looking at the gap between the respective marginal means, one could nevertheless suggest that these differences are relatively small—or at least that they are smaller than expected from the perspective of the self-interest and ideology predictions presented above.

There is, however, evidence from other sources suggesting that there is relatively less support for basic income schemes that are fully universal in terms of benefit entitlement. The most clear-cut evidence comes from a study by Bay and Pedersen (2006), in which they report the results of a so-called persuasion experiment that was conducted in May 2003 among a sample of approximately 1000 respondents living in Norway. In the experiment, respondents were first asked about their initial level of support for basic income, without any additional framing of the policy (see Fig. 2.6 for the results and question wording). After that, both the supporters and opponents of basic income were shown immigration-related arguments to see whether they could be persuaded to switch positions. Although the results show that most people maintained their original position after being exposed to the persuasion attempt, a substantial proportion of both the initial supporters and the initial opponents did change their mind. Among those who were initially in favour of basic income, about 34% switched to opposing it after being told that a basic income would also be paid to 'residents who are not Norwegian'. Conversely, when presented with the counter-framing that basic income could be given only to Norwegian citizens, about 26% of the initial opponents changed to supporting the policy proposal. Combined, these findings seem to suggest that a large number of the interviewed Norwegians were more likely to accept a citizenship-based basic income than a fully universal one for all residents.

In addition to Bay and Pedersen's (2006) experiment, there is some—albeit more circumstantial—evidence from other sources. Parolin and Siöland (2020), for example, show that the ideal-typical version of basic income, as defined in the 2016–2017 ESS (see Fig. 2.8), is significantly less popular among people who are more welfare chauvinistic—although this relationship is mostly restricted to countries with relatively high levels of social spending. Especially in these countries, the widespread prevalence of welfare chauvinism could pose a critical barrier to the acceptance of a fully universal basic income without any citizenship or residency requirements. Relatedly, there is also some evidence from opinion polls that many people seem to believe a basic income would in fact work like a welfare magnet, (undesirably) bringing migrants into the country. For example, in a survey conducted by Dalia Research in 2017 among approximately 11,000 respondents living in 28 different European countries, almost 40% agreed with the statement that 'foreigners could come to my country and take advantage of the [basic income] benefit' (see Fig. 4.4). I will return to the welfare magnet argument and its implications in Chapter 4. As shown by Delsen and Schilpzand (2019), however, this argument seems to have no significant effect on people's support for basic income, despite what one would perhaps intuitively expect. When taken together, most of the evidence from the survey experiments and other sources does nevertheless suggest that basic income varieties with citizenship or residency requirements are somewhat more likely to garner popular support than their fully universal counterparts.

All the studies and surveys discussed so far assume that basic income would be paid to the citizens or residents of a single country. However, as a basic income could also be implemented regionally—both within and across countries—it is worth investigating the popularity of basic income types that are not national in scope. Unfortunately, there is very little relevant opinion data available. One notable exception is a survey by Yougov on a European-wide basic income conducted among a sample of about 7,500 respondents living in France, Germany, Italy, Poland, Portugal and Spain. In the survey, respondents were asked whether they supported or opposed the introduction of an 'EU-wide Universal Basic Income, in which every EU resident receives a direct cash payment every month'. The total sample was split into two, and half of the respondents were invited to think about 'the Coronavirus pandemic and its impact on the economy' before answering the question. The other half of the respondents were not presented with this framing. As shown in Fig. 3.6, the level of support for an EU-wide basic income is—perhaps somewhat unexpectedly—very

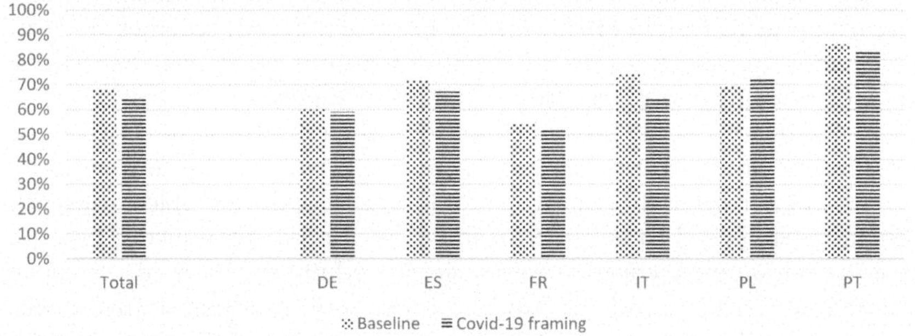

Fig. 3.6 Support for an EU-wide basic income, 2020 (*Source* Yougov [2020]. Question wording: '[Thinking about the Coronavirus pandemic and its impact on the economy]. To what extent do you support or oppose the following: the introduction of an EU-wide Universal Basic Income, in which every EU resident receives a direct cash payment every month'. The graph shows the percentage of respondents who [strongly] support this policy)

similar with or without the COVID-19 framing (at 65% and 68%, respectively). The only exception is Italy, where support in the COVID-19 framing group was 10% lower than in the baseline group. This finding is in stark contrast to evidence from other studies suggesting that the COVID-19 situation increased support for (a national) basic income in Belgium (Van Hootegem & Laenen, 2022), the UK and the US (Nettle et al., 2021; Weisstanner, 2022). Although most countries are relatively close to the average, support for a European basic income is overall much higher in Portugal (86%, without framing) and much lower in France (54%, without framing).

Turning to the second sub-dimension of universality, pertaining to benefit eligibility, expectations are more mixed. There are good reasons to believe that universal basic income schemes will be more popular than selective, means-tested alternatives. From a self-interest perspective, it has long been argued that because universal policies are to the personal advantage of relatively large segments of the population—including the middle classes—they tend to generate broad cross-class coalitions and thus high levels of popular support. By contrast, selective policies mostly serve marginal groups of poor people only, thereby providing little incentive for the broader population to show support on the basis of self-interest (Korpi & Palme, 1998). In addition, it has been argued that universal welfare schemes are also considered morally superior to selective ones. According to Rothstein (1998), this is because universal schemes are evaluated more positively on three moral dimensions. First, many see these policies as being more just, from a substantive perspective, because they treat all citizens equally instead of splitting the population into two separate groups as selective policies do (a poor and benefit-receiving minority versus a better-off and tax-paying majority). Second, the typical universal scheme is supposed to be superior in terms of procedural justice because it is much simpler, cheaper and easier to administer than its selective counterpart, which tends to produce more serious administrative problems such as benefit abuse (Roosma et al., 2016). Third, the universal approach is generally praised for yielding a fairer distribution of burdens, because it spreads the cost-benefit balance equally among the population: everyone pays taxes, but everyone also receives benefits. Yet, the same theoretical frameworks have been used to argue that selective welfare policies may be equally as (or even more) popular as universal ones (Laenen & Gugushvili, 2021). From a self-interest perspective, a universal system is not necessarily the most rational choice, at least not for middle-income and high-income earners, who may become net contributors rather than net beneficiaries if they pay more in taxes than they receive in benefits. Additionally, the moral superiority of the universal approach to welfare has been questioned, as many may feel that targeting the poor is actually fairer than distributing scarce public resources to all, including people who do not really need them (Goodin & Le Grand, 1987).

Despite the contrasting expectations, the evidence from the polls mostly points towards selective, means-tested basic income varieties being more popular than their fully universal counterparts (see also Seong Yoo et al., 2021a, 2021b for South Korea). First, the BNES experiment in Belgium (see Fig. 3.2) shows that popular support is slightly higher for basic income schemes that either include only the poor or exclude the rich, compared with schemes that are universally paid to all residents regardless of their financial means. This gap grew larger during the COVID-19 crisis, especially in the more-deprived region of Wallonia with regard to proposals that exclude the rich (the mean is 65), where full universality was the most popular option before the pandemic (56). In the wealthier region of Flanders, support for both the targeted and the universal basic income varieties dropped by nearly the same (somewhat marginal) amount. Second, the Rincon experiment in Spain shows that there was a somewhat higher level of support for a targeted basic income (the mean is 44.8) compared with a universal alternative (41.7). In Finland, it seems to be the other way round, but the difference is so small that it would be more appropriate to say that the different varieties of basic income are equally popular there. Third, an Ipsos MORI survey held in 2017 among approximately 1100 respondents living in the UK shows that a targeted basic income 'paid only to people with a low income' attracted greater support than the ideal-typical, universal basic income that is 'paid to all' (57% versus 49%, see Fig. 3.8). Fourth, the Survey on the Community Life and Welfare conducted in Japan in 2009 reports a significantly higher level of support for a negative income tax (45.6%) compared with a universal basic income (28.5%). It should be noted, however, that the survey asked about a negative income tax for working people only, and this might have increased support for the scheme. While basic income was defined as a 'minimum living expense for all citizens regardless of their income, assets or employment situation', negative income tax was described as a 'subsidy for working individuals whose annual income is below a certain standard' (Takamatsu & Tachibanaki, 2014). Fifth, Andersson and Kangas (2004) show that in

Finland there was a lower level of support for universal basic income (see Fig. 2.6 for question wording) than for a negative income tax (63% versus 76%). This was described as 'a system in which taxes and benefits are integrated so that those with very low incomes would automatically receive an income transfer instead of paying a tax'. The situation was different in Sweden, where the two policies were about equally popular (46% versus 43%). Sixth, the BABEL Survey found that more than half of the Belgian interviewees would rather support the introduction of a negative income tax (see Fig. 3.10), which was described as follows: 'Some people are proposing a negative income tax instead of a basic income. That is a system in which you get a basic income from the tax system in case your income is below a certain threshold. As your income increases, the basic income will decrease. When your income rises above the income threshold you start paying taxes again.'

Before turning to the next policy design dimension, it is lastly worth pointing out that access to a basic income scheme could in principle also be determined by eligibility criteria other than people's financial means, such as their age or employment status. Age-restricted basic income schemes have been suggested by some, either as end goals or as stepping stone policies towards a basic income for people of all ages (Torry, 2019). I will return to these later under the design dimension of duration, as one could see age-limited schemes as categorically universal schemes that cap the amount of years people are eligible for a basic income. Although less common, there have also been proposals for basic income varieties in which access is dependent on people being in paid work. Illustrative examples of these are some types of negative income tax—such as the Earned Income Tax Credit in the US (Leff et al., 2019)—and proposals for so-called 'sabbatical grants' (Offe & De Deken, 1999). Unfortunately, such basic income varieties have rarely featured in public opinion polls (with the exception of the Japanese survey mentioned above). Nevertheless, several surveys have included questions about basic income varieties that are not conditional on actual work but on people's intention to find work. This is discussed next, under the dimension of conditionality.

3.1.2 *Conditionality*

The second policy design dimension, conditionality, refers to so-called 'conditions of conduct' that are attached to benefit receipt (Clasen & Clegg, 2007). The ideal-typical definition of basic income is very clear on this: once entitlement and eligibility are established, the cash payment should be fully unconditional, with no requirements involved whatsoever. However, as discussed in Chapter 1, there have been alternative proposals for basic income varieties that do impose some form of conditionality on the recipients. The best-known of these is arguably the participation income originally formulated by Anthony Atkinson (1996) that is conditional on a number of agreed-upon, socially appreciated activities. In its most comprehensive form, a participation income can cover a very broad range of activities, including caring, training, working, volunteering and so on. In its strictest form, only the performance of paid work suffices to receive the benefit. Although many basic income proponents reject the idea of having any conditions attached to it, and especially any work-related conditions, some may accept such conditional types of basic income because they see them as a promising stepping stone policy towards the fully unconditional version.

This was not the case for Atkinson (1996), who proposed his participation income because he believed it would stand a better chance of being publicly accepted and thus being politically feasible. In fact, there are several signs in existing opinion research that suggest that Atkinson might have been correct. First, the literature on welfare deservingness shows that both control and reciprocity are hugely important normative criteria that people take into account when deciding who should get what from the welfare state (Laenen, 2020; van Oorschot, 2000). More concretely, this means that people are generally less supportive of welfare provisions for those who they see as not having contributed sufficiently (reciprocity) or as being responsible for their own neediness (control). Some even go as far as suggesting that it is a fundamental psychological trait of human beings to categorize help-seekers (and thus welfare claimants) into two distinct categories: first, those who are willing to contribute to the community but have been affected by unlucky circumstances beyond their control (the 'reciprocators'), and second, those who are unwilling to do so out of laziness (the 'cheaters') (Petersen, 2012). In this co-called 'deservingness heuristic'—which supposedly applies universally across countries, time periods and social groups (Aaroe & Petersen, 2014)—free-riding cheaters should be denied access to any welfare provision, presumably therefore including a basic income. Second, prior studies have shown that work ethics, understood as a set of values centred on the importance of employment in a productivist society, continue to be key in mainstream public opinion (Stam, 2015). Although post-productivist streams (which aim to de-emphasize the importance of wage labour in particular) are certainly emerging, these appear to be undercurrents at present, making it unlikely that the general public will readily accept a fully unconditional basic income (Kozàk, 2021).

Prior studies have consistently found overwhelming support for imposing work-related obligations on the (mostly able-bodied) recipients of current welfare benefits, and this is known to be strongly rooted in deservingness considerations and work ethics (Buss et al., 2017; Laenen & Meuleman, 2019). Accordingly, it makes sense to assume that conditional varieties of basic income will be more popular than their fully unconditional counterparts. By and large, this is also confirmed by the evidence from surveys, although there are important exceptions. Let us start with the BNES experiment conducted in Belgium, because it gauges (on a scale from 0 to 100) support for three types of schemes with varying degrees of conditionality: first, a fully unconditional basic income, second, a participation income that requires people to perform care tasks or to volunteer (if they are not in paid employment), and third, a basic income that is conditional on job-seeking efforts. Overall, the findings show that there is somewhat greater support for the conditional schemes (the mean is 53 for both schemes) than for the fully unconditional one (the mean is 47)—both before and during the COVID-19 pandemic (the reported means are pre-pandemic, see Fig. 3.2). There are nevertheless some interesting regional differences (see Fig. 3.3). While support for the three basic income varieties was relatively stable in the Dutch-speaking region of Flanders before and during the pandemic (except for a small decrease in support for the scheme that is conditional on job-seeking), there was a clear increase in support for all three types in the French-speaking part of Wallonia. This increase was larger for the unconditional variant (from 44 to 57) compared with the schemes that are conditional on job-seeking (from 54 to 63) or participation (from 55 to 60). However, as explained above, it is unclear whether these COVID-19 induced changes in support were also long term.

These findings are largely confirmed by the BABEL experiment, which also shows that a participation income (the mean level of support is 58 on a scale from 0 to 100) is more popular than an unconditional basic income (the mean is 51) in Belgium—again with very similar regional differences (see Fig. 3.1). The same pattern was found for the Netherlands in the BIN experiment, although the difference between the two options is much smaller there (the respective means are 65 and 63). This cross-national variation also becomes evident when looking at the results from the Rincon experiment (see Fig. 3.4). While a participation income is clearly more popular than an unconditional basic income in Spain, it appears to be the other way round in Finland. One potential explanation for these findings is that in both Finland (Kangas et al., 2021) and the Netherlands (van der Veen, 2019), there have been real-world policy experiments that suggest a basic income may not have the detrimental effects on employment that many assume it will. Although this reasoning is somewhat speculative at present, I demonstrate in Chapter 4 that people's support for basic income—including its unconditional variant—increases when they are told that it will not reduce the employment rate. That said, it does remain somewhat puzzling that conditional basic income schemes are more popular in Spain—where there has also been a similar experiment in Barcelona (Bollain et al., 2019)—and why a participation income is about equally as popular as an unconditional basic income in the UK—where no experiment has taken place. With regard to the latter, the same Ipsos MORI survey that was mentioned above asked respondents whether they would support the introduction of a basic income that is only 'paid to those who are in work, in training, doing voluntary work or pensioners', which about 52% did, compared with 48% for the unconditional option (see Fig. 3.8).

All in all, these findings suggest that there is significant variation between countries in the level of support for conditional vis-à-vis unconditional basic income types—which seems to go against the idea from the deservingness heuristic that people everywhere want to punish 'cheaters' for being lazy (Petersen, 2012). Nevertheless, out of all the countries discussed, it is only in Finland that unconditionality is actually *more* popular than conditionality. In all the others, an unconditional basic income is either equally or less popular than some of its conditional counterparts.

3.1.3 Uniformity

The third design dimension, uniformity, concerns the way in which the level of benefit is determined. Most basic income proposals assume that the amount will be equal for everyone who is both entitled and eligible (De Wispelaere, 2015). However, as explained in Chapter 1, there is nothing in the ideal-typical definition of basic income stating that it *has* to be equal for all. Instead, the amount could also be allowed to vary between individuals with different characteristics. Here, I consider the three characteristics that are arguably most often used in existing welfare states. The first of these refers to people's financial (or health) needs and usually implies that higher amounts will be paid to people in greater need. For example, one could imagine a basic income scheme in which everyone is given a basic amount, but in which supplements are provided for those who have a low income or face higher living costs because of having children or suffering from a disability. In social policy literature, this strategy is widely known as 'targeting within universalism' (Jacques & Noël, 2020; Skocpol, 1991). Alternatively, it is also possible for benefit access to be universal, but to make the level of basic income entirely dependent on people's financial means. A second conceivable characteristic to vary the amount of basic income between individuals is their work history. In this regard, it would also be possible to either pay supplements in addition to a basic amount or to vary the entire amount according to people's work record, with a longer work history presumably leading to higher benefits, as is the case in (Bismarckian) social insurance schemes (Clasen, 1997). The third characteristic, which is related to the other two but is able to combine them, is age. There are some who suggest that a basic income scheme should pay different amounts to different age groups. Most of these proposals argue that the amount should increase with age, with children receiving the lowest amount, elderly people the highest and the working-aged population somewhere in between (Torry, 2021). Varying the amount by age can either be promoted as an end goal to be pursued out of fairness considerations (mostly because both people's needs and work record are assumed to increase in line with their age), or as a stepping stone towards a flat-rate basic income. Of course, the same stepping stone logic can also apply to basic income schemes that vary the amount according to income or work history.

In light of the findings presented above, it seems plausible that support for basic income will increase when it compensates those in greater need and/or rewards those with a longer work record, as they are generally perceived as more deserving of social welfare (Laenen, 2020). If people are more willing to restrict access to those in need (cf. universality), they may also want higher benefits to be given to people in greater need. Likewise, if people prefer to limit access to those who are working or actively trying to find work (cf. conditionality), it follows that they may also be more supportive of a basic income that pays higher benefit amounts to people with a longer work history. Based on these considerations, I expect to find lower levels of support for a flat-rate basic income that is equal for all. However, the survey evidence in support of this expectation is scarce and not very strong. Although the BNES experiment in Belgium shows that people are less likely to support a flat-rate basic income compared with one that pays higher amounts to people with a longer work history, the difference is small, as shown by the respective mean scores both before (50 and 53) and during (54 and 59) the COVID-19 pandemic. In a similar vein, the popularity of a basic income that gives larger amounts to people with a lower income is very similar to that of its unconditional counterpart (see Fig. 3.2). There are again regional differences, in that support for basic income is generally higher in Wallonia than in Flanders, but the relative gaps between the three varieties of basic income are roughly the same in both regions (see Fig. 3.3).

A vastly different conclusion was produced by a very different type of survey experiment, conducted by Liebig and Mau (2004) in Germany immediately after the start of the new millennium. In the experiment, respondents were presented with descriptions of basic income *recipients* (rather than *schemes*) with varying characteristics. More specifically, these recipients were randomly varied in terms of their age, gender, employment/occupation status, income and number of children in the household. After seeing the description, respondents were asked to indicate whether they felt that the amount of basic income presented was fair. The authors found that while higher amounts were considered equitable for people who are older, have children or earn a low income, lower amounts were considered fair for those who had left their job voluntarily. These findings seem to suggest that a flat-rate payment of basic income is not the most popular approach, because if it were, then none of the characteristics should have had an effect on people's appraisal of the amount. Instead, the respondents differentiated notably between different types of recipients. This is a standard finding in similar types of vignette studies depicting recipients of existing welfare benefits (Baumberg Geiger, 2021; Castillo et al., 2019; Kootstra, 2016). Two important nuances should nevertheless be made here. First, the sample was very small, consisting of only 112 (employed) respondents—a number that is far too low to obtain reliable estimates of general public opinion. Second, the introductory text for the experiment referred more to a targeted basic income or a negative income tax than to a universal basic income (see Appendix 2). This implies that we do not know whether the respondents would have made similar distinctions between the recipients had they been presented with a basic income that is universal rather than selective.

3.1.4 Generosity

Similar to uniformity, the design dimension of generosity refers to the level of basic income. The difference is that generosity concerns how high a basic income will be, rather than how the level is determined (this section assumes a flat-rate basic income). As shown in Chapter 1, the ideal-typical definition of basic income does not stipulate the level at which it should be set. The main debate in this regard has taken place between proponents of a partial basic income and those who suggest a full basic income (Van Parijs & Vanderborght, 2017). A partial basic income is relatively low: possibly even lower than the current subsistence level or the least generous social benefit in a given society. Accordingly, on its own it is not high enough to live a decent life in that society. In neoliberal versions of a partial basic income, it is usually a standalone policy that is not topped up by any other social benefits, but only by market income (Murray, 2008). However, in most versions a partial basic income is in addition to other existing benefits. While some regard a partial basic income as the desired end goal, others see it as a more realistic stepping stone towards a full basic income that is much more generous; in other words, set higher than the subsistence level so that people can live on it. Further, a full basic income may or may not complement existing social benefits (Van Parijs & Vanderborght, 2017).

In terms of public opinion, it is difficult to predict what will be more popular: a lower, partial basic income or a higher, full basic income. Seen from a self-interest perspective, it may seem plausible that people will want basic income to be as generous as possible because they will want to receive higher amounts of money themselves. This argument is supported by research showing that those with a greater interest in a given welfare domain tend to be more supportive of higher benefits or more spending in that domain (Svallfors, 2012). Additionally, we know from empirical studies on distributive justice beliefs that most people do not want others to fall below a minimum level of income that would push them straight into poverty (Alves & Rossi, 1978; Gatskova, 2013). Although the level of this 'social minimum' is likely to vary across societies—and presumably also between different social groups—it does indicate that people may be reluctant to accept a basic income that is well below the current level of subsistence. At the same time, there are good reasons to believe that people may instead oppose a generous basic income that is on or above the subsistence level. In fact, it seems likely that most people will be aware of the relatively higher cost of a more generous basic income, and this could easily translate into lower support for it (van Oorschot & Meuleman, 2012). Many self-interested citizens could anticipate having to bear most of the additional costs through the tax system, turning them into net contributors to basic income rather than net beneficiaries of it. From a more ideological perspective, the higher cost of a more generous basic income may also be opposed on the grounds of sociotropic concerns, as people could worry that basic income (perhaps even the entire welfare state) would soon become unaffordable. Relatedly, many may believe that a generous basic income will decrease the competitive strength of the national economy and lead to lower employment rates through its allegedly detrimental effects on work incentives. This, in turn, is likely to decrease their support for basic income, as we will see in Chapter 4.

To examine which of these expectations is most accurate, let us first look at a number of survey experiments that have mentioned specific amounts of basic income. These all show that people seem to dislike basic income the most when the amount is below the current subsistence level. Basic income schemes with higher amounts are generally more popular (although there are sometimes limits to this). First, the BABEL experiment shows that support is greatest for a basic income of €1500 per month (the mean is 57.5), followed by one of €1000 (54.3) and lastly one of €500 (52.5). This is especially the case in the French-speaking region of Wallonia, where the respective means are 63.6, 58.1 and 54.1. Similarly, the BIN experiment in the Netherlands shows that support is lowest for the basic income of €500 (the mean is 61.5). However, in this case, support for the in-between option of €1000 (the mean is 66.5) is higher than support for the most generous option of €1500 (64.5). Given that €500 was well below the subsistence level in both countries at the time of the survey (while €1000 was close to it and €1500 was above it), this confirms the expectation that people are less supportive of a relatively low partial basic income than of a relatively high full basic income. Similar findings are observed in the Rincon experiment in Finland and Spain (see Fig. 3.4), and the Stadelmann-Steffen and Dermont experiment in Finland and Switzerland (see Fig. 3.5). In all these countries, the lowest level of support is found for basic income varieties that are (well) below the subsistence level. People thus generally appear to prefer higher amounts for basic income (see also Seong Yoo et al., 2021a, 2021b for South Korea).

In addition to the aforementioned experiments, two other surveys are worth discussing here. The first of these, reported in Andersson and Kangas (2004), was conducted in Finland and Sweden in 2002. Using an open question format, it asked respondents to indicate how high basic income should be. On average, the preferred amount was €970 in Sweden and €620 in Finland. In both countries, this amount is relatively high compared with the level of subsistence and the level of the least generous social benefits applicable at the time of the survey. The second survey, reported in Chrisp et al. (2020), was conducted in Finland in 2015 and presented respondents with six basic income varieties that differed in terms of their amount and whether they would replace or supplement other social benefits. As shown in Fig. 3.7, the highest level of support was found for a supplementary basic income of €560 per month (51%), followed by a supplementary basic income of less than €560 (33%). The other four options (presented in Fig. 3.7) are very close to each other in terms of popularity, at around 25%. In contrast to all the previous findings, the two most popular basic income varieties are both well below the subsistence level. This could suggest that relatively low amounts are acceptable to people when they are presented as

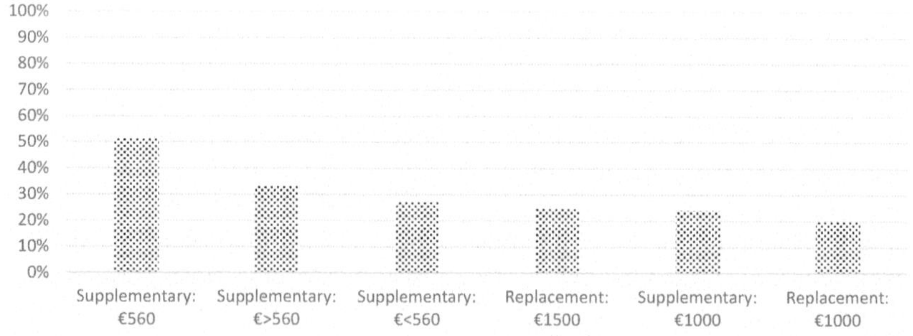

Fig. 3.7 Support for different basic income varieties in Finland, 2015 (*Source* Chrisp et al. [2020]. Question wording: see Pulkka [2019]. The questions are only available in Finnish. An English translation was not provided by the author. The graph shows the percentage of respondents who think the respective basic income variety is a good or very good idea)

a supplement to—rather than a replacement for—other social benefits. This form of interplay between the dimensions of generosity and integration is explored further below, where I examine a number of relevant combinations of policy design dimensions.

3.1.5 *Integration*

The design dimension of integration refers to the position a basic income will take within the broader welfare system. On the one hand, a basic income could come on top of existing welfare provisions, without changing anything. On the other hand, a more likely scenario is that a basic income would replace existing provisions, thereby freeing up public resources to then be used to finance the basic income. Some proposals suggest replacing all existing social benefits and services by a single (low level or high level) basic income scheme (Murray, 2008). By comparison, in most proposals the suggestion is to replace only a few specific cash transfer schemes, such as child allowances, old-age pensions, unemployment benefits and the like. Sometimes, these schemes would be allowed to remain in place, but with amounts that are reduced so that they would be supplementary to basic income (Van Parijs & Vanderborght, 2017). An alternative strategy is to provide top-ups to the basic flat-rate amount of basic income for those groups that have needs or costs that would have been covered by the transfers that will be replaced. For example, it would be possible to pay higher amounts of basic income to those with a disability or with children, who previously received disability benefits or child allowances, respectively. This is also a clear case of the 'targeting within universalism' strategy discussed above under the dimension of uniformity.

Building on the 'new politics of the welfare state' literature (Pierson, 1994, 2001), one could anticipate widespread opposition to a basic income that threatens to replace many existing welfare schemes, because these schemes have generated self-interested welfare constituencies. These constituencies will do everything they can to protect 'their' scheme against retrenchment, restructuring or perhaps even any change (regardless of its direction). Although a basic income can—depending on its level—either be a retrenchment or an expansion vis-à-vis the status quo, it will often be unclear to people whether they are likely to gain or lose from the reform. In such a scenario, it seems more likely that there will be opposition to basic income rather than support for it, as prior research suggests that people are generally more worried about potential losses than they are attracted by potential gains. This is known in psychological literature as 'negativity bias' (see Kahneman & Tversky, 1984). Accordingly, support for welfare reform—especially of the magnitude of basic income—may be impeded by a status quo bias, in which people prefer to hold on to what they have. The public opposition will be especially strong when basic income intends to replace existing welfare schemes with large and stable constituencies, such as old-age pensions. Conversely, when the welfare constituency is smaller and more fluid—for example, in the case of social assistance and unemployment benefits—opposition is likely to be weaker. A similar logic applies to basic income schemes that compensate existing welfare constituencies with supplements in addition to the flat-rate basic amount, thereby reducing opposition.

In contrast to the self-interest framework, opposing expectations emerge when things are considered from the perspective of ideology. On the one hand, there could be greater opposition to a basic income that replaces existing social benefits if these benefits are widely perceived to perform well in terms of reaching their social goals, to be administered fairly and correctly, and so on (Laenen & Gugushvili, 2022). In that case, people may be more willing to accept a basic income that complements rather than replaces existing welfare provisions. On the other hand, a basic income that only complements, while replacing nothing at all may be seen as expensive, wasteful or unnecessary. Which of these expectations is more likely depends both on the broader context and the specific benefits that are being replaced. With regard to the first, it seems plausible that there will be greater support for a basic income scheme designed to replace existing benefits in countries where the majority of the population is dissatisfied with the current performance of these benefits. In countries where evaluations of welfare performance are generally more positive, people are likely to be less supportive of a basic income that replaces existing benefits. However, there could be equally strong opposition to a purely complementary basic income, as this may be perceived as too costly and possibly a redundant reform proposal. With regard to the issue of which benefit schemes would be replaced, there are some studies showing that some types of schemes, such as old-age pensions, are generally perceived to function better than others, such as unemployment benefits (Laenen, 2018). Accordingly, it seems more likely that people will oppose a basic income if it aims to replace benefits that are evaluated more positively in terms of their performance. Further, it is also more likely that people will resist the replacement of schemes that are targeted at groups they consider highly deserving; for example, the elderly, the sick and the disabled. Conversely, there could be more support for a basic income that replaces schemes targeted at less deserving groups, such as the able-boded unemployed (Laenen, 2020; van Oorschot, 2006).

Empirically, there are three survey experiments offering some information about the popularity of basic income schemes that differ on the dimension of integration. First, the BNES experiment in Belgium included three different options: a basic income that would first, 'not replace any other social benefits', second, would 'replace all existing social benefits, such as pensions' and third, would 'replace all existing social benefits, such as unemployment benefits'. Although the latter two options are functionally the same, the experiment presented two very different benefit schemes (with different policy designs and target groups) as examples. This should lead to different levels of support according to both the deservingness and the self-interest perspective discussed above. Overall, the mean level of support for each of the three options is relatively close. The lowest level is found for a basic income that replaces all benefits and gives pensions as the example (the mean is 49), the highest level for one that replaces all benefits and gives unemployment benefits as the example (53) and an in-between level for a basic income that replaces no benefits (51). Interestingly, clear changes took place after the outbreak of the COVID-19 pandemic (see Figs. 3.2 and 3.3). What was the least popular option before the pandemic (replacing all benefits, with pensions as the example) became the most popular one during the pandemic—both in Flanders (where the mean score increased from 49 to 54) and in Wallonia (where it grew from 48 to 62). Although it is difficult to know why exactly this occurred, one possible explanation for the trend could be that people realized the economic crisis induced by COVID-19 increased resource scarcity and that pensions (by far the highest spending area in the Belgian welfare state) would have to be cut in order to finance a basic income.

The second and third experiments—included in the BABEL Survey in Belgium and the BIN Survey in the Netherlands, respectively—both had four different options: first, a basic income that 'replaces all existing benefits', second, one that 'replaces some existing social benefits, such as child allowances and sickness benefits', third, one that 'replaces some existing social benefits but provides top-ups for people with additional needs or costs (for example, people with children or disabled people)', and fourth, one that 'replaces no existing social benefits'. In the Belgian sample, support is greater for a basic income scheme that either replaces no other social benefits (the mean is 55.3) or provides supplements when it does (56.7) than for schemes that replace all or some benefits without providing top-ups (the means are 53.8 and 52.7, respectively). In this regard, again there are some regional differences. While not replacing any existing benefits is the most popular choice in Flanders (the mean is 55.3), the option to replace existing benefits but provide supplements for those in greater need is most popular in Wallonia (61.2). In the Netherlands, the most preferred option is to replace all existing benefits with a single basic income (the mean is 66), but this is closely followed by the option to replace some benefits while providing supplements (65). The third experiment, conducted by Stadelmann-Steffen and Dermont (2020) in Finland and Switzerland, shows that in both countries there is a slightly higher level of support for a supplementary basic income that cuts back on other social benefits/cash transfers compared with a basic income that would replace these benefits/transfers altogether. As shown in Fig. 3.5, these differences are nevertheless relatively small.

All in all, the results from the three survey experiments do not provide clear evidence for the expectation that people are least in favour of basic income schemes that replace some or all existing benefits (either because that is in their best interests or because they are motivated by ideological beliefs). At the same time, there is also little evidence in favour of the opposite expectation: that people prefer a basic income that is purely complementary to the existing welfare system. Instead, the differences between the options are usually relatively small, suggesting that the design dimension of integration may not be very important for public opinion. Although this may be true for the general population, it could still be that the integration of a basic income scheme is hugely important for certain sub-groups of that population—most notably the recipients of current welfare benefits. I will return to this issue below, when discussing individual differences in support for different varieties of basic income.

3.1.6 Financing

The financing dimension concerns the way in which a basic income is funded. This is left unspecified in the ideal-typical definition, but is of course hugely important. In broad terms, a basic income scheme can be financed from within and/or from outside an existing welfare system.

With regard to 'financing from within', two strategies (which can be combined) have been proposed. The first is to rely on the existing system of income (or payroll) taxes to fund a basic income. This usually implies that current taxes are either increased for everyone at the same rate or increased only for those at the top of the income distribution—the latter thus increasing the progressivity of taxes. Technically, it would also be possible to make the tax system more regressive in order to fund a basic income. Although such proposals are rare, some have suggested financing basic income from a proportional tax in which everyone pays the same tax share (Simon, 2001). This would be to the disadvantage of low-income earners in countries where income taxes are currently progressively designed. The second strategy to finance a basic income from within the existing welfare system is to cut expenditure elsewhere. This can be achieved by abolishing or reducing other social benefits (as well as tax exemptions and deductions) so that the resulting savings can be used to fund basic income. Relatedly, basic income could also be financed by budget cuts in other areas of public spending not related to welfare (such as defence or transport). Most of the proposals that plan to cut expenditure elsewhere do this with the aim of achieving approximate budget neutrality, meaning that the government budget will not have to increase to finance a basic income (Torry, 2016). Alternatively, there are many proposals to (partly) finance basic income with 'new' funding mechanisms that have been used little in modern-day welfare states—which mostly rely on income and payroll taxes (the latter typically being referred to as 'social security contributions') (Morel & Palme, 2012). Without going into full detail, these include a carbon tax, capital tax, inheritance tax, transaction tax and value-added tax (see Van Parijs & Vanderborght, 2017).

In terms of public opinion, it seems that (for the reasons mentioned above, under the dimension of integration) cuts in welfare expenditure will not be particularly popular among the public, unless the existing welfare system is seen as severely dysfunctional. In fact, previous opinion research has consistently found that most people are reluctant to cut back on social spending (Brooks & Manza, 2006; van Oorschot et al., 2022). Similarly, it seems unlikely that people will support an overall increase in income (or payroll) taxes for everyone to fund a basic income, as it is known that tax increases are generally opposed (Barnes, 2015). By contrast, it has been shown that progressive taxation, which levies a higher tax rate on those with a higher income, is hugely popular and also increases support for generous welfare provision (Barnes, 2015; Berens & Gelephitis, 2019; Edlund, 2003). Accordingly, raising taxes for the rich to finance a basic income could increase support for it—at least among the public at large, although possibly less so among high earners (see below). For most of the alternative funding mechanisms, it is more difficult to predict what will happen to popular support for basic income. Although it is informative to briefly look at some studies that examine the popularity of these mechanisms, it remains unclear how they are related to support for basic income. It could well be that a particular funding mechanism is relatively popular (such as a wealth tax, see Rowlington et al., 2021), but that people do not see it as desirable to use it in order to finance a basic income. Conversely, a less-popular mechanism (for example, inheritance tax: see Gross et al., 2017) may attract a higher level of support if it is used for the purpose of funding a basic income. Another take on the matter is that the specific funding mechanism is not that important for public opinion about basic income, as long as the mechanism promises to realize budget neutrality. In fact, it is possible that people support any funding mechanism as long as it does not increase the costs they incur (out of self-interest) or that society more broadly incurs (out of sociotropic concerns).

The idea that the specific funding mechanism is not particularly important for public opinion seems to be confirmed by the Stadelmann-Steffen and Dermont experiment in Finland and Switzerland. In the experiment, respondents were presented with basic income schemes that were either financed by an income tax, a transaction tax or a value-added tax. All of these alternatives prove virtually equally popular (see Fig. 3.5). However, most other surveys show that financing does matter for public opinion. In the BABEL experiment in Belgium and the BIN experiment in the Netherlands (see Fig. 3.1), increasing the current level of income taxes and social security contributions in order to finance a basic income is clearly the least popular option (the respective means are 51.6 and 61.4). Support increases somewhat (and to the same degree) if respondents are told that these taxes will 'stay as they are' and that 'potential additional costs are covered by a new tax on capital' or 'a new climate tax on CO_2 emissions'. A budget-neutral option was also included in the Netherlands, proving the most popular choice (with a mean of 65.7). The Rincon experiment in Finland and Spain also shows important differences in the level of support for different mechanisms to fund a basic income, while indicating that their relative popularity differs between the two countries (see Fig. 3.4). In Finland, the most popular option is to increase income taxes for the highest incomes—which boils down to making taxes more progressive. This is followed by an increase in taxes on capital and—perhaps unexpectedly—a general increase in income taxes for everyone. The least popular funding mechanism is clearly an increase in inheritance tax. The alternative mechanisms include cutting back on welfare expenditure or defence spending and increasing existing or introducing new environmental taxes, and are somewhere in-between the other options. In Spain, the most preferred option is also to raise the progressivity of income taxes, but the least preferred option is different to that in Finland: cutbacks in the welfare programmes that Rincon (2021) labels as 'universal' (old-age pensions, healthcare and education). By contrast, making budget cuts in so-called 'targeted' programmes—which include housing benefits, social assistance and unemployment benefits—is a more accepted strategy to fund a basic income. The same applies to cutting back on defence spending, taxing capital and introducing or increasing environmental taxes. Both a tax increase for everyone and an increase in inheritance tax are considered relatively unpopular ways to finance a basic income in Spain.

In addition to these experiments, there are two other, more traditional, surveys that tell us something about support for different mechanisms to fund a basic income. The first was conducted in 2017 in the UK by Ipsos MORI. It examined what would happen to people's support for (the ideal-typical) basic income when they were told that it would imply an increase in income taxes, cuts in social spending or both. As shown in Fig. 3.8, there is a significant drop in support, from 49 to 37%, 30% and 22%, respectively. In addition, the survey presented respondents with a list of options from which they could choose their 'most preferred way of mainly funding a basic income, if it was introduced' (regardless of whether they supported or opposed it). As shown in Fig. 3.9, the most popular option is to fund a basic income by 'increasing taxes on wealth' (34%), followed by 'cutting existing welfare benefits' and 'raising income tax' (12%). The remaining respondents either indicated 'don't know', 'none of these' or 'other' (14%, 9% and 3%, respectively). The second survey, held in the UK in 2018 by Populus, asked its respondents to perform a similar exercise, albeit with slightly different response options (see Fig. 3.9). In this case, the most popular funding mechanism is to 'raise progressive income taxes so the rich pay more into the scheme than they get out' (32%). This is closely followed by 'reducing the amount the government

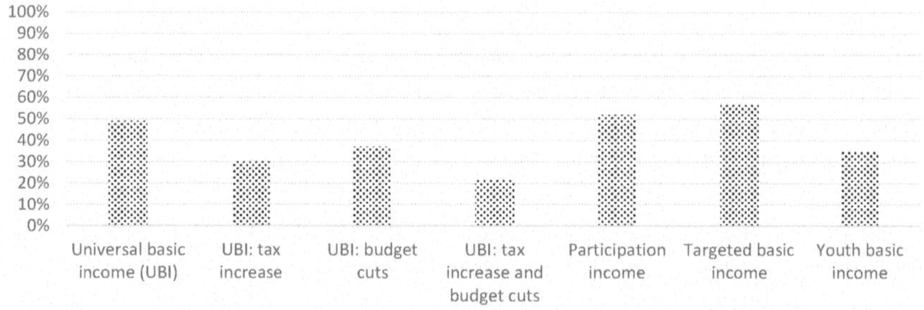

Fig. 3.8 Support for different basic income varieties in the UK, 2017 (*Source* Ipsos MORI [2017]. Question wording: 'As you may be aware, some countries are considering introducing a basic income. If introduced in the UK, this would provide a regular income paid in cash to every individual adult in the UK, regardless of their working status and income from other sources. In other words, it would be universal (i.e. paid to all), unconditional (i.e. paid without a requirement to work) and paid to individuals (rather than to a household). Assuming the level would be set roughly at the amount the UK government judged to be necessary to cover basic needs, e.g. food and clothing (but not housing costs), to what extent would you support or oppose the UK Government introducing a basic income (a) in general, (b) if it meant an increase in taxes from their current levels, (c) if it meant cuts in welfare benefits spending from their current levels and (d) if it meant both an increase in taxes and cuts in welfare benefits spending from their current levels'. 'The previous questions asked you about a basic income scheme that was universal, unconditional and with an equal amount paid to all individuals. To what extent would you support or oppose a basic income scheme that was (a) only paid to those who are in work, in training, doing voluntary work or pensioners, (b) only paid to those on low incomes and (c) only paid to young people (those aged 18–24) who are in work, in full-time education or in training?' The graph shows the percentage of respondents who support the respective basic income varieties)

spends on other benefits' and 'the creation of new funding streams like wealth taxes, carbon taxes, levies on data, or a sovereign wealth fund' (both 32%). The least popular options are to 'increase income tax rates for all if ordinary taxpayers gained overall' (19%) and to 'shrink the welfare state more broadly, possibly including cuts to social care, education or health' (7%). The remaining respondents chose 'none of these', but the question format makes it unclear whether these people are opposed to a

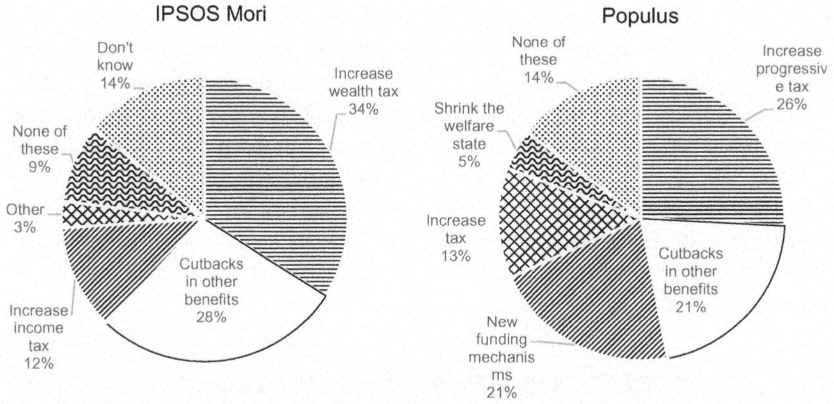

Fig. 3.9 Support for different funding mechanisms of basic income in the UK, 2017–2018 (*Source* Ipsos MORI [2017] and Populus [2018]. Question wording Ipsos MORI: 'Regardless of whether you support or oppose the UK Government introducing a basic income, which of the following, if any, would be your most preferred way of mainly funding a basic income, if it was introduced?' Question wording Populus: 'Which, if any, of the following funding options would you like to see used to fund a Universal Basic Income?' The charts present the percentage of respondents who selected a particular funding mechanism)

basic income or whether they just prefer a different funding mechanism that was not listed among the options.

Taken together, the evidence from the polls suggests that the dimension of financing is important with regard to public opinion on basic income. It is clear that popular support is greatest for basic income schemes that are funded by taxing the rich, put into practice either by making existing income taxes more progressive or by increasing taxes on capital or wealth, although not inheritance (however, see Seong Yoo et al., 2021a, 2021b for conflicting evidence on the popularity of an inheritance tax in South Korea). At the same time, there is also a relatively high level of support for cutting back on current welfare expenditure in order to finance a basic income. It, nevertheless, appears that people are more supportive of cutbacks in welfare provisions that are targeted more narrowly (such as social assistance and unemployment benefits) than they are of cutbacks in provisions that are more universal in design (such as healthcare and old-age pensions). Generally, the least popular strategy to fund a basic income seems to be an overall increase in income taxes for everyone, irrespective of their earnings. Support for new, alternative funding mechanisms—such as a climate tax—tends to be located somewhere in between. In addition to these general trends, the evidence also shows cross-national variation in the preferred mechanisms to fund a basic income. As shown by the Rincon experiment, for example, a general increase in taxes seems to be much more popular in Finland than in Spain. This demonstrates that the relative levels of support for different basic income varieties with varying funding mechanisms are very likely to be country specific.

3.1.7 Other Policy Design Dimensions

Although they are arguably important, there is much less information about public opinion regarding the six other policy design dimensions of basic income: administration, accumulation, duration, individuality, frequency and modality. In the following, I discuss the little survey evidence that is currently available, while acknowledging that much work remains to be done (see Chapter 5).

Let us start with the dimension of duration, which refers to the time period during which a person is entitled and eligible to receive a basic income. Although nothing in the ideal-typical definition states it would have a lifelong duration, most proposals assume this to be the case. However, there are some who want to limit the duration. This can be done by creating a temporary scheme that may only be paid for a certain number of years (for example, Offe & De Deken, 1999) or by introducing an emergency basic income during times of crisis (for example, George & Ortiz-Juarez, 2020). An alternative suggestion is to restrict a basic income to certain age categories, also thereby making it temporary by definition (Torry, 2019). With regard to the latter proposal, there is some evidence on public opinion from two different surveys. The first—albeit somewhat indirect—evidence comes from the Rincon experiment, in which respondents from Finland and Spain were presented with a basic income scheme that would only be accessible for people with underage children. Although this does not directly specify the age of the recipients, it seems to imply that basic income would mainly be paid out to younger parents with children, as a type of universal child benefit. While such a basic income for younger parents is *more* popular than a basic income for everybody in Spain, it is slightly *less* popular in Finland (see

Fig. 3.4). It seems likely that this difference between the countries is driven by the fact that Finland already has a universal child benefit system in place, whereas this is not the case for Spain, in which child benefits are currently means tested. The second source of—more direct—evidence is the BABEL Survey, which asked respondents to indicate their support (on a scale from 0 to 100) for three different schemes: a youth basic income (restricted to those between 18 and 25 years), a basic income for the working-age population (those between 18 and 65) and a basic pension (only for those aged 65 and above). As shown in Fig. 3.10, support increases by age group: while the mean score is 32.5 for a youth basic income, it is 40.7 for a basic income for the working-age population and 45 for a basic pension for the elderly. This is particularly true for the Dutch-speaking region of Flanders, where a basic income for the young attracts less support (25.7) than in the French-speaking region of Wallonia (40.7). This may have something to do with the fact that youth unemployment (measured as the proportion of unemployed people between the age of 15 and 24 out of the total number of people in that age group) has been about 10% lower in Flanders than in Wallonia over recent years (Statistics Belgium, 2022). It is possible that in this context, where the present (and the future) is looking brighter for younger people, a youth basic income is less popular among the public at large.

In the same survey, respondents were also asked about their opinion of a basic income that is paid 'once instead of monthly' (and that people can spend as they like). This type of basic income clearly relates to the policy design dimension of frequency, which concerns the regularity of payments. While most proposals seem to assume monthly (or weekly) instalments, there have been other suggestions for a so-called 'stakeholder grant' (or 'basic endowment') that people receive as a lump sum at one point in time (Ackerman & Alstott, 1999). As shown in Fig. 3.10, the results from the BABEL Survey suggest that popular support for this variant of basic income is relatively low in Belgium, with a mean score of 31.5 on a scale from 0 to 100. It is nevertheless difficult to evaluate this level of support in relative terms, as the survey did not include a regularly paid basic income as a reference point.

In addition to the frequency, there has been some discussion about which entity a basic income should be paid to. While the ideal-typical definition clearly states that it is for all *individuals*, there have also been proposals and experiments that take *households* (or families) as the unit

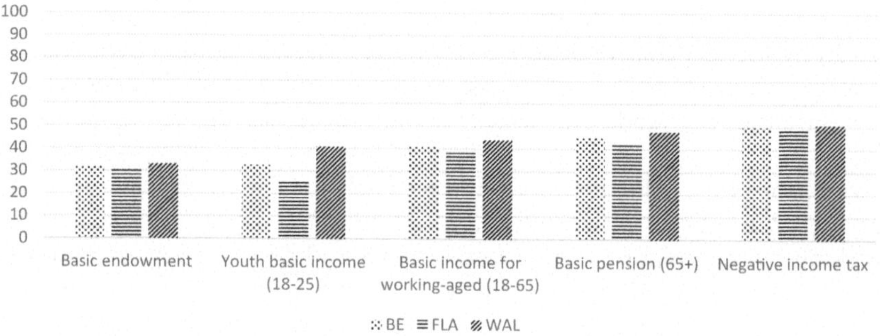

Fig. 3.10 Support for different basic income varieties in Belgium, 2021 (*Source* BABEL Survey [2021]. Question wording: [1] 'Some say that a basic income could also be paid once instead of monthly. Each citizen would then receive a basic endowment from the government once in his or her lifetime. People are free to choose how to spend that money. To what extent are you in favour or against the introduction of such basic endowment in Belgium?' [2] 'It has been suggested that a basic income should be restricted to certain age groups. To what extent are you in favour or against the introduction of a basic income only for young people between the ages of 18 and 25/people of working age, between 18 and 65/people over the age of 65?' [3] 'Some people are proposing a negative income tax instead of a basic income. That is a system where below a certain income threshold you get a basic income from taxes. As your income increases that basic income decreases. When your income rises back above the income threshold you start paying taxes again. To what extent are you in favour or against the introduction of such negative income tax in Belgium?' The answer scales ranged from 0 ['strongly against'] to 100 ['strongly in favour']. The graph presents the mean score on the scales for all respondents living in Belgium [BE], for the Dutch-speaking respondents living in Flanders [FLA] and for the French-speaking respondents living in Wallonia [WAL])

of entitlement (Sanzo & Pinilla, 2004). In this regard, the Rincon experiment presented respondents with basic income schemes that described recipients either as 'individuals' or as 'households'. Although the differences are relatively small, it appears that a basic income targeted at individuals is more popular in Finland, while the household alternative receives greater support in Spain (see Fig. 3.4). Once again, this may be due to differences in the context between the two countries. While Finland is typically classified as a social-democratic welfare regime in which social rights are granted universally on an individual basis, Spain is closer to the Mediterranean model where public welfare provision is less comprehensive and the (extended) family tends to fill the gaps (Esping-Andersen, 1990, 1999).

With regard to the dimension of accumulation, which concerns the extent to which basic income may be combined with earnings from other sources, most proposals suggest that there should be no limits. Nevertheless, some do suggest limits to accumulation. This is by definition the case for targeted versions of basic income (discussed under the dimension of universality), as these will be taken away once people's income reaches a certain level. Alternatively, it has also been suggested to claw back part of a basic income through the system by making it taxable, effectively meaning that it cannot be accumulated without limits (Meade, 1990). Leaving the actual mechanism unspecified, the BNES experiment presented respondents with a scheme that allows people to receive a basic income 'on top of the money they earn by working or in another way', and one in which the amount is reduced by the money earned elsewhere. As shown in Fig. 3.2, the two alternatives are very close to each other in terms of their popularity (the respective means are 52 and 51), although the gap grew somewhat larger during the COVID-19 pandemic (58 and 55). However, underlying these small differences there seems to be an increased polarization between the two main regions of Belgium. Starting from approximately the same level, support for a basic income in which accumulation is allowed and one in which it is not, both showed a decrease in Flanders (from 52 to 50 and 50 to 47, respectively) but an increase in Wallonia (from 51 to 62 and 51 to 59).

More generally, these findings demonstrate that there are also important differences between basic income varieties that vary with regard to some of the policy design dimensions that have hitherto been paid little attention in survey research. As with many of the dimensions discussed in the sections above, there appears to be some variation in public opinion both between and within countries, depending on the economic, political and institutional context people are exposed to. Much work still remains to be done in this regard. To the best of my knowledge, there are no surveys that have asked specifically about the policy design dimensions of administration (how and by whom?) and modality (what 'shape' should basic income take?). I will return to this issue in Chapter 5, where I identify important knowledge gaps and avenues for future research.

3.1.8 Some Relevant Policy Design Combinations

Up to this point, I have discussed the different policy dimensions of basic income separately. However, it seems highly likely that popular support hinges on specific *combinations* of these dimensions. In the following, I focus on a number of potentially relevant combinations between on the one hand, conditionality, uniformity and universality, and on the other hand, generosity, financing and integration. Although there are arguably other interactions that could be relevant, it would take too long to discuss all of them here (I will return to this issue in Chapter 5). To investigate the popularity of specific combinations of policy design dimensions, I mostly use data from the BNES and the BABEL experiment in Belgium, and the BIN experiment in the Netherlands. Additionally, I briefly refer to some of the findings from the survey experiments conducted in Finland, Spain and Switzerland, reported in Rincon (2021) and Stadelmann-Steffen and Dermont (2020). For methodological reasons, attention is limited here to so-called 'two-way combinations', meaning that I only analyse combinations of two design dimensions. Although combinations between three or more dimensions are arguably equally relevant, the number of respondents that evaluated these specific combinations is often too small to be able to attain reliable estimates.

I start with the combination between what are perhaps the two most central dimensions of basic income: its conditionality and universality. As seen above, it turns out that the level of support for basic income is lower when it is either fully universal or fully unconditional. Nevertheless, it could well be that people are more willing to accept universalism if basic income is made conditional on a socially appreciated activity. This is why Atkinson (1996) proposed his participation income. The underlying rationale here is that if there are at least some conditions attached to basic income, people will generally feel that *all* recipients are deserving of it because they all do something in return for the money. The other way round, it could also be that full unconditionality is accepted to a greater extent when a basic income has some restrictions that limit its universality. Many people may be more supportive of the unconditional version of basic income if it also sets residency or citizenship requirements, so that newly-arrived migrants cannot immediately receive obligation-free benefits. More generally, it is also worth asking whether people want multiple types of restrictions on top of each other in a basic income scheme—thus moving it further away from the universal and unconditional ideal type—or whether they are willing to accept just one restriction at a time.

To test this, I pinpoint the level of support for every possible two-way combination between the dimensions of conditionality, universality and uniformity, using data from the BNES experiment in Belgium. Table 3.1 shows the mean for each combination on a scale from 0 to 100, with larger scores indicating a higher level of support. Looking first at the set of combinations at the top of the table (between conditionality and universality), it is clear that a fully unconditional basic income is the least popular when it is universally paid to all residents (the mean is 43.9). Instead, people seem much more willing to accept full unconditionality if a residency requirement is set (the mean is 58.7). Seen from the other side, support for a fully universal basic income increases when it is made conditional on caring or volunteering (the mean is 51.6), or on job-seeking efforts (53.8). Of course, it has to be said that the one may (but need not) set limits on the other: if people are excluded because they fail to fulfil certain conditions of conduct, the scheme will no longer be fully universal. However, if everyone follows the 'rules of the game' and performs the required activities, the scheme will retain its fully universal character. We do not observe the same pattern for a basic income that is paid to everyone who meets the residency requirement. Here, support actually declines somewhat when benefit receipt comes with conditions of conduct. For the eligibility component of universality, the data shows that a fully unconditional basic income is more popular when it excludes the rich (the mean is 53.6) than when it is restricted to the poor (46.7) or when it is paid to all residents (43.9). As with full universality, support for a basic income that is targeted only at the poor increases when conditions of conduct are added.

The set of combinations displayed in the middle of Table 3.1, between conditionality and uniformity, paint a similar picture. A fully unconditional basic income is more popular when the amount received increases with recipients' work history (the mean is 54.2) compared with a flat-rate payment (45.8). Most people thus seem to think that if receiving the benefit is unconditional, its level should at least depend on prior contributions. The other way round, it is also the case that if basic income is equal for all, people seem to want job-seeking or caring/volunteering obligations to be imposed on its recipients (the means are 53.8 and 48,

Table 3.1 Combinations of conditionality, uniformity and universality

Conditionality → **Universality ↓**	Fully unconditional	Caring/volunteering required	Work required
All residents	43.9	51.6	53.8
Residency requirement	58.7	55.6	51.1
Excluding the rich	53.6	55.5	54.4
Only the poor	46.7	55.2	54.9
Conditionality → **Uniformity ↓**	Fully unconditional	Caring/volunteering required	Work required
Equality based	45.8	48.0	53.8
Need based	54.3	54.1	56.7
Equity based	54.2	54.9	54.5
Uniformity → **Universality ↓**	Equality based	Need based	Equity based
All residents	55.4	51.7	57.7
Residency requirement	48.9	52.3	49.6
Excluding the rich	52.5	51.7	54.3
Only the poor	50.5	55.1	57.4

Source BNES (2019/2020). Question wording: see Fig. 3.2 and Table A1.2

respectively). By contrast, when receipt of basic income is already conditional, people do not seem to see the need to also vary the amount it pays in line with the recipients' work history. Especially, when a basic income requires job-seeking efforts, there is very similar support for a flat-rate, a need-based and an equity-based amount (the means are 53.8, 56.7 and 54.5, respectively). This suggests that people set a limit to the number of work-related restrictions they are willing to accept, as they do not necessarily want to impose job-seeking requirements ***and*** make the level of basic income dependent on work history. With regard to the set of two-way combinations shown at the bottom of Table 3.1 (between uniformity and universality), the results indicate that a fully universal basic income is somewhat less popular if it is equal for all than if it pays higher amounts to those with a longer work record (the respective means are 54.5 and 57.7). Seen from the other perspective, a flat-rate basic income is most popular when it is fully universal. As could be expected, a basic income that varies the amount according to people's need is most popular when it is targeted only at the poor. An equity-based basic income, in which a higher amount is paid to people with a longer work record, is most popular when it is fully universal or targeted at the poor only (the respective means are 57.7 and 57.4). Further, support for a basic income that is targeted exclusively at the poor is higher if the amount is equity based, rather than flat rate or need based (the means are 57.4, 55.1 and 50.5, respectively).

The second batch of relevant policy design combinations concern the interplay between the generosity, financing and integration of basic income—which are strongly intertwined. As shown above, there tends to be lower support for a basic income that is well below the current subsistence level. One could argue that this is more likely if basic income is presented as a replacement for most existing social benefits, as that would leave many people—especially the poor—worse off. By contrast, if a basic income is seen as a supplement to the existing welfare system, people may be more inclined to accept a relatively low amount for it. Additionally, public opinion about both the generosity and the integration of basic income may also be closely related to the issue of financing. With regard to generosity, it seems highly likely that people will only be willing to accept an increase in income taxes or the introduction of new taxes if the proposed basic income is set at a relatively high level. In a similar vein, people may only support the replacement of other benefit schemes if the money saved as a result is directly used to fund a basic income. Using data from the BABEL experiment in Belgium and the BIN experiment in the Netherlands, Table 3.2 shows the average level of support for each two-way combination between the dimensions of generosity, financing and integration. Starting with the set of combinations presented at the top of the table (between generosity and integration), we can see that the Belgian case partly confirms the expectations. A basic income of €500 (which is well below any level of subsistence in Belgium) is slightly more popular when it supplements rather than replaces all or some of the existing social benefits (the means are 55.5, 51.4 and 48.3, respectively). This also applies to the Dutch case to some extent, where an amount of €500 is most accepted when basic income replaces other social benefits while at the same time providing top-ups for people in greater need (the mean is 64.1). That said, in both countries a basic income of €500 generally remains less popular than one of €1000 or €1500, irrespective of its integration into the existing system. With regard to the combinations between generosity and financing, the results indicate that, as expected, support for a basic income that is financed through an increase in income tax or the introduction of a new capital/climate tax generally increases with higher amounts. This pattern is found in both Belgium and the Netherlands and suggests that people prefer a generous basic income but

Table 3.2 Combinations of generosity, financing and integration

Generosity → **Integration ↓**	€500		€1000		€1500	
	BE	NL	BE	NL	BE	NL
All benefits replaced	51.4	62.2	53.6	70.2	56.6	65.8
Several benefits replaced	48.3	58.3	52.6	63.0	57.1	65.5
Replaces but supplements	51.4	64.1	56.4	66.1	60.2	64.9
No benefits replaced	55.5	61.8	54.1	66.9	56.1	61.4
Generosity → **Financing ↓**	€500		€1000		€1500	
	BE	NL	BE	NL	BE	NL
New climate tax	52.6	61.7	57.1	67.9	57.7	65.3
New capital tax	54.4	61.2	55.5	64.8	59.4	68.2
Tax increase	50.1	60.4	49.8	62.8	55.3	61.4
Financing → **Integration ↓**	New capital tax		New climate tax		Tax increase	
	BE	NL	BE	NL	BE	NL
All benefits replaced	53.0	68.0	56.0	66.8	52.0	63.4
Several benefits replaced	54.4	60.0	52.3	61.5	56.4	61.1
Replaces but supplements	57.3	66.1	60.8	65.7	52.5	62.4
No benefits replaced	58.7	65.8	59.2	64.8	51.2	58.8

Source BABEL Survey (2021) and BIN Survey (2021). Question wording: see Fig. 3.1 and Table A1.1

are to some extent also aware that this would most likely require a tax increase. For the combinations between financing and integration, people are, again as expected, less supportive of a basic income that requires a tax increase if no benefits are being replaced.

Overall, the data presented here shows that there are important differences in support for basic income schemes with varying combinations of policy design dimensions. These differences are sometimes larger than those found when looking at each dimension separately, and some combinations are clearly more popular than others. Most notably, the BNES experiment in Belgium shows that support for a basic income that is both fully unconditional and fully universal is generally lower than support for a basic income that sets limits on either aspect. While a fully universal basic income is more popular when it is conditional on job-seeking efforts, a fully unconditional basic income is supported more when it sets residency requirements. In a similar vein, a basic income that is fully universal or fully unconditional is more popular when it pays a higher amount to people with a longer work record compared with a flat-rate amount that is equal for all. Importantly, however, the experiment also shows that people do not always 'layer' multiple restrictions. For example, when basic income is already conditional on job-seeking efforts, there is no increase in support for also making the level of benefit dependent on recipients' work history.

It is very important to note that these findings do not necessarily apply to national contexts other than Belgium. In fact, there is some evidence that the popularity of basic income schemes with specific combinations of policy design dimensions varies between countries. Most notably, the Rincon experiment shows that people living in Finland and Spain prefer very different strategies to fund a fully universal basic income. While the Finnish respondents seem to want a 'take from all, give to all' type of basic income, in which full universality is financed by increasing income taxes for everyone at the same rate (Rincon et al., 2022), the Spanish respondents would rather have a 'Robin Hood for all' type of basic income that pays for full universality by increasing taxes for the rich (Rincon, 2022). Interestingly, in contrast to the findings from Belgium, in both Finland and Spain fully universal schemes do not receive a higher level of support when they are conditional on work-related obligations. Although the results from these survey experiments should not be directly compared, as they have dissimilar research designs, this does suggest that the popularity of different varieties of basic income—each of which have their own unique combination of policy design dimensions—is very much country specific. Previous research has hinted at a number of contextual factors that could explain this cross-national variation, and these factors mainly relate to existing welfare state policies (for example, the progressivity of income taxes), political discourse and media coverage (for example, the framing of basic income in public debates), culturally shared norms and values (for example, on the role of work in society) and the state of the economy (for example, the unemployment rate) (Laenen et al., 2022). Nevertheless, due to a lack of surveys charting popular support for differently designed basic income schemes across a wider range of countries, the type of research needed to unravel this cross-national variation is still very much in its infancy.

Summary Box 3.1 Across-the-Board Support for Different Varieties of Basic Income

Overall, the discussion of the across-the-board levels of support for different varieties of basic income demonstrates that some of these are clearly more popular than others.

Interestingly, it turns out that the basic income that comes closest to the ideal type—being universal, unconditional and equal for all—is often less popular than other varieties that deviate more significantly from the ideal type. For example, a targeted basic income that only includes the poor or excludes the rich is more popular than its fully universal counterpart without any means test. Similarly, there is often greater support for a basic income that is conditional on job-seeking efforts or other socially appreciated activities (such as caring or volunteering) compared with its fully unconditional counterpart. There also seems to be a higher level of support for a basic income that varies the amount according to recipients' needs or work record, compared with its flat-rate counterpart.

Furthermore, it seems that popular support is lowest when some of the core design features of the ideal-typical basic income appear in tandem. Most notably, the BNES experiment in Belgium shows that support for a basic income that is both fully unconditional and fully universal is lower than support for a basic income that sets limits on either of these aspects. Indeed, a fully universal basic income is more popular when it is conditional on job-seeking efforts, and a fully unconditional basic income is supported more when it sets residency requirements. In a similar vein, a basic income that is fully universal or unconditional is more popular when it pays a higher amount to people with a longer work record.

With regard to other important policy design dimensions of basic income, the results again show that some varieties are more popular than others. There is generally greater support for a relatively generous 'full' basic income that is at or above the current level of subsistence. However, lower amounts seem more acceptable when basic income is presented as a supplement to rather than a replacement for existing social benefits. In terms of financing, there seems to be relatively strong support for cutting back on welfare expenditure to fund a basic income. Nevertheless, it seems that the most popular funding mechanism is to increase taxes for the rich, either by making income taxes more progressive or by introducing or increasing taxes on capital and wealth.

Notwithstanding these general patterns, it is crucial to note that the evidence from the polls also demonstrates that the (relative) popularity of different varieties of basic income is very much context specific. More specifically, support appears to vary across countries, across regions within countries and over time. One example of cross-national variation is found in the Rincon experiment, which shows that while the Spanish prefer a basic income that is restricted to households with young children, the Finnish would rather have a basic income that is paid to all individuals irrespective of their family situation. An example of cross-regional variation comes from the BABEL Survey in Belgium, where a basic income restricted only to the young is more popular in the French-speaking region of Wallonia than it is in the Dutch-speaking region of Flanders. An example of over-time variation can be found in the BNES experiment, which shows that although support for basic income generally increased during the COVID-19 pandemic, the increase was larger for a basic income that excludes the rich than for its fully universal counterpart. This was, however, mainly due to a substantial increase in support for this type of basic income in Wallonia. Together, the evidence suggests that the popularity of different varieties of basic income follows a diverging over-time trajectory in different regions (and possibly also countries).

As alluded to above, these differences related to countries, regions and time are likely to be driven by variations in the cultural, economic, institutional and political context people are exposed to. However, the overall lack of surveys that have gauged people's opinion about different varieties of basic income in different countries, regions and years makes it difficult at present to reach empirically grounded conclusions in this regard.

3.2 Individual Differences

Although examining the across-the-board support for different basic income varieties is very informative, it seems highly likely that this support differs between individuals with diverging characteristics. The basic assumption in this regard is that people will express greater support for the types of basic income that they stand to benefit from personally (the self-interest factor) and/or that align with their political and ideological beliefs (the ideology factor). In the following, I first focus on the four individual characteristics for which there is enough data to be able to perform comparisons across the widest possible range of countries: age, gender, income and political ideology (with the latter measured on a left-right self-orientation scale). With the help of the above-discussed survey experiments (except the Rincon experiment, for which no information on respondents' characteristics is available), I compare the impact of these characteristics in four different countries: Belgium, Finland, Switzerland and the Netherlands. This comparison is important in light of the observation (made in Chapter 2) that the impact of people's characteristics on their support for basic income often varies between countries. After that, I focus more closely on a number of individual characteristics for which no (or a very limited) cross-national comparison is possible, but that are nonetheless highly relevant. Specifically, I use the BABEL Survey in Belgium (and to some extent also the BIN Survey in the Netherlands) to examine how support for different basic income varieties is related to voting intentions, trade union membership, welfare performance evaluations, benefit receipt and COVID-19 experiences. Although the main focus is on the survey experiments, I occasionally complement this with information from other, more-traditional surveys.

3.2.1 Age

In Chapter 2, it was shown that in almost all European countries, older (especially retired) people are less supportive of the ideal-typical basic income than their younger counterparts. From a self-interest perspective, this was interpreted as evidence that older people are generally less vulnerable on the labour market and experience less income insecurity because they are already covered by old-age pensions (which they do not want to lose). Additionally, it was argued that older people may be more opposed to basic income because they have a stronger status quo bias. It could be argued, however, that these mechanisms apply to different types of basic income to varying degrees. It could be that older people in particular are more supportive of a basic income that somehow takes into account prior contributions, given that they are more likely than younger people to have made such contributions (van Oorschot, 2006). For example, one would expect greater support among the elderly for a basic income that pays a higher amount to people with a longer work history, or for a basic income that sets (strict) residency requirements. Along similar lines, it seems plausible that the elderly will be less opposed to a basic income that is closer to the status quo, for example, because it does not replace existing social benefits (including old-age pensions). To test these assumptions, Table 3.3 shows the mean level of support per policy level within the survey experiments among those who are between 18 and 34 years of age (the 'young'), those between 35 and 64 years of age (the 'middle aged') and those above 65 years of age ('the elderly'). Generally, the data confirms that elderly people are less supportive of basic income than the young and the middle aged (as was also shown in Chapter 2). Nevertheless, it is still worth focusing more closely on the different policy design dimensions one by one.

Looking first at the dimension of conditionality, the general pattern is that a fully unconditional basic income tends to be less popular than its conditional counterparts in *all* age categories. Nevertheless, there is one important exception to this: the elderly in the Netherlands are equally supportive of an unconditional basic income and a conditional participation income (the respective means are 61.2 and 61.1). This is not the case for the middle aged and the young living in the Netherlands, who are somewhat more supportive of a conditional basic income.

With regard to the dimension of universality, we see that a fully universal basic income is generally less popular than a basic income that sets residency or nationality requirements, again across all the age groups. There are two notable exceptions to this, however. The first is found in the Netherlands, where only the elderly are more supportive of a restricted basic income. Here, both the young and the middle aged are most in favour of a fully universal basic income. The second exception is found in the BNES experiment in Belgium, where the elderly are less supportive of a basic income that sets residency requirements compared with a fully universal basic income. This is in contrast to the findings from the BABEL Survey, which show that the Belgian elderly are *more* supportive of residency requirements. Although it is difficult to tell with any certainty, these contrasting results could be due to differences in the question wording: while the BNES mentioned that basic income would be paid to 'all residents', the BABEL Survey made it clear that this would include 'newly-arrived migrants'. It could be that elderly people living in Belgium are especially opposed to basic income when migrants are framed as benefit recipients, thereby decreasing support for full universality relative to residency requirements. With regard to the eligibility component of universality, the data from the BNES experiment shows some differences between age groups. On the one hand, the elderly are more opposed to a basic income that is selectively targeted at the poor only (the mean is 50.1) compared with a basic income that is fully universal (54.5) or merely excludes the rich (57). On the other hand, young people in Belgium are less supportive of a fully universal basic income than a basic income that only includes the poor or excludes the rich (the means are 48.6, 53 and

Table 3.3 Support for different basic income varieties by age

	BE (BNES)			*BE (BABEL)*			*CH*			*FI*			*NL*		
	18–34	*35–64*	*65+*	*18–34*	*35–64*	*65+*	*18–34*	*35–64*	*65+*	*18–34*	*35–64*	*65+*	*18–34*	*35–64*	*65+*
Conditionality															
Unconditional	49.0	50.2	48.2	52.6	52.5	45.9							61.0	65.3	61.2
Conditional on participation	52.7	54.8	53.5	62.4	57.2	53.8							65.2	68.1	61.1
Conditional on job-seeking	56.7	55.0	55.5												
Universality															
All residents	48.6	52.2	54.5	56.3	53.5	46.4	41.1	42.9	35.2	52.8	48.7	44.7	64.0	69.8	57.5
Residency requirement	54.3	52.1	48.6	60.2	54.6	52.8	45.8	46.0	36.3	55.0	51.2	46.5	60.9	64.7	64.2
Nationality requirement				56.5	56.4	50.3							64.1	65.1	62.3
Excluding the rich	56.3	53.1	57.0												
For the poor only	53.0	55.8	50.1												
Generosity															
Low				58.4	51.5	46.3	43.8	41.8	33.5	52.9	48.1	46.3	57.3	63.5	6.16
Middle				55.6	55.1	50.1	44.8	45.9	35.9	54.5	50.8	46.3	66.6	69.2	61.4
High				59.3	58.3	53.0	43.5	45.9	38.9	55.0	51.6	44.8	65.4	66.9	60.6
Integration															
Replaces no benefits	49.9	53.0	51.1	59.5	54.2	52.0							62.9	64.8	61.9
Replaces some benefits				55.4	53.4	46.7							65.5	63.7	56.0
Replaces all benefits	55.0	53.5	53.0	54.7	55.5	47.8	44.0	44.5	34.3	53.8	49.2	45.8	63.2	68.5	63.9
Replaces but supplements				61.2	56.0	52.2							60.4	69.6	62.5

	BE (BNES)			*BE (BABEL)*			*CH*			*FI*			*NL*		
	18–34	*35–64*	*65+*	*18–34*	*35–64*	*65+*	*18–34*	*35–64*	*65+*	*18–34*	*35–64*	*65+*	*18–34*	*35–64*	*65+*
Cutbacks in benefits							44.4	45.2	37.6	54.8	51.5	46.1			
Financing															
Income tax							43.09	44.8	33.5	53.3	50.2	45.4			
Tax increase				53.5	52.0	48.3							62.1	63.8	57.2
Climate tax				58.6	56.8	47.9							70.2	64.9	61.4
Capital tax				60.4	55.4	52.8							57.1	68.3	63.8
Transaction tax							44.7	44.1	37.2	53.8	50.6	45.8			
Value-added tax							43.7	44.8	35.2	54.6	48.9	46.6			
Uniformity															
Equality based	47.4	53.7	51.3												
Need based	54.0	51.8	52.6												
Equity based	58.2	54.5	53.1												

Source BNES (2019/2020) and BABEL Survey (2021) for Belgium (BE), Stadelmann-Steffen and Dermont (S&D) (2020) for Finland (FI) and Switzerland (CH), and BIN Survey (2021) for the Netherlands (NL). The graph represents the mean score for each level in the experiment among the respective age groups. Notes on the policy design dimensions: (1) the dimension of accumulation in the BNES experiment is not included in the table; (2) the level 'replaces all existing benefits' is the average of the levels that give unemployment benefits and old-age pensions as respective examples (see Table A1.2); (3) the level 'residency requirement' in the S&D experiment is the average of the levels that propose respectively 5 and 10 years of residence (see Table A1.4); (4) the level 'middle' in the S&D experiment is the average of the two amounts that are given as middle options (see Table A1.4); (5) the dimension of integration in the S&D experiment refers to the replacement of social benefits generally instead of direct transfers only (see Table A1.4); (6) the funding mechanism of cutting back on government expenditure in the S&D experiment is not included in the table (see Table A1.4); (7) the budget-neutral option in the BIN Survey is not included in the table (see Table A1.1); and (8) the specific amounts for the dimension of generosity differ across the countries (see above)

56.3, respectively). The same is found for the middle aged, although the differences are smaller for this group.

With regard to the dimension of integration, there is little evidence for the hypothesis that older people are less supportive of a basic income that aims to replace existing social benefits. To the contrary, the highest level of support among the elderly is often found when a basic income replaces all social benefits (see the BNES experiment in Belgium and the BIN experiment in the Netherlands) or when it brings about cutbacks in social benefits (see the Stadelmann-Steffen and Dermont experiment in Switzerland). Nevertheless, the BABEL experiment in Belgium does confirm that elderly people are somewhat more supportive of a basic income that replaces no other benefits, or if it does, provides supplements to those in greater need. This may relate to the fact that the experiment mentioned the specific amount of basic income. As shown above, people are more reluctant to accept the replacement of other benefits if the amount of basic income is relatively low. It seems likely that the greater opposition to a benefit-replacing basic income among the elderly in the BABEL experiment is at least partly driven by the fact that a third of them were presented with an amount that is well below the subsistence level, which cannot easily be complemented with earnings from work. Interestingly, the young also generally seem somewhat more willing to accept a basic income that replaces (some or all) existing benefits. Overall, the middle aged do not have a particularly strong preference regarding the dimension of integration.

It is more difficult to discern general patterns for the dimension of financing. The BIN experiment in the Netherlands shows that the young mostly prefer a climate tax to fund a basic income (the mean is 70.2), followed by an increase in income or payroll taxes (62.1) and a capital tax (57.1). Among the middle aged and the elderly, a capital tax is the most popular funding mechanism (the means are 68.3 and 63.8, respectively), followed by a climate tax (64.9 and 61.4) and a tax increase (63.8 and 57.2). In Belgium, a capital tax is also the most popular option among the elderly and the young, but not among the middle aged. The Stadelmann-Steffen and Dermont experiment shows that in Switzerland, a transaction tax is the most popular funding mechanism among both young and old, and income tax is in particular an unpopular mechanism among the elderly. Other than that, the differences are relatively small. This is especially the case in Finland, where there are no notable age differences in terms of the preferred mechanism to finance a basic income.

Turning to the dimension of uniformity, we see that all age groups are most supportive of a basic income that is higher for those with a longer work record. While this was expected to be the case for the elderly (and perhaps also the middle aged), it is more surprising that an equity-based basic income is also more popular than its flat-rate counterpart among young people (the respective means are 58.2 and 47.4), who tend to have a relatively short work history and would thus receive lower amounts under such a system. A need-based basic income, which pays a higher amount to those in greater need, is the second most popular option among the young and the elderly, and the most popular one for the middle aged. It should nevertheless be noted that these findings only pertain to Belgium, as the dimension of uniformity was not included in the experiments in the other countries.

Lastly, it is interesting to examine whether the age groups vary in their support for different age-restricted basic income varieties—which are discussed above under the dimension of duration. On the one hand, one could possibly expect people to mainly support a basic income that is restricted to their own age group, because they may see themselves and/or their similar age peers as more deserving of it than other age groups (Laenen & Meuleman, 2017). In this scenario, the young will be most supportive of a youth basic income, the middle aged will be most supportive of a basic income for the working-age population and the elderly will be most supportive of a basic pension. On the other hand, it could be argued that the young will also have an interest in establishing a basic income for the other age groups, given that they will eventually receive it as they grow older. This is not the case for the elderly, who will of course never receive a youth basic income. Accordingly, elderly people may be strongly opposed to the introduction of a basic income for the young only. Similar mechanisms could be at play for the middle aged, who are too old to receive a youth basic income but may still hope to receive a basic pension in the future.

As shown in Fig. 3.11, these expectations are mostly confirmed by the data from the BABEL Survey in Belgium. The young are indeed more supportive of a youth basic income than the middle aged and the elderly (the means are 40.5, 30.2 and 26.7, respectively). A basic pension is also more popular among the elderly (the mean is 50.5) than it is among the middle aged (43.4) and the young (44). Further, a basic income for the working-aged is supported least by the only group that would be excluded from it: the elderly (the mean is 32.9). At the same time, however, a

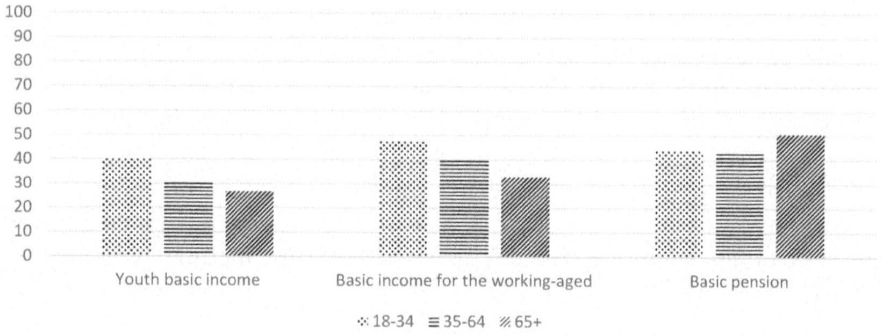

Fig. 3.11 Support for age-restricted varieties of basic income by age (*Source* BABEL Survey [2021]. Question wording: see Fig. 3.10. The answer scales ranged from 0 ['strongly against'] to 100 ['strongly in favour']. The graph presents the mean score on the scales in the respective age categories)

youth basic income is least popular among all age categories, including the young. Even this group would rather have a basic pension and even more so, a basic income for the working-age population (the mean is 47.3). For the elderly, the most popular basic income type is clearly the basic pension. The middle aged are most supportive of a basic pension, closely followed by a basic income for the working-age population (the mean is 40.1). The fact that the popularity of these two basic income varieties is so close to each other in the middle age group is probably due to the fact that one part of this group is very close to retirement or may already have reached early retirement (those in their late 50s and early 60s) while the other part is still relatively far removed from it (those in their 30s and 40s).

To sum up, there is some evidence that different age groups—especially the elderly—are most supportive of the basic income varieties that are in their best interests. Most notably, the elderly prefer a basic income that pays a higher amount to those with a longer work history (which many of them have) and would rather have a basic pension than a basic income for young people. However, the fact that young people also prefer an equity-based basic income to a flat-rate one suggests that this could be driven more by considerations of deservingness than by self-interest. Furthermore, it should be noted that these findings only apply to Belgium and have so far not been replicated in other countries. This is an important task for future research, because the evidence presented here clearly demonstrates that age differences in (relative) support for different types of basic income often vary across countries. Similarly, it seems likely that these age differences will also vary over time, perhaps pointing to generational gaps. Unfortunately, there is currently no longitudinal data available to examine this empirically.

3.2.2 Gender

In Chapter 2, we saw that men and women do not differ greatly in terms of their support for the ideal-typical basic income. When they do, it is often men who turn out to be somewhat more supportive. This goes against expectations, as it was assumed that women would support basic income more because they have greater self-interest in it and are generally more caring towards others (having been socialized accordingly). It seems plausible that men and women nevertheless think differently about various types of basic income with diverging policy designs. From a self-interest perspective, it seems likely that women are less supportive of a basic income in which access is conditional on job-seeking efforts compared with its fully unconditional counterpart, because they tend to have more and longer career breaks and greater overall vulnerability on the labour market. In a similar vein, we should expect to see a lower level of support among women for a basic income that varies the amount according to recipients' work history (compared with a flat-rate or a need-based basic income). Additionally, because women are more often employed in public welfare administration (for example, as social workers), they may be less supportive of a basic income that aims to replace many existing social benefits (as they could lose their job). From the perspective of caring, one would perhaps expect to find no gender differences in the relative popularity of different types of basic income, as women may simply be more willing to accept any type of basic income. As shown in Table 3.4, this hypothesis does not seem to hold, as there are some relevant differences between men and women concerning the types of basic income they support.

With regard to the dimension of conditionality, we see that women are *not* more supportive of a fully unconditional basic income. In fact, they seem to support it less—at least in Belgium and the Netherlands, where women prefer a conditional participation income to a fully unconditional one (see also Chrisp et al., 2020 for Finland and the UK). Relatedly, and against expectations, women show somewhat greater support for a basic

Table 3.4 Support for different basic income varieties by gender

	BE (BNES)		*BE (BABEL)*		*CH*		*FI*		*NL*	
	Men	*Women*	*Men*	*Women*	*Men*	*Women*	*Men*	*Women*	*Men*	*Women*
Conditionality										
Unconditional	49.4	49.4	50.1	52.2					64.3	61.8
Conditional on participation	54.1	55.1	58.0	58.1					66.3	64.1
Conditional on job-seeking	52.7	57.4								
Universality										
All residents	51.6	52.9	51.5	54.4	42.8	40.4	46.5	51.0	63.9	65.3
Residency requirement	49.6	53.9	57.2	54.9	45.1	45.1	49.1	52.9	66.0	61.4
Nationality requirement			54.3	56.2					65.8	61.8
Excluding the rich	54.0	55.9								
For the poor only	53.1	54.0								
Generosity										
Low			50.7	54.7	41.4	42.2	46.2	51.6	62.6	60.3
Middle			54.8	53.7	45.0	44.4	48.6	52.6	68.0	64.8
High			57.4	57.5	45.6	43.3	49.2	52.4	65.3	63.7
Integration										
Replaces no benefits	51.2	55.0	56.7	54.0					67.4	62.2
Replaces several benefits			50.2	54.9					58.7	64.7
Replaces all benefits	52.4	52.5	52.9	54.7	44.0	43.0	47.8	51.1	66.6	65.2
Replaces but supplements			56.6	56.9					67.7	59.2
Cutbacks in benefits					44.5	44.1	48.5	53.5		
Financing										
Income tax					44.1	42.6	47.9	51.7		
Tax increase			51.1	52.1					61.3	61.6
Climate tax			55.5	56.0					69.3	65.9
Capital tax			55.7	57.0					68.0	61.1
Transaction tax					44.3	43.3	47.1	53.3		
Value-added tax					44.0	42.5	48.8	50.9		
Uniformity										
Equality based	50.2	53.5								
Need based	51.2	53.9								
Equity based	54.8	55.1								

Source BNES (2019/2020) and BABEL Survey (2021) for Belgium (BE), Stadelmann-Steffen and Dermont (2020) for Finland (FI) and Switzerland (CH), and BIN Survey (2021) for the Netherlands (NL). The graph represents the mean score for each level in the survey experiment among the respective gender categories. See Table 3.3 for notes on the policy design dimensions shown in the table income that pays a higher amount to people with a longer work history (the mean is 55.1) than they do for a flat-rate (53.5) or a need-based (53.9) basic income. The same pattern is found for men.

Looking at the dimension of universality, men are almost always more opposed to a fully universal basic income and would instead rather impose residency or nationality requirements, or limit access to only the poor. For women, the evidence is much more mixed and seems to vary between countries. In Switzerland, similarly to their male counterparts, women are somewhat more in favour of setting a residency requirement (the mean is 45.1) than they are of making basic income fully universal (40.4). By contrast, in the Netherlands, women differ from their male counterparts in that they are most supportive of a fully universal basic income. In Belgium and Finland, women barely differentiate between basic income varieties that differ in terms of their universality.

For the dimension of integration, the evidence from the experiments does not provide strong evidence for the expectation that women are more opposed to a basic income that replaces many other social benefits. The BABEL experiment in Belgium shows that both men and women are somewhat more willing to accept a basic income that replaces other benefits if the basic income provides supplements to those in greater need. The BIN experiment in the Netherlands produced similar findings (for men at least). Among the female respondents in the Netherlands, a basic income that replaces but supplements existing benefits is actually the least popular option. In contrast to the gender differences found in Belgium and the Netherlands, the Stadelmann-Steffen and Dermont experiment shows that in Finland and Switzerland, both men and women differentiate little between basic income types that differ in terms of their integration into the existing welfare system.

With regard to the dimension of financing, men and women in Finland and Switzerland also make few distinctions between different funding mechanisms. In Belgium and the Netherlands, men mainly consider an increase in income or payroll taxes as less desirable than the introduction of new taxes on climate and capital. This is also true for women in Belgium, but not for women in the Netherlands, who are as supportive of a capital tax as they are of a tax increase to fund a basic income.

Lastly, for the dimension of generosity, it seems that both men and women are least in favour of a basic income when the amount it provides is well below the subsistence level.

In sum, there are only a few relevant differences in the types of basic income preferred by men and women. Most notably, men prove to be consistently opposed to a fully universal basic income, while for women this varies between countries. Other than that, men and women seem to have relatively similar preferences regarding different varieties of basic income.

3.2.3 Income

In Chapter 2, we saw that in most (European) countries, people earning a high income are less supportive of the ideal-typical basic income than their low-income counterparts, presumably because the former tend to see themselves as net contributors rather than net beneficiaries. Nevertheless, it seems plausible that the opposition from high-income earners will be stronger for some varieties of basic income than for others. Intuitively, people with a high income may be particularly opposed to a basic income if they are excluded from receiving it, either because it is targeted only at the poor or because it excludes the rich. There is a large body of literature suggesting that the upper (and also middle) classes will oppose highly selective, means-tested welfare schemes because they are unlikely to obtain any personal benefit from them (see Laenen & Gugushvili, 2021 for a review). However, as the middle classes will probably not see themselves as 'rich', it seems less likely that they will oppose a basic income that merely excludes the richest echelons of society. In a similar vein, high-income (and possible also middle-income) earners may be less supportive of a basic income that pays a larger amount to people with greater (financial) needs, as this implies that they would receive lower amounts. By contrast, people on a low income will presumably show greater support for such targeting within universalism.

It also seems unlikely that high-income earners will accept an increase in income and payroll taxes to fund a basic income. Although this probably also applies to low-income and middle-income earners, it seems plausible that the progressive nature of many contemporary tax systems means that in particular people with a high income will feel that the tax increase needed to fund basic income will increase their personal tax burden the most. This, in turn, could provoke this group's opposition to a basic income. Relatedly, high-income earners in particular may oppose a very generous basic income out of fear that it would make a tax increase inevitable. A similar logic could apply to a basic income that does not replace any existing social benefits, as this could be seen as too burdensome by high-income earners. For people on lower incomes, the cost aspect of a basic income scheme is probably somewhat less important, as they are more likely to be net beneficiaries. Therefore, I expect to find higher levels of support among low-income earners for generous basic income varieties that leave the existing benefit system more or less intact. Furthermore, given the fact that those on a low income are more likely to receive current social benefits, it seems plausible that they will be less supportive of a basic income that aims to replace 'their' benefits (Pierson, 1994, 2001).

Table 3.5 seems to confirm the previous finding that people earning a high income are generally less supportive of basic income than their low-income counterparts, regardless of the policy design. Importantly, however, this is not the case in the Netherlands, where high-income earners actually prove to be *more* supportive of some basic income varieties than low-income earners. In the other countries, high-income earners are always less supportive than low-income earners, but the gap between the two groups is clearly larger for some types of basic income than for others. In the following, I, therefore, examine in greater detail the income differences per policy design dimension.

Let us start with the dimension of conditionality, for which no expectations were formulated. For Belgium, both the BNES and the BABEL experiment show that low-income earners are more supportive of a basic income regardless of its degree of conditionality. However, the income-related gap is clearly larger in case of a fully unconditional basic income compared with its conditional counterparts. Using the BNES experiment as an example, we see that the gap between low-income and high-income earners is much smaller in the case of a basic income that is conditional on job-seeking efforts (the respective means are 55.5 and 54.4) compared with a fully unconditional basic income (52.7 and 45.1). Relatedly, although all the income groups prefer a conditional basic income, the difference with an unconditional one is larger for middle-income and especially high-income earners. Taking the BABEL experiment as a different example, we can see that the gap between a fully unconditional basic income and a conditional basic income is larger for high-income earners (the respective means are 48.9 and 58.4) than it is for people on low incomes (55.1 and 60.4). A similar pattern is observed in the BIN experiment in the Netherlands. Interestingly, it appears that Dutch high-income earners are—in absolute terms—nevertheless more supportive of

Table 3.5 Support for different basic income varieties by income

	BE (BNES)			*BE (BABEL)*			*CH*			*FI*			*NL*		
	Low	*Middle*	*High*	*Low*	*Middle*	*High*	*Low*	*Middle*	*High*	*Low*	*Middle*	*High*	*Low*	*Middle*	*High*
Conditionality															
Unconditional	52.7	46.6	45.1	55.1	51.3	48.9							62.4	64.0	61.4
Conditional on participation	55.5	53.3	51.3	60.4	57.7	58.4							62.5	68.1	69.2
Conditional on job-seeking	55.5	53.2	54.4												
Universality															
All residents	56.6	50.4	49.4	55.8	53.1	50.4	45.1	40.6	34.8	53.0	49.6	44.5	61.6	65.6	70.4
Residency requirement	51.1	51.5	48.6	61.4	54.9	57.6	49.8	43.6	36.4	54.9	51.4	47.7	62.7	65.8	58.1
Nationality requirement				56.9	55.6	53.6							63.1	66.7	65.3
Excluding the rich	54.8	52.0	54.4												
For the poor only	55.7	50.5	50.0												
Generosity															
Low				53.8	52.9	50.6	43.3	41.2	35.8	51.8	49.5	47.3	56.3	66.4	61.1
Middle				56.6	53.5	55.7	49.4	43.6	35.3	54.5	51.4	46.7	69.2	65.7	68.2
High				63.3	54.5	55.3	50.6	41.7	36.7	55.9	50.6	45.8	63.8	66.1	66.8
Integration															
Replaces no benefits	49.6	49.8	51.4	59.8	54.6	55.1							63.0	64.9	65.2
Replaces some benefits				59.3	52.0	51.9							59.1	65.4	56.9
Replaces all benefits	56.7	51.7	49.2	56.9	53.5	52.5	47.8	41.7	36.2	53.0	49.9	46.6	64.6	69.9	67.1
Replaces but supplements				55.5	57.5	55.6							63.1	64.3	71.0
Cutbacks in benefits							48.7	43.4	35.4	55.4	51.6	46.7			

	BE (BNES)			BE (BABEL)			CH			FI			NL		
	Low	*Middle*	*High*	*Low*	*Middle*	*High*	*Low*	*Middle*	*High*	*Low*	*Middle*	*High*	*Low*	*Middle*	*High*
Financing															
Income tax							48.1	44.6	34.3	54.7	49.7	45.4			
Tax increase				51.8	51.3	53.1							56.3	64.2	59.7
Climate tax				57.9	55.9	54.9							59.5	68.6	67.8
Capital tax				62.0	56.0	53.1							66.1	65.7	69.1
Transaction tax							48.8	41.5	36.9	54.6	51.0	45.7			
Value-added tax							47.1	41.3	34.5	52.4	51.0	48.0			
Uniformity															
Equality based	56.1	50.0	48.6												
Need based	54.1	49.5	49.5												
Equity based	53.8	53.9	53.3												

Source BNES (2019/2020) and BABEL Survey (2021) for Belgium (BE), Stadelmann-Steffen and Dermont (S&D) (2020) for Finland (FI) and Switzerland (CH), and BIN Survey (2021) for the Netherlands (NL). The graph represents the mean score for each level in the survey experiment among the respective income categories. In the BNES, income is measured as the annual net household income after taxes and transfers, with 'low' = < €20,650, 'middle' = €20,650–44,870 and 'high' = > €44,870. In the BABEL Survey, income is measured as the monthly net household income, with 'low' = < €1500, 'middle' = €1500–4000 and 'high' = > €4000. In the BIN Survey, income is measured as the yearly gross household income, with 'low' = < €36,500, 'middle' = €36,500–73,000 and 'high' = > €73,000. In the S&D experiment, income is measured as the monthly net household income, with in CH 'low' = < CHF5000, 'middle' = CHF5000-8999 and 'high' = > CHF8999 and in FI 'low' = < €1800, 'middle' = €1800–3400 and 'high' = > €3400. Please note that because the different surveys had pre-defined income categories, it was not possible to design completely uniform categories across countries. Furthermore, because only some of the surveys include information on the household size and composition, income was not calculated as household equivalent. See Table 3.3 for notes on the policy design dimensions shown in the table a participation income than their low-income counterparts (the respective means are 69.2 and 62.5). This is one of the few cases in which support for basic income is *not* greater among low-income earners.

With regard to the dimension of universality, the evidence presented in Table 3.5 does not support the hypothesis that people with a high income are more strongly opposed to targeted types of basic income. Instead, the BNES experiment in Belgium actually shows that high-income earners are somewhat more supportive of a basic income that excludes the rich (the mean is 54.4) compared with a fully universal one (49.4). Other than that, it seems that all income groups are more supportive of a basic income that sets residency requirements. However, there are two exceptions to this general pattern. The first is found in the BNES experiment in Belgium, where low-income earners appear to prefer a fully universal basic income (the mean is 56.6) to a basic income with residency requirements (51.1). This should be interpreted with caution, as it is not confirmed by the BABEL experiment (which was also conducted in Belgium). The second exception is found in the Netherlands, where high-income earners are more supportive of the fully universal option (the mean is 70.4) compared with a restricted basic income (58.1). In substantive terms, this is one of the largest differences in support for two basic income varieties found in any of the survey experiments.

Looking at the dimension of generosity, all the income groups prove to be least supportive of a relatively low basic income that is well below the existing subsistence level. Nevertheless, a closer look shows that in particular the low-income earners support a basic income below the subsistence level to a lesser extent than they support a more generous basic income (in all countries). By contrast, middle-income and high-income earners tend to make fewer distinctions between different basic income varieties with varying levels of generosity. For example, the Stadelmann-Steffen and Dermont experiment in Switzerland shows that while people on low incomes are significantly less supportive of the lowest amount (the mean is 43.3) than they are of the highest amount (50.6), high-income earners barely differentiate between the two (the means are 35.8 and 36.7, respectively). Overall, the data, therefore, does not confirm the expectation that high-income earners will oppose a generous basic income more fiercely than a low-level basic income because they strongly oppose the tax increase this would be likely to cause.

Turning to the dimension of integration, there is equally little support for the hypothesis that high-income earners will support a basic income that replaces existing social benefits whereas low-income earners will oppose this. Instead, the evidence from the survey experiments is mixed. The BNES experiment in Belgium shows that low-income earners are more supportive of a basic income that replaces all benefits (the mean is 56.7) compared with an equivalent that does not replace any benefits (49.6). For middle-income and high-income earners, the difference between the two basic income varieties is negligible. By contrast, the opposite pattern can be observed in the BABEL experiment, as low-income earners prove to be less supportive of a basic income that replaces other benefits. As argued above, this may be connected to the fact that the BABEL experiment specified the amount of basic income, whereas the BNES did not. In the BIN experiment in the Netherlands, both low-income and high-income earners are least supportive of a basic income that 'replaces some benefits'. Dutch high-income earners turn out to be most in favour of a basic income that replaces other benefits but provides supplements to those in greater need. No notable income differences are found in the Stadelmann-Steffen and Dermont experiment in Finland and Switzerland.

With regard to the dimension of financing, it can be seen that—as expected—the least popular option among all income groups is to increase the existing income or payroll taxes in order to finance a basic income. Nevertheless, do high-income earners oppose a tax increase to a comparatively greater degree than their low-income counterparts? Before answering that question, it should first be noted that *all* the financing mechanisms in the BABEL and the BIN experiment that are presented in Table 3.5 imply a tax increase of some form. This is because it was mentioned that a new capital or climate tax would come on top of existing income and payroll taxes (which would stay as they are) in order to cover the additional costs of implementing a basic income. Only the BIN experiment included the option that taxes would not increase. By contrast, in the Stadelmann-Steffen and Dermont experiment, respondents were only presented with three different funding mechanisms (income tax, transaction tax and value-added tax), without being told whether taxes would increase or not. This is probably the reason for the experiment finding no notable income differences with regard to the financing of basic income. With this information in mind, it seems that there is conflicting evidence for the hypothesis that people earning a high income will resist a tax increase more strongly than their low-earning counterparts. On the one hand, people on a low income seem to make the perfectly logical choice of preferring a capital tax to a climate tax—both in Belgium (the respective means are 62 and 57.9) and the Netherlands (66.1 and 59.5). This choice is logical because low-income earners are likely to have little capital to be taxed. This stands in contrast to their high-income counterparts, who barely distinguish between a capital and a climate tax. On the other hand, the BIN experiment shows that high-income earners are *not* most in favour of keeping taxes as they are (the mean is 63.7). Instead, the most popular option among high-income earners in the Netherlands is to introduce a new climate tax to finance a basic income (the mean is 68.6). Dutch low-income earners, by contrast, are most supportive of keeping taxes as they are (the mean is 66.9).

With regard to the dimension of uniformity, the BNES experiment in Belgium shows that high-income (as well as middle-income) earners prefer a basic income that pays a larger amount to those with a longer work history (the mean is 53.3) to a flat-rate (48.6) or a need-based (49.5) basic income. However, this is not the case for low-income earners, who differentiate somewhat less between the three proposals (the means are 53.8, 56.1 and 54.1, respectively). Although these findings seem to confirm the expectation that a need-based basic income is opposed more strongly by high-income earners, they do not confirm the expectation that low-income earners prefer this type of basic income.

Overall, the evidence from the survey experiments generally confirms that people on a low income are more supportive of basic income than their high-earning counterparts. At the same time, the data also shows that there are relevant income-related differences in support for different varieties of basic income with varying policy designs. In some specific cases (such as a conditional participation income in the Netherlands), support is greater among people on a high income than it is among their low-income counterparts. In some other cases, the income gap is clearly larger for some types of basic income than for others. The observed income-related differences nevertheless rarely accord with the expectations discussed above, which are mostly derived from self-interest theory. For example, there is little evidence that high-income earners oppose targeted types of basic income more strongly than people on a low income. This may indicate that we should perhaps look for answers elsewhere, moving away from the self-interest factor and closer to that of (political) ideology.

3.2.4 *Political Ideology*

In Chapter 2, I showed that people who identify as politically left wing are generally more supportive of the ideal-typical basic income than their right-wing counterparts. I now go on to explore whether this ideological gap depends on the type of basic income under consideration. Although it seems plausible that the political left will always be more supportive of basic income (regardless of its policy design), theoretically it could also be the case that some specific varieties receive more support from right-wingers than left-wingers. First of all, it has been argued that the political right would not be opposed to, or perhaps would even be in favour of, a basic income that is set at a relatively low level and/or replaces many existing social benefits (for a discussion, see Van Parijs & Vanderborght, 2017). In fact, these types of basic income have been proposed by some influential right-wing conservatives, who tend to see them as an ideal vehicle to dismantle the welfare state and to get rid of the associated government bureaucracy and control (see, for example, Friedman, 1962; Murray, 2008). By contrast, most proposals from left-wing progressives envision a world in which basic income is relatively generous and/or supplements rather than replaces existing benefits (Chrisp & Martinelli, 2019). Accordingly, there could well be a higher level of support for a low, benefit-replacing basic income among right-wingers than among their left-wing counterparts. Second, right-wingers may also be more supportive of more-restrictive basic income varieties that set limits on its conditionality and/or its universality (Laenen et al., 2022). Concretely, we could see a higher level of support for targeted and conditional types of basic income among right-wing people. Alternatively, it could be that left-wingers remain more supportive, but that right-wingers are closer to them in the case of restrictive basic income varieties compared with their fully universal or unconditional counterparts.

In its entirety, Table 3.6 demonstrates a very clear pattern, showing that left-wingers are *always* more supportive of basic income than their right-wing counterparts, regardless of the policy design. The gap also tends to be large—substantially larger than the previously examined characteristics. This suggests that individual differences in support for basic income are driven above all by people's ideological beliefs rather than their age, gender or income. Across all the survey experiments and all the countries, there is not a single exception to be noted. This observation immediately refutes the hypothesis that some types of basic income are more popular among right-wingers than among left-wingers. However, it does not counter the expectation that the gap between right-wingers and left-wingers is narrower for some types of basic income than for others. This makes it relevant to investigate—per policy design dimension—which types of basic income are supported most within the political left and the political right.

Starting with the dimension of conditionality, it can be seen from Table 3.6 that in Belgium, all three ideological groups are more supportive of a basic income that is conditional on caring/volunteering or job-seeking than they are of a fully unconditional basic income. Importantly, this also includes the political left. The BABEL experiment, for example, shows that those who identify as politically left wing prefer a conditional participation income (the mean is 65) to its fully unconditional counterpart (56.6). This is not the case in the Netherlands though, where those on the political left are approximately equally supportive of both basic income types (the respective means are 70.9 and 71.8). The same applies to centrists, but not to those on the right, who are more supportive of a conditional participation income.

For the dimension of universality, we see that all of the ideological groups make relatively few distinctions between different varieties of basic income. Accordingly, it is not the case that a fully universal basic income is always *most* popular among left-wingers and always *least* popular among right-wingers. There is nevertheless one noteworthy exception to this: the BNES experiment in Belgium shows that right-wingers are in fact less supportive of a fully universal basic income (the mean is 43.8) than they are of a basic income that excludes the rich (54), targets the poor only (47.4) or sets residency requirements (48.9). By contrast, their left-wing counterparts do not draw this sharp distinction between basic income types with diverging degrees of universality. A similar preference for a targeted version of basic income among conservative right-wingers has also been observed in Japan, where they are more supportive of a negative income tax (33% is in favour) than they are of a fully universal basic income (22.7%). Importantly, however, the same applies to their liberal, left-wing counterparts (50.5% versus 32.1%) (see Takamatsu & Tachibanaki, 2014).

With regard to the dimension of generosity, it turns out that left-wingers are always least supportive of the lowest proposed amount of basic income and most supportive of the highest amount. This pattern is observed in all the countries under consideration. This is not the case for

Table 3.6 Support for different basic income varieties by political orientation

	BE (BNES)			*BE (BABEL)*			*CH*			*FI*			*NL*		
	Left	*Centre*	*Right*	*Left*	*Centre*	*Right*	*Left*	*Centre*	*Right*	*Left*	*Centre*	*Right*	*Left*	*Centre*	*Right*
Conditionality															
Unconditional	58.2	48.4	42.2	56.6	52.8	44.5							71.8	62.6	55.6
Conditional on participation	61.2	53.1	52.0	65.0	59.5	49.8							70.9	63.2	62.6
Conditional on job-seeking	60.5	53.4	51.6												
Universality															
All residents	60.0	52.3	43.8	60.9	52.7	47.1	51.9	39.0	39.2	52.8	47.3	44.6	73.0	62.9	59.8
Residency requirement	58.2	49.3	48.9	61.7	57.4	48.9	55.1	42.6	42.8	55.9	49.5	46.7	69.7	63.2	58.5
Nationality requirement				60.3	58.5	45.6							71.5	62.5	58.3
Excluding the rich	61.0	52.1	54.0												
For the poor only	60.3	53.5	47.4												
Generosity															
Low				58.2	53.6	45.2	51.0	39.3	41.2	52.1	47.6	46.9	67.3	60.5	57.6
Middle				58.5	57.4	45.6	54.7	42.1	42.6	54.8	49.3	46.3	73.3	64.9	62.6
High				67.3	57.7	51.3	55.4	41.8	38.8	58.3	48.8	44.4	73.7	63.4	56.9
Integration															
Replaces no benefits	62.6	49.6	46.2	66.6	54.2	49.3							72.1	60.2	59.7
Replaces some benefits				58.3	54.2	46.0							66.6	60.8	58.7
Replaces all benefits	58.7	52.9	49.3	59.2	56.2	43.6	53.4	41.2	40.8	53.5	48.2	45.9	73.3	68.2	56.2
Replaces but supplements				59.3	60.0	49.3							74.3	62.2	61.2
Cutbacks in benefits							54.6	41.5	42.4	56.3	49.2	46.0			

(continued)

Table 3.6 (continued)

	BE (BNES)			*BE (BABEL)*			*CH*			*FI*			*NL*		
	Left	*Centre*	*Right*	*Left*	*Centre*	*Right*	*Left*	*Centre*	*Right*	*Left*	*Centre*	*Right*	*Left*	*Centre*	*Right*
Financing															
Income tax							53.3	40.6	40.5	56.2	48.4	43.1			
Tax increase				57.9	52.2	45.5							72.5	60.1	52.0
Climate tax				62.1	57.6	48.2							73.0	63.9	58.4
Capital tax				62.9	58.3	47.4							72.7	63.3	59.2
Transaction tax							53.5	41.0	43.0	54.0	49.0	46.1			
Value-added tax							52.7	40.8	41.3	53.5	48.1	48.0			
Uniformity															
Equality based	57.1	50.5	47.7												
Need based	60.1	51.6	46.8												
Equity based	62.5	53.2	51.0												

Source BNES (2019/2020) and BABEL Survey (2021) for Belgium (BE), Stadelmann-Steffen and Dermont (2020) for Finland (FI) and Switzerland (CH), and BIN Survey (2021) for the Netherlands (NL). The graph represents the mean score for each level in the survey experiment among the respective ideological groups. In each survey, political ideology was measured as a self-placement scale ranging from 'left' (0) to 'right' (10). In the table, 'left' includes all respondents with scores between 0 and 3, 'centre' includes all respondents with scores between 4 and 7, and 'right' includes all respondents with scores between 8 and 10. See Table 3.3 for notes on the policy design dimensions shown in the table right-wingers, who are by contrast *least* supportive of the highest amount in three of the four countries: Finland, Switzerland and the Netherlands. The sole exception to the rule is Belgium, where right-wingers also prefer the most generous basic income (the mean is 51.3) to its less generous counterparts (both around 45). Overall, the evidence nevertheless seems to confirm that right-wingers are somewhat less supportive of a very generous basic income. Those who identify as political centrists generally prefer the middle amount, although the differences are relatively small.

Turning to the dimension of integration, there is very little evidence for the expectation that right-wingers most strongly support a basic income that replaces existing social benefits. Indeed, those on the political right usually do *not* prefer a basic income that replaces all benefits to a basic income that replaces no other benefits. Likewise, there is little evidence that left-wingers are more supportive of a basic income that is completely complementary to the existing system. Belgium is again the exception in this regard, as left-wingers there prove to be more supportive of a basic income that replaces no other benefits. In general, those in the political centre do not appear to have strong opinions on the matter, except in the Netherlands, where they are more in favour of a basic income that replaces all other benefits compared with one that replaces only some or no benefits (the respective means are 68.2, 60.8 and 60.2).

With regard to the dimension of financing, both the BABEL and the BIN experiment show that an increase in income/payroll taxes is the least popular option among all ideological groups, compared with the introduction of a new capital or climate tax to cover the additional costs. The only exception in this regard is people on the political left in the Netherlands, who differentiate little between the three funding mechanisms. The findings from the Stadelmann-Steffen and Dermont experiment suggest that all three ideological groups lack a strong preference for a specific funding mechanism, especially in Switzerland. In Finland, the only notable observation is that the political left somewhat prefers income taxes while the political right somewhat favours a transaction tax or a value-added tax.

For the dimension of uniformity, we see that all three ideological groups have a slight preference for a basic income that rewards people who have a longer work history with a higher amount. Even among left-wingers, an equity-based basic income of this type (the mean is 62.5) is slightly more popular than its need-based (60.1) and flat-rate (57.1) counterparts. Perhaps somewhat counter-intuitively, it turns out that a flat-rate basic income is *not* the most popular option among left-wingers. Centrists and right-wingers seem to prefer an equity-based basic income, but they distinguish very little between a flat-rate and a need-based one.

In sum, the evidence from the survey experiments clearly confirms that left-wingers are more supportive of basic income than right-wingers (and centrists). Interestingly, however, left-wingers do not always prefer the type of basic income one could intuitively expect. For example, it is apparent that those on the political left are more supportive of a conditional participation income than they are of a fully unconditional basic income in Belgium, and that they are equally supportive of the two varieties in the Netherlands. In a similar vein, left-wingers do not prefer a basic income that is fully universal or one that leaves all existing social benefits intact. By contrast, right-wingers often have a preference for more-restrictive basic income varieties, as expected. Most notably, they always prefer a conditional to an unconditional basic income. Right-wingers are nevertheless not always more supportive of basic income varieties that set limits to universality or replace other benefits. The only expectation that seems to be fully supported by the data is the prediction that right-wingers are least likely to support a very generous basic income while left-wingers are most likely to do so.

3.2.5 *Voting Intentions*

It would perhaps be premature to end the discussion of political ideology and its influence on support for different basic income varieties here. 'Left', 'right' and 'centre' are arguably very broad categories that could mask important within-group variation. For example, it has been shown that most political support for basic income on the left has come from green parties and politicians rather than their socialist counterparts (Van Parijs & Vanderborght, 2017). Accordingly, it could well be that the electorates of these different left-wing parties have highly diverging opinions about basic income (Schwander & Vlandas, 2020). Likewise, it seems plausible that there is also some variation between the electorates of different right-wing parties—for example, between those who vote for the centre right and those who vote for the far right. To investigate this, I make use of the experiments included in the BABEL Survey in Belgium and the BIN Survey in the Netherlands. Both surveys are suited for this purpose because they asked respondents about their voting intentions, which can then be linked to their support for different varieties of basic income.

I first look at the results for Belgium, which are shown in Table 3.7. In the Belgian case, political parties can still be broadly classified from 'left' to 'right'. The most left-wing party is arguably the PVDA-PTB, which is nationally organized and adheres to a Marxist-socialist ideology. Although it has long been a relatively small party operating in the margins, recent electoral successes have made it a serious contender for the centre-left parties—the greens (Groen in Flanders and Ecolo in Wallonia) and in particular the traditional socialist parties (Vooruit in Flanders and PS in Wallonia). The parties that are historically closest to the political centre are the Christian democrats (CD&V in Flanders and CDH in Wallonia, although it should be noted that the latter have recently rebranded as Les Engagés). To the right of centre, we first find the liberal parties (Open VLD in Flanders and MR in Wallonia), followed by the Flemish nationalist N-VA. On the far-right, there is only Vlaams Belang. Neither N-VA nor Vlaams Belang has any real counterpart in Wallonia. Importantly, the radical right in Belgium is culturally rather than economically conservative. This means that it tends to be in favour of economic redistribution through the welfare state, albeit in a very chauvinistic way; that is, only for natives, not immigrants (Abts, Dalle Mulle, et al., 2021).

In terms of political support, basic income has mainly been endorsed by parties and politicians in Wallonia, although in very different forms (Geels, 2023). Most notably, Ecolo wants to introduce a youth basic income (between €460 and €600 per month) in the short term, with a truly universal basic income for people of all ages being the long-term goal. Alternatively, they are also in favour of something they call a 'universal solidarity capital', which is a basic endowment (of €30,000) paid to everyone at the age of 25. In both proposals, the cash payment would be delivered unconditionally, without any strings attached. This is different in the proposal of Les Engagés (formerly CDH) that involves a conditional participation income. Although the other parties in the French-speaking part of Belgium do not (yet) officially endorse a basic income scheme, the presidents of the two largest parties at the time of writing (Paul Magnette of PS and George-Louis Bouchez of MR) have recently expressed their support for some type of basic income. On the one hand, Bouchez proposes a 'social dividend' (of €1000 for those aged between 18 and 67 and €1600 for those above 67) that would replace most existing welfare benefits and services. He has in the past also shown support for a 'youth

Table 3.7 Support for different basic income varieties by voting intentions in Belgium

	Far left	*Greens*	*Socialists*	*Christian democrats*	*Liberals*	*Flemish nationalists*	*Far right*
Conditionality							
Unconditional	57.3	59.1	55.7	50.7	48.1	41.7	42.8
Conditional on participation	63.7	65.0	62.1	57.9	55.7	43.5	50.9
Universality							
All residents	57.7	62.9	57.6	50.9	46.6	43.6	48.7
Residency requirement	59.3	61.9	59.1	55.4	53.8	44.3	47.9
Nationality requirement	63.5	62.2	60.9	57.1	54.6	40.5	43.7
Generosity							
€500	55.2	58.6	55.2	56.7	50.1	43.1	40.2
€1000	57.8	64.3	60.2	53.4	52.4	41.4	48.4
€1500	67.5	64.8	62.6	53.2	51.8	43.7	51.1
Integration							
Replaces no benefits	60.2	67.6	63.2	54.9	47.6	37.8	50.4
Replaces some benefits	54.6	56.2	58.9	51.9	52.5	41.0	44.0
Replaces all benefits	60.1	62.7	53.8	55.4	47.3	46.3	43.1
Replaces but supplements	66.9	62.6	60.2	55.1	56.1	44.4	49.9
Financing							
Tax increase	54.4	57.0	60.5	49.4	48.9	39.3	50.3
Capital tax	59.1	62.1	62.4	56.0	52.1	47.6	44.2
Climate tax	67.4	67.8	54.6	57.5	53.0	41.9	47.0

Source BABEL Survey (2021). Question wording: 'Which political party would you vote for should the federal elections be held today?' The electoral groups in the table are: 'Far left' = PVDA-PTB; 'Greens' = Groen + Ecolo; 'Socialists' = Vooruit + PS; 'Christian Democrats' = CD&V + CDH/Les Engagés; 'Liberals' = Open VLD + MR; 'Flemish Nationalists' = N-VA; 'Far right' = Vlaams Belang. All respondents who indicated that they would vote for another political party (including DéFI), would vote blank/invalid or would not vote were treated as missing. The table presents the mean level of support for each policy design dimension in the survey experiment within the respective electoral groups

capital' of €25,000 that would (under certain conditions) be paid to all people aged between 18 and 25. On the other hand, Magnette wants to keep the existing welfare system intact but proposes a basic income (of €600) to build an additional layer on top of it. His proposal is restricted, however, to young people between the ages of 18 and 25. In the Dutch-speaking part of the country, basic income has occasionally been endorsed by individual politicians (mostly from Groen and Open VLD), but these were never political heavyweights as they were in the French-speaking part. Furthermore, no Flemish party has ever expressed official support for a basic income, except for Vivant, a very small party that no longer exists today in the Dutch-speaking or French-speaking part of Belgium (Vanderborght, 2004). Instead, most Flemish parties have to date been either opposed to basic income or indifferent about the issue. Nevertheless, when looking at the electorates of the different political parties (in Table 3.7), it does make sense to group Dutch-speaking and French-speaking respondents that belong to the same political 'family' (specifically, the far left, greens, socialists, Christian democrats and liberals). It should be noted that this is not the case for the Flemish nationalists and the far right, both of which consist of Dutch-speaking respondents only.

Table 3.7 first of all shows that in Belgium, basic income is most popular among those who intend to vote for the green parties. Indeed, almost every basic income variety under consideration receives the highest level of support among this particular electoral group. There are only three exceptions to this. The first is that green voters are *not* most supportive of a basic income that replaces only some of the existing social benefits (with or without supplements for those in greater need). These options are supported to a somewhat greater extent by the constituencies of the other left-wing parties. Green voters, by contrast, prefer a basic income that either replaces *no* other benefits or replaces *all* other benefits. Although this seems paradoxical, it could be that these voters mainly want a basic income that reduces administrative complexity, and both options would achieve this to a larger degree than the replacement of just a few benefits. The second exception is that the constituents of the green parties are *not* significantly more supportive of a basic income that is financed by a capital tax, which is equally popular among their socialist counterparts (the respective means are 62.1 and 62.4). In a similar vein, a basic income financed by climate tax is equally as popular among green voters as it is among far-left voters (the respective means are 67.8 and 67.4). The second-highest level of support for the different varieties of basic income is usually found among far-left voters or those who vote for the traditional socialists, who tend to be very close to each other. Within the political left, there are striking similarities as well as notable differences. The similarities are: first, each electorate prefers a conditional basic income to a fully unconditional one; second, they would all rather have a more generous basic income than a lower-than-subsistence alternative; third, they are all least supportive of a basic income that replaces only some benefits. The important differences are: first, unlike the greens, socialists and far-left voters prefer a basic income with residency or nationality requirements to a fully universal one; second, while far-left voters clearly prefer a basic income that replaces some benefits and provides supplements, the others do not; third, socialist voters prefer a capital tax (the mean is 62.4) or even an increase in income/payroll taxes (60.5) to a climate tax (54.6) as a funding mechanism for basic income, with the last of these being the most popular option among green and far-left voters.

Support is generally much lower among voters of centre and right-wing parties. This is especially the case for the Flemish nationalists, who are the most sceptical of basic income, as indicated by the fact that the mean level of support never reaches the mid-point of the scale. Compared with the Flemish nationalists, the Christian Democrats and liberals are more supportive of basic income. Most far-right voters find themselves somewhere in between. Within the political centre and right, there are clearly more differences than there are similarities. The only commonality is that (similar to their left-wing counterparts) they prefer a conditional participation income to a fully unconditional basic income. Other than that, these voters seem to support somewhat different basic income varieties. With regard to universality, both Christian democrats and liberals prefer to set residency or nationality requirements instead of allowing universal access. This is not found among right-wing voters—somewhat surprisingly, given the anti-immigration and welfare chauvinistic rhetoric of their parties (Abts, Dalle Mulle, et al., 2021). With regard to generosity, the far right in particular prefer a more generous basic income. Liberals and Flemish nationalists distinguish little between different amounts of basic income. Driven perhaps by the principle of subsidiarity, Christian-democratic voters have a slight preference for the least generous option. Looking at integration, Flemish nationalists are the least supportive of a basic income that replaces no other social benefits. This is the opposite for far-right voters, who are most supportive of a basic income that replaces nothing else (or provides supplements for the needy when it does). With regard to financing, a tax increase tends to be the least popular, except among far-right voters, who are most strongly opposed to a capital or climate tax. Flemish nationalists seem to prefer a capital tax to the two other funding mechanisms. Christian democrats and liberals do not have a clear preference in this regard.

Compared with Belgium, the Dutch political landscape is more scattered and volatile in the sense that the lower electoral threshold means that there are more (smaller) political parties, which tend to emerge or dissolve more quickly (Andeweg, 2005). Here, attention is limited to the constituencies of those political parties that were (electorally) most important in 2021, when the BIN Survey was fielded in the Netherlands. On the political left, these are the greens (GroenLinks, grouped together with the PvdD) and the socialists (PvdA and SP). On the right, these are the populist parties of PVV and FvD. In the political centre, we find the left-leaning social liberals (D66, grouped together with VOLT), the right-leaning liberals (VVD, grouped together with JA21) and the centre-seeking Christian democrats (CDA and CU). Political support for basic income has mostly come from the green party, which has advocated a fully unconditional and universal basic income in some of its election manifestos. Recently, D66 also included a basic income type proposal in its manifesto. More specifically, they argue for a (targeted) negative income tax that would abolish several existing social benefits (such as old-age pensions and social assistance) and that would be funded by a shift from income taxes to taxes on pollution and wealth. Two other parties (PvdD and PvdA) have also expressed their support for conducting basic income *experiments* (Roosma, 2022).

Table 3.8 shows that—as in Belgium—it is the green voters who tend to be most supportive of basic income in the Netherlands. There are nevertheless some notable exceptions. The first is that green voters are *not* most supportive of a fully unconditional basic income, although this is about equally popular among socialist and social-liberal voters. The same is true for a basic income that sets nationality requirements. The second exception is that green voters are *not* most supportive of a basic income that keeps all existing social benefits in place; a proposal that is actually the most popular among populist voters (the respective means are 70 and 74.5). The third exception is that green voters are *not* most supportive of a basic income that replaces some existing benefits but provides supplements to those in greater need; a system that is accepted most by socialist voters (the respective means are 68.4 and 75.1). Other than these exceptions, support for basic income is generally highest among green voters, followed by socialist, social-liberal and then Christian-democratic voters. Centre-right liberals and far-right populists tend to show the lowest level of support for basic income. Nevertheless, there are relevant differences

Table 3.8 Support for different basic income varieties by voting intentions in the Netherlands

	Greens	*Socialists*	*Social liberals*	*Christian democrats*	*Liberals*	*Populists*
Conditionality						
Unconditional	67.3	67.1	66.9	64.6	51.1	59.7
Conditional on participation	74.6	67.7	66.0	62.5	61.5	66.5
Universality						
All residents	74.9	65.7	66.6	63.8	58.0	61.2
Residency requirement	70.7	67.6	66.5	58.2	53.5	63.8
Nationality requirement	66.7	69.0	66.3	67.8	55.3	63.4
Generosity						
€500	68.1	60.8	62.5	61.6	54.4	59.2
€1000	71.6	68.6	71.2	66.7	57.4	66.9
€1500	72.8	72.3	65.5	62.4	55.8	62.1
Integration						
Replaces no benefits	70.0	63.6	69.7	63.3	51.2	74.5
Replaces some benefits	73.1	62.0	67.3	61.9	55.8	56.3
Replaces all benefits	71.8	70.2	61.9	61.8	57.1	63.7
Replaces but supplements	68.4	75.1	67.6	67.7	58.5	59.6
Financing						
Tax increase	71.8	68.5	63.6	59.7	49.4	62.5
Capital tax	68.5	67.8	69.0	68.4	55.1	63.5
Climate tax	75.4	67.0	69.3	65.8	57.6	62.4
Budget neutral	66.7	66.1	63.8	59.1	62.8	62.8

Source BIN Survey (2021). Question wording: 'If there were parliamentary elections today, which party would you then vote for?' The electoral groups in the table are: 'Greens' = GroenLinks + PvdD; 'Socialists' = PvdA + SP; 'Social liberals' = D66; 'Christian democrats' = CDA + CU; 'Liberals' = VVD; 'Populists' = PVV + FvD. All the respondents who indicated that they would vote for another political party, vote blank/invalid or not vote were treated as missing. The table presents the mean level of support for each policy design dimension in the survey experiment within the respective electoral groups

in the relative level of support for various types of basic income between the different electoral constituencies.

For the dimension of conditionality, it is apparent that green, liberal and populist voters clearly prefer a conditional participation income to an unconditional basic income. Interestingly, this pattern is not observed among socialist, social-liberal and Christian-democratic voters. With regard to universality, it appears that only green voters have a clear preference for a fully universal basic income. All the other voting groups distinguish little between basic income proposals with varying levels of universality, with the possible exception of the Christian democrats, who are less supportive of a basic income that sets residency (but not nationality) requirements. Looking at generosity, the data shows that a basic income set below subsistence level is least popular among all groups. Socialist voters in particular prefer the most generous basic income to the least generous one (the respective means are 60.8 and 72.3). It is more difficult to discern a general pattern for integration, but there are some interesting contrasts between parties that are relatively close to each other on the political spectrum. For example, while a basic income that replaces no other social benefits is the least popular option among centre-right liberals, it is actually the most popular option among far-right populists. In a similar vein, the replacement of all existing benefits is the second most popular option among socialist voters but the least popular among their social-liberal counterparts. With regard to the dimension of financing, there is a clear divide between on the one hand, liberal voters who prefer budget neutrality (the mean is 62.8) to an increase in income/payroll taxes (49.4) or the introduction of a new capital (55.1) or climate tax (57.6), and on the other hand, green, social-liberal and Christian-democratic voters, who are somewhat less concerned about budget neutrality. Social-liberal voters, and to some extent also Christian-democratic voters, have a slight preference for either a capital or a climate tax. Unsurprisingly, green voters are especially supportive of a climate tax to fund basic income, although a tax increase is also relatively popular in this group. Neither socialist nor populist voters seem to have a clear preference for a specific funding mechanism.

Overall, the evidence concerning voting intentions exposes two striking similarities. The first is that a fully unconditional basic income is never preferred to its conditional counterpart; even among left-wing voters. In Belgium, all the electoral constituencies, across the political spectrum, agree that basic income should be conditional on some type of participation. In the Netherlands, some constituencies (green, liberal and populist voters) also agree with this, while others have no clear preference (socialist, social-liberal and Christian-democratic voters). Second, almost all constituencies are least supportive of a basic income that is lower than the current subsistence level; including most right-wing voters (the only exception being the Flemish nationalists in Belgium). Other than that, the different constituencies prefer somewhat different basic income varieties. Interestingly, these varieties do not always match with the proposals put forward by the respective political parties or by prominent politicians within these parties. Perhaps the clearest example is the case of green support for basic income: whereas green parties (in both Belgium and the Netherlands) advocate a fully unconditional basic income, their voters clearly prefer a conditional version. Additionally, seemingly similar 'party families' can support different types of basic income in different countries. For example, while the Belgian socialists seem to oppose a climate tax to fund a basic income, their Dutch counterparts are much more receptive to the idea. This once again underlines the importance of investigating the determinants of popular support for different varieties of basic income in a cross-national setting.

3.2.6 Trade Union Membership

In addition to political parties and their electoral constituencies, there are other policy stakeholders, with opinions about basic income that are also important. These include trade unions and their members, who continue to play a pivotal role in many welfare states, especially those situated in the corporatist-conservative tradition (Palier, 2010). In Chapter 2, a number of reasons were listed why trade unions and their members may support or oppose the ideal-typical (that is, fully universal and fully unconditional) basic income. On the one hand, it was argued that trade unionists are strong supporters of a basic income because they may consider it will increase workers' (individual and/or collective) bargaining power, leading to higher wages and better working conditions. On the other hand, one could also expect trade unionists to oppose basic income, because they may think it will lead to lower wages, an erosion of the membership base and an increased tax burden for labour market insiders. Additionally, driven by their strong work ethic, trade unionists could feel unconformable about the unconditional aspect of basic income. Empirically, the data from the European Social Survey shows that in some countries, trade union members are mostly opposed to the ideal-typical basic income and less supportive than non-members. However, in most countries the difference between members and non-members is marginal.

It could well be that the gap in support between trade union members and non-members varies across different types of basic income. Building further on the reasons briefly outlined above, one could, for example, expect that trade unionists will be especially in favour of a more generous basic income because they believe that it would increase workers' bargaining power the most. Likewise, they could be more supportive of a basic income that seeks to introduce new taxes on capital and climate rather than increasing taxes on labour. It also seems plausible that trade union members will be more in favour of a basic income that is conditional on some type of participation, compared with a fully unconditional alternative. Lastly, given the fact that trade unions still play a regulatory and/or administrative role in many welfare states, their members may not want a basic income to replace all or some existing social benefits, as that could decrease the unions' power resources. To test these assumptions, I use data from the BABEL Survey conducted in Belgium, which includes about 1000 trade union members. Unfortunately, I could not use the BIN Survey in the Netherlands because the number of trade union members is too small to obtain reliable estimates.

As shown in Table 3.9, in most cases there is barely any difference between trade union members and non-members in terms of support for basic income. The two groups also seem to have relatively similar preferences with regard to different varieties of basic income. Both groups prefer a conditional to an unconditional basic income, and a more generous to a less generous alternative. The most notable difference pertains to the dimension of universality, as it appears that trade union members are less supportive of a fully universal basic income than non-members (the respective means are 51 and 57.2). Instead, members clearly prefer a basic income that sets residency (58.3) or nationality (58.2) requirements. Other than that, it can be seen that trade unionists are also somewhat less supportive of a climate tax to fund a basic income compared with non-members (the respective means are 54.3 and 58.2).

As with political ideology, it is probably premature to end the discussion of trade union membership after a simple comparison of members and non-members. This is because there is also substantial heterogeneity within the broader category of trade unions in most countries. In fact, different unions—often organized along sectoral, professional or ideological lines—could have very diverging interests in, and opinions about, basic income; as could their respective members. For the Belgian case, it makes sense to divide the different trade unions according to the various ideological pillars they traditionally belong to: first, the socialist pillar (ABVV in Flanders and FGTB in Wallonia), second, the Christian

Table 3.9 Support for different basic income varieties by trade union membership

	Non-members	*Members*	*Socialist*	*Christian*	*Liberal*
Conditionality					
Unconditional	52.7	51.8	52.4	51.3	56.4
Conditional on participation	60.0	60.0	62.0	58.0	59.6
Universality					
All residents	57.2	51.0	53.2	54.5	58.8
Residency requirement	55.0	58.3	58.1	55.0	60.7
Nationality requirement	56.0	58.2	60.6	54.1	54.1
Generosity					
€500	52.0	54.0	54.1	51.6	48.7
€1000	55.5	55.2	55.0	55.1	57.5
€1500	61.6	58.6	62.8	57.4	68.2
Integration					
Replaces no benefits	57.3	54.7	59.5	52.3	62.7
Replaces some benefits	52.7	54.2	52.2	51.7	59.2
Replaces all benefits	54.6	55.7	57.4	54.1	50.5
Replaces but supplements	59.3	58.6	58.9	58.9	58.9
Financing					
Tax increase	53.8	55.4	51.7	55.7	54.9
Capital tax	56.2	57.5	60.0	54.5	57.0
Climate tax	58.2	54.3	59.1	53.4	61.2

Source BABEL Survey (2021). Question wording: 'Are you currently a member of a trade union', 'Were you a member of a trade union in the past?', And 'Which trade union are/were you a member of?'. The categories in the table are: 'non-members' = not a member in the past or present, 'members' = member in the past or present, 'socialist' = ABVV + FGTB, 'Christian' = ACV + CSC, 'liberal' = ACLVB + CGSLB. The table presents the mean level of support for each policy design in the survey experiment within the respective categories

pillar (ACV in Flanders and CSC in Wallonia) and third, the liberal pillar (ACLVB in Flanders and CGSLB in Wallonia). As shown in Table 3.9, it proves true that trade unionists from the various pillars seem to prefer different basic income varieties. With regard to the dimension of conditionality, it is evident that in particular the members of the socialist and Christian unions prefer a conditional to an unconditional basic income. Although liberal trade unionists show the same preference, the difference between the two basic income varieties is much smaller in their case (the respective means are 59.6 and 56.4). Looking at universality, it is mainly the socialist members who prefer a basic income with nationality or residency requirements to a fully universal one (the means are 60.6, 58.1 and 53.2, respectively). For generosity, all trade union members are most supportive of the most generous basic income. Nevertheless, the difference between the lowest and the highest amount is especially large for the members of the liberal unions (the respective means are 48.7 and 68.2). With regard to integration, the liberal trade unionists in particular support a basic income that replaces no existing social benefits and oppose the alternative that replaces all of them (the respective means are 62.7 and 50.5). By contrast, the members of the Christian and socialist trade unions are not as strongly opposed to a basic income that would replace all other benefits. All three union groups have in common a preference for providing supplements to those in greater need if basic income were to replace other benefits. Turning to the dimension of financing, both socialist and liberal unionists most strongly oppose an increase in income/payroll taxes and would rather see basic income funded by a capital or climate tax. This is not found for the members of the Christian trade unions, who barely distinguish between the different funding mechanisms under consideration.

Overall, the data from the BABEL experiment shows relatively minor differences in the types of basic income preferred by trade union members and non-members, the only exception being that the former are less supportive of a fully universal basic income than the latter. Instead, it seems that there are larger differences *within* the category of trade union members. For the Belgian case, it is apparent that trade union members belonging to the various ideological pillars (socialist, Christian and liberal) prefer somewhat different basic income varieties. Although this finding is very relevant, it is important to note that it merely serves here as an illustration of a broader theme. It may well be that similar differences could be found in other countries where intra-union heterogeneity also exists (albeit perhaps in different ways). At the same time, it could also be that Belgium is unique in this regard. Although this seems somewhat unlikely, only future research will be able to establish this.

3.2.7 Welfare Performance Evaluations

In addition to general political ideologies and memberships, support for basic income is also influenced by more-specific beliefs about the functioning of the welfare state (Laenen & Gugushvili, 2022). In Chapter 2, it was shown that the ideal-typical basic income is least popular among those who are most critical of the current system—in an economic, moral and social sense. It seems likely, however, that these welfare critics oppose some types of basic income more than they do others. People who think that the existing welfare system is too expensive and thus harmful for the economy are probably less supportive of a basic income that is very generous, replaces no existing benefits or is financed by an increase in income/payroll taxes; all of which are likely to increase the fiscal burden, putting pressure on the economy. The introduction of a new capital tax to fund a basic income could also trigger opposition from those who criticize the welfare state on economic grounds, because they may fear that such a tax will make entrepreneurs move their businesses elsewhere. People who are morally critical of the welfare state—for example, because they think it saps work incentives and makes people lazy—are probably more in favour of a relatively low and conditional basic income than they are of a very generous and fully unconditional one, which they may see as *the* most dis-incentivizing policy imaginable. Although experts often argue that (the ideal-typical) basic income could actually increase work incentives compared with most means-tested schemes, because it takes away the high effective marginal tax rates for low-income households (see Van Parijs & Vanderborght, 2017), it seems somewhat unlikely that this expert vision has found its way into public opinion (see Chapter 4). Therefore, I consider it more plausible that a fully unconditional basic income is opposed more strongly by those who believe that the current welfare state demotivates people with regard to work. People who are critical of the welfare state in a social sense, most notably because they believe that it attracts too many immigrants, are probably less supportive of a fully universal basic income that is, on top of that, very generous. Additionally, it is possible that believers of the welfare magnet hypothesis (Borjas, 1999) are also less supportive of a fully unconditional basic income than a conditional one, if they tend to associate immigrant status with laziness and unwillingness to work (Gilens, 1999).

To test these expectations, for each basic income variety in the BABEL experiment I compare the mean level of support of those who are critical about the welfare state (for economic, moral or social reasons) and those who are not critical. As shown in Table 3.10, support is *always* lower among those who are critical of the existing system, regardless of the policy design of basic income. Furthermore, the difference between the critics and non-critics is often relatively large compared with some of the previously discussed characteristics. That said, it is still interesting to see the extent to which the expectations about relative support for different basic income types hold true. Based on the evidence from Belgium, only one of these can apparently be confirmed, in that there is a lower level of support for a fully unconditional basic income compared with a conditional one among those who are critical of the current welfare state. This is because they think it is too expensive (the respective means are 46.3 and 53.5), demotivates people to work (45.5 and 54.4) or attracts too many migrants (48.5 and 55.5). Importantly, this is also found among those who are not critical (although the difference is negligible for those who disagree with the statement that the welfare state attracts too many migrants). Remarkably, even those who think that the current welfare system does *not* undermine work incentives are still more supportive of a conditional participation income. All the other expectations are clearly not confirmed by the data. That is, support for basic income is *not* significantly lower among the economically critical when it is generous, fully universal, built on top of the existing system without replacing other benefits, or financed by a tax increase or a new capital tax. Likewise, neither the morally nor the socially critical are less supportive of a generous basic income. Those who believe the welfare magnet hypothesis are somewhat less in favour of a fully universal basic income, but the difference is very small.

All in all, it seems that those who are critical of the welfare state distinguish relatively little between different types of basic income (with the exception of conditionality). Instead, they are overall more strongly opposed to any basic income, regardless of its policy design. By contrast, those who are less critical of the welfare state seem to have clearer preferences, as they are somewhat more supportive of a basic income that is generous, does not replace any other benefits (or provides supplements to those in greater need when it does) and is financed by new taxes on capital or climate. Those who disagree with the statement that the welfare state is too expensive in particular are also more in favour of a basic income with residency or nationality requirements compared with a fully universal alternative (the means are 60.2, 58.6 and 54.2, respectively). Although it is difficult to tell with certainty, this may be because they think that full universality jeopardizes the affordability of the welfare state.

Table 3.10 Support for different basic income varieties by welfare performance evaluations

	The welfare state is too expensive		*The welfare state makes people lazy*		*The welfare state attracts too many migrants*	
	Agree	*Disagree*	*Agree*	*Disagree*	*Agree*	*Disagree*
Conditionality						
Unconditional	46.3	53.7	45.5	57.2	48.5	60.4
Conditional on participation	53.5	61.4	54.4	63.1	55.5	62.2
Universality						
All residents	49.1	54.2	48.3	58.6	49.9	61.0
Residency requirement	52.2	60.2	52.5	61.4	53.3	64.4
Nationality requirement	48.7	58.6	49.7	60.5	52.7	59.3
Generosity						
€500	48.8	55.5	49.1	54.6	50.5	56.8
€1000	50.1	57.6	49.1	62.5	50.8	62.4
€1500	50.9	60.1	51.9	64.3	54.5	66.4
Integration						
Replaces no benefits	48.8	59.9	48.2	64.2	51.8	63.5
Replaces some benefits	50.1	55.3	48.6	56.5	50.3	59.6
Replaces all benefits	47.5	56.7	50.9	58.6	51.7	58.6
Replaces but supplements	53.4	58.5	51.9	61.2	50.3	63.7
Financing						
Tax increase	48.1	54.9	48.2	55.9	48.7	58.3
Climate tax	51.7	58.3	50.7	61.3	53.6	61.9
Capital tax	49.9	59.6	50.9	63.0	53.2	63.7

Source BABEL Survey (2021). Question wording: 'To what extent do you agree or disagree with the following statements?' (a) 'Our social security system costs companies too much and damages our economy', (b) 'Our social security system makes people less motivated to work', and (c) 'Our social security system attracts too many migrants'. The graph represents the mean score for each policy design dimension in the survey experiment among the respective categories

3.2.8 *Benefit Recipiency*

I now look at the opinions of those who have more direct experience of the welfare state, most notably benefit recipients. This was not possible in Chapter 2 because the survey that was used (the European Social Survey) does not have reliable information on benefit recipiency. Nevertheless, the chapter did show that retired people in particular, most of whom presumably receive an old-age pension, are more strongly opposed to the ideal-typical basic income. The same was found for people with under-aged children, who probably receive child benefits—although the difference was much smaller and only apparent in a few countries. It was also shown that jobless people of working age, some of whom probably receive a social benefit (such as an unemployment or disability benefit), are more in favour of the ideal-typical basic income. Here, I explore whether actual benefit recipients differ from non-recipients in their support for different varieties of basic income, and whether there are also differences between recipients of different types of benefit (that is, child benefits, working-age benefits and old-age pensions). Two expectations guide these analyses. The first is that benefit recipients are expected to be less supportive of a basic income that replaces many or all of the existing benefits. This is mainly because these welfare constituencies will want to defend 'their' benefit from being replaced (Pierson, 1994, 2001). The second expectation is that benefit recipients are less supportive of a low basic income, as they often do not have income from any other sources (such as work) to accumulate this with, potentially leaving them worse off than before. This should nevertheless apply more to income-replacing benefits (for example, old-age pensions) than to cost-compensating benefits (such as child allowances). The interaction between the generosity and integration of basic income could be even more important, in that benefit recipients should be least supportive of a basic income that replaces many other benefits *and* is set at a low level. Conversely, they may be more willing to accept a basic income that replaces current benefits if it is very generous, or vice versa, a low-level basic income if it comes on top of the existing system.

To test these expectations, I make use of the BABEL Survey in Belgium, which asked respondents to indicate whether they or someone else in their household were receiving a social benefit (at the time of the survey). Respondents are classified as recipients if at least one of the following benefits was being received by at least one member of the household: a child benefit, an unemployment benefit (including furlough payments due to COVID-19), a sickness or disability benefit, a social assistance benefit, an old-age pension or an early retirement benefit. All the respondents who indicated that nobody in their household was in receipt of any of these benefits are categorized as non-recipients. In a second step, the recipients were divided into three groups: child benefits, working-age benefits (unemployment, sickness, disability and social assistance) and old-age pensions (including early retirement). It should be noted that this household perspective means that the different benefit categories are not mutually exclusive: respondents can, for example, receive both child benefits and an unemployment benefit, or they can receive a disability benefit while their partner receives a pension.

Table 3.11 shows the mean level of support for various types of basic income among the different benefit recipiency categories. To some extent, the evidence confirms the expectations. Most benefit recipients prefer a more generous version of basic income (albeit, as expected, pensioners to a lesser extent). Importantly, this is *not* the case for non-recipients. Likewise, most benefit recipients somewhat prefer a basic income that does not replace existing benefits, or alternatively, a basic income that replaces other benefits but provides supplements for those in greater need (which recipients often have themselves). For pensioners, however, the differences are marginal. Once again, non-recipients do not share this opinion: they are actually slightly *less* supportive of a basic income that does not replace anything else. Lastly, looking at the interaction between generosity and integration (see Appendix 3), it can be seen that benefit recipients (especially with regard to child or working-age benefits) are more likely to accept the replacement of all existing benefits if the amount of basic income is relatively high: support increases from a mean of 48.7 for an amount of €500, to 54.4 and 59.3 for an amount of €1000 and €1500, respectively. Interestingly, the opposite is found for non-recipients, for whom support decreases from 58.6 to 52 and 47.9, the more generous basic income becomes. Seen from the other side, benefit recipients are also more likely to accept a lower amount if no existing benefits are being replaced. That is, support for a lower than subsistence level basic income of €500 increases from 48.7 to 55.4 when it replaces no benefits compared with when it replaces all benefits—an increase that is not observed anymore for the highest amount of €1500 (the respective means are 59.3 and 58.2). This implies that integration into the existing system matters less for benefit recipients if basic income is very generous.

Beyond the dimensions of generosity and integration (and the interaction between them), a number of notable observations stand out from Table 3.11. First, it seems remarkable that the difference between recipients and non-recipients in their absolute level of support is relatively small in most cases. However, this is mainly because old-age pensioners are generally much closer to non-recipients than they are to their fellow recipients. Second, although all of the groups—non-recipients as well as the different types of recipients—are more supportive of a conditional participation income than they are of an unconditional basic income, this

Table 3.11 Support for different basic income varieties by benefit recipiency

	Non-recipients	*Recipients*	*Child benefits*	*Working-age benefits*	*Old-age pensions*
Conditionality					
Unconditional	49.7	51.7	55.0	56.1	48.3
Conditional on participation	54.1	59.6	61.0	63.2	56.2
Universality					
All residents	51.1	53.5	56.6	58.3	47.7
Residency requirement	54.5	56.5	59.3	58.7	54.2
Nationality requirement	50.7	57.1	58.4	62.3	54.8
Generosity					
€500	52.1	52.6	53.5	56.5	49.9
€1000	51.7	55.3	59.8	58.5	51.1
€1500	52.1	59.5	61.8	64.7	55.6
Integration					
Replaces no benefits	51.3	56.8	58.2	63.0	52.7
Replaces some benefits	50.5	53.4	57.0	55.9	49.8
Replaces all benefits	53.2	54.0	55.1	58.5	50.8
Replaces but supplements	52.6	58.3	61.5	61.5	54.9
Financing					
Tax increase	47.2	53.2	54.6	57.7	49.9
Capital tax	55.5	56.7	58.2	61.2	53.3
Climate tax	52.7	56.9	60.8	60.0	53.4

Source BABEL Survey (2021). Question wording: 'Which of the following social benefits have you or someone else in your household received in the past 12 months? Multiple answers are possible'. (a) 'an old-age pension', (b) 'an early retirement benefit', (c) 'an unemployment benefit', (d) 'a sickness or disability benefit', (e) 'a social assistance benefit', (f) 'a child benefit', (g) 'other' (with open response format), (h) 'nobody in my household has received a benefit'. The categories in the table are 'non-recipients' = (h), 'recipients' = (a) to (g), 'child benefits' = (f), 'working-age benefits' = (c), (d) and (e), 'old-age pensions' = (a) and (b). The table presents the mean level of support for each policy design dimension in the experiment within the respective categories

gap is especially large for the group of pensioners (the respective means are 56.2 and 48.3). In a similar vein, pensioners are also least in favour of a fully universal basic income (the mean is 47.7). Instead, they would rather set residency (54.2) or nationality (54.8) requirements in order to restrict access to a basic income. Third, although people in all the benefit recipiency categories would prefer the introduction of new taxes on capital and climate rather than increasing income/payroll taxes to fund a basic income, this opposition seems strongest among non-recipients, most of whom are in (full-time) paid employment (the means are 55.5, 52.7 and 47.2, respectively).

To sum up, the evidence from the BABEL experiment in Belgium confirms that current recipients of social benefits are less supportive of a relatively low basic income and of a basic income that replaces many of 'their' benefits. Interestingly, benefit recipients nevertheless also seem more willing to accept a low basic income when it does not replace other benefits. Likewise, they are more accepting of a basic income that replaces all existing benefits when it is relatively generous. These patterns apply mostly to recipients of child benefits and working-age benefits and less to recipients of old-age pensions, as the latter are more strongly opposed to basic income, especially its fully unconditional and fully universal versions. In absolute terms, pensioners' preferences tend to be closer to those of non-recipients than to their fellow benefit recipients. These non-recipients are overall the least supportive of a basic income, in particular when it is both highly generous and does not replace any existing benefits, or when it is financed by an increase in income/payroll taxes rather than by the introduction of new taxes on capital or climate. These findings seem to indicate that non-recipients are especially opposed to basic income types that would increase the tax burden on income from paid work.

3.2.9 COVID-19 Experiences

Lastly, we turn to looking at how the COVID-19 pandemic might have affected popular support for (different types of) basic income. Many people seem to think that basic income has gained considerable momentum during and after the pandemic, because it increased awareness that effectively everyone—including those who did not rely on any state support beforehand—is vulnerable to sudden and unforeseen crises. In addition to this, the associated economic recession vastly increased insecurity of income and employment for millions of people. The consequent direct cash payments to cope with these insecurities (such as furlough benefits in Europe and stimulus checks in the US) raised awareness that the universal and unconditional distribution of cash is possible and perhaps desirable (De Wispelaere & Morales, 2021; Johnson & Roberto, 2020). As discussed earlier, there is nevertheless conflicting empirical evidence regarding the question of whether the COVID-19 pandemic actually increased support for a basic income. Nettle et al. (2021) show that it has done so. These researchers asked (US and UK) citizens to retrospectively rate their support for basic income before the pandemic and compared it with their support during the pandemic. While Van Hootegem and Laenen (2022) confirm this finding in their natural experiment in Belgium, they also show that support for a basic income only increased among those who are relatively deprived, that the increase is not necessarily long term (because it decreased when the number of COVID-19 induced hospitalizations declined), and that the increase is mostly seen in relation to specific basic income varieties that are not fully universal or fully unconditional (see Sect. 3.1).

Here, I take a somewhat different approach to the issue by relating people's lived experiences during the pandemic to their support for different types of basic income. The basic expectation is that those who faced health and/or economic difficulties during the pandemic will be more supportive of basic income than those who did not. It could be that these people are either more supportive of all basic income varieties (regardless of their policy design) or that they support some specific varieties more than others. In particular, it seems plausible that those who experienced negative effects from the COVID-19 pandemic will be—relatively speaking—more in favour of a basic income that is fully unconditional and/or fully universal. It also seems likely that they will be more supportive of a basic income that is generous and/or does not replace existing social benefits (which function as a safety net in the event of economic or health issues). To test these expectations, I make use of the BABEL Survey, in which respondents from Belgium were asked whether they had encountered the following situations as a result of the COVID-19 pandemic: (a) hospitalization, (b) psychological problems, (c) financial problems, (d), temporary unemployment, (e) dismissal, (f) forced closure of their business. In addition, respondents were asked whether they or anyone in their household had been infected with COVID-19, and how their standard of living had evolved compared with the situation before the pandemic. Based on these questions, I constructed two (non-exclusive) groups with negative experiences: first, those who had experienced health issues (infection, hospitalization, or psychological problems) and second, those who had experienced economic issues (decreased living standard, financial problems, temporary unemployment, dismissal or been forced to close a business).

Table 3.12 compares the mean level of support for different varieties of basic income among those who had negative experiences related to the

Table 3.12 Support for different basic income varieties by COVID-19 experiences

	Health concerns		*Economic concerns*	
	Yes	*No*	*Yes*	*No*
Conditionality				
Unconditional	55.6	49.8	52.2	50.6
Conditional on participation	62.8	56.7	60.8	56.7
Universality				
All residents	58.0	51.3	54.2	52.0
Residency requirement	59.7	54.8	58.3	54.9
Nationality requirement	60.0	53.9	57.2	54.2
Generosity				
€500	59.4	50.3	52.7	52.4
€1000	55.7	53.8	55.0	53.9
€1500	63.0	56.0	62.2	55.0
Integration				
Replaces no benefits	60.5	53.9	58.2	53.7
Replaces some benefits	57.7	51.3	52.5	52.8
Replaces all benefits	61.8	51.1	57.6	51.5
Replaces but supplements	56.7	56.7	56.7	56.7
Financing				
Tax increase	56.7	50.0	53.0	50.9
Capital tax	60.3	55.3	58.3	55.2
Climate tax	60.7	54.2	57.6	54.9

Source BABEL Survey (2021). Question wording: 'Have you or anyone else from your household been infected with the COVID-19 virus?'. 'Try to remember what your standard of living was like before the COVID-19 outbreak. Compared to your current situation, do you feel that your living standard has deteriorated, improved or remained the same?'. 'Which of the following situations have occurred in your life as a result of the COVID-19 pandemic? Please indicate all situations that apply to you now or in the past'. (a) 'I was laid off by my employer', (b) 'I have been temporary unemployed', (c) 'I have been hospitalized due to COVID-19', (d) I had a hard time financially due to COVID-19, (e) 'I have had psychological problems due to COVID-19', (f) 'I was forced to close my business', (g) 'none of these situations'. The table presents the mean level of support for each policy design dimension in the survey experiment within the respective categories

COVID-19 pandemic and those who did not. In general, basic income appears to be more popular among those who experienced health or economic concerns during the pandemic. There are nevertheless a few exceptions to this, in which support is approximately equal in the different groups; for example, where a basic income replaces some existing benefits but provides supplements to those in greater need. In addition, the relative level of support for different basic income varieties is usually very similar among those who experienced negative consequences of the pandemic and those who did not. With regard to the dimension of conditionality, we can see that both camps prefer a conditional participation income to a fully unconditional basic income. Looking at universality, the fully universal option is supported the least by all the groups, although the differences tend to be relatively small. For the dimension of financing, everyone seems to oppose an increase in income/payroll taxes the most, but there is no clear preference for either a capital or a climate tax. In addition to these similarities, there are also some clear differences between those who did and who did not experience negative effects of the COVID-19 pandemic. Most notably, those who had encountered economic difficulties clearly prefer a more generous basic income, while those who did not experience such difficulties seem indifferent regarding the amount. This difference is not found with regard to health concerns. Looking at the dimension of integration, it is also apparent that there are somewhat diverging preferences. While those who experienced health or economic concerns either prefer a basic income that replaces no existing benefits or one that replaces all of the benefits, those who did not experience problems due to the pandemic favour a basic income that replaces other benefits while also providing supplements to people in greater need.

In sum, the evidence from the BABEL Survey in Belgium demonstrates that support for basic income was in general greater among those who had experienced economic or health difficulties during the COVID-19 pandemic than it was among those who did not experience these problems. In some ways, these results provide a micro-level foundation to the macro-level observation that popular support for basic income generally increased during the pandemic (Nettle et al., 2021). However, it is again apparent that this increase was mostly concentrated among the people facing the greatest structural and incidental precarity (see also Van Hootegem & Laenen, 2022). It will be a task for future research to investigate the extent to which these findings apply to contexts other than Belgium, and to study the longer-term impact of COVID-19 on support for different types of basic income.

Summary Box 3.2 Individual Differences in Support for Different Basic Income Varieties

Overall, the discussion about individual differences in support for the varieties of basic income with diverging policy designs uncovers some seemingly contrasting conclusions.

At first sight, it seems that individual differences are fairly robust in the sense that some groups are consistently more in favour of *all* basic income varieties than others, irrespective of the specific policy design. Most notably, younger people, those on a low income, benefit recipients, welfare state advocates and left-wing voters tend to be more supportive than their respective counterparts—older people, high-income earners, non-recipients, welfare critics and right-wing voters. There are nevertheless often important exceptions to this general pattern. For example, younger people in Belgium are *less* rather than more supportive of a basic pension than older people. Another example pertains to low-income earners in the Netherlands, who are *less* supportive of a conditional participation income than high-income earners, rather than more supportive. These examples demonstrate that specific types of basic income are not always most or least popular—in absolute terms, anyway—among the groups in which it could be expected.

In terms of the *relative* level of support for different basic income varieties, there are both notable differences and striking similarities between people with diverging characteristics. The differences sometimes confirm the prediction that people will mostly prefer the forms of basic income that are in their own best interests. For example, it is apparent that people who are currently in receipt of benefits are less likely to support a basic income that replaces 'their' benefits than are non-recipients (unless the amount is very high). Similarly, people who suffered economic problems as a result of the COVID-19 pandemic are relatively speaking more supportive of a generous basic income than those who did not experience any issues. In other cases, the differences seem more ideologically driven. For example, while left-wingers consistently prefer the most generous basic income proposal, this is not always the case for right-wingers. Other examples concern the fact that proponents of the welfare state have a clear preference for a basic income that leaves the existing benefit system intact (whereas welfare state critics do not), and the fact that trade union members of different ideological pillars prefer quite diverging types of basic income.

At the same time, there are many similarities in the types of basic income preferred by different social groups, and these similarities appear to cut across both interest-based and ideological divisions. Most strikingly, almost all groups—including those we would perhaps least expect, such as green voters, current benefit recipients and women—clearly prefer a conditional participation income to a fully unconditional basic income. There are relatively few deviations from this general trend, except in the Netherlands, where some specific groups, such as low-income earners and socialist voters, do not have a clear preference for either variety. There are nevertheless many other similarities that are often counter to people's material self-interest. For example, both low-income and high-income earners are opposed most strongly to an increase in income/payroll taxes to fund a basic income, despite the fact that the former would bear a comparatively smaller proportion of the increased tax burden than the latter (in a progressive tax system at least). In a similar vein, men and women tend to have very similar preferences concerning most policy design dimensions—including basic income's integration into the existing welfare system—despite having diverging interests in welfare provision.

Importantly, there is often cross-national variation in the relative level of support for different types of basic income between different social groups. For example, while men consistently oppose a fully universal basic income most strongly, women's opinion on the matter seems to vary between countries. Many other examples can be given here, but the main point is that individual differences in support for differently designed basic income varieties often vary between countries. In a similar vein, it seems likely that there is also variation over time in this regard. This is supported to some extent by the finding that those with negative experiences related to the COVID-19 pandemic support somewhat different varieties of basic income (in terms of their generosity and integration) than those without such experiences. It remains a major task for future research to investigate in much greater detail how and why individual differences in support for diverging types of basic income vary between countries and over time.

References

Aarøe, L., & Petersen, M. B. (2014). Crowding Out Culture: Scandinavians and Americans Agree on Social Welfare in the Face of Deservingness Cues. *The Journal of Politics, 76*(3), 684–697.

Abts, K., Dalle Mulle, E., van Kessel, S., & Michel, E. (2021). The Welfare Agenda of the Populist Radical Right in Western Europe: Combining Welfare Chauvinism, Producerism and Populism. *Swiss Political Science Review, 27*(1), 21–40.

Abts, K., Swyngedouw, M., Meuleman, B., Stefanelli, A., Wopereis, D., & Van Den Abbeele, J. (2021). *Belgian National Elections Study 2019. Codebook: Questions and Frequency Tables*. ISPO-KU Leuven.

Ackerman, B., & Alstott, A. (1999). *The Stakeholder Society*. Yale University Press.

Alves, W. M., & Rossi, P. H. (1978). Who Should Get What? Fairness Judgments of the Distribution of Earnings. *American Journal of Sociology, 84*(3), 541–564.

Andersen, J. G., & Bjørklund, T. (1990). Structural Changes and New Cleavages: The Progress Parties in Denmark and Norway. *Acta Sociologica, 33*(3), 195–217.

Andersson, J. A., & Kangas, O. (2004). Popular Support for Basic Income in Sweden and Finland. In G. Standing (Ed.), *Promoting Income Security as a Right: Europe and North America* (pp. 285–298). Anthem Press.

Andeweg, R. B. (2005). The Netherlands: The Sanctity of Proportionality. In M. Gallagher & P. Mitchell (Eds.), *The Politics of Electoral Systems* (pp. 491–510). Oxford University Press.

Atkinson, A. (1996). The Case for a Participation Income. *The Political Quarterly, 67*(1), 67–70.

Auspurg, K., & Hinz, T. (2015). *Factorial Survey Experiments*. Sage.

Barnes, L. (2015). The Size and Shape of Government: Preferences over Redistributive Tax Policy. *Socio-Economic Review, 13*(1), 55–78.

Baumberg Geiger, B. (2021). Disabled but Not Deserving? The Perceived Deservingness of Disability Welfare Benefit Claimants. *Journal of European Social Policy, 31*(3), 337–351.

Bay, A., & Pedersen, A. (2006). The Limits of Social Solidarity: Basic Income, Immigration and the Legitimacy of the Universal Welfare State. *Acta Sociologica, 49*(4), 419–436.

Berens, S., & Gelephitis, M. (2019). Welfare State Structure, Inequality, and Public Attitudes Towards Progressive Taxation. *Socio-Economic Review, 17*(4), 823–850.

Bollain, J., Groot, L., Miller, A., Schmidt, E., Tahiraj, E., Verlaat, T., & Yi, G. (2019). A Variety of Experiments. In M. Torry (Ed.), *The Palgrave International Handbook of Basic Income* (pp. 407–435). Palgrave Macmillan.

Borjas, G. J. (1999). Immigration and Welfare Magnets. *Journal of Labor Economics, 17*(4), 607–637.

Brooks, C., & Manza, J. (2006). *Why Welfare States Persist: The Importance of Public Opinion in Democracies*. Chicago University Press.

Buss, C., Ebbinghaus, B., & Naumann, E. (2017). Making Deservingness of the Unemployed Conditional. Changing Public Support for the Conditionality of Unemployment Benefits Across Europe. In W. van Oorschot, B. Meuleman, T. Reeskens, & F. Roosma (Eds.), *The Social Legitimacy of Targeted Welfare: Attitudes to Welfare Deservingness* (pp. 167–185). Edward Elgar Publishing.

Careja, R., & Harris, E. (2022). Thirty Years of Welfare Chauvinism Research: Findings and Challenges. *Journal of European Social Policy, 32*(2), 214–244.

Castillo, J. C., Olivos, F., & Azar, A. (2019). Deserving a Just Pension: A Factorial Survey Approach. *Social Science Quarterly, 100*(1), 359–378.

Chrisp, J., & Martinelli, L. (2019). Neither Left Nor Right. In M. Torry (Ed.), *The Palgrave International Handbook of Basic Income* (pp. 477–492). Palgrave Macmillan.

Chrisp, J., Pulkka, V. V., & Rincon, L. (2020). Snowballing or Wilting? What Affects Public Support for Varying Models of Basic Income? *Journal of International and Comparative Social Policy, 36*(3), 223–236.

Clasen, J. (1997). Social Insurance—An Outmoded Concept of Social Protection? In J. Clasen (Ed.), *Social Insurance in Europe* (pp. 1–13). The Policy Press.

Clasen, J., & Clegg, D. (2007). Levels and Levers of Conditionality: Measuring Change Within Welfare States. In J. Clasen & N. Siegel (Eds.), *Investigating Welfare State Change. The 'Dependent Variable Problem' in Comparative Analysis* (pp. 166–197). Edward Elgar Publishing.

Delsen, L., & Schilpzand, R. (2019). Individual Preferences for the Unconditional Basic Income in the European Union. In L. Delsen (Ed.), *Empirical Research on an Unconditional Basic Income in Europe* (pp. 29–60). Springer.

De Wispelaere, J. (2015). *An Income of One's Own? The Political Analysis of Universal Basic Income* (Unpublished doctoral dissertation). University of Tampere.

De Wispelaere, J., & Morales, L. (2021). Emergency Basic Income During the Pandemic. *Cambridge Quarterly of Healthcare Ethics, 30*, 248–254.

Edlund, J. (2003). Attitudes Towards Taxation: Ignorant and Incoherent? *Scandinavian Political Studies, 26*(2), 145–168.

Esping-Andersen, G. (1990). *The Three Worlds of Welfare Capitalism*. Princeton University Press.

Esping-Andersen, G. (1999). *Social Foundations of Postindustrial Economies*. Oxford University Press.

Friedman, M. (1962). *Capitalism and Freedom*. University of Chicago Press.

Gatskova, K. (2013). Distributive Justice Attitudes in Ukraine: Need, Desert or Social Minimum? *Communist and Post-Communist Studies, 46*, 227–241.

Geels, F. (2023). Assessing Basic Income Feasibility Political Parties' Positions on the French-Speaking Belgian Scene. *Politics of the Low Countries*. https://www.elevenjournals.com/tijdschrift/PLC/2023/Online%20First/PLC-D-22-00004 [onlinefirst]

George, G. M., & Ortiz-Juarez, E. (2020). *Temporary Basic Income: Protecting Poor and Vulnerable People in Developing Countries*. United Nations Development Programme.

Gielens, E., Roosma, F., & Achterberg, P. (2022). *Basic Income Netherlands (BIN) Survey*. School of Social and Behavioral Sciences, Tilburg University. https://dataverse.nl/dataset.xhtml?persistentId=doi:10.34894/2ZAVNQ

Gilens, M. (1999). *Why Americans Hate Welfare: Race, Media and the Politics of Antipoverty Policy*. University of Chicago Press.

Goodin, R., & Le Grand, J. (1987). *Not Only the Poor: The Middle Classes and the Welfare State*. Allen & Unwin.

Gross, C., Lorek, K., & Richter, F. (2017). Attitudes Towards Inheritance Taxation—Results from a Survey Experiment. *Journal of Economic Inequality, 15*, 93–112.

Hainmueller, J., Hopkins, D. J., & Yamamoto, T. (2014). Causal Inference in Conjoint Analysis: Understanding Multidimensional Choices via Stated Preference Experiments. *Political Analysis, 22*(1), 1–30.

Jacques, O., & Noël, A. (2020). Targeting Within Universalism. *Journal of European Social Policy, 31*(1), 15–29.

Johnson, A. F., & Roberto, K. J. (2020). The COVID-19 Pandemic: Time for a Universal Basic Income? *Public Administration and Development, 40*(4), 232–235.

Kahneman, D., & Tversky, A. (1984). Choices, Values, and Frames. *American Psychologist, 39*(4), 341–350.

Kangas, O., Jauhiainen, S., Simanainen, M., & Ylikännö, M. (2021). *Experimenting with Unconditional Basic Income. Lessons from the Finnish BI Experiment 2017–2018*. Edward Elgar Publishing.

Kootstra, A. (2016). (Un)Deserving Welfare Claimants in Britain and the Netherlands: Examining the Role of Ethnicity and Migration Status Using a Vignette Experiment. *European Sociological Review, 32*(3), 325–328.

Korpi, W., & Palme, J. (1998). The Paradox of Redistribution and Strategies of Equality: Welfare State Institutions, Inequality, and Poverty in the Western Countries. *American Sociological Review, 63*(5), 661–687.

Kozàk, M. (2021). Cultural Productivism and Public Support for the Universal Basic Income from a Cross-National Perspective. *European Societies, 23*(1), 23–45.

Laenen, T. (2018). Do Institutions Matter? The Interplay Between Income Benefit Design, Popular Perceptions, and the Social Legitimacy of Targeted Welfare. *Journal of European Social Policy, 28*(1), 4–17.

Laenen, T. (2020). *Welfare Deservingness and Welfare Policy. Popular Deservingness Opinions and Their Interaction with Welfare State Policies*. Edward Elgar Publishing.

Laenen, T., & Gugushvili, G. (2021). Are Universal Welfare Policies Really More Popular Than Selective Ones? A Critical Discussion of Empirical Research. *International Journal of Sociology and Social Policy, 41*(9/10), 1134–1147.

Laenen, T., & Gugushvili, G. (2022). Welfare State Dissatisfaction and Support for Major Welfare Reform: Towards Means-Tested Welfare or Universal Basic Income? *International Journal of Social Welfare*. https://doi.org/10.1111/ijsw.12546 [onlinefirst]

Laenen, T., & Meuleman, B. (2017). A Universal Rank Order of Deservingness? Geographical, Temporal and Social-Structural Comparisons. In W. van Oorschot, F. Roosma, B. Meuleman, & T. Reeskens (Eds.), *The Social Legitimacy of Targeted Welfare: Attitudes to Welfare Deservingness* (pp. 37–54). Edward Elgar Publishing.

Laenen, T., & Meuleman, B. (2019). Public Support for the Social Rights and Social Obligations of the Unemployed: Two Sides of the Same Coin? *International Journal of Social Welfare, 28*(4), 454–467.

Laenen, T., Mulayi, M. L., Francisco, C., & Van Lancker, W. (2021). *Basic Income in Belgium (BABEL) Survey Codebook V1.* Centre for Sociological Research, KU Leuven. https://osf.io/7ghfs/

Laenen, T., Van Hooteghem, A., & Rossetti, F. (2022). The Multidimensionality of Public Support for Basic Income: A Vignette Experiment. *Journal of European Public Policy*. https://doi.org/10.1080/13501763.2022.2055112 [onlinefirst]

Leff, B., Percy, A., Story, M., & Szlinder, M. (2019). Alternatives to Basic Income. In M. Torry (Ed.), *The Palgrave International Handbook of Basic Income* (pp. 213–231). Palgrave Macmillan.

Liebig, S., & Mau, S. (2004). A Legitimate Guaranteed Minimum Income? In G. Standing (Ed.), *Promoting Income Security as a Right: Europe and North America* (pp. 207–228). Anthem Press.

Meade, J. (1990). What Can We Learn from the Agathotopians? *Il Politico: rivista italiana di scienze politiche, 55*, 5–16.

Morel, N., & Palme, J. (2012). Financing the Welfare State and the Politics of Taxation. In B. Greve (Ed.), *The Routledge Handbook of the Welfare State* (pp. 400–409). Routledge.

Murray, C. (2008). Guaranteed Income as a Replacement for the Welfare State. *Basic Income Studies, 3*(2). https://doi.org/10.2202/1932-0183.1115 [online only]

Nettle, D., Johnson, E., Johnson, M., & Saxe, R. (2021). Why Has the COVID-19 Pandemic Increased Support for Universal Basic Income? *Humanities & Social Sciences Communications, 8*(1), 1–12.

Offe, C., & De Deken, J. (1999, November 5). *Work, Time, and Social Participation. Policy Options for Dealing with Labor Market Precariousness.* Paper Presented at the Workshop "Back to Full Employment? Employment Subsidies vs Sabbatical Grants", Brussels.

Palier, B. (Ed.). (2010). *A Long Goodbye to Bismarck? The Politics of Welfare Reform in Continental Europe*. Amsterdam University Press.

Parolin, Z., & Siöland, L. (2020). Support for a Universal Basic Income: A Demand–Capacity Paradox? *Journal of European Social Policy, 30*(1), 5–19.
Petersen, M. B. (2012). Social Welfare as Small-Scale Help: Evolutionary Psychology and the Deservingness Heuristic. *American Journal of Political Science, 56*(1), 1–16.
Pierson, P. (1994). *Dismantling the Welfare State? Reagan, Thatcher and the Politics of Retrenchment*. Cambridge University Press.
Pierson, P. (Ed.). (2001). *The New Politics of the Welfare State*. Oxford University Press.
Pulkka, V. V. (2019). "This Time May Be a Little Different"—Exploring the Finnish View on the Future of Work. *International Journal of Sociology and Social Policy, 39*(1/2), 22–37.
Rincon, L. (2021). *The Paradox of Universality: Preferences for Universal Basic Income in Finland and Spain* (Unpublished doctoral dissertation). Universitat de Barcelona.
Rincon, L. (2022). A Robin Hood for All: A Conjoint Experiment on Support for Basic Income. *Journal of European Public Policy*. https://doi.org/10.1080/13501763.2021.2007983 [onlinefirst]
Rincon, L., Vlandas, T., & Hiilamo, H. (2022). What's Not to Like? Benefit Design, Funding Structure and Support for Universal Basic Income. *Journal of European Social Policy, 32*(4), 467–483.
Roosma, F. (2022). A Struggle for Framing and Interpretation: The Impact of the 'Basic Income Experiments' on Social Policy Reform in the Netherlands. *European Journal of Social Security, 24*(3), 192–212.
Roosma, F., van Oorschot, W., & Gelissen, J. (2016). The Achilles' Heel of Welfare State Legitimacy: Perceptions of Overuse and Underuse of Social Benefits in Europe. *Journal of European Public Policy, 23*(2), 177–196.
Rothstein, B. (1998). *Just Institutions Matter. The Moral and Political Logic of the Universal Welfare State*. Cambridge University Press.
Rowlington, K., Sood, A., & Trinh, T. (2021). Public Attitudes to a Wealth Tax: The Importance of 'Capacity to Pay.' *Fiscal Studies, 42*(3/4), 431–455.
Sanzo, L., & Pinilla, R. (2004). A Household Basic Income. In K. Widerquist, J. A. Noguera, Y. Vanderborght, & J. De Wispelaere (Eds.), *Basic Income: An Anthology of Contemporary Research*. Wiley Blackwell.
Schwander, H., & Vlandas, T. (2020). The Left and Universal Basic Income: The Role of Ideology in Individual Support. *Journal of International and Comparative Social Policy, 36*(3), 237–268.
Seong Yoo, Y., Choi, G., & Yu, I. (2021a). *What Do People Think of Universal Basic Income? Findings of UBI Opinion Poll 2021: Part I* (GRI Issue & Analysis No. 455). Gyeonggi Research Institute.

Seong Yoo, Y., Choi, G., & Yu, I. (2021b). *What Do Koreans Expect of Basic Income? Findings of UBI Opinion Poll 2021: Part II* (GRI Issue & Analysis No. 456). Gyeonggi Research Institute.

Simon, H. A. (2001). UBI and the Flat Tax. In P. Van Parijs (Ed.), *What's Wrong with a Free Lunch?* Beacon Press.

Skocpol, T. (1991). Targeting Within Universalism: Politically Viable Policies to Combat Poverty in the United States. In C. Jencks & P. Peterson (Eds.), *The Urban Underclass* (pp. 411–436). Brookings Institution.

Spies-Butcher, B., Philips, B., & Henderson, T. (2020). Between Universalism and Targeting: Exploring Policy Pathways for an Australian Basic Income. *The Economic and Labour Relations Review, 31*(4), 502–523.

Stadelmann-Steffen, I., & Dermont, C. (2020). Citizens' opinions about basic income proposals compared – A conjoint analysis of Finland and Switzerland. *Journal of Social Policy, 49*(2), 383–403.

Stam, K. (2015). *The Moral Duty to Work: A Cross-National and Longitudinal Study of the Causes and Consequences of Work Ethic Values in Contemporary Society* (Unpublished doctoral dissertation). Ridderprint.

Statistics Belgium. (2022). *Employment and Unemployment*. https://statbel.fgov.be/en/themes/work-training/labour-market/employment-and-unemployment

Svallfors, S. (2012). *Contested Welfare States. Welfare Attitudes in Europe and Beyond*. Stanford University Press.

Takamatsu, R., & Tachibanaki, T. (2014). What Needs to Be Considered When Introducing a New Welfare System: Who Supports Basic Income in Japan? In Y. Vanderborght & T. Yamamori (Eds.), *Basic Income in Japan. Prospects for a Radical Idea in a Transforming Welfare State* (pp. 197–218). Palgrave Macmillan.

Torry, M. (2016). *The Feasibility of Citizen's Income*. Palgrave Macmillan.

Torry, M. (Ed.). (2019). *The Palgrave International Handbook of Basic Income*. Palgrave Macmillan.

Torry, M. (2021). *Basic Income: A History*. Edward Elgar Publishing.

Vanderborght, Y. (2004). *Universal Basic Income in Belgium and the Netherlands: Implementation Through the Backdoor?* (EUI Working Paper SPS, No. 2004/4). European University Institute.

van der Veen, R. (2019). Basic Income Experiments in the Netherlands? *Basic Income Studies, 14*(1). https://doi.org/10.1515/bis-2018-0023 [online only]

Van Hootegem, A., & Laenen, T. (2022). A Wave of Support? A Natural Experiment on How the COVID-19 Pandemic Affected the Popularity of a Basic Income. *Acta Politica*. https://doi.org/10.1057/s41269-022-00260-9 [online first] van Oorschot, W. (2000). Who Should Get What, and Why? On Deservingness Criteria and the Conditionality of Solidarity Among the Public. *Policy & Politics, 28*(1), 33–48.

van Oorschot, W. (2006). Making the Difference in Social Europe: Deservingness Perceptions among Citizens of European Welfare States. *Journal of European Public Policy, 16*(1), 23–42.

van Oorschot, W. (2008). Solidarity Towards Immigrants in European Welfare States. *International Journal of Social Welfare, 17*(1), 3–14.

van Oorschot, W., Laenen, T., Roosma, F., & Meuleman, B. (2022). Recent Advances in Understanding Welfare Attitudes in Europe. In K. Nelson, R. Nieuwenhuis, & M. Yerkes (Eds.), *Social Policy in Changing European Societies, Research Agendas for the 21st Century* (pp. 202–217). Edward Elgar Publishing.

van Oorschot, W., & Meuleman, B. (2012). Welfare Performance and Welfare Support. In S. Svallfors (Ed.), *Contested Welfare States: Welfare Attitudes in Europe and Beyond* (pp. 25–57). Stanford University Press.

Van Parijs, P., & Vanderborght, Y. (2001). From Euro-Stipendium to Euro-Dividend. *Journal of European Social Policy, 11*(4), 342–346.

Van Parijs, P., & Vanderborght, Y. (2017). *A Radical Proposal for a Free Society and a Sane Economy*. Harvard University Press.

Weisstanner, D. (2022). COVID-19 and Welfare State Support: The Case of Universal Basic Income. *Policy & Society, 41*(1), 96–110.

CHAPTER 4

Reasons for Supporting or Opposing Basic Income

While the previous chapters have described the level and structure of popular support for basic income, this chapter explores *why*—that is, for which *reasons*—people support or oppose it. This is important, because it offers valuable insights into the types of arguments that can be used in political framing to persuade people to endorse or reject the introduction of a basic income. Along broad lines, I make a distinction between so-called 'principled' reasons and 'practical' reasons for supporting or opposing basic income. Principled support (or opposition) occurs when people believe that basic income will promote (or demote) some general principle that they value, such as freedom, emancipation or equality. Practical support (or opposition), in turn, comes about when people believe basic income will lead to concrete outcomes that they see as positive (or negative). These outcomes can refer to people's personal life (for example, if people think they will personally have greater income security) or to society more generally (for example, if people think the overall level of poverty will be reduced). The current chapter focuses mostly on the arguments that have been included in opinion polls or have been raised spontaneously by people as part of their participation in qualitative research. This means that some specific arguments will not be dealt with in this chapter, as there is currently no information available about how these are perceived in public opinion. For a more comprehensive discussion about different arguments for and against basic income, I refer to

© The Author(s), under exclusive license to Springer Nature Switzerland AG 2023

T. Laenen, *The Popularity of Basic Income*, Exploring the Basic Income Guarantee, https://doi.org/10.1007/978-3-031-29352-8_4

other writings (see, for example, Afscharian et al., 2022; Van Parijs & Vanderborght, 2017; Wright & Przegalinska, 2022).

In the following, I first investigate different reasons for supporting or opposing basic income 'across the board', among the public at large. After that, I look more closely at individual differences, by analysing whether different groups of people endorse different types of arguments. To do so, I use information from three different types of data sources. The first of these are traditional opinion polls that ask respondents to what extent they agree with some of the arguments that have been made in favour of (or against) basic income, or ask them to predict the likely outcomes of introducing a basic income (for example, the effects on income inequality and employment). The second data source concerns survey experiments that randomly vary either the predicted policy outcomes of a basic income or the type of arguments used in favour of (or against) it. The third source involves qualitative research that tries to uncover which reasons people spontaneously use when justifying their support for (or opposition to) basic income. It should be noted, however, that most of the data focuses on the ideal-typical version of basic income. Whenever possible, this is complemented with information about reasons for supporting (or opposing) different varieties of basic income with diverging policy designs.

4.1 Across-the-Board

4.1.1 Evidence from Traditional Opinion Polls

To the best of my knowledge, the first poll providing information about the reasons why people support or oppose the introduction of a basic income was held in the Netherlands in 1995. After indicating whether they were for or against basic income (see Fig. 2.4), respondents were instructed to select a maximum of three reasons for their opinion from a pre-defined list of either pro-arguments or contra-arguments. Figure 4.1 shows the percentage of proponents and opponents endorsing the respective arguments. It should be noted that the number of proponents was relatively low, with only about 20% indicating that they were in favour of basic income. A far greater proportion of the Dutch population—in fact approximately half—opposed a basic income at the time. The main contra-arguments endorsed by the opponents clearly refer to some of the traditional objections that have been raised in relevant literature (for

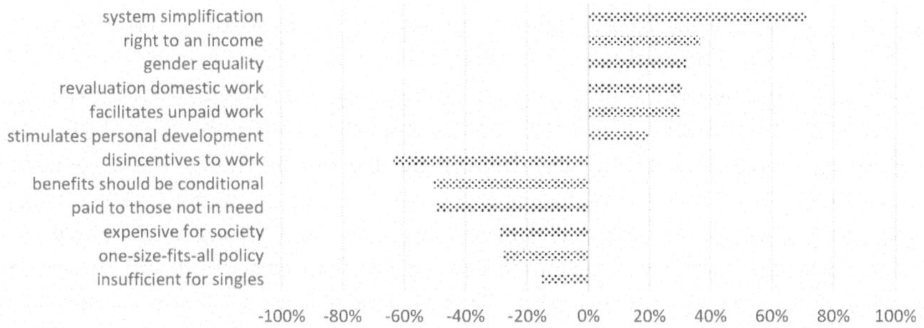

Fig. 4.1 Arguments for and against basic income in the Netherlands, 1995 (*Source* TISSER Solidarity Survey [1995]. Question wording: 'Which of the reasons below are the most important for you to be in favour of/against the introduction of a basic income?' Arguments: A basic income will: [1] 'make the system simpler and give less opportunity for abuse', [2] 'meet everyone's right to a personal income', [3] 'encourage a more fair division of informal and formal work between men and women', [4] 'also reward domestic work', [5] 'make it easier for people to do socially useful but unpaid work', [6] 'ensure that people have more time available for themselves and their personal development', [7] 'make the incentive to take on paid work too small', [8] 'go against the principle that you should not receive money from the government if you are unwilling to work', [9] 'also end up with people who don't need it at all', [10] 'cost society too much money', [11] 'give people who are in different circumstances all the same amount', and [12] 'not suffice for single people to get by'. The graph presents the percentage of proponents/opponents of basic income who endorsed the respective arguments in favour of/against it. Please note that negative percentages are used for the arguments against basic income)

a discussion, see Van Parijs & Vanderborght, 2017), namely that basic income will disincentivize work (63.3% of the respondents) and that it is wasteful because it is also paid to people with higher incomes who supposedly have no need for it (49.6%). Somewhat surprisingly, however, only a minority of the opponents (28.5%) endorsed the concern that a basic income would be far too costly (which is another frequently-cited contra-argument). There was also relatively little support for the argument that a basic income is too much of a one-size-fits-all policy that ignores the fact that people are in different circumstances and have different needs (27.9%), or for the argument that basic income is insufficient for singles because the flat-rate payment does not consider that these people are unable to benefit from economies of scale and may thus have greater needs (15.1%). The main argument in favour of basic income—endorsed by 71.6% of the proponents—was that it would simplify the existing social security system and limit people's opportunity to abuse it. This was followed, at some distance, by the simple argument that a basic income guarantees everyone the right to a personal income (36.5%). After that, proponents supported a basic income because they thought it promotes greater gender equality by reshuffling the division of formal and informal work between men and women (32.3%), rewards and revalues domestic work (30.6%), and facilitates commitment to socially useful but unpaid work such as caregiving or volunteering (29.7%). The least convincing argument for the proponents was clearly that a basic income would give people more time to pursue 'personal development' (19.9%).

It is difficult to tell, however, to what extent the findings from this early survey are specific to the place (the Netherlands) or to the time period in which it was held (1995). Unfortunately, it took about 20 years before other opinion polls started asking about people's arguments for and against basic income. Two of these were conducted in the UK, by Ipsos MORI in 2017 and Populus in 2018. The Populus survey is similar to the Dutch survey in the sense that it presented both arguments in favour of and arguments against basic income, but differs from it by asking all respondents—irrespective of whether they supported or opposed basic income (see Fig. 2.14)—to indicate whether they agreed or disagreed with the arguments. It is important to note here that the respondents showed much greater support than opposition to basic income (41% versus 17%), which is why the arguments in favour were generally also endorsed more than the opposing ones. As shown in Fig. 4.2, it is clear that the supporters mainly endorsed arguments in which basic income is presented as an alternative that is superior to the existing welfare system, which they seemed to see as at least somewhat dysfunctional. Indeed, arguments in favour of basic income that were given most support are the ones suggesting that it would: (1) 'provide more of an incentive to work because people wouldn't lose money if they got a job (as with many current benefits)' (56%), (2) 'reduce the stigma associated with receiving benefits' (49%), (3) 'give people the freedom to make the right decisions for themselves and their families to a greater extent than the current system allows' (47%) and (4) 'do a better job than the current system at providing a guaranteed basic level of security' (45%). It seems that people were less likely to support the arguments that a basic income

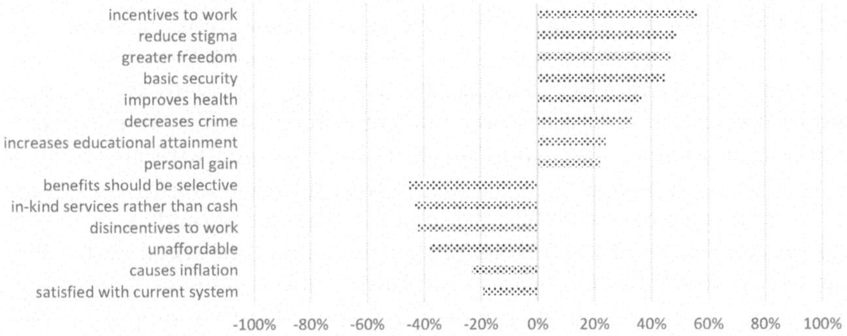

Fig. 4.2 Arguments for and against basic income in the UK, 2018 (*Source* Populus [2018]. Question wording: 'To what extent do you agree or disagree with the following statements about Universal Basic Income?' Arguments: [1] 'The payments would provide more of an incentive to work because people wouldn't lose money if they got a job (as with many current benefits)', [2] 'It would reduce the stigma associated with receiving benefits', [3] 'It could give people the freedom to make the right decisions for themselves and their families to a greater extent than the current system allows', [4] 'It would do a better job than the current system at providing a guaranteed basic level of security', [5] 'It would improve mental and physical health', [6] 'It would decrease crime by reducing destitution and extreme need', [7] 'It would increase educational attainment', [8] 'It would benefit me and my family', (9) 'The money spent giving everyone a basic income could be better targeted e.g. towards the very poorest alone', [10] 'Rather than cash, the state should provide citizens with basic food supplies and social housing to meet their needs', [11] 'If everyone received the payments it would create a disincentive to work, a risk that is too great compared with the current system', [12] 'It is unaffordable', [13] 'It causes inflation' and [14] 'The current system is working in the main so there is no reason to consider alternatives'. The graph presents the percentage of respondents who endorsed the respective arguments in favour of/against basic income. Please note that negative percentages are used for arguments against basic income)

would improve health (37%), decrease crime ('by reducing destitution and extreme need') (33%) and increase educational attainment (24%). This could be because the arguments do not frame basic income as a strategy to achieve these outcomes that is superior to the prevailing welfare system. It could, however, also mean that people find it less credible that a basic income would have a large effect on health, crime and educational attainment, or that these outcomes are considered less important. What also seems less important is the personal gain that people think they will have from a basic income, as only 22% believed it would 'benefit me and my family'. This number is especially low compared with the proportion of supporters of basic income (almost double the size, at 41%). This implies that a substantial group supports basic income without seeing it as offering any personal gain for themselves, thus seeming to go against the idea of self-interest. While this may be true, we should nevertheless be somewhat wary of the possibility that there could be social desirability bias at play here. In fact, even in a relatively anonymous survey setting, people may want to avoid giving the impression that they support a basic income simply because it is in their own best interests.

With regard to the contra-arguments, the Populus survey shows that the least supported suggestion was that 'the current [welfare] system is working in the main so there is no reason to consider alternatives' (19%). This again indicates that dissatisfaction with the prevailing system seems to be an important driver of support for basic income (at least in the UK), as was also suggested in Chapters 2 and 3. The most supported arguments against basic income were that social benefits should be targeted at those who need them, rather than giving them to everybody (45%), that the state should provide in-kind services, such as food supplies and social housing rather than cash (43%) and that a basic income would disincentivize work more than the current welfare system does (42%). With regard to the last, it is important to point out that the UK citizens interviewed within the context of the survey felt that compared with the existing welfare system, a basic income would actually be better at *encouraging* work than it would be at *discouraging* it (56% and 42%). This seems to indicate that people are well aware of the potential of a universal basic income to remove some of the unemployment traps that persist in the UK's (strongly means-tested!) welfare system (Martinelli, 2017). As we will see later on, it should nevertheless not necessarily be taken for granted that this awareness is also present in other countries. The economic contra-arguments that were presented to the respondents, stating that a basic income would be unaffordable and would cause inflation, were not given broad support (38% and 23%, respectively).

The other UK-based poll, which was conducted in 2017 by Ipsos MORI, only asked about people's agreement with a number of arguments in favour of basic income, after they had indicated their support for (49%) or opposition to (25%) such a scheme (see Fig. 3.8). As shown in Fig. 4.3, it appears there is always majority support for every argument presented in favour of a basic income. This is especially the case for the argument that a basic income would reward and encourage unpaid work such as caregiving or volunteering, to which 79% of the respondents (including some who did not support a basic income) agreed. A majority of respondents also agreed that a basic income would increase income security (67%), allow people to maintain their standard of living

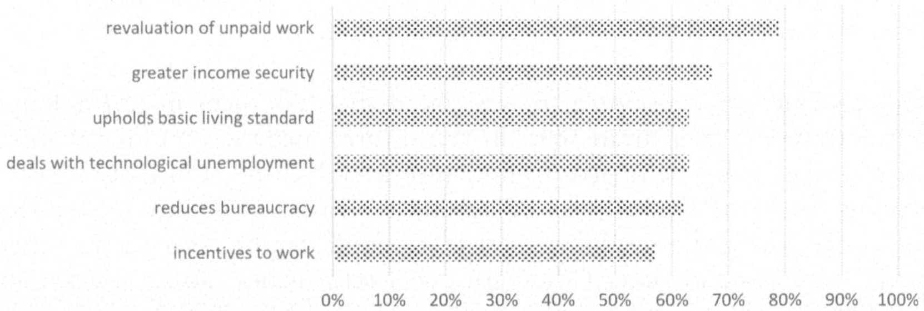

Fig. 4.3 Arguments for basic income in the UK, 2017 (*Source* Ipsos MORI [2017]. Question wording: 'Below are some arguments people have made in favour of introducing a basic income. Regardless of whether you support or oppose the UK Government introducing a basic income, how convincing, if at all, do you personally find each of these?' [1] 'Job security is increasingly a problem for many people. A basic income would provide income security to all who feel insecure about their job', [2] 'Advances in technology and automation will mean that, in the future, many people might lose their jobs and may be unable to find another job easily. A basic income would be a good way of dealing with this by providing a guaranteed income', [3] 'Conditions attached to welfare benefits and penalties for not meeting these are unfair and harsh. A basic income would ensure nobody fell below an adequate standard of living', [4] 'The current welfare system is very bureaucratic with programmes that help the wrong people or no one at all. A basic income would reduce bureaucracy and make the system more transparent', [5] 'Many people do very important work that is unpaid, such as caring or other voluntary work. A basic income would be a way of rewarding and encouraging others to do this type of work' and [6] 'Many unemployed people do not have an incentive to find a job because benefits they may currently be receiving are withdrawn. As everyone would receive it, a basic income would encourage unemployed people to get a job by allowing them to keep that basic income if they find work'. The graph presents the percentage of respondents who endorsed the respective arguments)

(63%), deal with increasing technological unemployment (63%), reduce welfare bureaucracy (62%) and incentivize work (57%). It seems plausible that in addition to the fact that about half of the respondents were already in favour of the introduction of a basic income, there are two other reasons why all these arguments were given majority support. The first is that—as in the Populus survey—many of the arguments presented basic income as a possible cure for some of the ills of the existing welfare system, such as its bureaucratic organization, strict benefit conditions and unemployment traps. The second reason is that the arguments suggest the existence of a social problem and to some extent also explain how a basic income could solve it. With regard to the argument about technological unemployment, for example, it was stated that 'advances in technology and automation will mean that, in the future, many people might lose their jobs and may be unable to find another job easily' and that 'a basic income would be a good way of dealing with this by providing a guaranteed income'. The results suggest that people can be convinced of the merits of a basic income if they are given information about the social problem a basic income is supposed to solve and how it aims to achieve that. This may well be a double-edged sword, however, if people are also easily convinced of the pitfalls of basic income when it is explicitly framed as aggravating existing social problems or creating new ones. This is hard to deduce from the Ipsos MORI survey, because it did not present contra-arguments. As shown below, this is nevertheless often the case.

At about the same time as the two UK-based polls, there were two cross-national surveys being conducted that tell us something about the reasons why people support or oppose basic income. The first of these was the Dalia survey, which presented a large sample of Europeans with a number of arguments for and against basic income and asked them to indicate the convincingness of these arguments. As shown in Fig. 4.4, none of the arguments listed was able to convince a majority of the Dalia respondents. With regard to the pro-arguments, the most convincing was the one maintaining that a basic income would 'reduce anxiety about basic needs' (40%). This was followed by the arguments that basic income would 'create more equality of opportunity' (31%), 'encourage independence and self-responsibility' (23%), 'increase appreciation for household work and volunteering' (21%), 'increase solidarity because it is funded by everyone' (21%) or would 'reduce bureaucracy and administrative expenses' (16%). This seems somewhat at odds with the fact that the majority of respondents (64%) actually supported the introduction of a

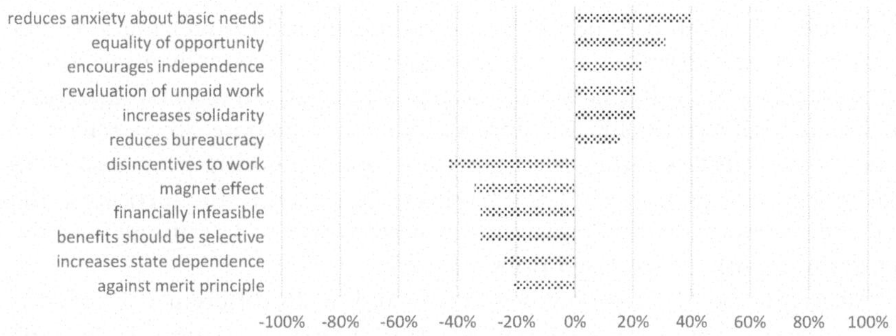

Fig. 4.4 Arguments for and against basic income in Europe, 2016 (*Source* Dalia Research [2015]. Question wording: 'Which of the following arguments for/against the basic income do you find convincing?' 'A basic income': [1] 'reduces anxiety about basic financing needs', [2] 'creates more equality of opportunity', [3] 'encourages independence and self-responsibility', [4] 'increases appreciation for household work and volunteering', [5] 'increases solidarity because it is funded by everyone', [6] 'reduces bureaucracy and administrative expenses', [7] 'encourages people to stop working', [8] 'encourages foreigners to come to my country to take advantage', [9] 'is impossible to finance', [10] 'is against the principle that only the people who need it most should get something', [11] 'increases dependence on the state' and [12] 'is against the principle of linking merit and reward'. The graph presents the percentage of respondents who endorsed the respective arguments. Note that negative percentages are used for the arguments against basic income)

basic income in their country (see Fig. 2.7). As suggested above, this could be because the Dalia survey did little to explain what the social problem is and how a basic income is supposed to solve it. However, it could also be that the survey simply did not mention the type of pro-arguments people find convincing. This interpretation is supported by the fact that 22% of the respondents indicated that they found 'none of these arguments' convincing. With regard to the contra-arguments, the most convincing was that basic income would 'encourage people to stop working' (43%). This was followed by the arguments that basic income would attract migrants (34%), is unaffordable (32%), goes against the principle that benefits should be selectively targeted at those who need it most (32%), increases people's dependence on the state (24%) and goes against the principle of 'linking merit and reward' (21%). Although the number of people who found none of the contra-arguments convincing is somewhat lower than for the pro-arguments (15%), it does draw attention to a potentially serious limitation of the type of top-down research discussed so far, in that arguments for and against basic income are determined a priori by pollsters rather than emerging spontaneously from people in bottom-up research. I will return to this issue below, in the section on the evidence from qualitative research. For now, however, I continue with the results from other top-down polls.

Although the Dalia survey was conducted in 28 different countries, it is not an ideal instrument to explore cross-national variation in the type of arguments people find convincing, because the sample size in most countries is too small to conduct statistically reliable analyses (in fact, often fewer than 200 respondents). The second cross-national poll, held by Ipsos in 2017, is better suited for that purpose. The Ipsos poll asked people from 11 different countries (Belgium, Canada, Germany, Spain, France, Italy, Mexico, Poland, Sweden, the UK and the US) to indicate their (dis)agreement with six different statements about basic income. I first look at the three statements that describe basic income as having positive social consequences. As shown in Fig. 4.5, the least supported argument in all countries was the one claiming that a basic income would 'allow people to be more involved in their local communities', ranging from a low of 28% in France to a high of 52% in Canada. People are generally more likely to think that a basic income will 'help to alleviate poverty' and 'allow people to spend more time with their families'. With the exception of France (45%) and Italy (47%), the poverty-reducing capacity of basic income was endorsed by the majority of respondents in all countries. This is most notable for Canada and Poland, where slightly over 60% agreed that basic income would alleviate poverty. The idea that basic income will encourage family life received majority support in all countries except Italy (48%) and France (41%).

For some countries, there is a relatively good match between the number of people who agree with the described positive outcomes of basic income and the number who support the introduction of a basic income (see Fig. 2.11). In Poland, for example, 60% support basic income, and the proportion of respondents agreeing with the positive outcomes is never far removed from that figure. In other countries, by contrast, there is often greater support for the positive outcomes of basic income than there is for basic income itself. In the US, for example, 61% believe basic income will help to alleviate poverty and 56% thinks

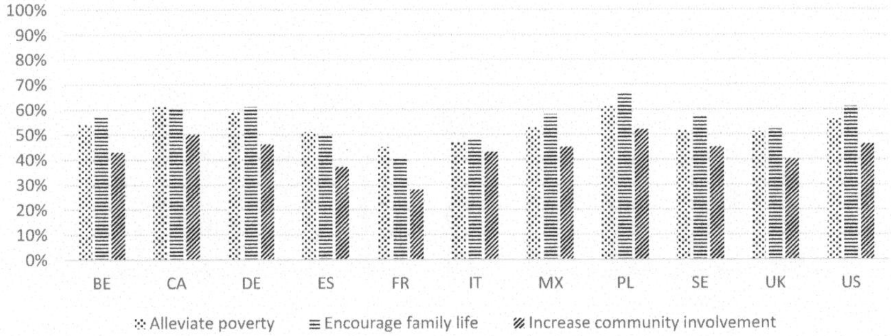

Fig. 4.5 Arguments for basic income in Europe, Canada, Mexico and the US, 2017 (*Source* Ipsos [2017]. Question wording: 'To what extent do you degree with the following statements on basic income?' Arguments: 'Basic income will': [1] 'help to alleviate poverty', [2] 'allow people to spend more time with their families' and [3] 'allow people to be more involved in their local communities'. The graph presents the percentage of respondents who endorsed the respective arguments in favour of basic income in the different countries)

it will encourage family life, but only 38% support the introduction of a basic income. A similar pattern can also be found in France and Spain (with support of 29% and 31%, respectively). One interpretation is that people living in these countries see some positives of basic income, but generally feel the perceived negatives outweigh them. This is difficult to confirm on the basis of the Ipsos data, because the respondents were not required to balance the pro-arguments and the contra-arguments against each other. Figure 4.6 nevertheless seems to indicate that in most countries there is a somewhat greater endorsement of the negative outcomes than the positive outcomes. This is especially the case in those countries in which the level of support for basic income is relatively low, such as France and the US. Overall, people are least likely to believe that a basic income will 'increase taxation to unaffordable levels', which aligns well with the earlier finding that basic income is not widely seen as too expensive by the general public. While in most countries about half of the respondents agree with the statement, this is somewhat higher in France (63%) and somewhat lower in Germany (42%). People are generally more likely to agree with the claim that basic income 'makes people reliant on the state for income' and/or 'discourages people from being in or seeking paid employment'. The concern that a basic income will create

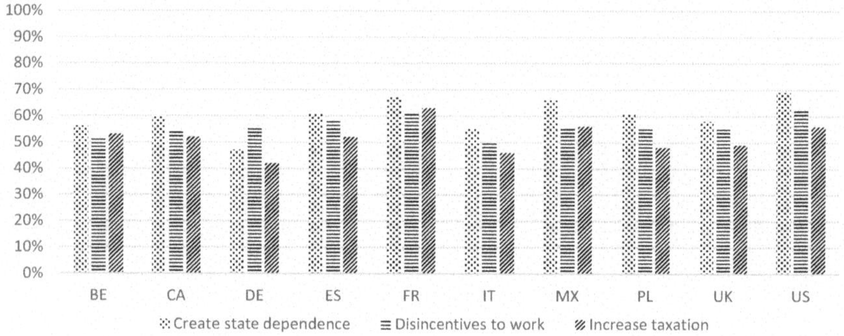

Fig. 4.6 Arguments against basic income in Europe, Canada, Mexico and the US, 2017 (*Source* Ipsos [2017]. Question wording: 'To what extent do you degree with the following statements on basic income?' Arguments: 'Basic income will': [1] 'make people reliant on the state for income', [2] 'discourage people from being in or seeking paid employment', and [3] 'increase taxation to unaffordable levels'. The graph presents the percentage of respondents who endorsed the respective arguments against basic income in the different countries)

state dependence is most common in the US (69%) and least common in Germany (47%). While the belief that basic income will disincentivize work is also most widely shared in the US (63%), it is the Italians who are least supportive of this argument (50%). These extremes clearly demonstrate that there is certainly some cross-national variation in the types of arguments about basic income the public endorses. There is, however, currently too little information from cross-national surveys available to explain *why* this is the case.

So far, the discussion has focused mostly on arguments related to the potential outcomes of basic income at the macro-level, pertaining to society as a whole. Nevertheless, there are also some polls that are informative about the perceived outcomes of basic income at the micro-level, which involves the personal consequences for individuals rather than societies. The most relevant in this regard is possibly the study by Richards and Steiger (2021), asking Americans about the predicted outcomes of basic income at both levels. In fact, for each macro-level outcome, the study presented an equivalent micro-level version of that outcome. Interestingly, the results—shown in Fig. 4.7—suggest that there is some discrepancy between the two levels. This is most obvious for the argument

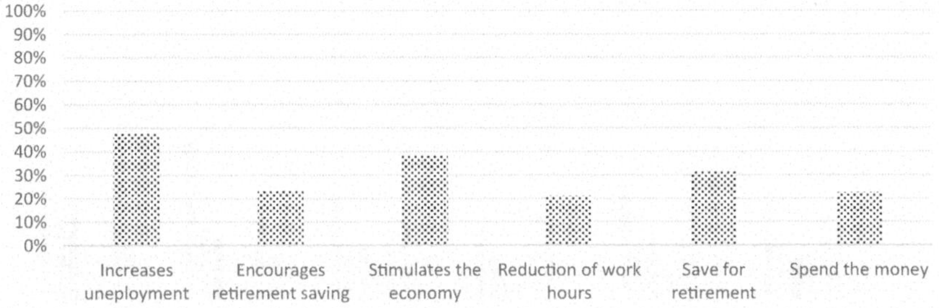

Fig. 4.7 Predicted outcomes of a basic income in the US, 2020 (*Source* Richards and Steiger [2020]. Question wording: 'The idea of a guaranteed annual income (also called universal basic income, basic income guarantee) is an idea that is beginning to be discussed in the United States and Europe. Some countries and some cities in the United States have been experimenting with it. The basic idea is that the government provides all eligible recipients with a minimum annual income no matter their employment status. For now, let us assume that every citizen, upon their 18th birthday, began receiving a GAI of $1000 per month'. Arguments: [1] 'The number of people not working would increase', [2] 'Most people would save their GAI for retirement', [3] 'Most people would spend the money, thus stimulating the economy', [4] 'I would decrease the number of hours I work if I received a guaranteed income of $1000 per month', [5] 'I would save the GAI for my retirement' and [6] 'I would spend the money, thus stimulating the economy'. The graph presents the percentage of respondents who endorsed the respective arguments

that basic income will disincentive work: while 48% believe that the introduction of basic income will increase the overall level of unemployment, only 21% indicate that they would reduce their own working hours. As we will see below, this belief that 'other people would stop working but not me' seems pervasive. In a similar vein, there is also some inconsistency between people's beliefs about what others would do with the money from a basic income and what they themselves would do with it. On the one hand, people seem inclined to believe that others would stimulate the economy by spending the money on consumption goods (38.5%) rather than save it for retirement (23%). On the other hand, people indicate that they themselves would be more likely to save basic income for retirement (31.5%) rather than spend the money (22.5%).

Although to the best of my knowledge there are no other opinion polls directly comparing the predicted macro-level and micro-level outcomes

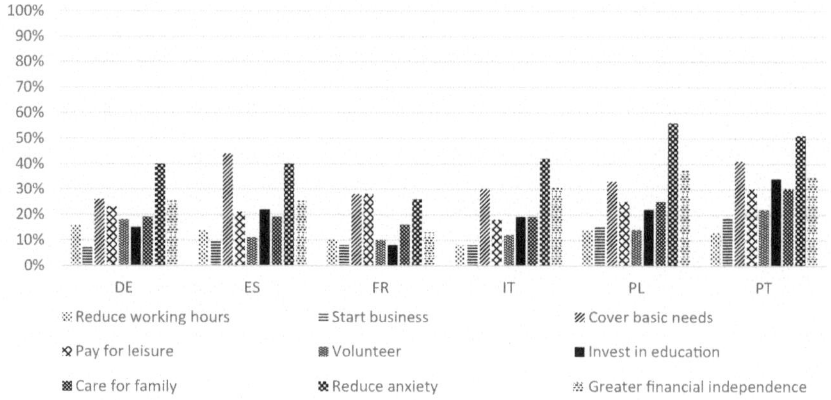

Fig. 4.8 Predicted micro-level outcomes of basic income in Europe, 2020 (*Source* Yougov [2020]. Question wording: 'For the following question, please imagine that the European Union did introduce a Universal Basic Income [i.e. an EU-wide scheme where every adult EU resident receives a direct cash payment every month]. Which, if any, of the following do you think would benefit you personally?' 'Basic income would': [1] 'allow me to reduce my current working hours', [2] 'give me the extra income I need to start my business', [3] 'allow me to pay for basic needs which I currently struggle to afford (e.g. food, clothing, rent, bills, healthcare, etc.)', [4] 'allow me to pay for leisure activities which I currently can't/struggle to afford', [5] 'give me more time to volunteer or get involved in activism', [6] 'provide me with money to invest in further education or training for myself', [7] 'give me more time to care for my family', [8] 'make me less anxious about my future than I currently am' and [9] 'give me more financial independence (i.e. being free from people I'm currently dependent on for money/security'. The graph presents the percentage of respondents who endorsed the arguments in the different countries)

of basic income, it is insightful to look at some other evidence about the micro-level and to contrast that evidence with the findings about the macro-level presented above. Figure 4.8 shows the results from a 2020 Yougov survey that was held in six different European countries and asked respondents to indicate how a (EU-wide) basic income would benefit them personally. In most countries, people generally seem most convinced by the statement that a basic income would make them less anxious than they currently are, which tends to be followed by the statement that basic income would allow people to pay for basic needs (such as 'food, clothing, rent, bills and healthcare') and the statement that a basic income would give them more financial independence (defined as 'being free from people I'm currently dependent on for money/security'). In Portugal, for example, the statements were endorsed by, respectively, 51%, 41% and 35% of the respondents. Similar relative preferences are found in Germany, Italy, Poland and Spain. This seems to confirm the previous finding that—at the macro-level—people generally do believe that a basic income will reduce the anxiety that exists in current societies by covering people's basic needs and increasing financial independence. The only clear exception in this regard is France, where all three statements were given a relatively low level of support (26%, 28% and 13%, respectively). Combined with the fact that all other micro-level outcomes were supported by a minority of the respondents in France, the available evidence suggests that the French are in general rather sceptical about the positive outcomes of a basic income compared with other Europeans—both at the micro and the macro-level (see Fig. 4.5).

The two micro-level outcomes that are least likely to occur in the public's eye both refer to behavioural changes that are related to the labour market. In fact, people generally do not believe that a basic income would allow them to reduce their working hours or give them the extra income they need in order to start their own business. With regard to the former, there are at least three possible interpretations of the finding that only a small minority in each country stated they would reduce their working hours (ranging from 8% in Italy to 16% in Germany). A first interpretation is that there is disbelief that the amount of basic income (which was not specified in the survey question) would be generous enough for people to have the luxury of reducing their working hours. It could in fact be that people believe retaining their current work intensity would still be necessary after a basic income has been introduced. A second interpretation is that people simply do not *want* to reduce their working hours, even if a basic income would allow them to do so. This could be because they need the money to maintain or improve their current standard of living, but it could also be because they adhere to the work ethic that is still very dominant in most European countries (Stam, 2015). A third interpretation is that people are somewhat dishonest when answering questions about their work intentions in a survey setting. Given the centrality of the work ethic, it may indeed be the case that there is a social desirability bias at play that prevents people from revealing their true intentions. Based on the evidence that is currently available, it is difficult to state which of these interpretations is most accurate. However, it is striking that these results once again point towards a discrepancy between the predicted outcomes of a basic income at the micro-level and at the macro-level, in the sense that most people believe a basic income will reduce other people's work intentions but not their own. For the time being, we cannot conclude the same for the statement related to people's intentions to start their own business, for the simple reason that there is no data available on the predicted effects of basic income on entrepreneurship at the macro-level. Figure 4.8 nevertheless shows that few people indicate a basic income would provide them with the help they need to start their own business, with the proportion ranging from 7% in Germany to 19% in Portugal. Although this may seem relatively low on a scale from 0 to 100, it can be argued that there would be a massive increase in economic activity if—as the numbers in Portugal suggest—one out of five citizens would actually start their own business after the introduction of a basic income.

The Yougov survey also presented respondents with a few other micro-level outcomes, which appear to be situated in between the most and least likely outcomes. There is a modest level of support for the statement that a basic income would 'allow me to pay for leisure activities which I currently can't or struggle to afford', ranging from a high of 30% in Portugal to a low of 18% in Italy. The same applies to the statements that a basic income would give people more time to volunteer or 'get involved in activism', or more time to care for their family (ranging between, respectively, 10% and 16% in France and 22% and 30% in Portugal). The final statement, which asserts that a basic income would 'provide me with money to invest in further education or training for myself', is also situated in between the two extremes, ranging from 8% in France to 34% in Portugal. Again, while most of these percentages seem relatively modest on a scale from 0 to 100, it can be argued that they represent meaningful and substantial increases in the number of people who would perform unpaid work (such as volunteering or informal caregiving) and invest in their human capital through education or training after the introduction of a basic income. This is especially the case in Portugal, which is a clear outlier with regard to people's intentions to perform unpaid work or invest in education. It should be noted, however, that questions such as the ones included in the Yougov survey only measure people's intentions and not their actual behaviour. As intentions and behaviour can (but need not) greatly differ, some caution is warranted when interpreting the results from surveys that ask people what they would do in the *hypothetical* situation of a basic income being introduced in their country.

Up to this point, the discussion of the reasons for supporting or opposing basic income has almost exclusively focused on its ideal-typical version, as the different polls typically describe basic income as a universal and unconditional cash benefit that is regularly paid to all individuals living in a specific country (or, in the case of the Yougov survey, all individuals living in the EU). However, we know that there are many different varieties of basic income that differ in terms of their policy design (see Chapter 1), and that these varieties are supported to somewhat differing degrees (see Chapter 3). For these reasons, it makes sense to investigate how various types of arguments play out in relation to different types of basic income. Unfortunately, there are almost no traditional opinion polls offering suitable information. To my knowledge, the only exception in this regard is the Public Perception Survey on Basic Income—an online survey that was conducted in 2021 among 10,000 South Koreans between the age of 20 and 69 by the Gyeonggi Research Institute (Seong Yoo & Jooyoung, 2021). Importantly, about half of the respondents were living in the province of Gyeonggi-do at the time of the survey, where a youth basic income programme has been in place since 2019 (Kim & Mah, 2021). The survey first presented respondents with a number of arguments related to the ideal-typical basic income, which was broadly described as: 'a fixed amount of money paid by the state or local governments to all members of society, unconditionally and regularly, regardless of their income or assets, whether or not they work. However, it is not determined in advance how much the payment should be'. After that, respondents were asked to indicate their support for a basic income of 200,000 won per month (71.7% were in favour) and a basic income of 500,000 won per month (59.4%). Those who supported either one of these two basic income types were then presented with a list of arguments in favour of a basic income, from which they had to select the most and the second-most important argument. Those who stated being against the scheme did the same with a list of contra-arguments. It should, however, be noted that at this point no differentiation was made between the higher and lower amount of basic income. Later on in the survey, respondents were able to indicate what they themselves thought was 'the appropriate amount of monthly basic income for every citizen'. The

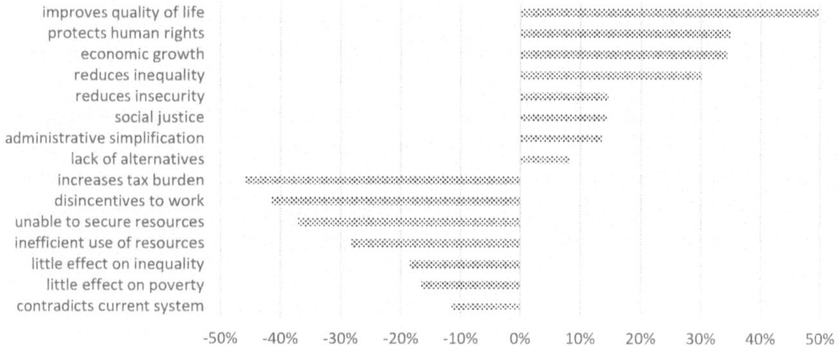

Fig. 4.9 Arguments for and against basic income in South Korea, 2021 (*Source* Public Perception Survey on Basic Income [2021]. Question wording: 'Basic income is a fixed amount of money paid by the state or local governments to all members of society, unconditionally and regularly, regardless of their income or assets, whether or not they work. However, it is not determined in advance how much the payment should be'. 'Why are you in favour of/against introducing the basic income system? Please rank the options in order of importance'. [1] 'Improving the overall quality of life', [2] 'Restoring basic human rights', [3] 'Boosting consumption and activating the domestic economy', [4] 'Addressing inequality and polarization', [5] 'Easing insecurity related to study and employment', [6] 'Implementing social justice through a common wealth dividend', [7] 'Saving administrative costs by streamlining the existing welfare system', [8] 'There are no better alternatives to basic income', [9] 'Resistance due to increasing burden on taxpayers', [10] 'Decreasing work motivation due to increase in non-work income', [11] 'Sufficient resources for funding not available', [12] 'Inefficient public spending', [13] 'Insignificant effect of alleviating social inequality and polarization', [14] 'No substantial help for low-income class', and [15] 'Conflict with the current welfare system'. The graph presents the percentage of respondents who selected the respective arguments as the most or second-most important argument for being for/against basic income. Please note that negative percentages are used for the arguments against basic income)

chosen amount was subsequently used as a basis for the respondents to assess the so-called 'social effects' of basic income.

Let us first briefly discuss the arguments related to a basic income that does not vary in terms of its generosity. As shown in Fig. 4.9, the most convincing argument in favour of basic income—chosen as the most or second-most important argument by about half of the respondents

(49.7%)—states that it will 'improve the overall quality of life'. This is followed by the arguments that basic income will 'restore basic human rights' (34.9%), 'boost consumption and activate the domestic economy' (34.4%) and 'address inequality and polarization' (30.1%). There is lower support for the arguments that basic income will 'ease the insecurity related to study and employment' (14.6%), 'implement social justice through a common wealth dividend' (14.3%) and 'save administrative costs by streamlining the existing welfare system' (13.5%). The least supported argument is that basic income is preferred simply because there are no better alternatives (8.2%). With regard to the contra-arguments, we see that South Koreans mainly oppose basic income because they think it will increase the tax burden (45.7%) and discourage paid employment (41.4%). This is followed by the concern that there will be insufficient resources to fund a basic income (37.1%) and the feeling that a basic income is an inefficient use of public spending (28.3%). The least important contra-arguments are the ones stating that a basic income would do little to reduce social inequality (18.5%), would be ineffective in improving the living standard of the low-income class (16.7%) and would be 'in conflict with the current welfare system' (11.6%).

As mentioned above, the respondents in the South Korean survey—including both supporters and opponents of basic income—were also asked about the predicted outcomes of a basic income, providing an amount they themselves saw as 'appropriate'. Table 4.1 reports the results of this exercise, by showing the percentage of respondents who think that the basic income amount of their choosing will have a positive effect on different policy outcomes. The table also shows the overall percentages, irrespective of the generosity of basic income. As can be seen, there is substantial variation in the overall perceived likelihood that basic income will produce the different outcomes. While a majority of the respondents feel that basic income will create economic growth (61.2%), reduce livelihood insecurity (60.9%), alleviate elderly poverty (59.3%) and expand basic economic rights (55.5%), there is only marginal support for the idea that basic income will improve educational issues (21.4%), help to solve ecological problems, such as the current climate crisis (22.4%), enhance women's rights (23.6), reduce income inequality (27.7%) and resolve marriage and birth problems (27.7%). There is a moderate level of support for the arguments that basic income will decrease income dependence on the main household breadwinner (46.6%), expand basic social rights (42.6%), increase socially beneficial activities (42.6%), boost social trust,

Table 4.1 Predicted outcomes of different basic income amounts in South Korea, 2021

	Overall	*Low*	*Medium*	*High*
'Boost the domestic economy'	61.2%	37.9%	67.5%	53.4%
'Ease livelihood insecurity'	60.8%	26.0%	72.0%	60.5%
'Alleviate poverty and lonely deaths among the elderly'	59.3%	30.1%	69.8%	53.3%
'Enhance the basic economic rights of individuals'	55.5%	28.4%	67.5%	53.0%
'Decrease income dependence on the main source of income in the household'	46.6%	20.1%	57.5%	51.9%
'Enhance the basic social rights of individuals'	46.1%	21.0%	56.7%	52.8%
'Increase socially beneficial activities'	42.6%	22.0%	50.1%	44.1%
'Enhance social trust, solidarity, and cohesion'	34.3%	16.0%	42.3%	43.0%
'Cultivate a sense of community'	32.5%	17.0%	42.5%	42.2%
'Realize social justice'	31.4%	14.4%	41.2%	41.4%
'Resolve marriage/birth problems'	27.7%	10.7%	38.4%	49.1%
'Narrow the income gap'	27.7%	9.7%	36.0%	45.1%
'Enhance women's rights and benefits'	23.6%	9.4%	30.8%	37.7%
'Help solve ecological problems, including the climate crisis'	22.4%	10.3%	28.9%	37.2%
'Improve educational issues such as competition for entrance exams'	21.4%	7.8%	28.9%	42.7%

Source Public Perception Survey on Basic Income (2021). Question wording: 'What do you think is the appropriate amount of monthly basic income for every citizen?' The categories are: 'low' = less than 100,000 won per month (n = 1732); 'medium' = between 310,000 and 400,000 won per month (n = 865); and 'high' = between 1,010,000 and 3,000,000 won per month (n = 619). 'When a basic income of ... [the amount selected in the previous question] is paid to all citizens, what kind of social effects do you think there would be?' The table presents the percentage of respondents who indicated that a basic income would lead to 'positive changes' or 'very positive changes' with regard to the respective outcomes

solidarity and cohesion (34.3%), cultivate a sense of community (32.5%) and bring greater social justice (31.4%).

Importantly, the perceived likelihood of the presented outcomes also varies across the different basic income amounts. Respondents who chose the lowest possible amount are clearly most sceptical of the idea that basic income will have any positive outcomes. In fact, even the outcome considered the most likely—that basic income will boost the economy—is only endorsed by a minority of those who prefer a very low basic income amount (37.9%). This is not surprising, as this group presumably includes many opponents of basic income, who also had to select a preferred amount. It is far more surprising that respondents who chose the highest possible amount are not necessarily the most convinced of the positive outcomes of basic income. Instead, many of the outcomes are seen as much more likely by those who prefer a medium amount than by those who prefer a high amount. This is especially the case for the most broadly supported arguments, which predict that basic income will boost the economy (67% vs 53%), increase income security (72% vs 60%), alleviate elderly poverty (70% vs 53%) and enhance basic economic rights (67% vs 53%). Conversely, the least supported outcomes overall are seen as more likely by those who prefer a high basic income amount than by those who prefer a medium amount. It, thus, seems that people who support a very generous basic income mainly do so because they think it will lead to specific (and perhaps somewhat atypical) outcomes that do not generally receive a high level of support in South Korea, such as reducing income inequality (45.1%) or contributing to solving ecological problems (37.2%).

The South Korean survey is innovative because it is the first, and to my knowledge only, traditional opinion poll that tells us something about the type of arguments people endorse in relation to different varieties of basic income with diverging policy designs. It is nevertheless limited to the specific dimension of generosity and constrained by the fact that respondents first had to choose their preferred basic income amount, rather than different amounts being randomly allocated. These shortcomings are addressed in the next section, which presents the results from the BABEL experiment conducted in Belgium. Here, I would like to highlight yet another innovation of the South Korean survey that merits attention. That is, the survey differs from most others in that it also asked respondents to indicate the *importance* they attach to different (positive and negative) outcomes of a basic income. In this way, it measures what people see as the *desired* outcomes of basic income, rather than its *likely* outcomes. This approach is unique in the field and has so far not been adopted by other traditional opinion polls. There are nevertheless other ways to discover the (relative) importance of different arguments for and against basic income. Some of these, notably the use of survey experiments and qualitative research methods, are discussed in the following sections. Here, I argue that the importance of different arguments can to some extent also be gauged by linking the arguments people endorse in traditional opinion polls to their support for basic income reported in those same polls. Unfortunately, this has rarely been carried out in prior research.

One notable exception in this regard is the study by Delsen and Schilpzand (2019) that uses data from the Dalia survey to test how different arguments are related to support for basic income. The study demonstrates that the presented arguments (see Fig. 4.4) tend to influence support, but that the strength of the relationship varies between the different arguments. It is true that support for basic income is greater among those who agree with the arguments in favour of basic income. There is nevertheless a relatively larger effect from the arguments that basic income will reduce anxiety about fundamental needs and will foster greater equality of opportunity; perhaps not coincidentally the two most supported arguments. The least supported argument—which claims that basic income will reduce bureaucracy and administrative expenses—seems unrelated to people's support for basic income. In a similar vein, Delsen and Schilpzand (2019) show that most of the contra-arguments decrease support for basic income. This is especially true for the argument that basic income goes against the principle of merit and reward—which was seen as the least convincing but appears to be the most consequential. Interestingly, the welfare magnet argument—that a basic income would attract migrants—did not influence people's support for basic income. Although this could indicate that the welfare magnet argument is not as important as the other contra-arguments, it should be kept in mind that we did see some evidence in Chapter 3 that people are generally more likely to support basic income schemes that are designed in such a way that they exclude newly-arriving migrants.

More broadly, Delsen and Schilpzand's (2019) findings demonstrate that people do care about the likely outcomes of basic income when deciding whether or not to support it. This basic interpretation is also backed up by other evidence. In the Dalia survey, for one example, respondents were also asked at what point they think their country should introduce basic income, to which about half replied that this should only happen 'after successful experiments' have been completed (either in their country or in other countries). By contrast, only 31% of the Dalia respondents indicated that a basic income should be introduced 'as soon as possible'. Other (albeit indirect) evidence comes from the surveys conducted within the Finnish experiment on basic income, which compare the opinions of people who were part of the experiment with those of a comparable control group (see Simanainen & Kangas, 2020). As shown in Fig. 4.10, it seems that participation in the experiment increased people's endorsement of different arguments in favour

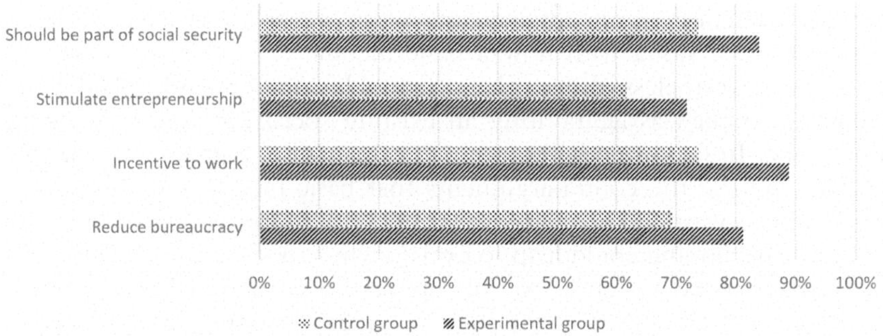

Fig. 4.10 Arguments for basic income in Finland, 2018 (*Source* Simanainen and Kangas [2020]. Question wording: [1] 'A basic income should be introduced as a permanent part of the social security system in Finland', [2] 'With a basic income, it would be easier to start your own business', [3] 'With a basic income, it would make more sense financially to accept a job offer' and [4] 'A basic income would reduce the bureaucracy involved in accepting a job offer'. The graph presents the percentage of respondents who agreed with the statements in the respective groups)

of basic income. In fact, compared with the control group, the experimental group appears more supportive of the arguments that a basic income would reduce bureaucracy (69.3% vs 81.2%), make it financially more attractive to accept a job offer (73.3% vs 88.9%) and make it easier to start a business (61.7% vs 71.8%). The participants in the basic income experiment were also more likely to support the permanent introduction of a basic income as part of the Finnish social security system (73.3% vs 83.9%). These results seem to indicate that participation in a basic income experiment makes people more supportive of basic income, because they gain first-hand experience of some of its (perceived) positive outcomes. It is nevertheless important to note that because the Finnish experiment was restricted to unemployed people (as was the control group: Kangas et al., 2021), these results should perhaps not be generalized to the broader population.

Taken together, the evidence from traditional opinion polls reveals something of a general pattern. It seems that people mainly endorse so-called 'practical' reasons that state basic income offers a practical solution to a concrete social problem, such as the alleviation of poverty or the revaluation of unpaid work. Furthermore, it appears that support for these practical arguments increases when the social problem is properly explained, along with how a basic income is supposed to solve it. This can nevertheless also work as a double-edged sword, when basic income is framed as aggravating an existing social problem or creating a new one. In fact, even without much explanation, a great many people already endorse the contra-arguments that basic income will discourage work and is wasteful because it also goes to those who do not really need it. This finding could help to explain why—as shown in Chapter 3—there tends to be a higher level of support for conditional and selective types of basic income than for their unconditional and universal counterparts. Interestingly, there is less support for the most cited economic contra-argument, which argues that a basic income would simply be unaffordable. It is also clear that people do not endorse the idea that basic income is not needed because the current welfare system is working as it should. On the contrary, people appear to become more supportive of pro-arguments when these are put in sharp contrast with the malfunctioning of the current system: for example, when it is argued that basic income will remove existing unemployment traps. However, this does not apply to the administrative arguments in favour of basic income (such as the reduction of bureaucracy and simplification of the system), as these are generally not seen as very convincing. Overall, people seem less likely to endorse so-called 'principled' reasons, which refer to broader values such as freedom or social justice. These may be too 'fluffy' to convince people compared with the 'practical' reasons. The only exceptions in this regard are arguments stating that basic income will increase 'basic security'. These types of arguments tend to be supported by a clear majority, even though they refer more to a general principle than to a concrete outcome.

In addition to the general pattern, there is also some evidence for variation between countries and types of basic income. With regard to the former, it was shown that in some countries (such as France) people are more sceptical about the positive outcomes of a basic income than in others (such as Poland). This applies both to macro-level outcomes that pertain to society as a whole (for example, that basic income would alleviate poverty) and micro-level outcomes that concern people's personal lives (for example, that basic income would cover their own basic needs). In most countries, there is nevertheless a discrepancy between the perceived outcomes of a basic income at the micro-level and at the macro-level. This is especially visible in relation to work intentions, as people seem to argue that most others would reduce their working hours while they would not. With regard to the second source of variation, it was shown that the perceived likelihood of the different outcomes varies between different basic income amounts. The most striking finding in this regard is that (South Korean) people who support a generous basic income seem to do so because they think it will lead to some specific outcomes that are generally not given a high level of support: for example, reducing income inequality or solving ecological problems such as the climate crisis.

While the existing traditional opinion polls have generated many insightful findings, they also have their shortcomings. One of these is that the polls tell us little about the relative importance of different arguments in determining people's support for the introduction of a basic income. This is mainly due to the fact that few surveys have directly asked their respondents how important a given argument is to them. However, even if a survey were to include this, it could still be argued that this approach falls short of uncovering the true importance of different arguments if the arguments are pre-defined by pollsters rather than created by people themselves. For this reason, we also need qualitative research in which people are able to decide for themselves which arguments they want to raise in relation to basic income. Another important shortcoming of the existing traditional polls is that they mostly focus on the ideal-typical version of basic income, rather than different varieties with diverging policy designs. These shortcomings will be addressed in the next sections.

4.1.2 Evidence from Survey Experiments

In addition to traditional opinion polls, there have been some survey experiments that are informative about the types of arguments people endorse in relation to basic income. These experiments typically investigate how a different framing of the potential policy outcomes of basic income affects its popular support. This was the case in the BABEL experiment in Belgium—which will be discussed in greatest detail, because the primary data is publicly available (Laenen et al., 2021)—and in three other experiments in the US that have been reported in prior studies (Jordan et al., 2022; Thomas et al., 2023; Yeung, 2022). However, two of the latter three experiments do not assess the across-the-board effects of different frames among the general population, but only examine their influence among specific ideological groups. For this reason, these experiments are not discussed here but in the section on individual differences in the reasons for supporting or opposing basic income.

It should be recalled from Chapter 3 that the BABEL experiment, conducted in 2021, presented respondents with a vignette description of a hypothetical basic income scheme that randomly varied in terms of its policy design characteristics. After reading the vignette, respondents had to indicate—on a scale from 0 to 100—the extent to which they supported the introduction of that particular basic income in Belgium. In addition, the respondents rated a second vignette (on the same scale) that randomly varied a number of important policy outcomes of that basic income. More specifically, the vignette varied the predicted effects of a basic income on poverty, income inequality, unemployment, entrepreneurship and informal care; that is, whether these would increase, decrease or stagnate (see Appendix 4 for the question wording). Respondents were told that the predicted outcomes were based on joint scientific research from different prominent Belgian universities. It is nevertheless important to note that the presented research results are fictive—something that the respondents were also informed about at the end of the survey, during the debriefing. This is because the actual outcomes of a basic income are still unknown in the context of the Belgian welfare state. The purpose of the BABEL experiment was to test which outcomes people consider important when thinking about a basic income and to see whether people change their mind about basic income when they are provided with information about its outcomes (rather than only its policy design). Additionally, the experiment makes it possible to expose the trade-offs people make between different policy outcomes of basic income as well as between its policy outcomes and policy design characteristics.

Let us first look at the average level of support for basic income for the different policy outcomes the BABEL respondents were presented with (shown in Fig. 4.11). As in Chapter 3, we again examine Belgium and its two main regions separately: Dutch-speaking Flanders and French-speaking Wallonia. Unsurprisingly, support for basic income is consistently higher if its outcomes are claimed to be positive. There are nevertheless some notable differences between the outcomes. Support is especially higher for a positive outcome than a negative outcome with regard to poverty, income inequality and unemployment. When poverty is said to decrease, support for basic income is greater than when it is said to increase (the respective means are 53.0 and 42.7). The same goes for income inequality (52.3 and 44.0) and unemployment (53.6 and 42.8). Stagnation in terms of poverty, income inequality or unemployment is always in between in terms of popular support (the means are 47.4, 46.8 and 46.9, respectively). For the two other outcomes, the differences are substantially smaller. Although support is higher when entrepreneurship is said to increase after the introduction of a basic income (49.9) compared with when it would decrease (44.4) or stagnate (48.8), the gap is smaller than for the previous outcomes. Similarly, there is barely any difference in support when informal caregiving is predicted to increase (49.7), decrease (46.3) or stagnate (47.3). This is remarkable when seen in light of the frequently-made arguments that basic income should be introduced because it will encourage economic risk-taking behaviour, such as entrepreneurship, while at the same time allowing people to provide more care for others (van Parijs & Vanderborght, 2017). The results from the BABEL experiment seem to suggest that when (Belgian) citizens decide to support or oppose basic income, they actually attach somewhat less importance to its effects on entrepreneurship and caregiving than they do to its effects on poverty, income inequality and unemployment.

Figure 4.11 also shows that there are again striking differences between the Dutch-speaking respondents living in Flanders and the French-speaking respondents living in Wallonia. First of all, support for basic income is always higher in Wallonia, regardless of its predicted outcomes. Remarkably, a basic income with *negative* outcomes is sometimes equally (or even slightly more) popular in Wallonia as a basic income with *positive* outcomes in Flanders. There is, for example, an approximately equal level of support for a basic income that *increases* poverty in Wallonia as there is for a basic income that *decreases* poverty in Flanders (the respective means are 48.2 and 50.2). Similar observations can be made for the outcomes of income inequality, unemployment, entrepreneurship and informal caregiving. This indicates that the baseline level of support for basic income—regardless of its outcomes—can vary across regions within countries (and presumably also between countries). A second relevant regional difference is that entrepreneurship seems to be more important in Dutch-speaking Flanders than in French-speaking Wallonia. In the former, support is clearly lower if basic income would decrease (39.7) rather than increase (47.0) entrepreneurship. In the latter, support for basic income is less affected by its expected effects on entrepreneurship (50.5 for a decrease and 53.7 for an increase). This also suggests that

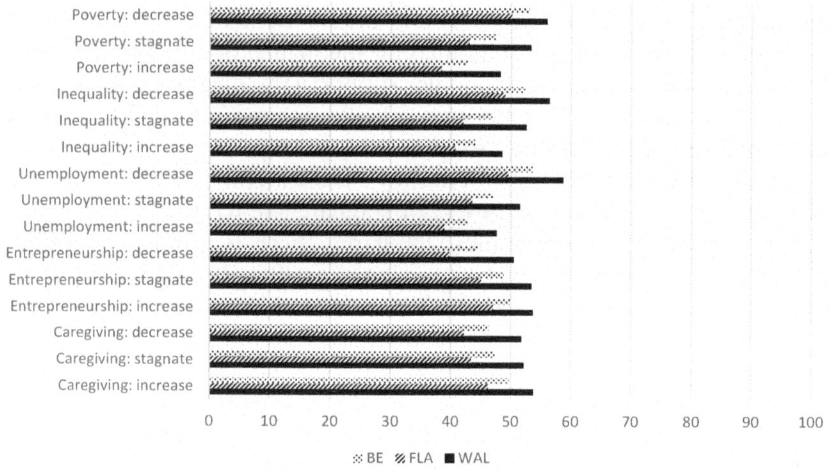

Fig. 4.11 Support for basic income with different policy outcomes in Belgium, 2021 (*Source* BABEL Survey [2021]. Question wording: 'In order to predict the consequences that the introduction of a basic income would have on Belgian society, the federal government has commissioned a study by several Belgian universities. This study shows that: [...]. With this knowledge in mind, we would like to ask you again to what extent you are in favour of or against the introduction of a basic income in Belgium?' The answer scale ranged from 'strongly against' [0] to 'strongly in favour' [100]. The graph presents the mean score for each outcome in the vignette experiment for all respondents living in Belgium [BE], the Dutch-speaking respondents living in Flanders [FLA] and the French-speaking respondents living in Wallonia [WAL])

the type of outcomes that people consider important varies within (and presumably between) countries.

One important advantage of the BABEL experiment is that it simultaneously showed multiple policy outcomes to respondents. This makes it possible to uncover how people react to specific combinations of outcomes, in terms of whether they make trade-offs between different policy outcomes of basic income. For example, are people willing to accept an increase in unemployment if it is compensated for by an increase in informal caregiving? Or, more generally, do people prioritize social outcomes (such as poverty, income inequality and informal caregiving) over economic outcomes (such as unemployment and entrepreneurship)?

Table 4.2 Combinations of unemployment/poverty with other policy outcomes

Unemployment → **Caregiving ↓**	Increase	Decrease
Increase	44.7	56.2
Decrease	40.1	52.5
Unemployment → **Entrepreneurship ↓**	Increase	Decrease
Increase	47.4	53.2
Decrease	41.7	48.1
Unemployment → **Inequality ↓**	Increase	Decrease
Increase	41.4	47.6
Decrease	48.0	57.5
Unemployment → **Poverty ↓**	Increase	Decrease
Increase	40.5	44.6
Decrease	47.6	60.4
Poverty → **Caregiving ↓**	Increase	Decrease
Increase	45.6	53.7
Decrease	42.4	51.6
Poverty → **Entrepreneurship ↓**	Increase	Decrease
Increase	44.7	55.3
Decrease	42.2	49.6
Poverty → **Inequality ↓**	Increase	Decrease
Increase	41.2	48.6
Decrease	46.8	58.7

Source BABEL Survey (2021). Question wording: see Fig. 4.11. The graph presents the mean score for the respective combinations of policy outcomes

Or vice versa? To test this, Table 4.2 shows the mean level of support for basic income for each possible combination of the respective outcomes of unemployment and poverty with all other policy outcomes. The results show that support is, as would be expected, always greater when both outcomes under consideration are positively framed than when they are both negatively framed; however, the differences in support are often significantly larger than those shown before, when the policy outcomes were viewed separately. For example, basic income proves to be much more popular when both poverty and unemployment are said to decrease

(60.4) rather than to increase (40.5). If one of the outcomes is positive and the other is negative, support for basic income is usually somewhere in between. Taking again the example of the combination between unemployment and poverty, we see that a basic income which increases the former and decreases the latter is about as equally popular as a basic income that does the exact opposite (means are 47.6 and 44.6). However, there are some instances in which one policy outcome seems to carry less weight than the other. This is particularly the case for informal caregiving, as the suggested result of an increase in the number of informal carers does little to enhance support for basic income when the other policy outcome is negative. For example, there is a lower level of support when basic income has a negative impact on unemployment but a positive one on caregiving (44.7), compared with when it has a negative impact on caregiving but a positive one on unemployment (52.5). This seems to indicate that people are not more willing to accept an increase in unemployment if this is the trade-off for an increase in informal, unpaid work. More generally, the findings refute the idea that people prioritize social over economic outcomes, or vice versa. Instead, both types of policy outcomes seem equally important in shaping people's support for basic income (with the exception of informal caregiving, which was given less weight by the respondents in the BABEL experiment).

Another advantage of the BABEL experiment is that it makes it possible to expose the potential trade-offs people make between the policy design features of basic income (that were varied in the first vignette, see Fig. 3.1) and its policy outcomes (which were varied in the second vignette). What happens to support for relatively unpopular types of basic income when their outcomes are predicted to be positive? For example, will a basic income that is well below the subsistence level become more popular if it is able to reduce poverty? Conversely, what happens to support for relatively popular basic income varieties when their outcomes are presented as negative? For example, will support for a conditional basic income decrease if the level of unemployment is claimed to increase? To address such questions, we can compare the mean level of support for different basic income varieties *before* the policy outcomes were presented, with the mean level of support for the same varieties *after* the outcomes were stated (on the same response scale). Table 4.3 shows the results of this exercise for the policy outcomes of poverty and unemployment on the one hand, and the policy design dimensions of generosity, integration and conditionality on the other hand. The table shows that popular

Table 4.3 Combinations of policy outcomes and policy design features

Poverty →	No information	Increase	Decrease
Generosity ↓			
€500	52.5	39.9	50.8
€1500	57.5	46.9	53.2
Unemployment →	No information	Increase	Decrease
Generosity ↓			
€500	52.5	40.3	52.4
€1500	57.5	45.5	53.5
Poverty →	No information	Increase	Decrease
Integration ↓			
Replaces all benefits	53.8	41.6	53.3
Replaces no benefits	55.3	43.2	52.5
Unemployment →	No information	Increase	Decrease
Integration ↓			
Replaces all benefits	53.8	40.6	54.8
Replaces no benefits	55.3	45.2	53.1
Poverty →	No information	Increase	Decrease
Conditionality ↓			
Unconditional	51.2	41.2	50.2
Conditional on participation	58.1	44.3	56.0
Unemployment →	No information	Increase	Decrease
Conditionality ↓			
Unconditional	51.2	39.5	53.4
Conditional on participation	58.1	45.8	53.8

Source BABEL Survey (2021). Question wording: see Fig. 4.11. The graph presents the mean score for the respective combinations of policy outcomes and policy design features

support consistently drops when the outcomes are negative, regardless of the policy design of the basic income. If poverty or unemployment is stated as increasing, there is always a much lower level of support compared with the baseline condition when no information about the outcomes was given to respondents. For example, both a basic income of €500 and one of €1500 decrease in popularity when poverty is predicted to increase (from 52.5 and 57.5, to 39.9 and 46.9, respectively). The same pattern can be observed for the policy design dimensions of integration and conditionality. Remarkably, however, there is no similar increase in support when the effects on poverty and unemployment are expected to be positive. Instead, support either remains very stable, or slightly decreases. Sticking to the same example, we see little change in the level of support for a basic income of €500 and one of €1500 after respondents have been told that these would decrease poverty (50.8 and 53.2, respectively). The same observation can be made for the design dimensions of integration and conditionality. Taken together, these findings suggest that support for relatively popular types of basic income can decrease when their effects on poverty and unemployment are negatively framed, but that—the other way around—support for relatively unpopular basic income types does not seem to increase when these effects are positively framed. This is indicative of a negativity bias in people's support for basic income, as they seem to be influenced more by negative than by positive outcomes.

Most of the above demonstrates that there are different levels of support for (different types of) basic income when the predicted outcomes differ. Nevertheless, this does not directly prove that people change their initial thoughts about basic income after they are informed about its potential outcomes. A closer analysis of the response patterns of the BABEL participants shows that about 60% change their opinion (by more than 5 points on a scale from 0 to 100) after reading the results of the (fictive) scientific research. This corresponds remarkably well with the number of respondents who consider these results to be trustworthy (58.4%). Importantly, those who changed their opinion mostly did so in a negative direction: while 40% decreased their support for basic income after being exposed to the research results, only 20% increased their support. This again suggests the existence of a negativity bias, in that support for basic income decreases if the policy is claimed to produce undesirable outcomes but does not increase if it is claimed to yield desirable outcomes.

This negativity bias is further supported by the results in Table 4.4, which shows the percentage of respondents who changed their opinion about basic income for each policy outcome separately. It can be seen from the table that the framing of negative effects leads to a larger *decrease* in support than the framing of positive outcomes leads to an *increase* in support. For example, while about 46% of the respondents become less supportive of basic income after they are told that poverty is likely to increase (a negative outcome), only 29% becomes more supportive after they are given the information that poverty is likely to decrease (a positive outcome). This also holds for all other policy outcomes. Remarkably, even when the outcome is presented as positive, there often is a larger proportion of respondents who become *less* rather than *more* supportive of basic income. For example, when entrepreneurship is said to increase after the introduction of a basic income, only 22% of the respondents increase their support, compared with 38% who decrease their support. A similar trend is observed for informal caregiving, unemployment and income inequality, but not for poverty. In the case of poverty, the number of respondents who increase or decrease their support when the outcome is framed in a positive way is almost equal, at 29% and 30%, respectively. The fact that for most policy outcomes people tend to become less rather than more supportive of basic income when presented with positive effects seems counterintuitive. However, this can be explained by the specific design of the survey experiment, as respondents were always shown *multiple* policy outcomes, some of which were positive, but some of which were likely to be negative. In light of people's negativity bias, it seems that negative outcomes generally take precedence when they decide whether or not to support basic income.

The negativity bias found in the BABEL experiment is confirmed by another survey experiment, conducted by Jordan and colleagues (2022) in November 2019 among a sample of 3600 respondents living in the US (who were recruited via Mechanical Turk). In the experiment, respondents were first given a short definition of universal basic income, describing it as a 'new policy that is being tested around the world which guarantees a payment of money to individuals from their government, regardless of need, qualification, or work'. After that, the respondents were shown two arguments about basic income, which were either only positive, only negative or a combination of a positive and a negative argument. More specifically, the two positive arguments shown in the experiment were that basic income would (1) 'help solve unemployment problems caused by increasing automation across a variety of industries' and (2) 'help make society fairer by reducing income inequality caused by automation across a variety of industries'. The negative arguments were that basic income would (1) 'be much too expensive to implement on a broad scale' and (2) 'encourage laziness by rewarding someone for not working'. After reading the different arguments, respondents were asked to indicate their support for the introduction of basic income. By comparing the level of support in the experimental groups with the level of support in the control group (who were not presented with any arguments in addition to the basic definition), Jordan et al. (2022) were able to test whether the positive and negative arguments had similar effects on people's support for basic income. Their main finding is that the negative arguments make people less supportive of basic income while the positive

Table 4.4 Opinion change after hearing about policy outcomes in Belgium, 2021

Policy outcomes	*Opinion change*		
	–	/	+
Poverty			
Increase	45.9%	39.2%	14.9%
Stagnate	44.9%	41.1%	14.0%
Decrease	29.7%	41.5%	28.7%
Inequality			
Increase	46.1%	38.3%	15.6%
Stagnate	40.0%	41.8%	18.2%
Decrease	34.2%	41.3%	24.5%
Unemployment			
Increase	48.5%	39.6%	11.9%
Stagnate	40.5%	41.0%	18.4%
Decrease	33.8%	39.1%	27.1%
Entrepreneurship			
Increase	37.8%	40.3%	21.9%
Stagnate	40.1%	42.4%	17.5%
Decrease	45.3%	36.8%	17.9%
Informal caregiving			
Increase	38.1%	38.9%	23.0%
Stagnate	40.2%	40.3%	19.5%
Decrease	44.7%	40.6%	14.7%

Source BABEL Survey (2021). Question wording: see Fig. 4.11. The graph presents the percentage of respondents who decreased (–) or increased (+) their support or did not change their opinion (/) after they were told about the respective policy outcomes

arguments do not make people more supportive. The authors take this as evidence that there is a negativity bias at play. Nevertheless, there are two important nuances to this interpretation that are worth mentioning here. The first is the possibility that the positive arguments were less influential because they both refer to the controversial concept of automation, which might in itself have been questioned by many respondents (Herke & Vicsek, 2022). Given that the debate about the magnitude and effects of automation is ongoing even among expert scholars (Arntz et al., 2016; Frey & Osborne, 2017), it seems reasonable that many citizens have difficulties imagining that automation will actually lead to higher levels of unemployment and income inequality. The second nuance is that the reported negativity bias was only found among specific ideological groups.

I will return to the role played by political ideology in more detail below, when discussing individual differences in people's reasons for supporting or opposing basic income.

In sum, the findings from the BABEL experiment demonstrate that support for basic income does, as expected, tend to be greater when people are told that its introduction will have positive rather than negative outcomes. However, this applies much more to poverty, income inequality and unemployment than it does to entrepreneurship and informal caregiving, which seem to be less relevant when people decide whether or not they would support basic income (although entrepreneurship is somewhat more important for the Dutch-speaking respondents than it is for their French-speaking counterparts). Conversely, negative outcomes also appear to decrease support for basic income, but importantly, there is some evidence that the impact of negative outcomes on people's support for basic income is generally greater than that of positive outcomes. Both the BABEL experiment in Belgium and the experiment by Jordan et al. (2022) in the US point towards some negativity bias, by showing that people become *less* supportive of basic income after being exposed to negatively framed arguments, but not necessarily *more* supportive of it when exposed to positively framed arguments.

4.1.3 Evidence from Qualitative Research

The quantitative evidence presented above, stemming from both traditional polls and survey experiments, offers valuable insights into the perceived plausibility and importance of different arguments about the potential outcomes of basic income. However, one key limitation of this type of evidence is that the arguments are always pre-defined by researchers rather than spontaneously suggested by citizens. In fact, it could be argued that to uncover the real importance people attach to different arguments, we should investigate which arguments they themselves offer to justify their position concerning basic income. This bottom-up approach is followed in a few qualitative studies into people's support for basic income that typically give people the opportunity to freely discuss why they are for and/or against its introduction. In this section, I consider the results of four qualitative studies, conducted in Belgium (Legein et al., 2018), the Netherlands (Rossetti et al., 2020), Germany and Slovenia (Zimmermann et al., 2020), and Hungary (Herke & Vicsek, 2022). Before discussing these studies in more detail, it is worth noting that their results should not be directly compared, because they pertain to very specific groups that are by no means representative of the general population in these countries. Accordingly, the arguments raised by the respondents in these qualitative studies should not be taken as representative of the arguments endorsed by the general population. That said, qualitative research is actually *not* intended to be representative of a broader population. Instead, the more modest goal is to find out which types of arguments spontaneously emerge when people talk about basic income.

The first study, by Legein and colleagues (2018), is a qualitative experiment conducted in 2015 among 686 students from different disciplines at two universities in the French-speaking part of Belgium. In the experiment, respondents were presented with a description of basic income that randomly varied the arguments and metaphors used to frame the policy. More specifically, a fictive news article was shown that reads as follows: 'Some people propose the idea of a universal grant, also called—depending on the country—basic income, unconditional basic income or citizen's income, which can be defined as an income paid by a political community to all its members on an individual basis, without means-test or work requirements. Although this idea has long been connected to a gentle utopia entertained by intellectuals (but supported by numerous Nobel Prize winners in Economic Sciences), it slowly gained ground. It has been tested briefly in Canada, the US, and India; has been launched by Lula in Brazil; and in Alaska, it exists by means of a redistribution of oil profits by the state'. To this fixed description, the researchers added a specific argument or a metaphor to frame basic income. These mentioned that basic income could be seen as: (1) 'an income supplied by the state so that citizens can freely live their life without having to be concerned about material constraints' [freedom argument], (2) 'an income that citizens receive from the state by the very fact that they are members of it' [unconditionality argument], (3) 'a base frame supplied by the state so that citizens can build their life freely without having to be concerned about material constraints' [base frame metaphor], (4) 'a springboard supplied by the state so that citizens can freely launch themselves into life without any material constraints' [springboard metaphor] and (5) 'pocket money that citizens receive from the state in the same way that children are given this by the very fact that they are members of the family' [pocket money metaphor]. The respective arguments and metaphors were randomly allocated to respondents, so that each respondent was presented with either one argument or one metaphor. There was also a control group of respondents who were not given any information in addition to the original article. Although this research design seems similar to the survey experiments discussed above, the crucial difference is that respondents were asked an open-ended rather than a closed question after reading the article, by simply asking 'What do *you* think?' The respondents could therefore freely speak their mind about basic income. The answers they gave were subsequently coded and interpreted by the researchers.

Most basically, the results show that people were more likely to cite arguments related to the one they had been exposed to in the news article on basic income. With regard to unconditionality, for example, respondents referred more frequently to arguments related to the conditions under which access to a basic income should be granted. For the metaphors, it appears that only the pocket money metaphor had an influence on the types of arguments the respondents endorsed (compared with the control group). In fact, framing basic income as pocket money appears to increase the use of negative arguments about the policy—in particular, the arguments that basic income is unaffordable and should be restricted to Belgian citizens, who are viewed as part of 'the family'. Legein and colleagues (2018) seem to take these findings as clear evidence that the framing of basic income in media and political discourse can influence the types of arguments that citizens endorse. At the same time, they also show that some arguments are not affected at all by the different frames presented in the study. On the one hand, there are arguments that are always somewhat prevalent, regardless of the specific framing. This is the case, for example, for the argument that basic income would decrease work incentives and make people lazy (see quote 1.1 in Table 4.5). This fear that basic income will cause laziness is—as we will see below—perhaps the most frequently cited and pervasive argument against the policy idea. On the other hand, some arguments were not frequently put forward, such as the idea that people have a natural right to basic income because they are entitled to their share of the publicly owned commons (Standing, 2020). This could be because the specific frames in this study did not trigger the use of these arguments, or because people generally consider them less important in relation to basic income. Unfortunately, the study by Legein et al. (2018) cannot provide the answer.

Table 4.5 Example quotes from study participants in qualitative studies on arguments about basic income

Study		*Quote*
1. Legein et al. (2018)	1.1	'Work is an integral part of our society and it is the basis of its smooth running but also of numerous quarrels. The big question is to know if receiving this basic income would encourage people to work less, so contenting themselves with the benefits.' (p. 9)
2. Rossetti et al. (2020)	2.1	'Of course you will always have people who can't work for medical reasons, so you shouldn't bother those people. But people who are able to work and who simply don't do anything, and think "with this money, oh well, I don't have to do anything" [...] you should make them work, through mandatory voluntary work, or something similar. I think this is a condition that can be applied to it [basic income], because so many volunteers are also needed everywhere.' (p. 291)
	2.2	'Me too? So even if I go to work, would I also get this basic income? So I would be very well off? That sounds nice. I want to participate. But who will pay for it??' (p. 292)
3. Zimmermann et al. (2020)	3.1	'If my ex-husband—who was a craftsman—and I, back then, had been provided with a basic income by the state at the same amount, we'd only have had to decide which one of us would work a bit extra, and I would not have had to go to work while still breastfeeding.' (p. 308)
	3.2	'No, people would have to earn it [basic income] in a sense. It would start after they get German citizenship. Without that, they'd not get this money.' (p. 308)
	3.3	Also, self-employed people could not profit from working illegally. They are now working illegally in order to not have to pay for childcare. So, if they don't have to do those things and they receive the social benefit instead [...] there would be none of that anymore. They would receive €500 whether they would be working or not, end of story. It would be better if they would work, wouldn't it?' (p. 309)
	3.4	'But then the difference between the minimum wage and this benefit should be, let's say, very large [...] so as to not, I don't know, encourage laziness.' (p. 310)

(continued)

Table 4.5 (continued)

Study		*Quote*
4. Herke and Vicsek (2022)	4.1	'It [basic income] would surely be better than receiving nothing, because that [being unemployed] would not be a solution for the situation that people do not have the opportunity to work because of artificial intelligence and robots. But I am still saying that we should work on creating workplaces and opportunities instead of allocating free money.' (p. 7)
	4.2	'There was already such a [basic income] system in history: it was called socialism, and it did not really work. I think that it is an idealistic concept that is impossible to realize, and which will always lead to the extreme, and it will finally end in a totalitarian dictatorship or something like that.' (p. 8)
	4.3	'One thing that I thought is that for a transitional period, while someone is learning a new profession that they could use in a new environment, then for that time it [basic income] could certainly be good.' (p. 8)

The second study, by Rossetti and colleagues (2020), reports the results of a series of in-depth interviews about basic income conducted in 2018–2019 with 49 randomly selected residents of the city of Tilburg in the Netherlands. The specific context of Tilburg was chosen because it was part of a larger policy experiment that allowed local municipalities to (temporarily) relax the strict work obligations attached to the receipt of means-tested social assistance benefits. Although these local experiments were restricted to social assistance recipients and are broadly referred to as 'trust experiments', some see them as a litmus test of introducing an unconditional basic income (Roosma, 2022; van der Veen, 2019). At the start of the interview, respondents were asked how they would describe a basic income in their own words. The responses made it clear that most did not know what a basic income is, as many people incorrectly defined it as a minimum wage or as their own household budget. Some even interpreted basic income as a strictly equal income for all, as it would be under communist rule, and therefore, immediately opposed it. To deal with this lack of prior knowledge, the researchers defined basic income as 'a monthly income paid by the government on which you can live frugally. It will be the same amount for everyone, paid to all adult residents of the Netherlands. The payment is without conditions and is not dependent on income, assets or work situation. It partially replaces other benefits and allowances, such as social assistance'. After checking whether the description had been understood correctly, the interviewers asked respondents whether they would support or oppose the introduction of a basic income, and to indicate their reasons for doing so.

The results first of all show that respondents' support for basic income was mainly motivated by the idea that it would provide basic security to them as well as to others. With regard to the latter, the most favoured aspect of a basic income is arguably that it would improve the circumstances of the poor, for whom the prevailing social benefits and wages are considered as too low to lead a life with dignity. At the same time, basic income was also heavily criticized by the respondents on various grounds. On the one hand, there was widespread opposition to the inclusion of people who are seen as undeserving of state support. This mostly refers to so-called 'freeriders' who are deemed capable of making a meaningful contribution to Dutch society through paid work or other socially appreciated activities (such as caregiving or volunteering), but are unwilling to do so (see quote 2.1 in Table 4.5). In this regard, it is clear from the interviews that most respondents strongly oppose a fully unconditional basic income, but would be more willing to accept some kind of participation income (Atkinson, 1996). In a similar vein, respondents often object to a fully universal basic income because they consider it unfair to give the money to higher-income groups that do not really need it (so it is claimed). On the other hand, basic income was also opposed for practical reasons. Most notably, respondents tended to immediately question the financial feasibility of implementing a basic income, and worried about the tax increase they thought would be necessary to fund it (see quote 2.2 in Table 4.5). Although it was acknowledged that basic income would simplify the existing social security system, some respondents also saw it as somewhat pointless administrative work for the state to pay money to people, only to claw it back later via the tax system. This was succinctly described by one respondent as 'moving cash around', but was generally regarded as a somewhat inefficient use of government resources. Respondents generally also found it difficult to imagine that a flat-rate benefit such as basic income would be successful in decreasing income inequality.

The third study, by Zimmermann and colleagues (2020), reports the results of a series of group discussions (in this case, democratic fora and focus groups) on the future of the welfare state that were held in 2015–2016 in Germany and Slovenia within the framework of the 'Welfare State Futures: Our Children's Europe' (WelfSOC) project (Taylor-Gooby & Leruth, 2018). In these discussions, respondents were invited to envision what the welfare state would ideally look like in the future. Importantly, the topics to be discussed were not pre-defined by the researchers but were left to the participants. In some group discussions, basic income was suggested—mostly by well-informed respondents from the middle class—as a promising scenario for the future. In most discussions, however, the topic of basic income was not spontaneously raised by the participants, suggesting that the policy had a relatively low public salience, or was not seen as a serious alternative to the existing welfare system. This is especially the case in the three other participating countries in the WelfSOC project—Denmark, Norway and the UK—where none of the respondents even mentioned the issue of basic income. From the discussions in Germany and Slovenia, we can nevertheless distil the types of arguments people spontaneously cite for and against the introduction of basic income. We can also examine whether these arguments differ between the countries. It is important to note that because basic income was raised by the respondents themselves, no definition of it was offered by the researchers. This implies that the respondents did not talk about a well-defined basic income scheme, but instead discussed the general principles behind the policy—such as its universality and unconditionality.

The results show that the respondents from Germany mainly like the idea of basic income because they think it would increase individual freedom. More specifically, the respondents argued that a basic income would give people greater freedom to choose the work they really *want* to do, and greater freedom to be with and provide care for their family (see quote 3.1 in Table 4.5). However, many respondents were against the idea of a fully universal and fully unconditional basic income that is equal for all. Some of the respondents proposed excluding migrants (or newly-arrived migrants) from a basic income scheme, because they have not yet contributed anything to German society and because there is concern over a welfare magnet effect (see quote 3.2 in Table 4.5). Most respondents also preferred to make basic income conditional on the demonstration of job-seeking efforts. This call for conditionality is driven by the concern that a basic income would otherwise decrease incentives to work, but also by the expectation that people should contribute to society before they are able to receive money from the government. This demand for reciprocity can also be seen in the widespread opposition to the idea of a flat-rate basic income. Most respondents argued that the level of basic income should be linked to people's prior investments (such as their education) and achievements (for example, their work record). Overall, the principle of equality played a very marginal role in the German debates on basic income, as it was rarely referred to as 'a good thing'. Most respondents were—as was shown in the Dutch interviews—also somewhat sceptical of the suggestion that a basic income can reduce income inequality. Again, it seems that people find it counterintuitive that a flat-rate benefit could close the gap between the rich and the poor in society. From a more-practical point of view, the German respondents argued that a basic income would reduce administrative complexity, but many saw it as unaffordable in the existing economic context.

The results from Slovenia are very different from those observed in Germany. Most of the Slovenian respondents found the universal access and flat-rate amount of basic income attractive, because it would lead to much-desired equality of treatment and would supposedly increase social cohesion. In addition to these principled arguments, the respondents often raised more-practical arguments, which actually dominated the group discussions in Slovenia. More specifically, basic income was widely praised for its potential to decrease state bureaucracy, government corruption and benefit abuse by citizens (see quote 3.3 in Table 4.5). Basic income was thus seen as a promising tool to fix a welfare system perceived as being broken. However, this does not mean that basic income did not attract any criticism. In fact, there was also a genuine fear among the Slovenian respondents that a basic income would make people lazy, and hence, reduce their motivation to work. To maintain this motivation, however, the Slovenian respondents did not suggest making basic income conditional on job-seeking efforts (as their German counterparts did). Instead, they argued for a relatively low amount of basic income that would only cover people's basic needs and thereby keep their work incentives intact (see quote 3.4 in Table 4.5).

Zimmermann and colleagues (2020) demonstrate that there are important country differences in the types of arguments that are cited to support or oppose basic income and suggest that these differences can be understood by looking at the existing welfare state context. Their argument is that citizens tend to refer to the normative principles that are embedded most strongly in the welfare institutions of their respective countries. It should indeed come as no surprise that the German respondents—who live in a corporatist-conservative welfare regime dominated by the social insurance logic, which prescribes that social benefits ought to be conditional on work (Esping-Andersen, 1990)—are less supportive of a fully unconditional basic income that is equal for all, regardless of prior achievements, contributions and investments. By the same token, it seems logical that their Slovenian counterparts—who live in a post-communist country with a welfare system that is more equality-oriented (Stambolieva, 2019)—are more appreciative of the equality of treatment provided by basic income. More broadly, these findings suggest that the (existing, as well as past) welfare state context to which people are exposed influences the type of basic income they prefer, and the type of arguments they raise in order to defend their opinions (see also Laenen et al., 2022).

The fourth and final qualitative study that is considered here, by Herke and Vicsek (2022), reports the results of 30 in-depth interviews with Hungarian university students about the introduction of a basic income in the context of automation. Although the interviews took place in spring 2020, respondents were asked to imagine the hypothetical scenario that by the year 2060, there would be massive technological unemployment in Hungary due to automation-induced job losses. More specifically, respondents were given the following instruction: 'Please imagine that we are in 2060. The unemployment level is high, robots and Artificial Intelligence are carrying out many jobs. There is a debate in parliament about whether to introduce a basic income for everyone. The basic income scheme would include all of the following: (a) the government pays a monthly income to everyone to cover essential living costs, (b) it replaces many other social benefits, (c) the purpose is to guarantee everyone a minimum standard of living, (d) everyone receives the same amount regardless of whether or not they are working, (e) people also keep the money they earn from work or other sources, and (f) this scheme is paid for by taxes. The government would ask the public about their support for this, and they would also ask you. What would you reply? What would your arguments be?' Although the description of basic income is the same as used in the European Social Survey (see Fig. 2.8), the difference is that the respondents in Herke and Vicsek's study were given an open-ended question inviting them to freely express their thoughts on basic income.

The results first and foremost show that most of the respondents simply refused to believe, or did not accept, the scenario they were presented with. Most were actually highly sceptical of the idea that automation would lead to massive unemployment, as they argued that such a pessimistic scenario had been predicted numerous times in the past, but had not happened as yet ('so why would it happen in the future?'). Additionally, they claimed that automation would also create new types of work, and that their own future jobs—which were less likely to be routine jobs because of their higher level of education—would be relatively safe from automation. Regardless of whether the threat of technological unemployment was perceived as real or not, most respondents nevertheless agreed that it *should* not be real. It was in fact broadly claimed that the government has the responsibility to ensure that there is always enough work in society (irrespective of the level of automation), because work is regarded as something that gives meaning to life. Accordingly, basic income is not seen as an adequate solution to automation, because automation itself is not seen as a problem. Instead, the respondents seemed to prefer some type of guaranteed employment scheme over a guaranteed basic income scheme (see quote 4.1 in Table 4.5). Irrespective of the future scenario that was presented, respondents were often highly critical of the introduction of a basic income in Hungary. Two reasons for their opposition stand out. The first is that the Hungarian respondents associated basic income with communism, and therefore, opposed it on principle. The underlying rationale was that a basic income would ultimately lead to a loss of individual freedom, as was the case under the former communist and totalitarian regime (see quote 4.2 in Table 4.5). The second contra-argument that was often raised by the respondents was that basic income would have a negative impact on people's work incentives. This sparked strong opposition to a fully unconditional and generous basic income that would be paid throughout people's lives. If the respondents accepted any form of basic income at all, there was a clear preference for a temporary scheme with an income that would be low enough so as to sustain the incentive to work. This short-term basic income could then be used to cover people's basic needs during periods of transition, for example, the move to a new profession via vocational training (see quote 4.3 in Table 4.5).

Taken together, the qualitative evidence presented here shows that people advance different types of arguments to justify their support for, or opposition to, basic income. Some of the arguments are broadly shared by people living in vastly different contexts. Most notably, people very often base their opposition to a basic income on the idea that it would encourage laziness and reduce the willingness to work. Although most agree that this is a potential problem, the proposed solutions to the problem diverge widely. For example, while some argue for the imposition of work or other obligations, others maintain that a basic income can be unconditional, but should in that case be relatively low and/or temporary. Other types of contra-arguments—such as the unaffordability of basic income, its negative association with communism and its limited potential to reduce income inequality—were also used in different contexts to argue against the introduction of basic income. It seems that the most commonly used arguments in favour of basic income tend to vary somewhat more between different contexts. For example, while the German respondents in the study by Zimmermann and colleagues (2020) mainly favoured basic income because it would increase individual freedom, the Slovenian respondents mainly supported basic income because they saw it as a cure for some of the ills of the prevailing welfare system (such as corruption and benefit abuse).

At least equally important—although emphasized less in the above discussion—are the arguments that were *not* spontaneously offered by the respondents in the respective studies. For example, people rarely seemed to refer to basic income as a potential solution to the threat of automation-driven unemployment, or to basic income as a dividend to be paid because 'we', the people, have a natural right to society's public resources. Although these (and other) types of arguments are frequently put forward in academic and political debates (Afscharian et al., 2022), they do not yet seem to have found their way into the discourse of ordinary citizens. This could be because citizens are generally unaware of these arguments, or because they consider them as less important when forming their opinion about basic income. However, it is important to reiterate that the respondents from the qualitative studies are by no means representative of the general population, because they constitute small, specific subgroups. It, nevertheless, remains relevant to see which arguments are spontaneously raised in relation to basic income, and which ones are not.

Summary Box 4.1 Across-the-Board Reasons for Supporting or Opposing Basic Income

Overall, the discussion shows that—across the board—people have many different reasons for supporting or opposing basic income. However, these are not all of equal importance.

The most consistent argument against the introduction of a basic income (and an argument that is found by all the studies mentioned, irrespective of their research design) is that it would make people lazy and discourage work. Many people, therefore, argue that a basic income should not be implemented at all, or alternatively, that it should be designed in such a way that it will maintain work incentives—for example, by making basic income conditional on job-seeking efforts, low enough to cover only basic needs or limited in time. Interestingly, there is a striking discrepancy between the macro-level and the micro-level in this regard: while people generally think that most others will reduce their work if a basic income is introduced, they simultaneously claim that they would not do so themselves. Although people also endorse many other arguments against basic income, these are raised far less consistently. Basic income is often opposed because it is allegedly unaffordable, because it is claimed to work as a welfare magnet, because it wastes scarce resources on well-off people, because it is associated with communism, and so on. These types of contra-arguments nevertheless appear to different degrees depending on the context.

By contrast, it is more difficult to pinpoint the most consistently supported argument in favour of basic income, as people give a wide variety of reasons. For example: because basic income is thought to bring down poverty, provide basic security, revalue unpaid work such as care-giving or volunteering activities, reduce the administrative complexity of the current welfare system, and so on. Other arguments that are often put forward by basic income advocates seem to receive little support in public opinion. For example, people rarely refer to the threat of automation-induced unemployment as a reason to introduce a basic income. There are also very few indications from the evidence presented above that people support basic income purely out of self-interest (although this could be the result of social desirability bias). Importantly, the arguments in favour of basic income seem to be outweighed by the arguments against it. There is some evidence (from survey experiments in Belgium and the US) for a negativity bias, as people are more likely to decrease their support after hearing about negative outcomes than they are to increase it after hearing about positive outcomes.

Lastly, the evidence suggests that the perceived plausibility and importance of different arguments for and against basic income can vary between countries as well as between regions within countries. With regard to cross-national variation, it has been shown, for example, that scepticism about the positive outcomes of basic income is much more common in some countries (such as France) than it is in others (such as Poland). With regard to cross-regional variation, it was demonstrated, for example, that basic income's impact on entrepreneurship is considered much more important in the Dutch-speaking region of Belgium (Flanders) than in the French-speaking region (Wallonia). It should nevertheless be noted that our knowledge about the degree and the determinants of the contextual variation in the types of arguments people endorse in relation to basic income is still very limited. Improving that knowledge is an important task for future research.

4.2 Individual Differences

In addition to the across-the-board perspective, this chapter also investigates individual differences in the types of arguments people endorse or find important in relation to basic income. It concentrates on three specific individual characteristics: age, gender and political ideology. Attention is limited to these characteristics because they are often included in, and can easily be compared between, a number of publicly available surveys conducted in different countries. In the following, I focus only on the evidence from traditional opinion polls and survey experiments. There is no additional evidence presented from qualitative studies, as the number of respondents is typically too small to draw reliable comparisons between various groups with different characteristics.

4.2.1 Age

In the previous chapters, it was shown that young people are often more supportive of different types of basic income than their older counterparts. I argued that this higher level of support among the young is mainly because they have more to gain from the introduction of a basic income, and in particular, from the fully universal and unconditional ideal type. Many of the above-discussed arguments for basic income seem to work mostly in favour of young people, as they are more likely to need a basic income to compensate for their under-protection in existing social security systems, to guarantee greater income security in case of unstable employment, to protect them against the uncertainties associated with automation-driven unemployment, to provide a springboard for starting their own business or investing in their human capital through education, and so on. These arguments apply less to elderly people, because most of them are no longer active on the labour market and are already in receipt of an old-age pension. It, thus, seems plausible that the elderly will be less likely to consider a basic income as being of personal benefit to them. There is nevertheless one important exception: a basic income could benefit elderly people if it encouraged working-age people to provide more informal care for their elderly relatives. Therefore, the revaluation of unpaid work by rewarding caregivers with a regular cash payment could be of substantial importance to elderly people in particular. By contrast, young people may attach more importance to policy outcomes that directly affect them, such as basic income's impact on employment, educational attainment, entrepreneurship and so on. That said, both younger and older people can also support basic income for sociotropic reasons, as something that will improve society as a whole (for example, because it reduces poverty or income inequality). Nevertheless, it seems more likely that young people are generally more positive about the predicted outcomes of introducing a basic income than their elderly counterparts.

There are only a few surveys that can provide insights into possible age differences in the support for different arguments related to basic income. The first is the Tisser Solidarity Survey conducted in 1995 in the Netherlands. As discussed above, respondents were first asked whether they were in favour of or against the introduction of a basic income scheme and could then select a maximum of three reasons to justify their opinion. It should be remembered that support for basic income was relatively low, with only 19.1% of the respondents indicating that they were in favour (see Fig. 2.4). The level of support was nevertheless somewhat higher among those aged between 18 and 34 (21.2%) than those above the age of 65 (13.9%). People aged between 35 and 64 were closer to the youngest age category in terms of their support for basic income, at 20%. As shown in Fig. 4.12, the elderly respondents who opposed basic income mainly did so because they thought it would discourage work (64.4%), because they felt it should not be paid to those who are not in need of it (62.4%) and because they were of the opinion that social benefits ought to be conditional on the willingness to work (54.5%). These arguments

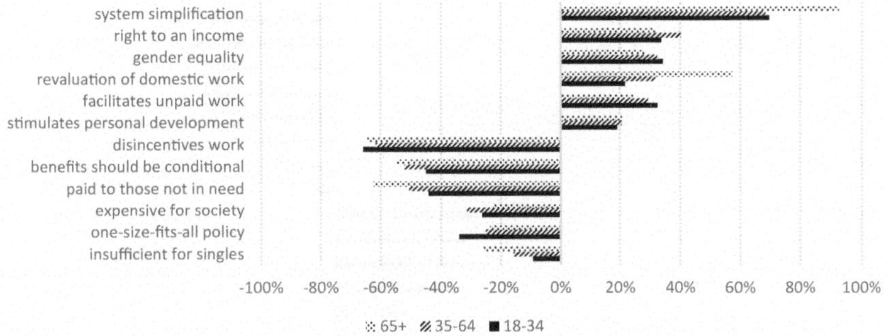

Fig. 4.12 Arguments for and against basic income in the Netherlands, by age (*Source* TISSER Solidarity Survey [1995]. Question wording: see Fig. 4.1. The graph presents the percentage of proponents/opponents of basic income who endorsed the respective arguments in favour of/against basic income per age category. Please note that negative percentages are used for the arguments against basic income)

were also supported most by the younger respondents, although to a lesser extent (except for the argument that basic income would discourage work, with which 61.6% of the youngest age category agreed). Although younger and older people thus seem to oppose basic income for the same principle reasons, there are also notable age differences. The youngest respondents were more often against basic income because they see it as a one-size-fits-all policy that treats different types of people equally (34% compared with 23.5% among the elderly). The elderly more often criticized basic income for providing insufficient income security to single persons (25.8% compared with 9.2% among the young). The argument that basic income is too costly was supported slightly more by younger age groups (especially by the middle age group, at 31.4%) than the elderly (22.6%). This could be because they already bear the heaviest tax burden, as they are of working age.

With regard to the arguments in favour of basic income, it is clear that the few elderly people who supported basic income mainly did so because they see it as a simplification of the existing social security system (92.5%). A little more than half of the elderly respondents who were in favour of basic income also supported it because of the belief that it will revalue domestic work (57.4%). All the other arguments were supported considerably less by the elderly (with the proportion always below 30%). Similarly,

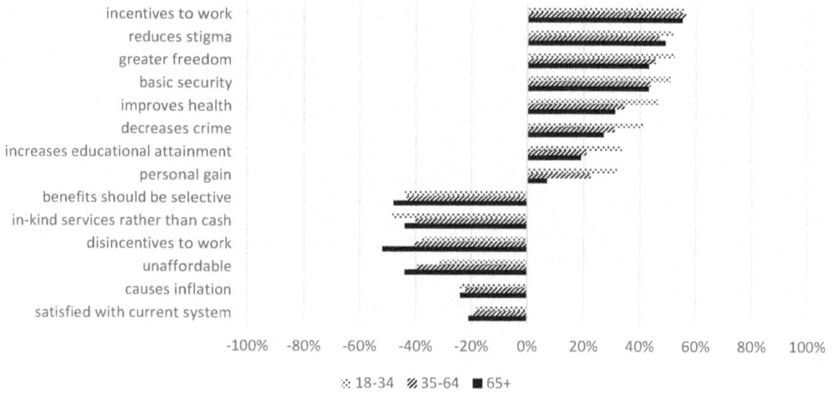

Fig. 4.13 Arguments for and against basic income in the UK, by age (*Source* Populus [2018]. Question wording: see Fig. 4.2. The graph presents the percentage of respondents who endorsed the respective arguments in favour of/against basic income per age category. Please note that negative percentages are used for arguments against basic income)

the young also supported basic income mainly because they feel it would simplify the existing social security system; however, the proportion is much lower (68.2%) than among the elderly. Young people were also less likely to stress the revaluation of domestic work (21.7%) compared with their elderly counterparts. The middle age group is somewhere in between these extremes with regard to the argument that a basic income would revalue domestic work (57.4%). This group was also more likely to support basic income simply because it provides the basic right to an income (40.2%). None of the age groups seem to think that the stimulation of personal development is an important argument in favour of basic income (with the proportions always around 20%).

After the Tisser Solidarity Survey, there was a long period during which (at least to my knowledge) no opinion surveys were held that provide information on how various age groups evaluate different arguments in favour of or against basic income. This changed when the Ipsos MORI and Populus surveys were conducted in the UK in 2017 and 2018, respectively. As shown in Fig. 4.13, the results from the Populus survey demonstrate that all age groups were most supportive of the argument that basic income would encourage work more than the existing welfare system. People of different ages also agreed that a basic income would reduce the stigma that is attached to current social benefits. Other than that, there are clear age differences, in that young people were always considerably more supportive of the arguments in favour of basic income than elderly people. The size of the gap, nevertheless, differs between the arguments. While young people were more likely to think that basic income would bring greater freedom and income security, the difference with their elderly counterparts is in both cases lower than 10 percentage points. This gap is larger with regard to the other arguments, as elderly people were significantly less likely to agree that a basic income would reduce crime, increase educational attainment and improve health. The most striking difference is related to the perceived personal gain: while 32.1% of the youngest age group thought a basic income would benefit them and their family, this was only 7% among the elderly. As argued above, this is probably due to the fact that most people above the age of 65 are no longer active on the labour market and already receive a state pension. Accordingly, it seems that elderly people's opposition to a basic income is to a large extent driven by considerations of self-interest.

Additionally, the opposition from elderly people also comes from the fact that many of them agreed with the statements that a basic income would disincentivize work (52%), that social benefits should be selectively targeted at poor people rather than universally granted to everyone (48%), that basic income is unaffordable (44%) and that welfare support should be provided through in-kind services rather than cash payments (44%). Young people were less convinced of the assumption that basic income would reduce work incentives (37.7%) and would prove too expensive (31.6%). By contrast, they were more in favour of the idea that social benefits should be selective (44.2%) or be provided in kind (48.8%). This suggests that a considerable proportion of young people may be equally (or more) supportive of policies that could be seen as alternatives (or supplements) to a basic income, including means-tested social assistance and universal basic services (Gough, 2019). The other arguments against basic income that were presented in the Populus survey—which argued that it would cause inflation and that there is no need for it because the current welfare system works well—were endorsed least by all age groups.

As shown in Fig. 4.14, the results from the Ipsos MORI survey demonstrate that there are barely any age differences in the perceived convincingness of the different arguments in favour of basic income. For most of the arguments, the difference between the age groups is not much

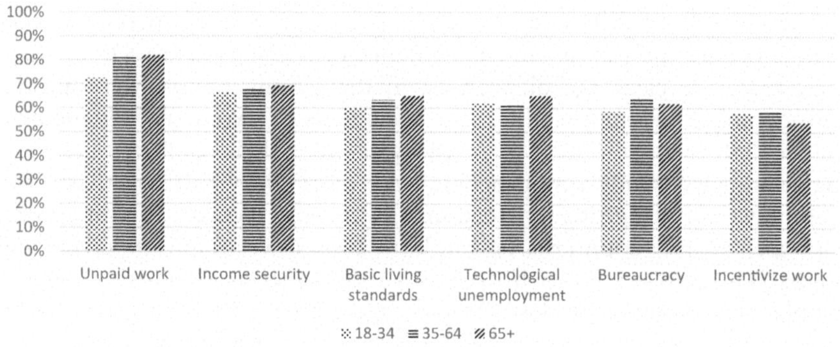

Fig. 4.14 Arguments for basic income in the UK, by age (*Source* Ipsos MORI [2017]. Question wording: see Fig. 4.3. The graph presents the percentage of respondents who endorsed the respective arguments within the respective age groups)

larger than 5 percentage points. This means that young people were not more supportive of the specific arguments in favour of basic income that were presented in this survey than they were of the arguments presented in the surveys discussed above. However, this does not necessarily mean that the findings from the different surveys contradict each other. In fact, there are some notable similarities. For example, both the Ipsos MORI and the Populus survey show that people of different ages have relatively similar opinions about basic income's ability to provide greater incentives to work than the existing welfare system. In a similar vein, both the Ipsos MORI and the Tisser Solidarity survey demonstrate that elderly people are more likely to endorse the revaluation of unpaid domestic work as an argument in favour of basic income. The only substantial age difference found among the Ipsos MORI respondents is that elderly people were more likely than younger people to think that a basic income would encourage unpaid work (the means are 82% and 72.4%, respectively). This could indicate that elderly people care more about the impact of basic income on unpaid work than their younger counterparts, who may consider other policy outcomes as more important.

Whether different age groups emphasize different policy outcomes when shaping their support for or opposition against basic income is an empirical question that can be assessed with the help of the BABEL experiment, conducted in 2021 in Belgium. As explained earlier, the experiment asked respondents to re-evaluate their support for basic income after they had been informed about the results of a (fictive) scientific study on the likely outcomes of introducing a basic income in Belgium. Table 4.6 shows the mean level of support for basic income per policy outcome included in the experiment on a scale from 0 to 100 and seems to confirm that elderly people attach greater value to the impact that a basic income would have on unpaid work in the form of informal caregiving. When it was suggested that the number of carers would increase, elderly people supported basic income to a greater extent than when it was suggested to decrease or stagnate (the respective means are 48, 41.4 and 40.9). This pattern is not found among younger age groups, who were about equally supportive of a basic income that increases, decreases or stabilizes the number of informal caregivers active in Belgium.

Table 4.6 Support for basic income with different policy outcomes, by age

	18–34	*35–64*	*65+*
Poverty			
Decrease	57.0	53.1	47.9
Stagnate	52.3	46.5	42.9
Increase	42.3	44.5	38.5
Income inequality			
Decrease	59.5	50.7	46.0
Stagnate	45.8	49.4	41.8
Increase	45.6	43.9	42.4
Unemployment			
Decrease	57.3	53.4	49.2
Stagnate	46.5	42.5	43.7
Increase	47.3	48.3	37.5
Entrepreneurship			
Decrease	48.1	44.1	40.0
Stagnate	52.6	48.6	44.1
Increase	50.8	50.9	46.2
Informal caregiving			
Decrease	49.3	46.7	41.4
Stagnate	52.4	46.9	40.9
Increase	49.6	50.4	48.0

Source BABEL Survey (2021). Question wording: see Fig. 4.11. The table presents the mean score for each outcome in the experiment for the respective age groups

The BABEL experiment also demonstrates that elderly people care somewhat more than young people about the effects of basic income on entrepreneurship. Table 4.6 shows that the elderly (as well as the middle age group) were slightly more supportive of basic income if it would increase rather than decrease the number of entrepreneurs in Belgium (the respective means for the oldest category are 46.1 and 40). This is not the case for young people, who seem to care somewhat more about the outcomes of basic income in terms of poverty and income inequality. If young people are told that these would increase after a basic income scheme has been introduced, there is a significant decrease in their support level. The same holds for elderly people, but to a lesser extent. With regard to poverty, young people showed less support for a basic income that increases rather than decreases the number of poor people in Belgium (the mean is 42.3 and 57, respectively). This difference is slightly smaller among elderly people (the respective means are 38.5 and 47.9). A similar pattern is observed for income inequality, as the decrease in support in case of a negative outcome is larger for young people than for their elderly counterparts (the respective means are 45.6 and 59.5, and 42.4 and 46). For unemployment, both young people and elderly people are equally less in favour of a basic income that increases rather than decreases the number of unemployed people in Belgium. Hence, the importance of this particular policy outcome does not seem to differ between the age groups.

These results suggest that elderly people's opposition to a basic income scheme can be weakened if they are told that it would yield positive policy outcomes. It should nevertheless be noted that elderly people continue to be less supportive of basic income than their younger counterparts, even when its outcomes are predicted to be positive. In fact, support for basic income never reaches the mid-point of the response scale (which ranged from 0 to 100) for the elderly. This may relate to the fact that elderly people are less likely to see basic income as offering them any personal gain (as shown earlier). This interpretation is supported by the data from the BABEL experiment, in which respondents were also asked to what extent they think that introducing a basic income would be of personal benefit to them. The results clearly show that elderly people were less likely to think that they would benefit from a basic income than their younger counterparts. On a scale from 0 ('no personal benefit') to 100 ('a lot of personal benefit'), the mean score for people aged between 18 and 34 is 51.2, it is 44.3 for people between 35 and 64, and only 28.9 for people above the age of 65. This again confirms the theory that elderly people mainly oppose basic income out of self-interest.

To sum up, the evidence from the polls reveals both similarities and differences between age groups with regard to the types of arguments they endorse in relation to basic income and the importance they attach to various policy outcomes. Despite having different levels of support for basic income, young people and their elderly counterparts often agree on the predicted outcomes of introducing a basic income. For example, in the Tisser Solidarity Survey, all the different age groups most often selected the statement that basic income would reduce work incentives as their main argument for being against the introduction of the policy proposal. Likewise, all age groups in the Ipsos MORI and Populus surveys were equally convinced of the statement that a basic income would increase work incentives compared with the prevailing (largely means-tested) welfare system. Furthermore, the BABEL experiment shows that the different age groups were also affected in roughly the same way when provided with scientific information about the predicted outcomes of a basic income: when these are positive, support clearly increases (and vice versa). However, the different age groups seem to value different policy outcomes. It appears that the revaluation of unpaid work, in particular, is important for elderly people when shaping their support for basic income. Young people seem to attach somewhat greater importance to the effects of basic income on poverty and income inequality. Although the elderly also become relatively more supportive of basic income if it will yield positive outcomes, they generally remain opposed to the policy. This opposition seems first and foremost rooted in considerations of self-interest, in that most elderly people fail to see how they would personally benefit from the introduction of a basic income scheme.

4.2.2 Gender

In Chapters 2 and 3, it was shown that there are seldom large differences between men and women in support for various types of basic income. It could, nevertheless, be that men and women have very different reasons for supporting or opposing the policy proposals. For example, it seems plausible that women will mainly support basic income because it rewards unpaid work activities, such as informal caregiving for children or elderly relatives, which they still perform disproportionately more than men, despite women's vastly increased labour market participation and the changed gender roles (Shelton, 2006). Because of this, men may attach less importance to the impact of basic income on unpaid work, focusing instead on other policy outcomes, such as employment or entrepreneurship. At the same time, it could also be that many women fear that a basic income will become a form of subsidy for domestic work, pushing them back into the role of a housewife and out of the labour market. From that perspective, women may be more prone to *oppose* basic income because it rewards and encourages (mostly female-provided) informal caregiving. This type of feminist critique has been suggested by scholars (for example, Robeyns, 2000), but it remains unclear how this resonates with the opinions of 'the woman on the street'. In the following, I investigate the extent to which there are gender differences in the arguments people endorse or find important with regard to basic income. This analysis is explorative in nature, as it is difficult to formulate clear hypotheses about such gender differences. Empirically, I rely on the same set of surveys as in the previous section.

The first of these is the Tisser Solidarity Survey conducted in 1995 in the Netherlands. In line with the findings from the previous chapters, the survey shows that men are slightly more supportive of basic income than women, although the difference is relatively small (22% and

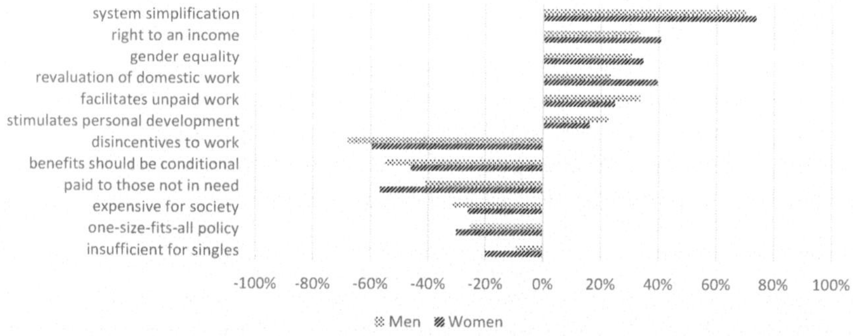

Fig. 4.15 Arguments for and against basic income in the Netherlands, by gender (*Source* TISSER Solidarity Survey [1995]. Question wording: see Fig. 4.1. The graph presents the percentage of proponents/opponents of basic income who endorsed the respective arguments in favour of/against basic income per gender. Negative percentages are used for the arguments against basic income)

16.5%, respectively). As shown in Fig. 4.15, there are also some gender differences in the arguments people selected to justify their support for or opposition to the introduction of a basic income scheme. Although men and women agreed that the most important argument in favour of basic income was the simplification of the existing social security system, women were more likely than men to select the revaluation of domestic work as a reason to support basic income (39.6% and 23.6%, respectively). Women also more often than men chose the argument about the right to a personal income for everyone as a reason to support basic income (40.7% and 33.3%, respectively). Interestingly, there was no gender gap with regard to the argument that a basic income would 'encourage a more fair division of informal and formal work between men and women'. Furthermore, men more often based their support for basic income on the argument that it would 'make it easier for people to do socially useful but unpaid work' than women (33.5% and 24.8%, respectively). With regard to the arguments against basic income, men more often than women selected the statement that social benefits should be conditional on work willingness (55% and 46.1%, respectively), and that a basic income would reduce work incentives (67.9% and 59.5%, respectively). By contrast, with regard to the universality aspect women appear to oppose basic income more than men do, as they were more likely to choose the argument that social benefits should be restricted to those in need (56.7% and 41.1%, respectively). Women were also more likely than men to oppose basic income because it would 'not suffice for single people to get by' (20.1% and 9.1%, respectively). This is probably due to the fact that female-headed single households have traditionally faced a significantly higher risk of poverty than their male-headed counterparts (Kramer et al., 2015).

Whereas the Tisser Solidarity Survey reveals some clear gender differences, these are practically non-existent in other, more recent surveys. As shown in Fig. 4.16, the results from the Populus survey (conducted in the UK in 2018) show that men tend to be somewhat more likely than women to think that basic income would have positive policy outcomes. With regard to the arguments against basic income, it can be seen that men were somewhat more likely to believe that it would cause inflation or that it would be unaffordable. Women were somewhat more likely to argue that a basic income should not be implemented because it is better to provide in-kind services than cash benefits. However, the differences are always small, at around 5 percentage points. The data from the UK also does not support the earlier finding (from the Tisser survey) that women are more likely to think that social benefits should be selectively targeted at poor people rather than universally granted to all. Overall, the findings from the Populus survey show barely any substantial gender differences in the arguments endorsed in relation to basic income. A similar pattern is observed in the Ipsos MORI survey, conducted in the UK in 2017, in that there are also no notable gender differences in the perceived convincingness of different arguments in favour of basic income (see Appendix 5 for the results). Strikingly, men and women do not differ with regard to the extent to which they agree with the statement that a basic income would reward and encourage unpaid work (77% and 80%, respectively), such as caregiving or voluntary work. In addition, the BABEL experiment, conducted in Belgium in 2021, also does not reveal any substantial gender differences in the type of policy outcomes (including informal caregiving) people attach importance to when shaping their support for basic income (see Appendix 5 for the results).

Overall, most of the available survey evidence suggests that men and women do not differ much in the arguments they endorse or find important in relation to basic income. This confirms the conclusion made in the previous chapters that gender alone is not an important factor determining support for basic income.

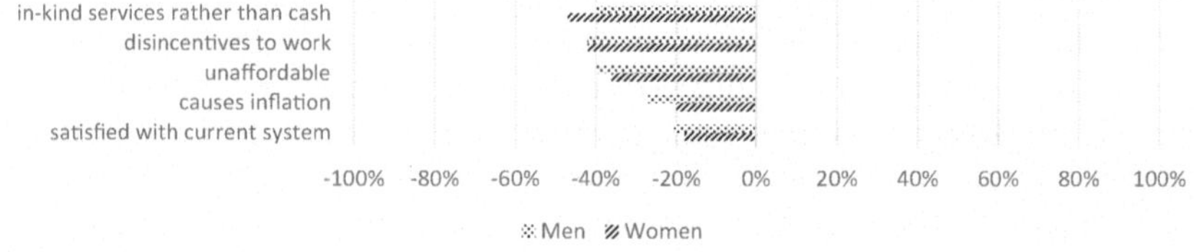

Fig. 4.16 Arguments for and against basic income in the UK, by gender (*Source* Populus [2018]. Question wording: see Fig. 4.2. The graph presents the percentage of respondents, by gender, who endorsed the respective arguments in favour of/against basic income. Please note that negative percentages are used for arguments against basic income)

4.2.3 *Political Ideology*

With regard to political ideology, the previous chapters have demonstrated that right-wing voters are consistently less supportive of basic income than their left-wing counterparts. It is less clear, however, *why* this is the case. Which types of arguments lie beneath the right-wing opposition? Do right-wing people dislike basically everything about basic income, or do they also see some positives? If so, what are these positives? Conversely, what makes left-wing voters more supportive of basic income? Which arguments do they find convincing or unconvincing? Furthermore, can the initial positions of these respective ideological groups be altered through the political framing of basic income? Can right-wing conservatives be persuaded to support basic income if they receive information that it would produce positive results on policy outcomes they may value, such as a reduction in state bureaucracy, an increase in entrepreneurship, a strengthening of individual financial freedom or a revaluation of unpaid work and family life? Similarly, to what extent would left-wing liberals reduce their support when they are told that basic income could also have negative consequences, such as an increase in poverty or unemployment? In the following, I mainly address these issues with the help of survey experiments that randomly vary the potential outcomes of a basic income between respondents with a different political ideology. This is because, much to my surprise, most of the traditional opinion polls discussed earlier to describe the arguments people endorse for and against basic income do not include a suitable measurement of political ideology.

A clear exception in this regard is the Ipsos MORI survey in the UK, as this asked respondents about their voting intentions. Here, the focus is on comparing those who intended to vote for the right-wing Conservative Party with those who intended to vote for the left-wing Labour Party. These were by far the two largest political parties in the UK at the time of the survey (2017). As would be expected, support for the introduction of a basic income was considerably lower among Conservative voters (40%) than among Labour voters (63%). Accordingly, it is no surprise that the former were more sceptical about the positive outcomes of basic income than the latter. As shown in Fig. 4.17, Labour supporters seemed convinced by all the arguments in favour of basic income presented in the survey. This notably applies to the idea that a basic income would reward and encourage unpaid work, such as caregiving or volunteering (which 86% of Labour voters agreed with). People who intended to vote

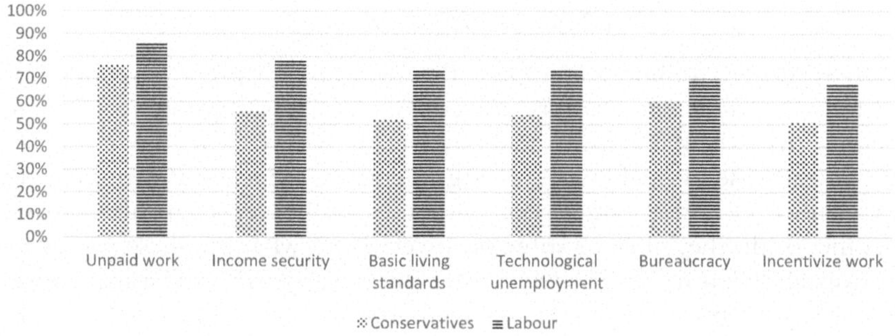

Fig. 4.17 Arguments for basic income, by political ideology (*Source* Ipsos MORI [2017]. Question wording: see Fig. 4.3. The graph presents the percentage of respondents who endorsed the respective arguments within the respective political groups)

for the Labour Party also believed that basic income would help to reduce income insecurity (78%), increase basic living standards (74%), deal with the problem of technological unemployment (74%) and reduce bureaucracy (70%). The least convincing argument—although still supported by 68% of Labour voters—was that basic income would do away with the prevailing unemployment traps by proving greater incentives for people (on a low-income) to work. By contrast, Conservative voters generally found these arguments less convincing (with most arguments being endorsed by about 50%). There are nevertheless two clear exceptions to this. First, most supporters of the Conservative Party (76%) agreed that a basic income would lead to a revaluation of unpaid work. It is here that the political left and the political right in the UK seem to find common ground regarding the outcomes of basic income. The same applies—although to a lesser extent—to for the idea that a basic income would reduce bureaucracy, which was endorsed by 60% of Conservative voters. It seems no coincidence that these particular arguments find greater support among Conservative voters, as they clearly relate to justifications that are often used by right-wing political elites in support of basic income, arguing that it could restore family life and make the welfare state less bureaucratic (for example, Murray, 2008).

Notwithstanding some important exceptions, the results from the Ipsos MORI survey in the UK demonstrate that right-wing voters are generally more sceptical about the positive outcomes of basic income

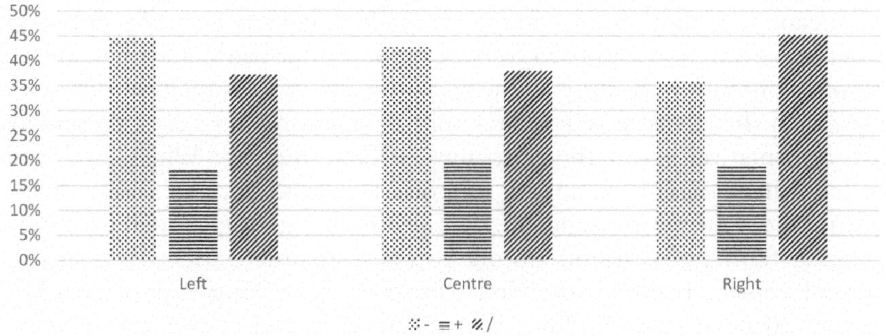

Fig. 4.18 Opinion change after hearing about policy outcomes, by political ideology (*Source* BABEL Survey [2021]. The graph presents the percentage of respondents who decreased [−] or increased [+] their support, or did not change their opinion [/] after they were told about the policy outcomes of basic income within the respective ideological groups)

than their left-wing counterparts. For the time being, we can only assume that this ideological cleavage also exists in countries other than the UK. Although the previous chapters have shown that support for basic income is often lower among right-wing voters (especially in Western European countries), the scarcity in available data prevents us from making the same claim about the arguments in favour of basic income. The fact of the matter is that we currently do not know whether left-wing voters are always more likely to think that basic income will have positive outcomes whereas right-wing voters are more likely to see negative outcomes. There is nevertheless some research that has investigated the extent to which right-wing voters can be persuaded of the positive outcomes of basic income, or vice versa, whether left-wing voters can be convinced to go along with its negative outcomes. The results from the BABEL experiment, conducted in Belgium in 2021, seem to suggest that the former is harder to achieve than the latter.

As explained earlier, the BABEL experiment asked respondents to re-evaluate their support for basic income after they had been informed about the results of a (fictive) scientific study on the likely outcomes of introducing a basic income in Belgium. As shown in Fig. 4.18, almost half of the right-wing voters (45.2%) did not change their opinion after seeing these potential outcomes. Those who did so, mostly became less supportive (35.7%) rather than more supportive (19.1%). Taken together, this means that most right-wing voters either remained equally opposed or became even more opposed to basic income after being informed about its policy outcomes. Among left-wing voters, we see a somewhat different pattern, in that there was a greater shift in opinion after being presented with information about the outcomes of basic income. While 44.7% of the left-wing voters became less supportive of basic income, only 18.2% became more supportive and 37.1% did not change their initial position. A similar tendency is found among voters who situate themselves in the political centre, being neither left-wing nor right-wing supporters. My interpretation of these findings is that left-wing and centre voters more easily withdraw their (relatively greater) support for basic income if they are told that it could also have negative consequences. Right-wing voters, by contrast, seem less sensitive to this type of information. If this interpretation is correct, it would mean that the above-discussed negativity bias in support for basic income applies more to left-wing and centre voters than it does to their right-wing counterparts.

Table 4.7, which shows the mean level of support for basic income per policy outcome included in the BABEL experiment, to some extent supports the interpretation that left-wing voters are more likely to withdraw their support if basic income would yield negative outcomes. This is especially the case concerning poverty, as support among left-wing voters is much lower when basic income is said to increase poverty compared with when it is claimed to decrease poverty (the respective means are 42 and 62, on a scale from 0 to 100). Although basic income is widely seen (mainly by its advocates) as a promising instrument to fight poverty, some microsimulation studies have shown that under certain conditions, poverty could also increase after the introduction of such a scheme (for example, Browne & Immervoll, 2017). If this were to happen, left-wing voters would presumably be quick to withdraw their support. Although the same pattern is observed for centre and right-wing voters, the reduction in support in the case of a poverty increase is markedly smaller than among left-wing voters. Furthermore, while support also decreases among left-wingers if basic income is said to increase income inequality or unemployment, this decrease is not as sharp as with poverty. Left-wing people's opinion about basic income does not seem influenced by the outcomes it could produce in terms of entrepreneurship or informal care.

Right-wing voters, by contrast, seem somewhat more sensitive to the effects of basic income on entrepreneurship, which can be inferred from the fact that support was slightly greater among this group if there would be an increase rather than a decrease in the number of entrepreneurs active in Belgium (the respective means are 45 and 38). However, it seems that right-wing voters care even more about the effects a basic income would have on the level of unemployment. Among this ideological group, support for basic income was much lower when it was stated that it would increase the number of unemployed people compared with if it would decrease (the respective means are 34 and 48). Right-wing voters also reduced their support for basic income if it meant an increase in poverty or income inequality, but this reduction is smaller than for the unemployment outcome. The potential impact of basic income on the number of informal caregivers did not seem to be an important consideration for right-wing voters. For voters who situated themselves in the political centre, the effects of basic income on informal care also did little to change their support for the policy idea. Other than that, these voters

Table 4.7 Support for basic income with different policy outcomes, by political ideology

	Left	*Centre*	*Right*
Poverty			
Decrease	62.0	53.2	47.1
Stagnate	53.4	48.9	38.0
Increase	42.1	45.2	38.6
Income inequality			
Decrease	56.3	54.2	45.4
Stagnate	52.8	48.9	38.0
Increase	49.4	44.0	40.5
Unemployment			
Decrease	60.5	54.0	48.2
Stagnate	50.2	47.9	42.5
Increase	48.4	45.5	34.2
Entrepreneurship			
Decrease	52.1	45.0	38.3
Stagnate	53.9	51.1	40.9
Increase	52.3	51.3	45.0
Informal caregiving			
Decrease	51.0	47.7	40.2
Stagnate	53.7	48.1	41.4
Increase	53.6	51.4	43.0

Source BABEL Survey (2021). Question wording: see Fig. 4.11. The table presents the mean score for each outcome in the experiment for the respective ideological groups do not seem to prioritize one particular policy outcome over the others in the way their left-wing and right-wing counterparts do (with poverty and unemployment, respectively). More generally, these findings suggest that different policy outcomes carry a different weight for different ideological groups in shaping their support for the introduction of a basic income.

In addition to the BABEL experiment, there are three other survey experiments (conducted in the US) that are informative about the way in which different ideological groups respond to the political framing of basic income. The first of these, by Jordan and colleagues (2022), was already mentioned earlier when discussing the presence of a negativity bias in support for basic income (see Sect. 4.1.2). The study nevertheless found that only certain ideological groups reacted more strongly to negative than to positive frames about basic income. More specifically, it turns out that this negativity bias was restricted to conservative Americans. Importantly, this not only included Republican voters, but also those who identified as conservative Democrats or as conservative Independents. All three groups became significantly *less* supportive of basic income after being presented with negative frames about it. They did not, however, change to being *more* supportive after being given positive frames. By contrast, Americans who categorized their political views as 'liberal' were unmoved by both negative and positive framing of basic income. These findings from the US seem to point in the opposite direction to the BABEL experiment in Belgium, which showed that left-wing voters are *more* rather than *less* prone to negativity bias than their right-wing counterparts. It could well be that the difference in the findings is (at least partly) due to the fact that the respective experiments presented different types of arguments against basic income. In the study by Jordan et al. (2022), the negatively framed arguments were that basic income would encourage laziness and is too costly. Both of these have frequently been cited as reasons to oppose basic income by right-wing elites, in the US and elsewhere. The results might have been very different if the study had also included the argument that a basic income would not reduce or could even increase, the existing level of poverty. In such a scenario, in which the critique is much more left-wing oriented, liberal Americans might equally have reduced their support for basic income (as shown by the BABEL experiment). Hence, it seems reasonable to assume that whether the negativity bias in support for basic income differs across ideological groups depends to a large extent on the specific contra-arguments that are presented. Nevertheless, we cannot exclude the possibility that the differences may also stem from the fact that the experiments were conducted in two countries with highly diverging political contexts: Belgium and the US. Unfortunately, there currently is no cross-national data available to test this proposition.

The second survey experiment, conducted in 2021 by Yeung (2022) among a sample of 2,530 Americans (who were recruited via Lucid), was also inspired by the idea that left-wing liberals and right-wing conservatives may react very differently to political frames about basic income. The experiment aimed to uncover whether conservatives can be persuaded to give up their resistance to a basic income scheme if the policy is framed as being in line with supposedly core conservative values, such as equality of opportunity, self-responsibility and laissez-faire government. All the respondents were first told that 'In the United States, some cities are considering—or have already started—to implement pilot programs for universal basic income (UBI)'. They were then given a description of basic income that matches the one in the European Social Survey (see Fig. 2.8). While the control group was not presented with any further information, the two experimental groups were each given a different framing of the likely advantages of basic income. Participants in the first experimental group were presented with an equalizing-opportunity frame, which stated that 'an important future of UBI is that it will create a level playing field because poor households will also be financially empowered. This encourages people to be more self-reliant and self-responsible'. The second experimental group was given a limiting-government frame, stating that 'an important feature of UBI is that it will limit government because some existing government programs for the poor will be cut or replaced by UBI. This helps to minimize government bureaucracy'. The underlying assumption was that these specific frames would increase conservatives' support for basic income (because these align with the values they hold) more than they would increase liberals' support for the policy. To see whether this was the case, respondents from all three groups were asked to indicate their support for the introduction of a basic income scheme in the US, on a scale from 0 (strongly against) to 6 (strongly in favour).

The results from Yeung's experiment clearly refute the hypothesis that positive framing of basic income could increase the level of support among conservatives. Compared with the control group (1.28), the average level of support for basic income was 1.36 in the equalizing-opportunity frame and 1.39 in the limiting-government frame. Although there was thus a small increase in support, the conclusion is that most conservatives continued to oppose the introduction of basic income even after they were exposed to arguments that were supposedly tailored to core conservative values. This confirms the findings from the BABEL experiment in Belgium and the experiment by Jordan et al. (2022), both of which demonstrate that right-wing conservative voters are unlikely to abandon their opposition to basic income even if they are told that it will yield positive outcomes. According to Yeung (2022), this is because most respondents who identify as conservative (75% to be exact), who are also Republicans, tend to associate the concept of basic income with the Democratic Party. It could, therefore, be that the conservatives in Yeung's study were not persuaded by the positive frames because they disagreed with the message, but because they disliked the alleged messenger—Democratic politicians. It would be interesting to see what happens to conservatives' support for basic income when not only the message but also the messenger of the political frame is specified. It is possible that the positive frames would have had an effect on the support of conservative voters if they had been put forward by representatives of the Republican Party. For the time being, we know little about such messenger effects in the political framing of basic income, as there are no studies that have investigated this.

The evidence from the third survey experiment, conducted in 2021 by Thomas et al. (2023) among a sample of 628 Americans (recruited via MTurk), suggests that some messages nevertheless can persuade conservatives to support the introduction of a basic income. In this experiment, respondents were randomly assigned to one of three groups. The first, the control group, is only given a description of basic income, stating: 'The Basic Income policy would streamline many government programs and provide a single, efficient monthly payment to all citizens, regardless of employment status, sufficient to cover basic needs.' The second group were presented with the additional information that 'Freedom is an important value for Americans. The goal of this "Financial Freedom" policy is to get the government out of deciding which services are available to people and instead enable individuals to decide for themselves how to best meet their needs'. According to Thomas and colleagues (2023), this 'financial freedom' message should convince conservatives to support basic income because it fits with the core conservative value that citizens ought to be economically independent from the government. American liberals, as was argued, also value freedom, but more in a social than an

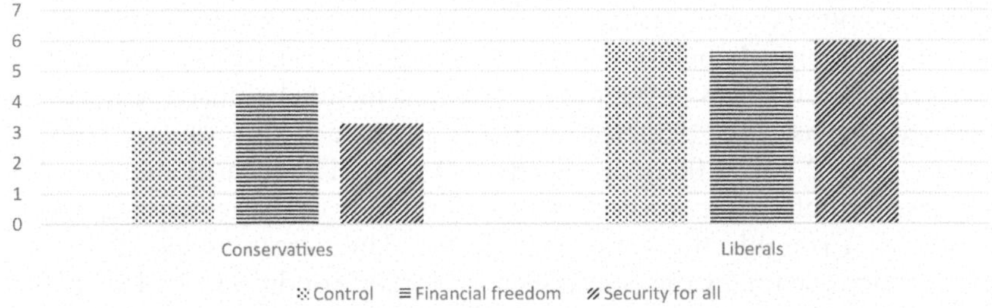

Fig. 4.19 Support for basic income with different political framing, by political ideology (*Source* Thomas et al. [2022]. Question wording: 'To what extent do you support or oppose this Basic Income policy?' The graph presents the mean score for basic income among the respective ideological groups)

economic sense and should therefore not be triggered as much by this particular message. The third group were given the additional information that 'Security is an important value for Americans. The goal of this 'Social Security for All' policy is to protect Americans and their families against financial shocks such as job losses'. Here, the assumption is that this 'social security for all' message should mainly increase support for basic income among liberals (because it reflects their desire to provide care for the needy and vulnerable), and less so among conservatives. To test this, respondents were asked to indicate their support for basic income on a scale from 0 ('oppose a great deal') to 7 ('support a great deal'). Respondents were also asked a range of other questions about basic income, including the perceived fit of the policy with their values, their stance towards some common arguments against basic income, their stereotypes about the recipients of basic income, their desire to receive the benefit themselves and the perceived effectiveness of the policy.

As shown in Fig. 4.19, the expectations of Thomas et al. (2023) are confirmed by the experimental evidence. American conservatives who were exposed to the message about financial freedom were more supportive of basic income compared with the conservatives in the control group, who were not given any additional information (on the scale from 0 to 7, the respective means are 4.24 and 3.08). Although the difference may seem small, the freedom message was able to change conservatives' position from moderate opposition to moderate support for basic income. Furthermore, the results show that the freedom message also increased conservatives' resistance to contra-arguments, rejection of negative stereotypes of benefit recipients, desire to receive a basic income and perceived effectiveness of the policy. This was mainly because the freedom message increased the perceived moral fit of basic income among conservatives (from 2.4 to 3.08 on a scale from 0 to 5). The security message did not have a similar effect on conservatives' support for basic income, which remained at roughly the same level (3.28). The perceived moral fit also did not increase under the 'social security for all' condition (2.41). People who identified as politically liberal were unaffected by both messages. Instead, liberals were relatively supportive of basic income and reported a substantial moral fit for each condition.

In sum, the evidence presented here first of all demonstrates that right-wing voters are generally more sceptical about the positive outcomes of basic income than their left-wing counterparts—at least in the UK, although with some exceptions, such as its potential to revalue unpaid work. Most of the evidence also suggests that it is difficult to persuade right-wing voters to support basic income through political framing. The BABEL experiment in Belgium shows that most right-wingers either do not change their opinion or become less supportive of basic income after they are informed about its potential outcomes. There is a significant decrease in support among right-wing voters in particular when basic income is stated to increase unemployment. The experiment by Jordan et al. (2022) in the US confirms that conservatives reduce their support for basic income if they are told that it would encourage laziness or that it is too expensive. The same conservatives do not increase their support for basic income when they are presented with positively framed arguments stating that basic income would help to reduce automation-induced income inequality and unemployment. In a similar vein, Yeung (2022) finds that American conservatives do not become more supportive of basic income after being exposed to core conservative values stressing the potential of the policy to equalize opportunities, increase self-responsibility and limit government bureaucracy. By contrast, Thomas et al. (2023) observe that American conservatives can be persuaded to support basic income if they are told that it would increase personal financial freedom, which appears to have a significant moral fit with conservative values. American liberals are largely unaffected by both positively and negatively framed arguments about basic income. This differs from the findings in the BABEL experiment, which show that left-wing voters become less supportive of basic income after hearing about its potential (negative) outcomes. In particular when basic income is said to increase poverty, there is a substantial decrease in support among left-wing voters.

Summary Box 4.2 Individual Differences in Reasons for Supporting or Opposing Basic Income

Overall, the available survey evidence suggests that there are both notable differences and striking similarities between various groups with different characteristics in terms of the arguments they endorse or find important in relation to basic income.

With regard to age, it is found that despite having different levels of support, younger and older people can have relatively similar opinions concerning the predicted outcomes of basic income. For example, in the UK all age groups seem to agree that a basic income would provide greater work incentives than the existing (largely means-tested) welfare system. At the same time, there are also clear age differences: while young people are more positive about some outcomes (for example, the potential of basic income to increase educational attainment), their elderly counterparts are more positive about other outcomes (for example, basic income's potential to reward and encourage unpaid work). More generally, this points towards the fact that different age groups value different policy outcomes in relation to basic income. It should nevertheless be noted that elderly people always remain relatively opposed to basic income, even in the scenario that it would yield positive outcomes. This is mainly because they do not see it as offering any personal benefit.

With regard to political ideology, it is found that right-wing voters are considerably more sceptical about the positive outcomes of a basic income—which is fully in line with their lower level of support reported in the previous chapters. It also proves rather difficult to persuade right-wing voters to support a basic income with political frames that highlight its positive policy outcomes, even if those outcomes are designed to align with core conservative values, such as equality of opportunity, self-responsibility and limited government. The only exception in this regard is the finding that conservative voters in the US seem to slightly increase their support for basic income when they are presented with a message claiming that it would increase people's personal financial freedom. By contrast, it seems easier to further decrease right-wing voters' support, using negatively framed arguments about basic income, especially when these arguments suggest that there would be a reduction of work incentives. Such negativity bias is also found for left-wing voters, at least in Belgium, where they become less supportive of basic income after being exposed to a scenario in which it would have negative policy outcomes. This occurs in particular when basic income would cause an increase in poverty.

With regard to gender, most of the evidence points towards the conclusion that there are barely any differences between men and women in terms of the arguments they endorse or find important in relation to basic income. This fits well with the finding from the previous chapters that gender is not a strong determinant of support for basic income.

Importantly, the available evidence can nevertheless only show the tip of the iceberg, as the number of surveys that provide information on both the reasons people have for supporting or opposing basic income and their individual characteristics is severely limited. Cross-national surveys—along the lines of the European Social Survey—that have standardized measurements for respondents' characteristics are thus greatly needed. This would allow future research to investigate in greater detail if, how, when, where and why various social groups differ in the reasons they have for supporting or opposing basic income in different countries.

References

Afscharian, D., Muliavka, V., Ostrowski, M. S., & Siegel, L. (2022). The State of the UBI Debate: Mapping the Arguments for and Against UBI. *Basic Income Studies, 17*(2), 213–237.

Arntz, M., Gregory, T., & Zierahn, U. (2016). *The Risk of Automation for Jobs in OECD Countries: A Comparative Analysis* (OECD Social, Employment and Migration Working Papers, No. 189). OECD Publishing.

Atkinson, A. (1996). The Case for a Participation Income. *The Political Quarterly, 67*(1), 67–70.

Browne, J., & Immervoll, H. (2017). Mechanics of Replacing Benefit Systems with a Basic Income: Comparative Results from a Microsimulation Approach. *The Journal of Economic Inequality, 15*(4), 325–344.

Delsen, L., & Schilpzand, R. (2019). Individual Preferences for the Unconditional Basic Income in the European Union. In L. Delsen (Ed.), *Empirical Research on an Unconditional Basic Income in Europe* (pp. 29–60). Springer.

Esping-Andersen, G. (1990). *The Three Worlds of Welfare Capitalism*. Princeton University Press.

Frey, C. B., & Osborne, M. A. (2017). The Future of Employment: How Susceptible Are Jobs to Computerisation? *Technological Forecasting and Social Change, 114*, 254–280.

Gough, I. (2019). Universal Basic Services: A Theoretical and Moral Framework. *The Political Quarterly, 90*(3), 534–542.

Herke, B., & Vicsek, L. (2022). The Attitudes of Young Citizens in Higher Education Towards Universal Basic Income in the Context of Automation—A Qualitative Study. *International Journal of Social Welfare, 33*(3), 310–322.

Jordan, S., Ferguson, G., & Haglin, K. (2022). Measuring and Framing Support for Universal Basic Income. *Social Policy & Administration, 56*(1), 138–147.

Kangas, O., Jauhiainen, S., Simanainen, M., & Ylikännö, M. (2021). *Experimenting with Unconditional Basic Income. Lessons from the Finnish BI Experiment 2017–2018*. Edward Elgar Publishing.

Kim, D., & Mah, J. S. (2021). Basic Income Policy of Korea. *Journal of Poverty, 27*(1), 15–32.

Kramer, K. Z., Myhra, L. L., Zuiker, V. S., & Bauer, J. W. (2015). Comparison of Poverty and Income Disparity of Single Mothers and Fathers Across Three Decades: 1990–2010. *Gender Issues, 33*, 22–41.

Laenen, T., Mulayi, M. L., Francisco, C., & Van Lancker, W. (2021). *Basic Income in Belgium (BABEL) Survey Codebook V1.* Centre for Sociological Research, KU Leuven. https://osf.io/7ghfs/

Laenen, T., Van Hooteghem, A., & Rossetti, F. (2022). The Multidimensionality of Public Support for Basic Income: A Vignette Experiment. *Journal of European Public Policy*. https://doi.org/10.1080/13501763.2022.2055112 [onlinefirst]

Legein, T., Vandeleene, A., Randour, F., Heyvaert, P., Perrez, J., & Reuchamps, M. (2018). Framing the Basic Income: An Experimental Study of How Arguments and Metaphors Influence Individuals' Opinion Formation. *Basic Income Studies, 13*(2). https://doi.org/10.1515/bis-2018-0010 [online only]

Martinelli, L. (2017). *Assessing the Case for a Universal Basic Income in the UK* (IPR Policy Brief). University of Bath.

Murray, C. (2008). Guaranteed Income as a Replacement for the Welfare State. *Basic Income Studies, 3*(2). https://doi.org/10.2202/1932-0183.1115 [online only]

Richards, D. R., & Steiger, T. L. (2021). Value Orientations and Support for Guaranteed Income. *Social Science Quarterly, 102*(6), 2733–2751.

Robeyns, I. (2000). Hush Money or Emancipation Fee? A Gender Analysis of Basic Income. In R. van der Veen & L. Groot (Eds.), *Basic Income on the Agenda. Policy Objectives and Political Chances* (pp. 121–136). Amsterdam University Press.

Roosma, F. (2022). A Struggle for Framing and Interpretation: The Impact of the 'Basic Income Experiments' on Social Policy Reform in the Netherlands. *European Journal of Social Security, 24*(3), 192–212.

Rossetti, F., Roosma, F., Laenen, T., & Abts, K. (2020). An Unconditional Basic Income? How Dutch Citizens Justify Their Opinions About a Basic Income and Work Conditionality. *Journal of International and Comparative Social Policy, 36*(3), 284–300.

Seong Yoo, Y., & Jooyoung, M. (2021). *The Public Perception Survey on Basic Income*. Gyeonggi Research Institute.

Shelton, B. A. (2006). Gender and Unpaid Work. In J. Saltzman Chafetz (Ed.), *Handbook of the Sociology of Gender* (pp. 375–390). Springer.

Simanainen, M., & Kangas, O. (2020). Speaking to Those Who Know It Best: Does Participation in an Experiment Explain Citizens' Attitudes to Basic Income? *Journal of International and Comparative Social Policy, 36*(3), 269–283.

Stambolieva, M. (2019). *Welfare State Transformation in the Yugoslav Successor States: From Social to Unequal*. Routledge.

Stam, K. (2015). *The Moral Duty to Work: A Cross-National and Longitudinal Study of the Causes and Consequences of Work Ethic Values in Contemporary Society* (Unpublished doctoral dissertation). Ridderprint.

Standing, G. (2020). *Battling Eight Giants: Basic Income Now*. I.B. Taurus.

Taylor-Gooby, P., & Leruth, B. (2018). *Attitudes, Aspirations and Welfare: Social Policy Directions in Uncertain Times*. Palgrave Macmillan.

Thomas, C. C., Walton, G. M., Reinhart, E. C., & Markus, H. R. (2023). Mitigating Welfare-Related Prejudice and Partisanship Among U.S. Conservatives with Moral Reframing of a Universal Basic Income Policy. *Journal of Experimental Social Psychology, 105*. https://doi.org/10.1016/j.jesp.2022.104424 [online only]

van der Veen, R. (2019). Basic Income Experiments in the Netherlands? *Basic Income Studies, 14*(1). https://doi.org/10.1515/bis-2018-0023 [online only]

Van Parijs, P., & Vanderborght, Y. (2017). *A Radical Proposal for a Free Society and a Sane Economy*. Harvard University Press.

Wright, R. E., & Przegalinska, A. (2022). *Debating Universal Basic Income. Pros, Cons, and Alternatives*. Palgrave Macmillan.

Yeung, E. S. (2022). Can Conservatives Be Persuaded? Framing Effects on Support for Universal Basic Income in the US. *Political Behavior*. https://doi.org/10.1007/s11109-022-09824-z [online first]

Zimmermann, K., Boljka, U., Rakar, T., & Filipovic Hrast, M. (2020). The Social Legitimacy of the Universal Basic Income from a Social Justice Perspective: A Comparative Analysis of Germany and Slovenia. *Journal of International and Comparative Social Policy, 36*(3), 301–331.

CHAPTER 5

Conclusion: Implications for the Political Feasibility of Basic Income

In this chapter, I discuss the implications of the most consistent and important findings from the previous chapters in terms of the political feasibility of introducing a basic income in the real world. More specifically, I identify eight political challenges that advocates of a basic income (in particular, in its fully universal and unconditional ideal-typical form) are likely to face. These are, to paraphrase Guy Standing (2020), 'eight giants' that will often have to be battled and defeated by those who seek to establish a basic income in a given context. Most of these relate to prospective constraints that have to be dealt with *before* a basic income could be introduced, in order to increase the likelihood of it happening. There will of course also be retrospective challenges that influence the performance and sustainability of a basic income *after* its implementation (De Wispelaere & Noguera, 2012). Although these are arguably important, I focus on prospective challenges, because the first task at hand for policy entrepreneurs is to get a basic income through the democratic decision-making process.

At the same time, each political challenge also comes with some political opportunities that basic income advocates may—now or in the future—be able to exploit. However, to find out whether these opportunities are likely to materialize, more research is needed. In light of this, I put forward a research agenda that aims to inspire future studies on the popularity and political feasibility of basic income. A key theme, cutting

© The Author(s), under exclusive license to Springer Nature Switzerland AG 2023

T. Laenen, *The Popularity of Basic Income*, Exploring the Basic Income Guarantee, https://doi.org/10.1007/978-3-031-29352-8_5

across the discussion of the political challenges and opportunities, as well as the presentation of the research agenda, is that basic income's popularity and political feasibility is very much context specific, as these things vary between countries, between regions within countries, and over time.

5.1 Eight Political Challenges and Their Opportunities

5.1.1 Political Opportunity Costs

The empirical analyses presented in this book suggest that basic income (the ideal-typical version of it in particular) faces relatively high political opportunity costs, because it is rarely *more* popular than some of the relevant competing policies. This is especially problematic for the political feasibility of basic income when those competing policy schemes already exist. In that case, policymakers will see little electoral gain from implementing a brand new basic income policy, as it does not offer the competitive advantage of being more popular among the general public. In such a scenario, not implementing a basic income will be free from electoral losses (which would only occur if basic income was considerably *more* popular than the existing policies). As a result, policymakers are more likely to stick to the status quo, since they lack a clear popular mandate to change it. In the event that a basic income is no more popular than a potential policy competitor, there is an equal playing field in which public opinion will not tip the balance to one side or the other. However, if basic income is *less* popular than the policy competitor, it is already fighting an uphill battle, because public opinion and political feasibility will rule in favour of the competing scheme.

Throughout the book, I have compared the popularity of basic income with that of several other policy schemes. Some of these are very different to a basic income. For example, the data from the International Social Survey Programme (ISSP) shows that in most countries, a guaranteed *income* scheme (although admittedly vaguely described) is about equally as popular as a guaranteed *employment* scheme (equally vaguely defined) that promises to provide everyone with a job rather than a cash payment. Accordingly, basic income does not have the competitive advantage of being more popular than a policy that some see as a more suitable alternative (Leff et al., 2019). The same applies to the idea of making the welfare state fully means tested, as data from the European Social Survey

(ESS) shows that in most countries, the popularity of mean-tested welfare is similar to that of a universal basic income. Likewise, the book demonstrates that the ideal-typical version of basic income—which is both fully universal and unconditional—is usually not more popular than other basic income types or cognates, and is often actually less popular. In particular, the survey evidence suggests that targeted types of basic income (that only include poor people or that exclude the rich) are somewhat more popular than their fully universal counterpart. This also applies to a negative income tax, which in the rare cases when it has been included in a survey has proved to be given a somewhat higher level of support than a universal basic income. Accordingly, these targeted versions of basic income have a competitive advantage in that they are more popular and thus politically more feasible. In a similar vein, I find that conditional types of basic income (which make access to the benefit, or the benefit level dependent on work-related or other activities) tend to be more popular than their fully unconditional counterpart. This mainly refers to a participation income (Atkinson, 1996), which is universally accessible in principle but in practice may exclude those who do not comply with the obligation to perform some kind of socially appreciated activity (such as caregiving, volunteering or working). There is also some evidence that (at least in Belgium) people would rather vary the amount of basic income according to work history than pay a flat-rate amount to everyone—as most existing social insurance schemes do. Lastly, it was also shown that basic income schemes for specific age groups—such as the elderly or people with under-age children—are more popular than a basic income for everyone. This suggests that categorically universal schemes, such as a universal child benefit or a people's pension, have greater political feasibility than a non-categorical, universal basic income.

Taken together, these findings imply that a basic income does not have the competitive advantage of being more popular than competing policies, some of which already exist and would thereby burden the potential policy with high political opportunity costs. Importantly, these include the three constellations that are most common in modern-day welfare states: contribution-based social insurance, means-tested social assistance and universal but categorical schemes (Clasen & van Oorschot, 2002). Given that these types of welfare schemes are not significantly *less* popular than a basic income, it seems unlikely that electorally motivated policymakers would abandon them any time soon. At the same time, the survey findings may also offer some hope to advocates of a basic income, in particular to those who seek to introduce the ideal-typical version of it. This is because basic income is hardly ever as highly ***unpopular*** as one may have expected it to be. Surveys often show that about half of the respondents support a basic income, suggesting that there is rarely fierce opposition among the general public. In fact, in some countries (such as Lithuania) or regions (such as the French-speaking part of Belgium), support is significantly higher, which suggests that the political feasibility of basic income is also relatively high there. As I explain below, these contexts are nevertheless often characterized by a demand-capacity conflict, in which popular demand for basic income outweighs the institutional capacity to implement it. The fact that basic income is not inherently unpopular in most contexts does, however, provide fertile ground on which policy entrepreneurs can build to create further support. I will offer some suggestions on how to possibly achieve that in the next sections.

5.1.2 The Problem of Cheap Support

Although basic income may be given relatively high levels of support in surveys, this could still turn out to be what De Wispelaere (2015) has called 'cheap support'. Saying 'yes' to a basic income in a survey setting does not necessarily mean also saying 'yes' to it in a concrete, real-life context (for example, at the ballot box). The existing survey measurements are also somewhat limited in this regard, as they mostly ask about people's principled support for the introduction of a basic income scheme in their country, but generally do not ask about their intended political behaviour. For example, would people vote for a political party if it were to propose a basic income scheme, or vice versa, withdraw their vote for that party? Furthermore, are people willing to support (or oppose) basic income through political acts, such as signing or starting a petition, writing a letter to a politician and organizing or participating in a public rally? Unfortunately, the survey evidence presented in this book cannot indicate whether the observed support for basic income is 'cheap'. There is nevertheless one highly relevant source of information that suggests this may be the case: the 2016 Swiss referendum. In that legally binding referendum, citizens could cast their vote on the possible inclusion of a new article in the Swiss constitution that would guarantee the right to a basic income, loosely defined as a monthly cash payment to all adult residents without any means test or work requirement (in line with the ideal-typical version of basic income). With only 23% of the participants voting 'yes' (Colombo et al., 2016), the outcome was clear: the Swiss did not *really* want to introduce a basic income. However, the relatively low proportion of people voting for basic income in the referendum stands in stark contrast to the numbers observed in surveys that tend to be higher (including in Switzerland: see, for example, Stadelmann-Steffen & Dermont, 2019).

There are at least two possible interpretations of this observation. The first is that surveys overestimate the actual level of popular support for basic income, because of the relative ease with which people can say 'yes' to something that has no direct consequences in real life—either for them or for society as a whole. If this interpretation is correct, one could argue that support for basic income as expressed in surveys is indeed to some extent 'cheap'. The second interpretation is that referenda may underestimate the actual level of support for basic income, because they are usually not representative of the whole population. In fact, only about 47% of the eligible population participated in the Swiss referendum, and voter turnout was disproportionally higher among those who tend to oppose basic income more strongly, such as high-income earners (see Sect. 5.1.6) and older people (Sect. 5.1.5) (Colombo et al., 2016). For now, it is impossible to tell whether one of these interpretations is more accurate than the other, or whether they are both correct. Nevertheless, they do indicate that if and when policy entrepreneurs manage to have some type of basic income assessed at the ballot box rather than in a survey, it is crucial that they put sufficient effort in mobilizing the groups that are most in favour of it. These are often specific to the context and the type of basic income, but—as discussed below—often include young people (see Sect. 5.1.5), those on a low income (Sect. 5.1.6) and left-wing voters (Sect. 5.1.7). If advocates succeed in having these groups represented (and perhaps even overrepresented), they stand a far better chance of winning the popular vote in favour of a basic income.

5.1.3 The Universality-Unconditionality Impasse

As mentioned in Sect. 5.1.1, the evidence presented in this book suggests that there is often greater popular support for basic income varieties that deviate from the ideal-typical version. In particular, support seems to increase if limits are set to either the universality or unconditionality of a basic income scheme. With regard to the former, people seem to have a slight preference for basic income schemes that are limited in terms of universality, because they exclude (newly arrived) migrants by setting residency or citizenship requirements, or because they are restricted to certain income groups by targeting poor people only ('poverty testing') or leaving out the rich ('affluence testing'). With regard to unconditionality, people generally favour schemes that are conditional on socially appreciated activities, such as caregiving, volunteering or working (as in a participation income). This preference for targeted and conditional types of basic income is probably due to the fact that these schemes are able to exclude groups that are generally considered less deserving of social welfare, because they are perceived to make limited contributions to society or are not seen as being in need of assistance (Laenen et al., 2022). Further, having both at the same time—that is, a basic income that is fully universal *and* fully unconditional—tends to be the least preferred option. Importantly, this pattern is not only observed among the public at large, but also among the political constituencies that are most likely to support the introduction of a basic income, such as young people (see Sect. 5.1.5), low-income groups (see Sect. 5.1.6) and left-wing voters (see Sect. 5.1.7). It, therefore, seems that the ideal-typical version of basic income has the least favourable prospects with regard to political feasibility.

This is highly problematic for its proponents, who typically insist that a basic income should be both universal and unconditional in order to reach its full potential (Van Parijs & Vanderborght, 2017). At the same time, it also offers political opportunities for those who are willing to compromise on one of these two core components of the ideal type. Advocates who are prepared to accept a basic income that is fully universal but not unconditional (as is the case in proposals for a participation income) stand a better chance of finding political approval for their plan than those who oppose any form of conditionality. Similarly, it seems that a basic income that is fully unconditional but not universal (for example, a negative income tax) has a higher likelihood of being politically feasible. Although the 'full package' will not be attained in either of these scenarios, it would bring most existing welfare systems considerably closer to the ideal-typical basic income as envisioned by its advocates. For the time being, those advocates may—with an eye on political feasibility—be better off if they either give up their demand for full universality or their demand for full unconditionality. This is not to say that the idea of combining full universality with full unconditionality should be abandoned permanently. In fact, this could remain the desired end goal in the long term. In order to reach this goal, it, nevertheless, seems more sensible to promote stepping stone policies that are more popular and thus politically more feasible than the ideal-typical basic income. For example, one could first argue for the introduction of a conditional participation income, and once that policy is established, try to convince people that it should be made fully unconditional.

5.1.4 Demand-Capacity Conflicts

Throughout the book, there are signs of several demand-capacity conflicts, in which popular demand for basic income is likely to be higher than the financial or administrative capacity that is available to implement it. Here, I identify three of these conflicts.

The first is related to the above-discussed finding that a conditional participation income is more popular and thus politically more feasible than a fully unconditional basic income. From this perspective, it seems that a participation income is more likely to be introduced by electorally-motivated policymakers. At the same time, many commentators have described a participation income as an administrative nightmare, as it would require an enormous and costly bureaucracy to monitor whether all its recipients are complying with their obligation to perform some kind of socially appreciated activity (De Wispelaere & Stirton, 2007; Torry, 2016). In other words, while a participation income is popular and politically feasible, it may be highly problematic from an administrative point of view. Hence, there is a situation of high popular demand but limited capacity to meet that demand. There are several potential solutions to this problem. One solution is to do without the strict monitoring of people's behaviour, so that there is a participation income on paper but not in practice. However, this would be likely to stir public opposition as it means that there would in reality be a fully unconditional basic income in place, which was not very popular to begin with because people prefer to exclude those who do not make a supposedly meaningful contribution to society. Another solution would be to improve the administrative feasibility of a participation income, by limiting the number of activities that qualify as 'participation', clearly defining these activities and possibly placing time limits on them (as is the case for many cash-for-care schemes, such as parental leave), and creating well-considered procedures to automatically check the activities. It is clearly beyond the scope of this book to investigate the administrative feasibility of a participation income in detail, but the main challenge for its advocates is to take steps forward so that the policy is not only popular and politically feasible, but also practical.

The second demand-capacity conflict concerns the generosity and financing of basic income—aspects that are not always aligned in popular preferences. On the one hand, the survey evidence shows that people tend to favour a relatively generous full basic income over a partial one that is well below the current level of subsistence in their country. On the other hand, people do not always support the tax increase or the replacement of existing welfare schemes that may be needed to make a generous basic income financially feasible (Torry, 2016). This is perfectly illustrated by the finding that the respondents in the BIN experiment in the Netherlands preferred a relatively high amount (of €1000), but at the same time also wanted budget neutrality and lacked a clear preference for replacing existing social security programmes. In a similar vein, an Ipsos MORI Survey in the UK found that there was a significant drop in support for basic income (from 45 to 22%) once it was clear to respondents that a tax increase and budget cuts would be required to fund this. Both examples suggest that popular demand for basic income is not always in tune with the available financial capacity to implement it. One possible way out of this would be to increase the capacity to finance a basic income by strengthening the commitment to two of the most popular funding mechanisms: increasing the progressivity of income taxes and introducing or expanding taxes on capital. Both boil down to increasing taxes on the rich in order to redistribute resources to poorer people. It should nevertheless be noted that this is also a risky strategy with regard to political feasibility, as it could well even further strengthen the opposition of high-income earners (a politically powerful group) to a basic income (see Sect. 5.1.6).

The third demand-capacity conflict, originally formulated by Parolin and Siöland (2020), holds that support for basic income is generally greatest in contexts where the administrative and financial capacity to implement it is lowest. At the country level, it was shown that support is in fact greatest in countries with lower levels of economic development and in less mature welfare states—such as Lithuania, Hungary and Slovenia. Here, political feasibility appears to be substantial, but the financial feasibility to actually implement a full-blown basic income scheme is relatively low (Hanna & Olken, 2018; Ravallion, 2009). This demand-capacity conflict also applies to regions within countries, as well as to time periods. With regard to the first, there is evidence that popular demand for basic income is greater in poorer than in richer regions. For example, the level of support is consistently higher in the French-speaking part of Belgium than in the Dutch-speaking part, and this is probably due to the fact that the former is in a worse economic situation than the latter. A similar story applies to the eastern and western part of Germany, respectively. With regard to time, there is evidence that support for basic income increased during the COVID-19 pandemic, especially among those who already felt relatively deprived and experienced economic or health concerns. However, while popular demand for a basic income may increase in times of crisis, it seems likely that the financial capacity to implement it tends to shrink during economic slumps (De Wispelaere & Morales, 2021). One could argue that this type of demand-capacity conflict will solve itself from the moment a country or region reaches the level of economic development needed to finance a basic income. This, nevertheless, seems somewhat optimistic, as the economic development could also dampen popular demand. In that case, the financial feasibility of basic income would increase, but its political feasibility would decrease. Furthermore, it is also evident that in more-deprived countries, regions or time periods, not only basic income but also other welfare schemes—such as means-tested social assistance—are highly popular. Accordingly, basic income still faces the political opportunity costs discussed above (see Sect. 5.1.1), especially when the competing policies are cheaper to implement.

5.1.5 Age Politics

One of the most consistent findings, observed across many opinion polls conducted in different countries and years, is that elderly people (in particular those in receipt of a pension) are markedly less supportive of basic income than their younger counterparts. I have argued that this is mostly due to the fact that elderly people are less likely to believe a basic income will benefit them personally, because most of them are no longer active in the labour market and already receive an old-age pension. This means that elderly people generally have lower levels of job and income insecurity than younger people. Such self-interested opposition to basic income is also confirmed by survey evidence, with elderly people being less likely to see basic income as offering any personal gain to them. For example, a Populus survey in the UK shows that less than 10% of those above the age of 65 thought a basic income would benefit them and their family (compared with about 30% of those between 18 and 34). This is highly problematic for basic income advocates, because elderly people are a politically powerful group in most democracies, for several reasons. The most obvious one concerns the fact that elderly people constitute—at least in ageing societies—a large voting bloc that could easily veto the introduction of a basic income. Additionally, the elderly are also a stable constituency ('once a pensioner, always a pensioner') whose members have a great deal of time on their hands (because they no longer work) to actively put pressure on policymakers. Further, in many countries elderly people are well represented by strong, organized interest groups (such as the National Council of Ageing in the US) and sometimes even have their own political parties (for example, 50PLUS in the Netherlands). Taken together, this makes it very likely that electorally motivated policymakers will be highly responsive to the opinions of elderly people (Schneider & Ingram, 1997). Accordingly, it seems that basic income faces gloomy prospects of being implemented from the perspective of 'age politics' (Pampel & Williamson, 1985).

The other side of the coin is that younger people are generally more supportive of basic income. In fact, it could be argued that all basic income advocates have to do is to wait until generational replacement creates a society that is much more open to the idea. As today's older generations disappear, so too may the persistent idea that welfare provision ought to be conditional and selective. However, this interpretation is premature, given that there is currently no evidence whatsoever that the higher level of support among the young is actually a cohort effect rather than an age effect (as there is no longitudinal data available to test this). If it proves to be the latter, then younger people could well reduce their support in the future as they grow older. Even if it proves to be a cohort effect, this would not necessarily increase the political feasibility of the ideal-typical version of basic income. This is because young people also often prefer basic income varieties that deviate from the ideal type, such as a participation income, a targeted basic income or a basic income that pays a higher amount to those with a longer work record. Interestingly, elderly people tend to have similar relative preferences for different varieties of basic income. Thus, while the old and the young differ in their absolute levels of support, they seem to be similar in terms of which types of basic income they prefer. This offers some opportunities for intergenerational coalition building and could enhance the political prospects of implementing basic income schemes that are preferred by all generations.

Again, these can be considered either as the ultimate end goal or as a stepping stone policy towards the introduction of the ideal-typical version of a basic income.

One strategy to avoid strong political opposition from the elderly and their interest groups is thus to propose basic income schemes that are, relatively speaking, the most popular among this group. One highly relevant candidate in this regard is a basic income that makes the benefit amount dependent on people's work history. For example, it would be possible to put in place a scheme with a basic amount that is equal for all and that is then increased by a fixed amount for every x number of working years. This may weaken the opposition from elderly people, who would typically be paid a higher amount than their younger counterparts in such a system. This strategy of 'reciprocity within universalism' could be especially attractive in countries where the existing old-age pension, or the welfare system more broadly, is organized along the principles of contribution-based social insurance (Laenen et al., 2022). In addition to compensation, there are other strategies of blame avoidance (Pierson, 1994, 2001) that policy entrepreneurs could apply to soften the opposition from elderly people. One is to opt for the long-term implementation of basic income, for example, by introducing a basic income scheme from a certain generation onwards. Importantly, this is not the same as a youth basic income, which can only be received until a certain age and is thus restricted in time. The limited evidence that is currently available—from the BABEL Survey in Belgium—suggests that a basic income limited only to young people is strongly opposed by the elderly, who would rather have a basic pension or a basic income for working-aged people. Furthermore, even though support is higher among young people, they also prefer a youth basic income the least. Accordingly, the introduction of a youth basic income does not rank high in terms of political feasibility. It would possibly make more sense, at least politically, to propose a basic income that is paid for life, but only from today's young generation onwards. This would leave the current older generations—who have more vested interests in the existing social protection system—unaffected, thereby increasing the political feasibility of introducing a basic income. However, this would also mean (at least in pay-as-you-go systems) that some of the younger generations would be burdened with a 'double pay problem', as they may have to pay for the newly established basic income scheme alongside current old-age pensions. Unfortunately, the available survey evidence is unable to determine the degree to which young people would be willing to accept such a double payment burden in order to introduce a basic income.

Another strategy to break the united front of elderly opposition would be to take away some of the uncertainty that comes with the introduction of a basic income. At the moment, most elderly people seem to believe they would not benefit from a basic income. It is plausible that this is to some extent driven by the fact that it is relatively difficult for them to assess whether their financial situation would improve or deteriorate if a basic income were to replace the old-age pension. Faced with such uncertainty, elderly people may prefer to stick to what they currently have. If policy entrepreneurs could succeed in reducing that uncertainty (for example, by creating tools that help people to evaluate whether they would win or lose financially from a basic income scheme), they may be able to build support among those elderly who mistakenly thought they would be worse off after the introduction of a basic income. This could convert some risk-averse pensioners from opposition to support. At the same time, such an information campaign could also work as a double-edged sword, if the presumed losers start to oppose basic income even more than they did before. According to the new politics of the welfare state theory (Pierson, 1994, 2001), this could have a detrimental impact on the political feasibility of basic income, as people typically react more strongly to the potential losses than to the potential gains of a welfare reform (this is known as 'negativity bias', see also Sect. 5.1.8). In light of this, policy entrepreneurs would be well advised to also draw attention to the societal rather than the personal effects of basic income. In particular, elderly people's opposition could be weakened if advocates stress its potential to revalue unpaid work, such as informal caregiving or volunteering. Survey data shows that the elderly attach a relatively high level of importance to this policy outcome, presumably because it also benefits them personally.

Most of the above is based on the idea that—at least in countries with relatively generous contributory pensions—many elderly people will oppose basic income because it could be perceived as a retrenchment of 'their' welfare benefits (Lynch & Myrskylä, 2009). As a natural reaction, basic income advocates may try to counter that perception, by denying or hiding the fact that certain groups within the elderly population will indeed lose out financially. The notion of retrenchment could nevertheless possibly also be used to build support for a basic income, if it is presented as a reform that is needed to make the existing pension system financially sustainable, which is a commonly shared concern in public opinion (see, for example, European Commission, 2020). Although it is not often recognized, a basic income (or basic pension) could actually cut costs in countries where a large proportion of social spending is allocated to generous pension insurance for people who previously had relatively high wages. As a basic income would effectively put a ceiling on all pension benefits, advocates could also promote the policy as a cost-cutting measure, thereby justifying the fact that it would mean a retrenchment for large groups of elderly people (Green-Pedersen, 2002). This could, nevertheless, also lead to increased opposition from high-income earners, who will be the ones losing out (see Sect. 5.1.6).

5.1.6 Class Politics

In addition to age politics, it seems that the introduction of a basic income will also be difficult to achieve from the perspective of 'class politics'. This is because in most countries and across different types of basic income, there is a considerably lower level of support among high-income earners compared with their low-income counterparts. Furthermore, basic income tends to be supported less by people with stable jobs (the so-called 'labour market insiders') and is often less popular among the higher educated. Taken together, this implies that the upper classes are mostly opposed to basic income, while the lower classes are more supportive of it. I suggest that this is mainly because the former see themselves as net contributors to a basic income scheme, while the latter believe they will be net beneficiaries. If a basic income is to be financed by (progressively designed) income taxes, this perception is probably accurate. Additionally, people from the upper classes experience markedly less job and income insecurity than their lower-class counterparts, who are more likely to be without a job or to have a precarious, low-paid one. Accordingly, it makes a great deal of sense that these so-called 'labour market outsiders' are *the* prime constituency of a basic income.

With an eye on political feasibility, it may nevertheless be bad news that the upper classes oppose basic income more strongly. In fact, there is mounting evidence that policymakers and the public policies they design are more responsive to citizens with higher incomes and a higher level of education than they are to their lower-income and lower-educated counterparts (Elkjaer & Klitgaard, 2021; Elsässer et al., 2021). In political science literature, this phenomenon is generally known as 'unequal responsiveness' (Gilens, 2012) and there are two main pathways through which it comes into being. The first, labelled here as 'descriptive representation', refers to the fact that policymakers themselves are usually members of the upper class. Hence, it is logical that most of them have similar ideas and interests to those of their higher-income and higher-educated citizen peers. The second pathway, which I term 'substantive representation', refers to the fact that wealthy and well-educated people tend to have greater monetary and informational resources at their disposal to persuade policymakers to serve their interests. Furthermore, it is well established that voter turnout tends to be higher among the upper classes (Franko et al., 2016), making them more important to electorally motivated policymakers. With regard to labour market position, there is also evidence that trade unions are more likely to protect the interests of 'insiders' rather than 'outsiders' (Rueda, 2007). Accordingly, if labour market insiders oppose basic income, there is a higher likelihood that the trade unions they are represented by will do the same.

The good news for (at least some) basic income advocates is that the upper-class opposition is not observed always and everywhere. In fact, there are important exceptions. In some countries, high-income earners and higher-educated people are equally or even more supportive of basic income than their low-income, lower-educated counterparts. A case in point is the Netherlands, where several surveys show that those with tertiary education and a high income are relatively supportive of basic income, although not necessarily of the ideal-typical version (see Sect. 5.1.1). In such countries, policy entrepreneurs could exploit the fact that the upper classes are not as opposed to basic income, to make the phenomenon of unequal responsiveness work for instead of against them. The same advocates should also be alert to societal developments that could shift the balance in their favour. Obvious examples in this regard are the COVID-19 pandemic and the energy crisis caused by the Russian invasion of Ukraine. Both have resulted in greater job and income insecurity for millions of citizens who had previously believed they were relatively safe from those issues. This could, in turn, increase popular support for basic income. In addition, the rapidly accelerating flexibilization and automation of labour could provide similar opportunities. At present, there is little evidence that people see basic income as an effective policy to cushion the effects of technological unemployment, and there are no higher levels of support among groups that are more vulnerable to such unemployment (such as low-skilled routine workers) (Busemeyer &

Sahm, 2022; Dermont & Weisstanner, 2020). If automation does lead to massive job losses in the future, this could nevertheless increase support for basic income (as it is independent of work status). However, it could potentially also increase opposition from people whose jobs are largely unaffected by automation (such as high-skilled labour market insiders). In this event, the phenomenon of unequal responsiveness could once again block the introduction of a basic income.

There are several other opportunities for basic income advocates to exploit from the perspective of class politics. Above all, it is important to take note of the fact that there are some groups that are not particularly opposed to basic income, even though it could be expected of them. The first group comprises trade unionists, who according to some should be against a basic income because it could negatively affect the collective bargaining power of trade unions (and thus go against their interests) or because it clashes with the work ethic (and thus conflicts with their ideology). However, strong opposition from trade unionists is not found in most countries. It could, therefore, be that trade unions are also less opposed to basic income than is often assumed (Vanderborght, 2006), or that they will decrease their opposition once they find out about the opinions of their members (Cigna, 2022). The second group concerns the recipients of social benefits other than old-age pensions (for example, those in receipt of disability or unemployment benefits). From the perspective of the new politics of the welfare state (Pierson, 1994, 2001), one could assume that these welfare constituencies would feel threatened by the idea that a basic income would replace 'their' benefits, potentially making them worse off. However, this is not supported by the evidence from polls. In fact, it seems that working-age benefit recipients are generally *more* supportive of basic income rather than less supportive. The third group involves the middle class. Depending on the precise funding mechanism for a basic income scheme, some members of the middle class will be net contributors, whereas others will be net beneficiaries. It is nevertheless relatively difficult for people in this group to determine which side they will ultimately end up on, if a basic income is introduced. In light of people's general tendency to react more strongly to potential losses than to potential gains (also known as 'negativity bias'—see Sect. 5.1.8), one could expect the middle class to mainly oppose basic income. The available survey evidence, nevertheless, seems to indicate that middle-class citizens are neither strongly against basic income nor strongly in favour of it. This provides opportunities for policy entrepreneurs, as the middle class constitutes a large and electorally important constituency waiting to be persuaded of the added value of basic income.

5.1.7 Party Politics

From the perspective of 'party politics', I distinguish three key difficulties that advocates for basic income will often have to overcome. One of these issues concentrates on reducing the opposition from right-wing voters, while the other two pertain to sustaining the support of left-wing voters.

First of all, the available survey evidence consistently shows that in most countries, support for basic income is considerably lower among right-wing voters than their left-wing counterparts. Even when presented basic income schemes match well with right-wing proposals for a basic income—because they offer a relatively low amount and/or replace many existing social benefits, thereby dismantling the welfare state—there continues to be greater opposition from right-wing voters. This is in large part because right-wingers are less committed to promoting equality of outcomes and because they dislike the idea that a basic income would also be paid to people who they consider undeserving of social welfare (Laenen et al., 2022). In particular, this includes people who are seen as unwilling to work (who are given a 'free pass' under an unconditional basic income scheme) and migrants (who could be drawn to the country once a basic income is in place, acting as a welfare magnet) (Borjas, 1999). Right-wing voters are—at least in the UK—also more sceptical about the predicted positive effects of basic income on relevant policy outcomes, such as its potential to increase, rather than decrease, work incentives. Furthermore, it proves somewhat difficult to persuade right-wing people to abandon their opposition to a basic income. Several survey experiments, conducted in Belgium and the US, demonstrate that right-wing voters fail to increase their support for basic income after being exposed to positive frames about the policy. By contrast, they often do react to negative frames by decreasing their (already relatively low level of) support for basic income. This suggests that right-wing voters are susceptible to negativity bias when shaping their opinion about basic income (see Sect. 5.1.8).

All of this is highly problematic for the political feasibility of basic income, as it seems that broad political coalitions are needed for such a scheme to be implemented and sustained (De Wispelaere, 2015). If right-wing voters—and by extension the political parties they are represented by—continue to oppose basic income after a left-wing government has been able to introduce the policy, it will probably not take long for the scheme to be retrenched after a right-wing government subsequently takes power. There is nevertheless one survey experiment, conducted in the US, that proves some specific arguments can and do convince right-wing voters to (moderately) support the introduction of a basic income (Thomas et al., 2023). In particular, it appears that US conservatives were persuaded by the argument that a basic income would increase people's freedom from the government—a factor they considered as fitting in with their moral values. This finding suggests that if policy entrepreneurs manage to frame basic income as a tool to promote values endorsed by right-wing ideology—such as individual freedom and limited government—there could be a significant reduction in right-wing opposition. This should in turn increase the chances of building the sufficiently large and stable political coalition that is needed to implement a basic income scheme.

It would nevertheless be a mistake to focus exclusively on how to persuade right-wing voters to abandon their opposition to basic income. In fact, there are two political challenges that are specific to left-wing voters that basic income advocates should take seriously. The first of these concerns the fact that left-wing voters' support for basic income is also likely to be susceptible to negativity bias. In fact, there is evidence—from the BABEL experiment in Belgium—that left-wing voters also reduce their support for basic income if they are told that the policy would have negative policy outcomes. In particular, there is evidence of a dramatic decrease in left-wing support if the introduction of a basic income would increase the poverty rate—which some microsimulation studies suggest could well happen under certain circumstances (for example, Browne & Immervoll, 2017). A similar, albeit somewhat weaker, reduction was observed for the policy outcomes of income inequality and employment (but not for entrepreneurship and informal caregiving). Although other survey experiments—conducted in the US—suggest that left-wing voters are immune to the political framing of basic income (because they support it anyway), the Belgian experiment clearly shows that in some specific contexts, particular frames can erode left-wing support. Accordingly, it seems that if the opponents of basic income succeed in convincing left-wing voters that it could also have negative effects, such as an increase in poverty, they will be able to put a serious dent in its political feasibility.

To avoid this, basic income advocates are advised to extensively test the potential impact of basic income with the help of policy experiments and microsimulations in order to provide evidence-based arguments that it will *not* have the negative outcomes that left-wing voters fear the most. Importantly, this means that the predicted outcomes of basic income also ought to be compared with those of its main policy competitors, such as means-tested social assistance (see also Sect. 5.1.8).

There is one other political challenge that advocates of the ideal-typical version of basic income in particular are confronted with: left-wing voters do not necessarily prefer the ideal type. In fact, the evidence from the polls indicates that they often favour basic income types that deviate significantly from the ideal-typical version. In particular, it was shown that left-wing people from different political strands—voting for green or socialist parties alike—prefer a conditional participation income to a fully unconditional basic income. In a similar vein, there is some evidence from Japan (see Takamatsu & Tachibanaki, 2014) that left-wing voters favour a targeted negative income tax over a fully universal basic income. Other evidence (from Belgium) shows that left-wingers do not have a strong preference for either a targeted or a universal basic income, and that they (slightly) favour a scheme that varies the amount according to people's financial needs or work history over a flat-rate payment. Taken together, these findings indicate that the ideal-typical version of basic income is—even among its core political constituencies—not *more* popular than some of the other types with which it will have to compete. This is likely to increase the political opportunity costs faced by advocates of the ideal type (see Sect. 5.1.1). At the same time, it also provides opportunities to build large cross-party coalitions to support other basic income types. One obvious candidate in this regard is a participation income, because this is the more popular option among both left-wing voters and their right-wing counterparts. Accordingly, it seems that it is not—as often suggested (Chrisp & Martinelli, 2019)—basic income but rather participation income that is 'neither left nor right'. However, as noted above (see Sect. 5.1.4), the greater political feasibility of participation income could be offset by its lower administrative feasibility.

5.1.8 Negativity Bias

This book shows that people have many different reasons for supporting or opposing basic income. At the same time, most people seem susceptible to negativity bias, in the sense that they are more likely to decrease their support for basic income when they are told that it would yield negative outcomes than they are to increase their support if the outcomes are predicted to be positive. More specifically, support is significantly reduced (among left-wing voters in particular, see Sect. 5.1.7) if basic income is framed as increasing the existing levels of poverty and income inequality. Similarly, support strongly decreases if basic income is claimed to decrease the employment level. This is observed among left-wing voters, but even more so among their right-wingers counterparts (who are also less supportive of basic income if entrepreneurship would decrease). This finding is indicative of the fear that a basic income would reduce labour market participation—a concern that seems to be shared by most of the population. Interestingly, there is nevertheless a clear discrepancy between the predicted impact of a basic income at the macro level and at the micro-level, in the sense that most people believe a basic income will reduce other people's work intentions but not their own.

This negativity bias is problematic for the political feasibility of basic income, because it makes it easier for opponents to discredit the policy in their political framing than it is for proponents to promote it. Furthermore, it comes on top of the previously discussed type of negativity bias, which assumes that people react more strongly to personal financial losses than to personal financial gains. It, therefore, appears that basic income advocates will have to deal with negativity bias at both the personal level and the societal level. With regard to the personal negativity bias, it will be crucial to convince sections of the middle class and the elderly population that they and their families would also gain from the introduction of a basic income. The societal negativity bias could be dealt with by conducting policy experiments and microsimulation studies to provide evidence-based information about the likely effects of introducing a fully-fledged basic income in a given context. It is nevertheless crucial that these experiments and simulations are successful, in the sense that they mostly (perhaps even only) show positive outcomes. At a bare minimum, they should show that labour market participation would not decrease, as this seems to be an important outcome for people from all walks of life. To convince left-wing voters, these scientific assessments should also confirm that poverty and income inequality would not increase (see Sect. 5.1.7). To persuade their right-wing counterparts, they should probably also be able to take away the fear that basic income would damage the economy and attract new migrants to the country. To win over elderly people, it should perhaps also be shown that basic income will have positive effects on one of the policy outcomes that they attach a relatively high level of importance to: informal caregiving (see Sect. 5.1.5). In that sense, popular support for basic income seems overall to be more practical than principled.

It will also be important to demonstrate that basic income—and the ideal-typical version in particular—does not perform worse, and preferably performs even better, than the existing welfare system. For example, if it can be shown that a universal basic income does a better job of improving work incentives or alleviating poverty than the existing system, public opinion may shift in favour of basic income. There are some hints of this in the available survey evidence; in particular in the UK, where a large proportion of the population already think that a basic income would boost work incentives more than the current (largely means-tested) system. In a similar vein, experiments and simulations will need to compare the predicted effects of the ideal-typical version of basic income with those of its potential policy competitors (such as a guaranteed employment programme, a participation income or a negative income tax). Only when the ideal type can yield demonstrably better results than both the existing system and the competing schemes will its introduction no longer be hampered by the negativity bias discussed here.

This will of course require rigorous scientific testing of the predicted impact of different policy schemes on a broad range of policy outcomes, and this may not always be administratively or financially feasible. It is nevertheless crucial for the political feasibility of basic income that policy entrepreneurs can rely on evidence-based information to refute claims that it will have negative effects, as these claims will surely be put forward by those who oppose the policy. If anything, it seems that policy entrepreneurs should first and foremost advocate basic income *pilots* rather than basic income *schemes*. There is also some evidence—from the Dalia survey conducted in 28 European countries—that citizens would prefer a basic income to be introduced only after it has been successfully tried and tested. In light of this, it is also telling that the participants in the Finnish experiment with basic income—arguably the largest of its type—are considerably more positive about the policy than their otherwise similar peers who did not take part in the experiment (Simanainen & Kangas, 2020). Taken together, the evidence suggests that—under the right circumstances—pilots can increase the popularity and political feasibility of basic income, and thereby, have a real impact on politics and policy (Chrisp & De Wispelaere, 2022).

5.2 A Research Agenda

In this book, I have provided the most comprehensive, detailed and up-to-date overview of the popularity of basic income and have reflected extensively on the implications for its political feasibility. At the same time, I fully acknowledge that—mainly due to limited data availability—current knowledge about the popularity and political feasibility of basic income only represents the tip of the iceberg. In fact, there are still many unknowns to be explored in future research. Here, I sketch out a research agenda to help navigate that journey into the unknown. It serves as a roadmap for future scholars, allowing them to ask new research questions with the help of innovative data and methods. I consider it the task of the academic community to reveal ever more parts of the iceberg that are currently hidden. Additionally, the agenda is also intended as a source of inspiration for policy entrepreneurs who seek to introduce a basic income in the real world. I highly recommend these entrepreneurs to take the popularity of basic income and its political implications seriously in the feasibility assessment of their policy proposals, in addition to analyses of the administrative and financial feasibility. Even proposals that are very well thought out, administratively and financially, can fail to be implemented in the end due to a lack of public and political support.

The research agenda is summarized in Fig. 5.1, which presents a conceptual model visualizing the relationship between the popularity of basic income and its real-world implementation (as described in this book). The model starts from the assumption that—as the different chapters have shown—people's support for (different varieties of) basic income is associated with individual characteristics, such as their age, income and political ideology. This popular support, in turn, is seen as an important factor influencing the political feasibility of basic income, because it supposedly affects policymakers' positions towards it through various mechanisms of policy responsiveness. As argued in the introduction, public opinion could also influence the administrative and financial feasibility of basic income (for example, if opposition turns into tax evasion).

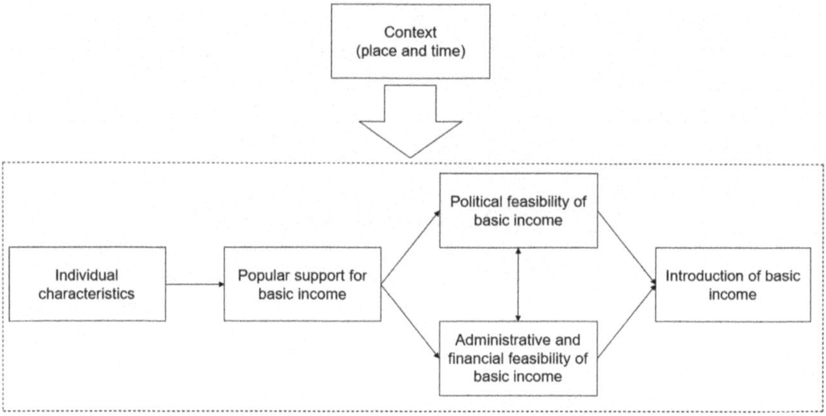

Fig. 5.1 Summary of the research agenda

The different types of feasibility—administrative, financial and political—also feed back into one another and jointly determine whether a basic income can be introduced (and sustained). This whole process is considered to be very much context specific, as it varies across both place and time. In the following, I identify the most pressing knowledge gaps with regard to the different components and relationships included in the conceptual framework, so that these can be addressed in future research.

5.2.1 *Exploring the 'Causes' of Support for Basic Income*

This book has tried to identify the determinants or 'causes' of popular support for different types of basic income, at both the individual level and the contextual level. With regard to the former, it was shown that people's socio-demographic characteristics (such as their age and income) and ideological beliefs (such as their political orientations) can influence how they think about basic income. Future research should nevertheless continue the search for new and improved individual-level determinants of support for basic income.

To begin with, there is a need to develop more detailed and precise measurements of some of the individual characteristics discussed in this book. For example, it would be highly relevant to use a more disaggregated measurement of the employment sector to predict support for basic income than the simple distinction between the private and the public sector. In the public sector, there may be some specific subsectors that are more opposed to the introduction of a basic income, because it threatens to make their jobs obsolete (for example, civil servants working in social security administration, or social workers employed in public assistance agencies). Similarly, some private subsectors may be more supportive of basic income than others, for example, depending on the degree to which automation or flexibilization of labour has penetrated the sector. Another example relates to benefit recipiency, which is measured rather crudely in most existing surveys, as they rarely ask respondents to indicate *how much* money they (and other members of their household) receive from social benefits. This is nevertheless crucial information, because it determines to a large extent whether benefit recipients will win or lose (financially) from the introduction of a particular basic income scheme. Such information is also needed to test some of the propositions from the new politics of the welfare state theory (Pierson, 1994, 2001). For example, will benefit recipients oppose a basic income and punish the politicians responsible for it at the ballot box if it constitutes a retrenchment of 'their' benefits? Further, is it true—in relation to the introduction of a basic income—that these welfare constituencies react more strongly to financial losses than to financial gains, as assumed by the idea of personal negativity bias (see Sect. 5.1.8)?

To better understand who supports basic income and who opposes it (and why), future research should also examine the role of other individual characteristics that have not been accounted for in this book. There are some socio-demographic characteristics that have yet to be explored, but could be highly relevant in understanding popular support for basic income. One relevant example concerns whether people own capital and property assets, such as a house or stocks and shares (Lux & Mau, 2021). Likewise, there are some ideological beliefs that have been paid little attention in prior research. A relevant example in this regard involves conspiracy beliefs about basic income, which some believe are on the rise and pose an eminent threat to its popularity and political feasibility. For the time being, it is nevertheless unclear how prevalent such conspiracy beliefs are and how they relate to people's support for the policy. There are also some unexplored individual characteristics that lie somewhere in between people's socio-demographic features and their ideological views. One pertinent example is people's perceived risk of losing their job due to automation. While some studies have used the risk of automation (as projected by experts) as a predictor (Busemeyer & Sahm, 2022; Dermont & Weisstanner, 2020), we know little about how people perceive that risk themselves, and how that feeds into their position towards basic income. Although there is some evidence that citizens refuse to accept a scenario in which 'robots take over our jobs' and do not see basic income as a good solution if that were nonetheless to happen, the evidence is restricted to a small sample of Hungarian university students (Herke & Vicsek, 2022). We clearly need more research, with larger samples in multiple countries, to understand how perceptions of automation are linked to support for basic income.

Another path for future research to pursue would be the inclusion of intersections between different individual characteristics—for example, between gender and other socio-demographic features. Throughout the book, it is shown that men and women do not differ substantially in terms of their support for different types of basic income, or in the related arguments they endorse or find important. This seems to indicate that gender as such is not particularly relevant for the political feasibility of basic income. However, it could well be that gender plays a more important role when it is linked to other characteristics, such as household composition. For example, a basic income could be particularly beneficial to—and thus supported by—single mothers, as they tend to have greater income insecurity (Kramer et al., 2015). Unfortunately, such intersections are difficult to account for from a methodological point of view, because the number of respondents is often too small to obtain reliable statistical estimates. This is the case for most of the surveys used in this book, as they are designed to represent the general population rather than specific segments of it (such as single mothers). One notable exception in this regard is the BABEL Survey in Belgium, which over-sampled trade union members making it possible to investigate the extent to which basic income is supported by trade unionists from different ideological strands. Future research should further explore how specific segments of the population think about basic income, either by over-sampling these groups in general population surveys or by conducting highly targeted surveys. Other examples of groups that could be important for the political feasibility of basic income but are often under-represented and thus overlooked in survey analyses are radical-right (or left) voters, self-employed people, migrants and ethnic minorities and residents of care facilities. Reaching such 'hard-to-survey populations' (Tourangeau et al.,

2014) will add important insights to our current knowledge about the popularity and political feasibility of basic income.

A further task for future research—which is especially relevant for our fundamental knowledge base—would be to expose the theoretical mechanisms that lie behind popular support for basic income. In this book, I have made the assumption that such support is driven by (possibly a combination of) considerations of self-interest and ideology. This assumption is based on decades of research investigating popular attitudes towards the welfare state (van Oorschot et al., 2022). I have been less concerned with testing theories, as the book is not only targeted at scholars, but also at policy entrepreneurs who may be more interested in finding out *who*—that is, which identifiable political constituencies—support (or oppose) basic income, rather than knowing *why*—that is, through which theoretical mechanisms—they do so. For example, while the book clearly shows that elderly people are less supportive of basic income, it does not provide clear-cut evidence for why this is the case. There are some signs that the elderly oppose basic income out of self-interest, but it cannot be ruled out that their opposition is also (and perhaps more strongly) rooted in ideological conservatism. Nevertheless, as an academic, I consider it important that future research further theorizes why people support (or oppose) different types of basic income and puts these theories to the empirical test. Multiple regression analyses with (preferably longitudinal) survey data offer one way of getting closer to the theoretical dynamics behind popular support for basic income. Another promising approach would be to deploy qualitative research methods (such as content analysis of focus groups and in-depth interviews), which can generate valuable insights into the reasoning behind people's position towards a basic income (as shown in Chapter 4).

The book clearly demonstrates that individuals' characteristics often influence support for basic income differently in different countries. A case in point is education, which increases support in some countries while in others, it decreases it. Similar observations are found for many other individual characteristics. This important finding has nevertheless remained under the radar in most prior studies, because they were either limited to single countries or lumped all countries together in a pooled cross-national analysis. Nevertheless, it currently remains unclear how and why the impact of individual characteristics differs across countries. I consider it a key task for future research to uncover the factors explaining such cross-national variation. One important aspect could be countries' existing tax-transfer systems, which are likely to affect citizens' normative beliefs and cost-benefit calculations related to the introduction of a basic income through various mechanisms of policy feedback (Busemeyer et al., 2021; Pierson, 1993). For example, the progressivity of income taxes and social transfers may to a large extent shape the self-interest considerations of different income groups (Korpi & Palme, 1998), which would in turn influence their support for basic income. In a similar vein, varying levels of welfare state generosity could be a factor influencing how particular social groups think about basic income in different countries. For example, it seems plausible that the generosity of pension benefits (or the lack thereof) shapes elderly people's opinions about basic income, and thereby potentially also the size of the gap in support between the old and the young. In addition to existing welfare state policies, it seems likely that economic (for example, the level of unemployment), cultural (for example, the religious heritage of a country), demographic (for example, the degree of population ageing) and political factors (for example, a partisan discourse) will also affect who supports and who opposes basic income in different contexts. This 'context' not only concerns countries, but also regions within countries and developments over time. Accordingly, future research should explore how and why the impact of people's individual characteristics on their support for basic income varies between regions and over time. The element of time is particularly important to consider in future studies. As discussed above, it is consistently found that young people are more supportive of basic income than their elderly counterparts (see Sect. 5.1.5), but we do not know whether this is a cohort effect or an age effect. This is nevertheless hugely important for the political prospects of basic income, as the former implies that popular support is likely to increase in the future due to generational replacement, whereas the latter suggests that the higher level of support among the young is likely to decrease as they grow older. To be able to determine which scenario is most probable, we need longitudinal data allowing us to track how the support for basic income of individuals (or groups) evolves over time. Unfortunately, this data is currently not available.

The context can also influence across-the-board support for basic income. The different chapters have shown that support is higher in some countries, regions and time periods than in others. Using data from the ESS, it was also shown that the level of economic development and of social spending help to explain such contextual variation, with support for the ideal-typical version of basic income being lower in countries where both the economy and the welfare state are less developed (see Sect. 5.1.4). Future research should, nevertheless, explore other contextual determinants of popular support for basic income, as economic development and social spending do not come near to explaining all the observed variation between different countries. Here, I refer to the importance of the same contextual factors as discussed above. These include other elements of the welfare state (for example, the tax burden), other economic conditions (for example, the rate of inflation), cultural characteristics (for example, the centrality of work), demographic features (for example, the influx of refugees) and political factors (for example, the state structure). With regard to the last of these, it will be particularly important to assess how experiments, pilots and simulations influence support for basic income (before, during and after they are conducted). While we know from the Finnish experiment that the participants in the experimental group were more positive about basic income than a comparable control group, both groups, nevertheless, consisted only of unemployed people. What is needed are studies that investigate how experiments affect across-the-board support among the general population. More research is also needed about the impact that time developments and events—in particular economic, health and other crises—have on popular support for (different types of) basic income, relative to competing policy schemes (such as means-tested social assistance).

At the same time, we should not expect to *fully* explain the variation present between countries, regions and time periods. Empirical analyses usually uncover a number of general patterns, from which there are always context-specific deviations. These deviations can nevertheless be hugely important for the political feasibility of basic income in that specific context. For example, it could be that there are some countries with a high level of economic development *and* a high level of support for basic income. In that case, there is no demand-capacity conflict of the type discussed above. Knowing about the patterns is thus interesting, but not indispensable for policy entrepreneurs who seek to put in place a basic income in their particular context. Instead, I strongly recommend that those entrepreneurs always conduct a context-specific analysis of the popularity of their policy proposal, and reflect on the context-specific implications for the political feasibility of that proposal. In fact, I consider this equally as important as analysing the administrative and financial feasibility of basic income proposals. For policy entrepreneurs in the Global

North (Western Europe and the US in particular), there may already be some survey evidence available to evaluate the popularity and political feasibility of policy proposals. In the Global South, such evidence is largely absent, which I believe is mainly due to a lack of resources and infrastructure to field large-scale surveys, rather than due to a lack of interest in basic income. In fact, there are plenty of basic income advocates in Africa and Latin America (Murray & Pateman, 2012), most of whom are currently in the dark about who supports which types of basic income in their country. Although there is somewhat more information available for policy entrepreneurs in Asian (Japan and South Korea in particular) and Eastern European countries, they are also less well-equipped to assess the popularity and political feasibility of basic income in their specific context. In this light, I seize the opportunity to call for the inclusion of detailed items on basic income in international surveys that also cover the regions that have been underexposed in prior research (for example, the Afrobarometer, the ISSP and the World Values Survey).

5.2.2 Measuring Support for Basic Income

Future research should also continue to pay due attention to the proper measurement of popular support for basic income. As a minimum, what a basic income is should always be explained, as citizens often lack prior knowledge about it. This can involve giving relatively broad definitions of the ideal-typical version of basic income (or other types, such as a participation income) to assess support for a general policy *idea*. Alternatively (or additionally), information can be given about the specific design features of a concrete policy *proposal*—such as its amount, eligibility rules, funding mechanism and integration within the existing welfare system. In this book, data limitations restricted me to focusing mainly on the policy design dimensions of universality, conditionality, financing, generosity, integration and uniformity. Future research would benefit from also analysing the effects of dimensions that have remained underexplored in public opinion studies, such as the administration, duration, individuality, frequency and modality of basic income. It is also important to keep taking stock of possible interactions between different policy design features to reveal how people react to trade-offs (for example, between the generosity and conditionality of basic income). Analysing these interactions not only generates fundamental knowledge about the popularity of basic income, but also allows us to identify with greater accuracy the political constituencies that can be mobilized in favour of (or against) differently designed types of basic income in different countries, regions and time periods.

There is nevertheless a limit to the number of policy design features that can be included in descriptions of basic income in public opinion research. Providing detailed information about the proposed policy scheme is often a good thing, but can also be damaging if the description is so complex that people feel cognitively overburdened. To confirm whether people have understood the definition that is provided and are able to respond to questions about it, I highly recommend that preparatory cognitive interviews and pilot studies should be conducted (see Laenen et al., 2021 for an example). Further, it would also be valuable to assess—preferably in an open-answer format—people's initial perceptions of basic income, before a definition is provided: what do they *think* it is? This can help to expose the familiarity with the concept of basic income in public opinion and some of the stereotypical images that may be used to describe it. As a general rule, researchers should nevertheless always make a common definition of basic income available to respondents, so that they are at least all 'talking about the same thing'. The empirical analyses in this book have nevertheless made it very clear that the chosen definition can colour the results. For example, surveys often describe basic income as a solution to a particular social problem (such as poverty or technological unemployment), which in all likelihood increases the level of support—either across the board or among specific groups, such as low-skilled workers—compared with a situation in which no explanation is offered with regard to the problem(s) basic income supposedly solves. Importantly, this implies that the level of support observed in different surveys (which often use differently worded questions) cannot and should not be directly compared unless the differences between them are extremely small. Instead, I strongly advise the development of standardized measurements of popular support for basic income that can be reliably compared (for example, between countries or over time).

Other than that, I formulate five additional recommendations to improve our measurement, and thus our understanding, of popular support for basic income. The first is to conduct—if feasible—surveys among samples that are representative (to the extent this is possible) of the larger population whose support for basic income one aims to measure. If it is the general public that is of interest, the recommendation is to randomly select a (relatively large) sample of the public by using, for example, population registers. When this is not possible—possibly due to a lack of administrative or financial resources—it should at least be recognized that the respondents are part of a convenience sample that is not representative of the public as a whole. Similarly, even when a survey is targeted at a specific segment of the general population (such as trade union members), it should be evaluated how representative of that segment the sample actually is. This is of course a standard recommendation for any survey research, but is worth repeating for the case of popular support for basic income, which is often gauged in surveys by using convenience samples that are not representative of the entire population (without this being properly acknowledged). For the time being, we, nevertheless, have to make do with the surveys that are currently available, even if they are often not entirely representative of any broader population. This pragmatic approach is also adopted in the book.

The second recommendation is to measure popular support for basic income *relative* to support for other, competing policy schemes, such as conditional and means-tested social assistance (see also Rincon, 2021). This can either be performed directly, by forcing people to rank different schemes, or indirectly, by asking them to rate different schemes separately on a common scale. While the first option has the advantage of uncovering popular preferences with regard to policy priorities, the second also allows people to be equally supportive of—or possibly indifferent about—various policy schemes (because they are not forced to rank them). Although the measurement of relative levels of support is of course not a strict requirement, it does allow evaluation of the potential political opportunity costs involved in introducing a basic income in a particular context (see Sect. 5.1.1). Furthermore, it can help to tackle what seems an obvious reaction from political opponents, who could recognize the fact that basic income is relatively popular but question whether it is also *more* popular than its policy competitors (in particular those that already exist, such as conditional, means-tested social assistance). For this reason, I argue that it should be standard practice to compare the popularity of basic income with that of its main policy competitors. More generally, surveys should also ask people whether they consider the implementation of a basic income as an improvement (or conversely, a deterioration) of the existing welfare system.

The third recommendation is to develop indicators that measure intended political behaviour in relation to basic income. The standard approach in existing survey research is to ask people the extent to which they support or oppose the introduction of a basic income scheme in their country (as most surveys discussed in this book have done). However, this does not capture people's willingness to *act* in support of (or against) basic income. In light of this, future research should first and foremost ask respondents whether they would vote for (or against) a party or a politician that proposes (or opposes) the introduction of a basic income. Additionally, it would be beneficial to ask people whether they would, for example, sign a petition or take part in a public protest in favour of (or against) basic income, contact a policymaker directly to advocate (or oppose) basic income, vote for (or against) basic income in a referendum if one were to be organized, become or remain a member of a trade union or other interest organization if it would propose (or oppose) a basic income, and so on. This type of information is presumably more relevant for policy entrepreneurs who seek to put in place a basic income, as it allows a more precise assessment of the political implications of public opinion than a simple measurement of people's stated support. It could also help to detect cases of 'cheap support' for basic income (see Sect. 5.1.2), as one could argue that people who state that they support the introduction of a basic income but are unwilling to carry out any political act on behalf of it are arguably not all that supportive of the policy.

The fourth recommendation is to more closely capture the reasons underlying popular support for (or opposition to) a basic income. As shown in Chapter 4, some surveys have probed the perceived convincingness and importance of different arguments and outcomes associated with the introduction of a basic income. While I advise future research to continue along the same path, there are some issues that require specific attention. Most importantly, there is a pressing need to increase our understanding of the impact that different arguments about basic income and its predicted outcomes have on popular support. It is particularly important for policy entrepreneurs to know whether and how they can overcome the negativity bias that was uncovered in this book (see Sect. 5.1.8). That is, which types of arguments are able to persuade people to support the introduction of a basic income, and does this vary between individuals with different characteristics (for example, depending on their political ideology) and across contexts (for example, between countries with diverging levels of economic development). In addition, it is very relevant to investigate whether the *messenger* (rather than the message) of the political framing also has an effect on support for basic income. For example, do people react differently when the arguments are put forward by scientists or by politicians? If the latter proves to be the case, does it make a difference whether the arguments are communicated by someone who is seen as a political ally or as a political opponent?

For obvious reasons, having this evidence-based knowledge about the impact of political framing is vital for any policy entrepreneur who seeks to sway public opinion to support basic income. It is nevertheless equally crucial for those entrepreneurs to have an accurate picture of the arguments that are already widely supported by (specific parts of) the population, irrespective of the framing. In this light, more research is needed with regard to who endorses which arguments, and in which contexts. The arguments included in surveys should nevertheless not only be determined by people who are experts on the topic of basic income, as they may not be fully aware of the (mis)conceptions that are prevalent among non-experts (who actually comprise the majority of the population). Instead, it is crucial to conduct exploratory qualitative studies that would allow us to uncover the types of arguments and outcomes people *spontaneously* think of in relation to basic income (for example, using in-depth interviews or focus groups). Although the insights gained from such qualitative inquiry can serve as valuable input for quantitative surveys, this bottom-up strategy has rarely been applied in prior research (however, see Chapter 4 for some notable exceptions).

The fifth and final recommendation is to measure people's support for basic income in settings that are (or feel) more 'natural' to them. Most existing studies tend to pull people out of their everyday life and place them in an unfamiliar research environment so that they can be asked about their attitudes towards basic income. This is the case with traditional polls and survey experiments, but also with qualitative techniques such as in-depth interviews and focus groups. I consider it a major task for future research to also investigate people's opinions about basic income in habitats that are much more familiar to them. Promising techniques to achieve this—which have so far rarely been used in research—are (non-)participatory observation and social media analyses (for an excellent example of the latter, see Gielens et al., 2022). Both methods can even be applied in such a way that people are unaware that their opinions about basic income are under scientific investigation, which could severely reduce social desirability bias and allow us to study these opinions as they naturally unfold.

5.2.3 Exploring the 'Consequences' of Support for Basic Income

Despite its importance, there is surprisingly little research on the 'consequences' of popular support for basic income, making it unclear whether and how such support affects the different types of feasibility depicted in Fig. 5.1. Future research should, therefore, investigate how public opinion could influence the administrative, financial and political feasibility of basic income.

With regard to the administrative and financial aspects, a highly relevant question to address in future research is the extent to which people's support for basic income influences their (actual or intended) tax behaviour: are supporters also willing to pay taxes for it and would opponents try to evade them? Similar questions can be asked about the relationship between people's support for basic income and their (actual or intended) labour market participation and compliance with possible requirements (as present in a participation income, for example). Questions of this nature can be addressed with the help of traditional opinion polls, survey experiments or qualitative methods, such as in-depth interviews. However, it seems likely that these methods will suffer from social desirability bias, especially on the part of those who would indeed evade taxes, stop working or disregard any of the participation requirements. Therefore, future research should also rely on analytical techniques that are somewhat less vulnerable to this bias. These include, first of all, policy field experiments that make it possible to observe—using, for example, administrative records—people's real-world behaviour. However, ethical requirements mean that participation in such experiments tends to be completely voluntary, and researchers often need participants' informed consent to use sensitive personal data such as tax and work records. This is problematic, because it tends to exclude the group of people researchers are perhaps most interested in, in view of administrative and financial feasibility: opponents of basic income (who may refuse to participate *because* they dislike the policy) and those who would demonstrate undesirable behaviour, such as tax evasion (who might fear that study participation would expose them and lead to possible sanctions). This is less of a problem in lab experiments, in which participants are aware that the situation is purely hypothetical. Although experiments of this type can potentially reveal some fundamental tendencies of how people would react to the introduction of a basic income, their greatest weakness is arguably the fact that the situation is not 'real', in the sense that the results are fabricated in a controlled laboratory environment (thereby undermining its so-called 'ecological validity').

It will be even more important for future research to investigate how public opinion about basic income influences its political feasibility, which no empirical study has done to date. In this book, I have made the assumption that there is in fact a relationship between the two, in the sense that public opinion affects policymakers' (strategic) positions towards a basic income. Importantly, this assumption is shared by most scholars investigating the politics of basic income (see, for example, De Wispelaere & Noguera, 2012; Laenen et al., 2022; Torry, 2016). It is usually justified by referring to the long-established political science literature on policy responsiveness, as this argues that policymakers tend to take public preferences into account because they want to be re-elected, or they see it as their moral duty to do so (Page & Shapiro, 1983). It can be argued that basic income is—like most other social policies—hugely important to people (and policymakers), because it would directly affect the life of almost everyone living in the society in which it is implemented. Accordingly, this creates great incentives for policymakers to—at least rhetorically (see Hobolt & Klemmensen, 2008)—respond to public opinion, making basic income a likely candidate for responsiveness to occur. From this perspective, the case of basic income would simply add to the mounting empirical evidence showing that policymakers are indeed to some extent responsive to public opinion, including in the domain of social policy (Brooks & Manza, 2006; Schakel et al., 2020).

At the same time, basic income could also be seen as a somewhat unlikely case for responsiveness to occur, compared with most other social policies. This is because it performs worse on the three main factors that political scientists have recognized as explaining why responsiveness is more likely for some policy issues than for others: 'issue salience', 'opinion coherence' and 'policy radicalness' (Manza & Cook, 2002; Page & Shapiro, 1983). With regard to the first, it can be argued that basic income is less salient, visible and proximate than most other, existing social policies, because people generally lack direct experience of a basic income (which does not currently exist anywhere; see Chapter 1). Accordingly, it also seems likely that public opinion about basic income is less coherent compared with public opinion about existing social policies. This is again because people lack real, on-the-ground experience of a basic income, which they do have this with existing policies (for example, as benefit recipients or taxpayers). Furthermore, basic income is to some extent fighting an uphill battle, because most politicians appear to have a strong status quo bias (Gilens & Page, 2014) and much policymaking is a path-dependent endeavour (Pierson, 2000). This makes it less likely that public opinion will be followed when there is a radical overhaul of the existing system at stake, as would be the case with a basic income. If implemented, a basic income (the ideal-typical version in particular) would in fact radically transform 'welfare as we know it' in most countries, because it departs from the dominant view of making social benefits conditional on work requirements and/or selectively targeted at low-income groups through means testing. The radical nature of basic income may make it a less likely candidate for policy responsiveness compared with existing social policies, which can be reformed more incrementally.

This makes basic income a challenging case with regard to policy responsiveness, because it confronts us with a theoretical puzzle that has hitherto not been addressed empirically—as no study has ever investigated whether policymakers' positions towards a basic income are influenced by public opinion. Future research should nevertheless go further than the simple yes-or-no question of whether policy responsiveness occurs. Instead, the broader objective should be to uncover ***under which conditions*** (that is, who, when, where, why and how) such responsiveness is more likely or less likely to occur. With regard to the 'who' aspect, the goal should be to find out whether certain policymakers are more/less responsive to public opinion about basic income than others. More specifically, we would learn a great deal by comparing different types of policymakers with different characteristics and roles, for example, including incumbent politicians, trade union representatives and representatives of employers' organizations. Furthermore, the 'who' aspect should also address the issue of who—that is, which people—policymakers respond to: the general public or specific constituencies? The 'when' and 'where' aspects relate to the broader context in which policymakers operate. Future research should examine policymakers' responsiveness to public opinion about basic income in different countries, regions and time periods, as we know from prior research that such responsiveness is context specific (see, for example, Hobolt & Klemmensen, 2008; Wlezien & Soroka, 2012). Lastly, the 'how' and 'why' aspects refer to the micro-mechanisms behind policymakers' responsiveness (or lack thereof) to public opinion about basic income: ***why*** are they (un)responsive, and *how* do they collect and process information about public opinion? These are also questions that cannot be answered on the basis of prior research and should thus be part of future inquiries linking public opinion about basic income to its political feasibility.

Taken together, this book thus ends by questioning the very reason it was written in the first place; that is, because public opinion is assumed to influence the administrative, the financial and above all the political feasibility of basic income. In the end, however, this remains very much an open question that needs to be investigated further in future research.

References

Atkinson, A. (1996). The Case for a Participation Income. *The Political Quarterly, 67*(1), 67–70.

Borjas, G. J. (1999). Immigration and Welfare Magnets. *Journal of Labor Economics, 17*(4), 607–637.

Brooks, C., & Manza, J. (2006). *Why Welfare States Persist: The Importance of Public Opinion in Democracies*. Chicago University Press.

Browne, J., & Immervoll, H. (2017). Mechanics of Replacing Benefit Systems with a Basic Income: Comparative Results from a Microsimulation Approach. *The Journal of Economic Inequality, 15*(4), 325–344.

Busemeyer, M., Abrassart, A., & Nezi, R. (2021). Beyond Positive or Negative: New Perspectives on Feedback Effects in Public Opinion on the Welfare State. *British Journal of Political Science, 51*(1), 137–162.

Busemeyer, M., & Sahm, A. (2022). Social Investment, Redistribution or Basic Income? Exploring the Association Between Automation Risk and Welfare State Attitudes in Europe. *Journal of Social Policy, 51*(4), 751–770.

Chrisp, J., & De Wispelaere, J. (2022). Parading Utopia on the Road to Nowhere? An Introduction to the Special Issue on the Policy Impact of the European Basic Income Experiments. *European Journal of Social Security, 24*(3), 167–176.

Chrisp, J., & Martinelli, L. (2019). Neither Left Nor Right. In M. Torry (Ed.), *The Palgrave International Handbook of Basic Income* (pp. 477–492). Palgrave Macmillan.

Cigna, L. M. (2022). Looking for a North Star? Ideological Justifications and Trade Unions' Preferences for a Universal Basic Income. *European Journal of Industrial Relations, 28*(2), 129–146.

Clasen, J., & van Oorschot, W. (2002). Changing Principles in European Social Security. *European Journal of Social Security, 4*(2), 89–115.

Colombo, C., De Rocchi, T., Kurer, T., & Widmer, T. (2016, Juni). *Analyse der eidgenössichen Abstimmung vom 5*. GfS Bern.

European Commission. (2020). *Attitudes Towards Adequacy and Sustainability of Social Protection Systems in the EU*. Publications Office.

Dermont, C., & Weisstanner, D. (2020). Automation and the Future of the Welfare State: Basic Income as a Response to Technological Change? *Political Research Exchange, 2*(1). https://doi.org/10.1080/2474736X.2020.1757387 [online first]

De Wispelaere, J. (2015). *An Income of One's Own? The Political Analysis of Universal Basic Income* (Unpublished doctoral dissertation). University of Tampere.

De Wispelaere, J., & Morales, L. (2021). Emergency Basic Income During the Pandemic. *Cambridge Quarterly of Healthcare Ethics, 30*, 248–254.

De Wispelaere, J., & Noguera, J. (2012). On the Political Feasibility of Universal Basic Income: An Analytic Framework. In R. Caputo (Ed.), *Basic Income Guarantee and Politics. International Experiences and Perspectives on Income Guarantee* (pp. 17–39). Palgrave Macmillan.

De Wispelaere, J., & Stirton, L. (2007). The Public Administration Case Against Participation Income. *Social Service Review, 81*(3), 523–549.

Elkjaer, M. A., & Klitgaard, M. B. (2021). Economic Inequality and Political Responsiveness: A Systematic Review. *Perspectives on Politics*. https://doi.org/10.1017/S1537592721002188 [onlinefirst]

Elsässer, L., Hense, S., & Schäfer, A. (2021). Not Just Money: Unequal Responsiveness in Egalitarian Democracies. *Journal of European Public Policy, 28*(12), 1890–1908.

Franko, W. W., Kelly, N. J., & Witko, C. (2016). Class Bias in Voter Turnout, Representation, and Income Inequality. *Perspectives on Politics, 14*(2), 351–368.

Gielens, E., Roosma, F., & Achterberg, P. (2022). More Than a Free Lunch: A Content Analysis of the Controversies Surrounding Universal Basic Income on Dutch Twitter. *Social Policy and Society*. https://doi.org/10.1017/S1474746422000422 [onlinefirst]

Gilens, M. (2012). *Affluence & Influence. Economic Inequality and Political Power in America*. Princeton University Press.

Gilens, M., & Page, B. I. (2014). Testing Theories of American Politics: Elites, Interest Groups, and Average Citizens. *Perspectives on Politics, 12*(3), 564–581.

Green-Pedersen, C. (2002). *The Politics of Justification. Party Competition and Welfare-State Retrenchment in Denmark and the Netherlands from 1982 to 1998*. Amsterdam University Press.

Hanna, R., & Olken, B. A. (2018). Universal Basic Incomes Versus Targeted Transfers: Anti-Poverty Programs in Developing Countries. *Journal of Economic Perspectives, 32*(4), 201–226.

Herke, B., & Vicsek, L. (2022). The Attitudes of Young Citizens in Higher Education Towards Universal Basic Income in the Context of Automation—A Qualitative Study. *International Journal of Social Welfare, 33*(3), 310–322.

Hobolt, S. B., & Klemmensen, R. (2008). Government Responsiveness and Political Competition in Comparative Perspective. *Comparative Political Studies, 41*(3), 309–337.

Korpi, W., & Palme, J. (1998). The Paradox of Redistribution and Strategies of Equality: Welfare State Institutions, Inequality, and Poverty in the Western Countries. *American Sociological Review, 63*(5), 661–687.

Kramer, K. Z., Myhra, L. L., Zuiker, V. S., & Bauer, J. W. (2015). Comparison of Poverty and Income Disparity of Single Mothers and Fathers Across Three Decades: 1990–2010. *Gender Issues, 33*, 22–41.

Laenen, T., Mulayi, M. L., Francisco, C., & Van Lancker, W. (2021). *Basic Income in Belgium (BABEL) Survey Codebook V1.* Centre for Sociological Research, KU Leuven. https://osf.io/7ghfs/

Laenen, T., Van Hooteghem, A., & Rossetti, F. (2022). The Multidimensionality of Public Support for Basic Income: A Vignette Experiment. *Journal of European Public Policy*. https://doi.org/10.1080/13501763.2022.2055112 [onlinefirst]

Leff, B., Percy, A., Story, M., & Szlinder, M. (2019). Alternatives to Basic Income. In M. Torry (Ed.), *The Palgrave International Handbook of Basic Income* (pp. 213–231). Palgrave Macmillan.

Lux, T., & Mau, S. (2021). Homeownership and Social Policy Preferences. In T. Laenen, B. Meuleman, A. Otto, F. Roosma, & W. Van Lancker, *Leading Social Policy Analysis from the Front. Essays in Honour of Wim van Oorschot* (pp. 333–345). Centre for Sociological Research, KU Leuven.

Lynch, J., & Myrskylä, M. (2009). Always the Third Rail? Pension Income and Policy Preferences in European Democracies. *Comparative Political Studies, 42*(8), 1068–1097.

Manza, J., & Cook, F. L. (2002). A Democratic Polity? Three Views of Policy Responsiveness to Public Opinion in the United States. *American Politics Research, 30*(6), 630–667.

Murray, M., & Pateman, C. (Eds.). (2012). *Basic Income Worldwide. Horizons of Reform.* Palgrave Macmillan.

Page, B. I., & Shapiro, R. Y. (1983). Effects of Public Opinion on Policy. *American Political Science Review, 77*(1), 175–190.

Pampel, F. C., & Williamson, J. B. (1985). Age Structure, Politics, and Cross-National Patterns of Public Pension Expenditures. *American Sociological Review, 50*(6), 782–799.

Parolin, Z., & Siöland, L. (2020). Support for a Universal Basic Income: A Demand–Capacity Paradox? *Journal of European Social Policy, 30*(1), 5–19.

Pierson, P. (1993). When Effect Becomes Cause: Policy Feedback and Political Change. *World Politics, 45*(4), 595–628.

Pierson, P. (1994). *Dismantling the Welfare State? Reagan, Thatcher and the Politics of Retrenchment*. Cambridge University Press.

Pierson, P. (2000). Increasing Returns, Path Dependence, and the Study of Politics. *American Political Science Review, 94*(2), 251–267.

Pierson, P. (Ed.). (2001). *The New Politics of the Welfare State*. Oxford University Press.

Ravallion, M. (2009). *Do Poorer Countries Have Less Capacity for Redistribution?* (Policy Research Working Paper). World Bank Group.

Rincon, L. (2021). *The Paradox of Universality: Preferences for Universal Basic Income in Finland and Spain* (Unpublished doctoral dissertation). Universitat de Barcelona.

Rueda, D. (2007). *Social Democracy Inside Out: Partisanship and Labor Market Policy in Advanced Industrialized Democracies*. Oxford University Press.

Schakel, W., Burgoon, B., & Hakhverdian, A. (2020). Real but Unequal Representation in Welfare State Reform. *Politics & Society, 48*(1), 131–163.

Schneider, A., & Ingram, H. (1997). Social Construction of Target Populations: Implications for Politics and Policy. *American Political Science Review, 87*(2), 334–347.

Simanainen, M., & Kangas, O. (2020). Speaking to Those Who Know It Best: Does Participation in an Experiment Explain Citizens' Attitudes to Basic Income? *Journal of International and Comparative Social Policy, 36*(3), 269–283.

Stadelmann-Steffen, I., & Dermont, C. (2019). Citizens' Opinions About Basic Income Proposals Compared—A Conjoint Analysis of Finland and Switzerland. *Journal of Social Policy, 49*(2), 383–403.

Standing, G. (2020). *Battling Eight Giants: Basic Income Now*. I.B. Taurus.

Takamatsu, R., & Tachibanaki, T. (2014). What Needs to Be Considered When Introducing a New Welfare System: Who Supports Basic Income in Japan? In Y. Vanderborght & T. Yamamori (Eds.), *Basic Income in Japan. Prospects for a Radical Idea in a Transforming Welfare State* (pp. 197–218). Palgrave Macmillan.

Thomas, C. C., Walton, G. M., Reinhart, E. C., & Markus, H. R. (2023). Mitigating Welfare-Related Prejudice and Partisanship Among U.S. Conservatives with Moral Reframing of a Universal Basic Income Policy. *Journal of Experimental Social Psychology, 105*. https://doi.org/10.1016/j.jesp.2022.104424 [online only]

Torry, M. (2016). *The Feasibility of Citizen's Income*. Palgrave Macmillan.

Tourangeau, R., Edwards, B., Johnson, T., Wolter, K., & Bates, N. (Eds.). (2014). *Hard-to-Survey Populations*. Cambridge University Press.

Vanderborght, Y. (2006). Why Trade Unions Oppose Basic Income. *Basic Income Studies, 1*(1). https://doi.org/10.2202/1932-0183.1002 [online only]

Van Parijs, P., & Vanderborght, Y. (2017). *A Radical Proposal for a Free Society and a Sane Economy*. Harvard University Press.

van Oorschot, W., Laenen, T., Roosma, F., & Meuleman, B. (2022). Recent Advances in Understanding Welfare Attitudes in Europe. In K. Nelson, R. Nieuwenhuis, & M. Yerkes (Eds.), *Social Policy in Changing European Societies, Research Agendas for the 21st Century* (pp. 202–217). Edward Elgar Publishing.

Wlezien, C., & Soroka, S. N. (2012). Political Institutions and the Opinion-Policy Link. *West European Politics, 35*(6), 1407–1432.

APPENDICES

APPENDIX 1: THE SURVEY EXPERIMENTS IN CHAPTER 3

See Tables A1.1, A1.2, A1.3, and A1.4.

Table A1.1 Wording of the levels in the vignette experiment in the BABEL/BIN Survey

Dimensions	*Levels*	*Wording*
Amount	500	*The Belgian government provides a monthly income of €500*
	1000	*The Belgian government provides a monthly income of €1000*
	1500	*The Belgian government provides a monthly income of €1500*
Universality	Everyone, including newcomers	*That amount is paid to all adult residents in Belgium, including newcoming migrants*
	Residency requirement	*That amount is paid to all adults living in Belgium, on the condition that they have been in the country for a few years*
	Nationality requirement	*That amount is paid to all adults living in Belgium, on the condition that they have the Belgian nationality*

(continued)

© The Editor(s) (if applicable) and The Author(s), under exclusive license to Springer Nature Switzerland AG 2023

T. Laenen, *The Popularity of Basic Income*, Exploring the Basic Income Guarantee, https://doi.org/10.1007/978-3-031-29352-8

Table A1.1 (continued)

Dimensions	*Levels*	*Wording*
Conditionality	Fully unconditional	*People who are not working are not obliged to search for a paid job*
	Caring/volunteering required	*People who are not working are obliged to perform voluntary work or to take up caring responsibilities*
Integration	All benefits replaced	*The basic income replaces all existing social benefits*
	Several benefits replaced	*The basic income replaces some existing social benefits, such as child allowances and sickness benefits*
	Replaces but supplements	*The basic income replaces some existing social benefits but provides top-ups for people with additional needs or costs (e.g. people with children or disabled people)*
	No benefits replaced	*The basic income replaces no existing social benefits*
Financing	Climate tax	*The basic income is paid for by income taxes and social security contributions, which stay as they are. Potential additional costs are covered by a new climate tax on* CO_2 *emissions*
	Capital tax	*The basic income is paid for by taxes and social security contributions, which stay as they are. Potential additional costs are covered by a new tax on capital*
	Tax increase	*The basic income is paid for by income taxes and social security contributions, which will increase in the future*
	Budget neutral (only in BIN)	*The basic income is paid for by taxes and social security contributions, which will stay as they are*

Notes The total number of unique combinations in the BABEL Survey is $3 \times 3 \times 2 \times 4 \times 3 = 216$. The total number of unique combinations in the BIN Survey is $3 \times 3 \times 2 \times 4 \times 4 = 288$. One policy design dimension, that of accumulation, was held constant across the vignettes. This means that all respondents were told that 'people who work will receive the money they earn elsewhere on top of the basic income'. See Laenen et al. (2021) and Gielens (2022a) for more information about the BABEL Survey and the BIN Survey, respectively

Table A1.2 Wording of the levels in the vignette experiment in the BNES

Dimension	*Level*	*Wording*
Universality	All residents	*The Belgian government pays a monthly income to all residents*
	Residency requirement	*The Belgian government pays a monthly income to all residents, if they have lived in our country for a couple of years*
	Excluding the rich	*The Belgian government pays a monthly income to all residents, except to those who have a lot of money*
	Only the poor	*The Belgian government pays a monthly income only to residents who have little money*
Uniformity	Equality-based	*The amount is equal for everyone*
	Need-based	*The amount decreases as people earn more*
	Equity-based	*The amount increases as people have worked longer*
Conditionality	Fully unconditional	*People who are not working are not obliged to search for a paid job*
	Work required	*People who are not working are obliged to search for a paid job*
	Caring/volunteering required	*People who are not working are obliged to perform voluntary work or to take up caring responsibilities*
Integration	Replaces no benefits	*The basic income does not replace any other social benefits*
	Replaces all benefits, incl. pensions	*The basic income replaces all existing social benefits, such as pensions*
	Replaces all benefits, incl. unemployment benefits	*The basic income replaces all existing social benefits, such as unemployment benefits*
Accumulation	Allowed	*People receive the basic income on top of the money they earn by working or in another way*
	Not allowed	*The basic income is reduced by the money people earn by working or in another way*

Notes The total number of unique combinations is $4 \times 3 \times 3 \times 3 \times 2 = 216$. One policy design dimension, that of financing, was held constant across the vignettes. This means that all respondents were told that 'the basic income will be paid for through taxes'. See Abts, Swyngedouw, et al. (2021) for more information about the BNES

Table A1.3 Wording of the levels in the conjoint experiment by Rincon

Dimension	*Level*	*Wording*
Universality (target population)	Everyone	*To whom the benefit is directed: everyone*
	Only with minors	*To whom the benefit is directed: those with minors*
	Only with family dependents	*To whom the benefit is directed: to those with dependent family members*
	Only the poor	*To whom the benefit is directed: to those under the poverty threshold*
Universality (legal requirements)	Residency requirement 6 months	*Legal requirements: having a residence permit (since at least 6 months ago)*
	Residency requirement 1 year	*Legal requirements: having a residence permit (since at least 1 year ago)*
	Residency requirement 5 years	*Legal requirements: having a residence permit (since at least 5 years ago)*
	Citizenship	*Legal requirements: citizenship*
Conditionality	Fully unconditional	*Conditions to receive the benefit: unconditional*
	Full-time employment	*Conditions to receive the benefit: being in full-time employment*
	Self-employment	*Conditions to receive the benefit: being in self-employment*
	Part-time employment	*Conditions to receive the benefit: being in part-time employment*
	Volunteering	*Conditions to receive the benefit: involved in volunteering or community work*
	Training/education	*Conditions to receive the benefit: involved in training or education*
	Unable to work	*Conditions to receive the benefit: unable to work*
	Unemployed—searching for job	*Conditions to receive the benefit: being unemployed but looking for employment*
	Unemployed—not searching for new job	*Conditions to receive the benefit: being unemployed but not looking for employment*
Individuality	Individuals	*Benefit recipients: individuals*

(continued)

Table A1.3 (continued)

Dimension	*Level*	*Wording*
	Households	*Benefit recipients: families/households*
Generosity	€200	*Amount: €200*
	€500	*Amount: €500*
	€900	*Amount: €900*
	€1200	*Amount: €1200*
	€1500	*Amount: €1500*
Financing	Increase corporate tax	*How it will be funded: increase taxes for corporations*
	Increase capital tax	*How it will be funded: increase capital income tax*
	Introduce technology tax	*How it will be funded: introduce a tax on technology*
	Introduce transaction tax	*How it will be funded: introduce a tax on inter-bank financial transactions*
	Introduce environmental tax	*How it will be funded: introduce a new environmental tax*
	Increase environmental tax	*How it will be funded: increase environmental taxes on excise liquid fuels (FI)/hydrocarbons (ES)*
	Increase inheritance tax	*How it will be funded: increase inheritance tax*
	Increase income tax for everyone	*How it will be funded: increase personal income tax for everyone*
	Increase income tax for the rich	*How it will be funded: increase personal income tax for the highest incomes*
	Cutting unemployment benefits	*How it will be funded: cutting unemployment benefits*
	Cutting social assistance	*How it will be funded: cutting social assistance for low-income families*
	Cutting housing benefits	*How it will be funded: cutting housing benefits*
	Cutting pension spending	*How it will be funded: cutting pension spending*
	Cutting health spending	*How it will be funded: cutting spending on health*
	Cutting education spending	*How it will be funded: cutting spending on education*
	Cutting defence spending	*How it will be funded: cutting spending on defence*

Notes The total number of unique combinations is $4 \times 4 \times 9 \times 2 \times 5 \times 16 = 23{,}040$. Because of the very high number of unique combinations, the different levels in the conjoint experiment were grouped into meaningful categories. See Rincon (2021) for more information about the experiment

Table A1.4 Wording of the levels in the conjoint experiment by Stadelmann-Steffen and Dermont

Dimension	*Level*	*Wording*
Universality	Permanent residents	*Entitlement: permanent residents*
	Residency requirement of 5 years	*Entitlement: after 5 years of residence*
	Residency requirement of 10 years	*Entitlement: after 10 years of residence*
Generosity (adults)	Very low	*Amount for adults: CHF 1000 per month (CH)/€560 per month (FI)*
	Low	*Amount for adults: CHF 1750 per month (CH)/€1200 per month (FI)*
	Middle	*Amount for adults: CHF 2500 per month (CH)/€1750 per month (FI)*
	High	*Amount for adults: CHF 3000 per month (CH)/€2300 per month (FI)*
Generosity (children)	Low	*Amount for children: CHF 250 per month (CH)/€170 per month (FI)*
	Middle	*Amount for children: CHF 450 per month (CH)/€300 per month (FI)*
	High	*Amount for children: CHF 625 per month (CH)/€430 per month (FI)*
Integration	Replaces social benefits	*Social security and welfare programmes: basic income replaces all existing measures*
	Cutbacks in social benefits	*Social security and welfare programmes: existing measures are cut back and additional to basic income*
	Replaces cash transfers	*Direct payments: basic income replaces direct payments*
	Cutbacks in cash transfers	*Direct payments: existing measures are cut back and additional to basic income*
Financing	Cutting back expenditure	*Financing: cutting back other government expenses*
	Income tax	*Financing: income tax*
	Value-added tax	*Financing: value-added tax*
	Transaction tax	*Financing: transaction tax*

Notes The total number of unique combinations is 3 × 4 × 3 × 4 × 4 = 576. See Stadelmann-Steffen and Dermont (2020) for more information about the experiment

Appendix 2: The Introductory Text in the Survey Experiment by Liebig and Mau

1. Introduction

In Germany we have a number of different types of social welfare payments which provide those who are needy with a decent standard of living e.g. unemployment payments, retirement pension, benefit payment, housing subsidies etc. Recently, politicians have been discussing different ways of simplifying the whole German system of social welfare transfers. One suggestion made within these debates was to replace the different types of payments with a general income subsidy. All citizens who are needy would get a fixed amount of money from the State and all other types of social welfare payments would be abolished. Those citizens who have a job but whose income is very low also get an income subsidy from the State. With this new regulation everybody in Germany would have a guaranteed minimum income.

The question now is, what should be the amount on income subsidy provided by the State and should these payments differ according to the individual situation of the person subsidized? In the following we are going to present you with a number of examples of fictitious persons who may get a State-financed income subsidy. We want to know if, in your opinion, the amount of income subsidy is just and fair or if you think the income subsidy is unjust. The only thing we are interested in is your personal opinion and your views on how just or unjust the particular income subsidies in the presented examples are.

Source Liebig and Mau (2004: 214).

Appendix 3: Interaction Between Generosity and Integration, by Benefit Recipiency

See Table A3.1.

Table A3.1 Combinations of generosity and integration by benefit recipiency category

Generosity → *Integration ↓*	*€500*		*€1000*		*€1500*	
	Non-recipients	*Recipients*	*Non-recipients*	*Recipients*	*Non-recipients*	*Recipients*
All benefits replaced	58.6	48.7	52.0	54.4	47.9	59.3
Several benefits replaced	44.0	49.6	55.2	51.8	51.5	59.2
Replaces but supplements	48.3	56.4	53.8	57.4	56.5	61.5
No benefits replaced	55.7	55.4	45.8	57.3	51.9	58.2
Generosity → *Integration ↓*	*€500*		*€1000*		*€1500*	
	Child benefits	*Working-age benefits*	*Child benefits*	*Working-age benefits*	*Child benefits*	*Working-age benefits*
All benefits replaced	50.0	50.8	54.9	59.9	62.8	65.3
Several benefits replaced	53.1	51.1	59.7	52.1	59.5	64.4
Replaces but supplements	53.0	64.5	63.3	58.2	69.3	62.2
No benefits replaced	58.3	59.6	60.5	63.9	55.5	66.3
Generosity → *Integration ↓*	*€500*		*€1000*		*€1500*	
	Old-age pensions		*Old-age pensions*		*Old-age pensions*	
All benefits replaced	46.9		52.6		53.1	
Several benefits replaced	45.9		47.4		56.4	
Replaces but supplements	54.1		52.7		57.7	
No benefits replaced	52.1		51.8		54.7	

Appendix 4: The 'Policy Outcomes Part' of the BABEL Experiment

See Table A4.1.

Table A4.1 Wording of the policy outcomes in the BABEL experiment

Dimensions	*Levels*	*Wording*
Poverty	Increase	*The level of poverty will increase in Belgium*
	Decrease	*The level of poverty will decrease in Belgium*
	Stagnate	*The level of poverty will remain more or less the same in Belgium*
Income inequality	Increase	*The gap between the rich and the poor will increase in Belgium*
	Decrease	*The gap between the rich and the poor will decrease in Belgium*
	Stagnate	*The gap between the rich and the poor will remain more or less the same in Belgium*
Unemployment	Increase	*The number of unemployed people will increase in Belgium*
	Decrease	*The number of unemployed people will decrease in Belgium*
	Stagnate	*The number of unemployed people will remain more or less the same in Belgium*
Entrepreneurship	Increase	*The number of entrepreneurs will increase in Belgium*
	Decrease	*The number of entrepreneurs will decrease in Belgium*
	Stagnate	*The number of entrepreneurs will remain more or less the same in Belgium*
Informal care	Increase	*The number of informal caregivers will increase in Belgium*
	Decrease	*The number of informal caregivers will decrease in Belgium*
	Stagnate	*The number of informal caregivers will remain more or less the same in Belgium*

Notes The total number of unique combinations in the BABEL Survey is $3 \times 3 \times 3 \times 3 \times 3 = 243$. 'Informal caregivers' were described in a footnote as 'people who provide voluntary and unpaid care to people with physical, mental or (social) psychological disabilities in their family, household or other social networks'.

Appendix 5: Gender Differences in the Reasons to Support or Oppose Basic Income

See Table A5.1 and Fig. A5.1.

Table A5.1 Support for basic income with different policy outcomes, by gender

	Men	*Women*
Poverty		
Decrease	52.5	54.6
Stagnate	56.9	53.9
Increase	53.1	57.0
Income inequality		
Decrease	55.4	55.7
Stagnate	52.2	55.3
Increase	54.7	54.3
Unemployment		
Decrease	55.2	56.3
Stagnate	53.5	53.9
Increase	53.7	55.1
Entrepreneurship		
Decrease	51.9	52.9
Stagnate	56.1	56.5
Increase	54.3	56.0
Informal care		
Decrease	55.5	55.5
Stagnate	51.9	53.7
Increase	54.8	56.3

Source BABEL Survey (2021). Question wording: see Fig. 4.11 and Appendix 4. The table presents the mean score for each outcome in the experiment for each gender

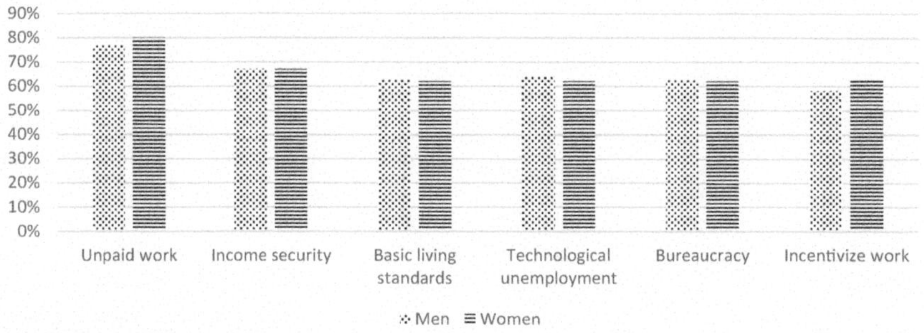

Fig. A5.1 Arguments for basic income in the UK, by gender (*Source* Ipsos MORI [2017]. Question wording: see Fig. 4.3. The graph presents the percentage of respondents who endorsed the respective arguments, by gender)

References

Aarøe, L., & Petersen, M. B. (2014). Crowding Out Culture: Scandinavians and Americans Agree on Social Welfare in the Face of Deservingness Cues. *The Journal of Politics, 76*(3), 684–697.

Abts, K., Dalle Mulle, E., van Kessel, S., & Michel, E. (2021). The Welfare Agenda of the Populist Radical Right in Western Europe: Combining Welfare Chauvinism, Producerism and Populism. *Swiss Political Science Review, 27*(1), 21–40.

Abts, K., Swyngedouw, M., Meuleman, B., Stefanelli, A., Wopereis, D., & Van Den Abbeele, J. (2021). *Belgian National Elections Study 2019. Codebook: Questions and Frequency Tables*. ISPO-KU Leuven.

Ackerman, B., & Alstott, A. (1999). *The Stakeholder Society*. Yale University Press.

Adriaans, J., Liebig, S., & Schupp, J. (2019). In Germany, Younger, Better Educated Persons, and Lower Income Groups Are More Likely to Be in Favor of Unconditional Basic Income. *DIW Weekly Report, 15*, 127–134.

Afscharian, D., Muliavka, V., Ostrowski, M. S., & Siegel, L. (2022). The State of the UBI Debate: Mapping the Arguments for and Against UBI. *Basic Income Studies, 17*(2), 213–237.

Alesina, A., & Fuchs-Schündeln, N. (2005). Goodbye Lenin (or Not?): The Effect of Communism on People's Preferences. *The American Economic Review, 97*(4), 1507–1528.

Alves, W. M., & Rossi, P. H. (1978). Who Should Get What? Fairness Judgments of the Distribution of Earnings. *American Journal of Sociology, 84*(3), 541–564.

© The Editor(s) (if applicable) and The Author(s), under exclusive license to Springer Nature Switzerland AG 2023

T. Laenen, *The Popularity of Basic Income*, Exploring the Basic Income Guarantee, https://doi.org/10.1007/978-3-031-29352-8

Andersen, J. G., & Bjørklund, T. (1990). Structural Changes and New Cleavages: The Progress Parties in Denmark and Norway. *Acta Sociologica, 33*(3), 195–217.

Andersson, J. A., & Kangas, O. (2004). Popular Support for Basic Income in Sweden and Finland. In G. Standing (Ed.), *Promoting Income Security as a Right: Europe and North America* (pp. 285–298). Anthem Press.

Andeweg, R. B. (2005). The Netherlands: The Sanctity of Proportionality. In M. Gallagher & P. Mitchell (Eds.), *The Politics of Electoral Systems* (pp. 491–510). Oxford University Press.

Arntz, M., Gregory, T., & Zierahn, U. (2016). *The Risk of Automation for Jobs in OECD Countries: A Comparative Analysis* (OECD Social, Employment and Migration Working Papers, No. 189). OECD Publishing.

Atkinson, A. (1996). The Case for a Participation Income. *The Political Quarterly, 67*(1), 67–70.

Auspurg, K., & Hinz, T. (2015). *Factorial Survey Experiments*. Sage.

Barnes, L. (2015). The Size and Shape of Government: Preferences over Redistributive Tax Policy. *Socio-Economic Review, 13*(1), 55–78.

Baumberg Geiger, B. (2021). Disabled but Not Deserving? The Perceived Deservingness of Disability Welfare Benefit Claimants. *Journal of European Social Policy, 31*(3), 337–351.

Bay, A., & Pedersen, A. (2006). The Limits of Social Solidarity: Basic Income, Immigration and the Legitimacy of the Universal Welfare State. *Acta Sociologica, 49*(4), 419–436.

Berens, S., & Gelephitis, M. (2019). Welfare State Structure, Inequality, and Public Attitudes Towards Progressive Taxation. *Socio-Economic Review, 17*(4), 823–850.

Bollain, J., Groot, L., Miller, A., Schmidt, E., Tahiraj, E., Verlaat, T., & Yi, G. (2019). A Variety of Experiments. In M. Torry (Ed.), *The Palgrave International Handbook of Basic Income* (pp. 407–435). Palgrave Macmillan.

Borjas, G. J. (1999). Immigration and Welfare Magnets. *Journal of Labor Economics, 17*(4), 607–637.

Brooks, C., & Manza, J. (2006). *Why Welfare States Persist: The Importance of Public Opinion in Democracies*. Chicago University Press.

Browne, J., & Immervoll, H. (2017). Mechanics of Replacing Benefit Systems with a Basic Income: Comparative Results from a Microsimulation Approach. *The Journal of Economic Inequality, 15*(4), 325–344.

Busemeyer, M., Abrassart, A., & Nezi, R. (2021). Beyond Positive or Negative: New Perspectives on Feedback Effects in Public Opinion on the Welfare State. *British Journal of Political Science, 51*(1), 137–162.

Busemeyer, M., & Sahm, A. (2022). Social Investment, Redistribution or Basic Income? Exploring the Association Between Automation Risk and Welfare State Attitudes in Europe. *Journal of Social Policy, 51*(4), 751–770.

Buss, C., Ebbinghaus, B., & Naumann, E. (2017). Making Deservingness of the Unemployed Conditional. Changing Public Support for the Conditionality of Unemployment Benefits Across Europe. In W. van Oorschot, B. Meuleman, T. Reeskens, & F. Roosma (Eds.), *The Social Legitimacy of Targeted Welfare: Attitudes to Welfare Deservingness* (pp. 167–185). Edward Elgar Publishing.

Caputo, R. (Ed.). (2012). *Basic Income Guarantee and Politics.* Palgrave Macmillan.

Careja, R., & Harris, E. (2022). Thirty Years of Welfare Chauvinism Research: Findings and Challenges. *Journal of European Social Policy, 32*(2), 214–244.

Castillo, J. C., Olivos, F., & Azar, A. (2019). Deserving a Just Pension: A Factorial Survey Approach. *Social Science Quarterly, 100*(1), 359–378.

Chrisp, J., & De Wispelaere, J. (2022). Parading Utopia on the Road to Nowhere? An Introduction to the Special Issue on the Policy Impact of the European Basic Income Experiments. *European Journal of Social Security, 24*(3), 167–176.

Chrisp, J., & Martinelli, L. (2019). Neither Left Nor Right. In M. Torry (Ed.), *The Palgrave International Handbook of Basic Income* (pp. 477–492). Palgrave Macmillan.

Chrisp, J., Pulkka, V. V., & Rincon, L. (2020). Snowballing or Wilting? What Affects Public Support for Varying Models of Basic Income? *Journal of International and Comparative Social Policy, 36*(3), 223–236.

Cigna, L. M. (2022). Looking for a North Star? Ideological Justifications and Trade Unions' Preferences for a Universal Basic Income. *European Journal of Industrial Relations, 28*(2), 129–146.

Clasen, J. (1997). Social Insurance—An Outmoded Concept of Social Protection? In J. Clasen (Ed.), *Social Insurance in Europe* (pp. 1–13). The Policy Press.

Clasen, J., & Clegg, D. (2007). Levels and Levers of Conditionality: Measuring Change Within Welfare States. In J. Clasen & N. Siegel (Eds.), *Investigating Welfare State Change. The 'Dependent Variable Problem' in Comparative Analysis* (pp. 166–197). Edward Elgar Publishing.

Clasen, J., & van Oorschot, W. (2002). Changing Principles in European Social Security. *European Journal of Social Security, 4*(2), 89–115.

Coêlho, D. B. (2012). Brazil: Basic Income—A New Model of Innovation Diffusion. In M. C. Murray & C. Pateman (Eds.), *Basic Income Worldwide. Horizons of Reform* (pp. 59–77). Palgrave Macmillan.

Cole, G. D. H. (1935). *Principles of Economic Planning*. Macmillan & Co.

Colombo, C., De Rocchi, T., Kurer, T., & Widmer, T. (2016, Juni). *Analyse der eidgenössichen Abstimmung vom 5.* GfS Bern.

Cunliffe, J., & Erreygers, G. (2001). The Enigmatic Legacy of Charles Fourier: Joseph Charlier and Basic Income. *History of Political Economy, 33*(3), 459–484.

Cunliffe, J., & Erreygers, G. (Eds.). (2004). *The Origins of Universal Grants. An Anthology of Historical Writings on Basic Capital and Basic Income*. Palgrave Macmillan.

Delsen, L. (2019). *Empirical Research on an Unconditional Basic Income in Europe*. Springer.

Delsen, L., & Schilpzand, R. (2019). Individual Preferences for the Unconditional Basic Income in the European Union. In L. Delsen (Ed.), *Empirical Research on an Unconditional Basic Income in Europe* (pp. 29–60). Springer.

Dermont, C., & Weisstanner, D. (2020). Automation and the Future of the Welfare State: Basic Income as a Response to Technological Change? *Political Research Exchange, 2*(1). https://doi.org/10.1080/2474736X.2020.1757387 [online first]

De Wispelaere, J. (2015). *An Income of One's Own? The Political Analysis of Universal Basic Income* (Unpublished doctoral dissertation). University of Tampere.

De Wispelaere, J., & Morales, L. (2021). Emergency Basic Income During the Pandemic. *Cambridge Quarterly of Healthcare Ethics, 30*, 248–254.

De Wispelaere, J., & Noguera, J. (2012). On the Political Feasibility of Universal Basic Income: An Analytic Framework. In R. Caputo (Ed.), *Basic Income Guarantee and Politics. International Experiences and Perspectives on Income Guarantee* (pp. 17–39). Palgrave Macmillan.

De Wispelaere, J., & Stirton, L. (2004). The Many Faces of Universal Basic Income. *The Political Quarterly, 75*(3), 266–274.

De Wispelaere, J., & Stirton, L. (2007). The Public Administration Case Against Participation Income. *Social Service Review, 81*(3), 523–549.

Dolezal, M. (2010). Exploring the Stabilization of a Political Force: The Social and Attitudinal Basis of Green Parties in the Age of Globalization. *West European Politics, 33*(3), 534–552.

Edlund, J. (2003). Attitudes Towards Taxation: Ignorant and Incoherent? *Scandinavian Political Studies, 26*(2), 145–168.

Elkjaer, M. A., & Klitgaard, M. B. (2021). Economic Inequality and Political Responsiveness: A Systematic Review. *Perspectives on Politics*. https://doi.org/10.1017/S1537592721002188 [onlinefirst]

Elsässer, L., Hense, S., & Schäfer, A. (2021). Not Just Money: Unequal Responsiveness in Egalitarian Democracies. *Journal of European Public Policy, 28*(12), 1890–1908.

Esping-Andersen, G. (1990). *The Three Worlds of Welfare Capitalism*. Princeton University Press.

Esping-Andersen, G. (1999). *Social Foundations of Postindustrial Economies*. Oxford University Press.

ESS ERIC. (2021). *The Human Values Scale: Findings from the European Social Survey*. ESS ERIC.

European Commission. (2020). *Attitudes Towards Adequacy and Sustainability of Social Protection Systems in the EU*. Publications Office.

Ezrow, L., De Vries, C., Steenbergen, M., & Edwards, E. (2010). Mean Voter Representation and Partisan Constituency Representation: Do Parties Respond to the Mean Voter Position or to Their Supporters? *Party Politics, 17*(3), 275–301.

Franko, W. W., Kelly, N. J., & Witko, C. (2016). Class Bias in Voter Turnout, Representation, and Income Inequality. *Perspectives on Politics, 14*(2), 351–368.

Frey, C. B., & Osborne, M. A. (2017). The Future of Employment: How Susceptible Are Jobs to Computerisation? *Technological Forecasting and Social Change, 114*, 254–280.

Friedman, M. (1962). *Capitalism and Freedom*. University of Chicago Press.

Garand, J. C., Xu, P., & Davis, B. C. (2017). Immigration Attitudes and Support for the Welfare State in the American Mass Public. *American Journal of Political Science, 61*(1), 146–162.

Gatskova, K. (2013). Distributive Justice Attitudes in Ukraine: Need, Desert or Social Minimum? *Communist and Post-Communist Studies, 46*, 227–241.

Geels, F. (2023). Assessing Basic Income Feasibility Political Parties' Positions on the French-Speaking Belgian Scene. *Politics of the Low Countries*. https://www.elevenjournals.com/tijdschrift/PLC/2023/Online%20First/PLC-D-22-00004 [onlinefirst]

George, G. M., & Ortiz-Juarez, E. (2020). *Temporary Basic Income: Protecting Poor and Vulnerable People in Developing Countries*. United Nations Development Programme.

Gielens, E., Roosma, F., & Achterberg, P. (2022a). *Basic Income Netherlands (BIN) Survey*. School of Social and Behavioral Sciences, Tilburg University. https://dataverse.nl/dataset.xhtml?persistentId=doi:10.34894/2ZAVNQ

Gielens, E., Roosma, F., & Achterberg, P. (2022b). More Than a Free Lunch: A Content Analysis of the Controversies Surrounding Universal Basic Income on Dutch Twitter. *Social Policy and Society*. https://doi.org/10.1017/S1474746422000422 [onlinefirst]

Gilens, M. (1999). *Why Americans Hate Welfare: Race, Media and the Politics of Antipoverty Policy*. University of Chicago Press.

Gilens, M. (2012). *Affluence & Influence. Economic Inequality and Political Power in America*. Princeton University Press.

Gilens, M., & Page, B. I. (2014). Testing Theories of American Politics: Elites, Interest Groups, and Average Citizens. *Perspectives on Politics, 12*(3), 564–581.

Gilligan, C. (1982). *In a Different Voice: Psychological Theory and Women's Development*. Harvard University Press.

Goodin, R., & Le Grand, J. (1987). *Not Only the Poor: The Middle Classes and the Welfare State*. Allen & Unwin.

Gough, I. (2019). Universal Basic Services: A Theoretical and Moral Framework. *The Political Quarterly, 90*(3), 534–542.

Green-Pedersen, C. (2002). *The Politics of Justification. Party Competition and Welfare-State Retrenchment in Denmark and the Netherlands from 1982 to 1998*. Amsterdam University Press.

Grog, C., & Erickson, G. (2012). The Improbable but True Story of How the Alaska Permanent Fund and the Alaska Permanent Fund Dividend Came to Be. In K. Widerquist & M. W. Howard (Eds.), *Alaska's Permanent Fund Dividend. Examining its Suitability as a Model* (pp. 15–39). Palgrave Macmillan.

Gross, C., Lorek, K., & Richter, F. (2017). Attitudes Towards Inheritance Taxation—Results from a Survey Experiment. *Journal of Economic Inequality, 15*, 93–112.

Haarmann, C., Haarmann, D., & Nattrass, N. (2019). The Namibian Basic Income Grant Pilot. In M. Torry (Ed.), *The Palgrave International Handbook of Basic Income* (pp. 357–472). Palgrave Macmillan.

Hainmueller, J., Hopkins, D. J., & Yamamoto, T. (2014). Causal Inference in Conjoint Analysis: Understanding Multidimensional Choices via Stated Preference Experiments. *Political Analysis, 22*(1), 1–30.

Hanna, R., & Olken, B. A. (2018). Universal Basic Incomes Versus Targeted Transfers: Anti-Poverty Programs in Developing Countries. *Journal of Economic Perspectives, 32*(4), 201–226.

Herke, B., & Vicsek, L. (2022). The Attitudes of Young Citizens in Higher Education Towards Universal Basic Income in the Context of Automation—A Qualitative Study. *International Journal of Social Welfare, 33*(3), 310–322.

Hobolt, S. B., & Klemmensen, R. (2008). Government Responsiveness and Political Competition in Comparative Perspective. *Comparative Political Studies, 41*(3), 309–337.

Jacques, O., & Noël, A. (2020). Targeting Within Universalism. *Journal of European Social Policy, 31*(1), 15–29.

Johnson, A. F., & Roberto, K. J. (2020). The COVID-19 Pandemic: Time for a Universal Basic Income? *Public Administration and Development, 40*(4), 232–235.

Jordan, S., Ferguson, G., & Haglin, K. (2022). Measuring and Framing Support for Universal Basic Income. *Social Policy & Administration, 56*(1), 138–147.

Kahneman, D., & Tversky, A. (1984). Choices, Values, and Frames. *American Psychologist, 39*(4), 341–350.

Kangas, O., Jauhiainen, S., Simanainen, M., & Ylikännö, M. (2021). *Experimenting with Unconditional Basic Income. Lessons from the Finnish BI Experiment 2017–2018*. Edward Elgar Publishing.

Karshenas, M., & Tabatabai, H. (2019). Basic Income by Default: Lessons from Iran's 'Cash Subsidy' Program. In M. Torry (Ed.), *The Palgrave International Handbook of Basic Income* (pp. 339–356). Palgrave Macmillan.

Kim, D., & Mah, J. S. (2021). Basic Income Policy of Korea. *Journal of Poverty, 27*(1), 15–32.

King, J. E., & Marangos, J. (2006). Two Arguments for Basic Income: Thomas Paine (1737–1809) and Thomas Spence (1750–1814). *History of Economic Ideas, 14*(1), 55–71.

Kootstra, A. (2016). (Un)Deserving Welfare Claimants in Britain and the Netherlands: Examining the Role of Ethnicity and Migration Status Using a Vignette Experiment. *European Sociological Review, 32*(3), 325–328.

Korpi, W., & Palme, J. (1998). The Paradox of Redistribution and Strategies of Equality: Welfare State Institutions, Inequality, and Poverty in the Western Countries. *American Sociological Review, 63*(5), 661–687.

Kozàk, M. (2021). Cultural Productivism and Public Support for the Universal Basic Income from a Cross-National Perspective. *European Societies, 23*(1), 23–45.

Kramer, K. Z., Myhra, L. L., Zuiker, V. S., & Bauer, J. W. (2015). Comparison of Poverty and Income Disparity of Single Mothers and Fathers Across Three Decades: 1990–2010. *Gender Issues, 33*, 22–41.

Laenen, T. (2018). Do Institutions Matter? The Interplay Between Income Benefit Design, Popular Perceptions, and the Social Legitimacy of Targeted Welfare. *Journal of European Social Policy, 28*(1), 4–17.

Laenen, T. (2020). *Welfare Deservingness and Welfare Policy. Popular Deservingness Opinions and their Interaction with Welfare State Policies.* Edward Elgar Publishing.

Laenen, T., & Gugushvili, G. (2021). Are Universal Welfare Policies Really More Popular Than Selective Ones? A Critical Discussion of Empirical Research. *International Journal of Sociology and Social Policy, 41*(9/10), 1134–1147.

Laenen, T., & Gugushvili, G. (2022). Welfare State Dissatisfaction and Support for Major Welfare Reform: Towards Means-Tested Welfare or Universal Basic Income? *International Journal of Social Welfare.* https://doi.org/10.1111/ijsw.12546 [onlinefirst]

Laenen, T., & Meuleman, B. (2017). A Universal Rank Order of Deservingness? Geographical, Temporal and Social-Structural Comparisons. In W. van Oorschot, F. Roosma, B. Meuleman, & T. Reeskens (Eds.), *The Social Legitimacy of Targeted Welfare: Attitudes to Welfare Deservingness* (pp. 37–54). Edward Elgar Publishing.

Laenen, T., & Meuleman, B. (2019). Public Support for the Social Rights and Social Obligations of the Unemployed: Two Sides of the Same Coin? *International Journal of Social Welfare, 28*(4), 454–467.

Laenen, T., Mulayi, M. L., Francisco, C., & Van Lancker, W. (2021). *Basic Income in Belgium (BABEL) Survey Codebook V1.* Centre for Sociological Research, KU Leuven. https://osf.io/7ghfs/

Laenen, T., Van Hooteghem, A., & Rossetti, F. (2022). The Multidimensionality of Public Support for Basic Income: A Vignette Experiment. *Journal of European Public Policy.* https://doi.org/10.1080/13501763.2022.2055112 [onlinefirst]

Le Clainche, C. (2004). Public Support for Basic Income Schemes and a Universal Right to Health Care: What the French People Think. In G. Standing (Ed.), *Promoting Income Security as a Right: Europe and North America* (pp. 401–426). Anthem Press.

Lee, S. (2018). Attitudes Toward Universal Basic Income and Welfare State in Europe: A Research Note. *Basic Income Studies, 13*(1). https://doi.org/10.1515/bis-2018-0002 [online only]

Leff, B., Percy, A., Story, M., & Szlinder, M. (2019). Alternatives to Basic Income. In M. Torry (Ed.), *The Palgrave International Handbook of Basic Income* (pp. 213–231). Palgrave Macmillan.

Legein, T., Vandeleene, A., Randour, F., Heyvaert, P., Perrez, J., & Reuchamps, M. (2018). Framing the Basic Income: An Experimental Study of How Arguments and Metaphors Influence Individuals' Opinion Formation. *Basic Income Studies, 13*(2). https://doi.org/10.1515/bis-2018-0010 [online only]

Liebig, S., & Mau, S. (2004). A Legitimate Guaranteed Minimum Income? In G. Standing (Ed.), *Promoting Income Security as a Right: Europe and North America* (pp. 207–228). Anthem Press.

Lux, T., & Mau, S. (2021). Homeownership and Social Policy Preferences. In T. Laenen, B. Meuleman, A. Otto, F. Roosma, & W. Van Lancker, *Leading Social Policy Analysis from the Front. Essays in Honour of Wim van Oorschot* (pp. 333–345). Centre for Sociological Research, KU Leuven.

Lynch, J., & Myrskylä, M. (2009). Always the Third Rail? Pension Income and Policy Preferences in European Democracies. *Comparative Political Studies, 42*(8), 1068–1097.

Martinelli, L. (2017). *Assessing the Case for a Universal Basic Income in the UK* (IPR Policy Brief). University of Bath.

Manza, J., & Cook, F. L. (2002). A Democratic Polity? Three Views of Policy Responsiveness to Public Opinion in the United States. *American Politics Research, 30*(6), 630–667.

Meade, J. (1990). What Can We Learn from the Agathotopians? *Il Politico: rivista italiana di scienze politiche, 55*, 5–16.

Miller, A., Yamamori, T., & Zelleke, A. (2019). The Gender Effects of a Basic Income. In M. Torry (Ed.), *The Palgrave International Handbook of Basic Income* (pp. 133–153). Palgrave Macmillan.

Milner, M., & Mabel, E. (1918). *Scheme for a State Bonus*. Simpkin, Marshall & Co.

Morel, N., & Palme, J. (2012). Financing the Welfare State and the Politics of Taxation. In B. Greve (Ed.), *The Routledge Handbook of the Welfare State* (pp. 400–409). Routledge.

Murray, C. (2008). Guaranteed Income as a Replacement for the Welfare State. *Basic Income Studies, 3*(2). https://doi.org/10.2202/1932-0183.1115 [online only]

Murray, M., & Pateman, C. (Eds.). (2012). *Basic Income Worldwide. Horizons of Reform*. Palgrave Macmillan.

Nettle, D., Johnson, E., Johnson, M., & Saxe, R. (2021). Why Has the COVID-19 Pandemic Increased Support for Universal Basic Income? *Humanities & Social Sciences Communications, 8*(1), 1–12.

Offe, C., & De Deken, J. (1999, November 5). *Work, Time, and Social Participation. Policy Options for Dealing with Labor Market Precariousness*. Paper Presented at the Workshop "Back to Full Employment? Employment Subsidies vs Sabbatical Grants", Brussels.

Page, B. I., & Shapiro, R. Y. (1983). Effects of Public Opinion on Policy. *American Political Science Review, 77*(1), 175–190.

Palier, B. (Ed.). (2010). *A Long Goodbye to Bismarck? The Politics of Welfare Reform in Continental Europe*. Amsterdam University Press.

Pampel, F. C., & Williamson, J. B. (1985). Age Structure, Politics, and Cross-National Patterns of Public Pension Expenditures. *American Sociological Review, 50*(6), 782–799.

Parolin, Z., & Siöland, L. (2020). Support for a Universal Basic Income: A Demand–Capacity Paradox? *Journal of European Social Policy, 30*(1), 5–19.

Petersen, M. B. (2012). Social Welfare as Small-Scale Help: Evolutionary Psychology and the Deservingness Heuristic. *American Journal of Political Science, 56*(1), 1–16.

Pierson, P. (1993). When Effect Becomes Cause: Policy Feedback and Political Change. *World Politics, 45*(4), 595–628.

Pierson, P. (1994). *Dismantling the Welfare State? Reagan, Thatcher and the Politics of Retrenchment*. Cambridge University Press.

Pierson, P. (2000). Increasing Returns, Path Dependence, and the Study of Politics. *American Political Science Review, 94*(2), 251–267.

Pierson, P. (Ed.). (2001). *The New Politics of the Welfare State*. Oxford University Press.

Pogge, T. W. (2001). Eradicating Systemic Poverty: Brief for a Global Resources Dividend. *Journal of Human Development and Capabilities, 2*(1), 59–77.

Pulkka, V. V. (2019). "This Time May Be a Little Different"—Exploring the Finnish View on the Future of Work. *International Journal of Sociology and Social Policy, 39*(1/2), 22–37.

Raes, K. (1988). Basic Income and Social Power. In A. G. Miller (Ed.), *Proceedings of the First International Conference on Basic Income, Louvain-la-Neuve, Belgium, 4–6 September 1986* (pp. 106–122). Basic Income European Network.

Ravallion, M. (2009). *Do Poorer Countries Have Less Capacity for Redistribution?* (Policy Research Working Paper). World Bank Group.

Rennwald, L. (2020). *Social Democratic Parties and the Working Class*. Springer Nature.

Rhys Williams, J. (1943). *Something to Look Forward To. A Suggestion for a New Social Contract*. Macdonald & Co.

Richards, D. R., & Steiger, T. L. (2021). Value Orientations and Support for Guaranteed Income. *Social Science Quarterly, 102*(6), 2733–2751.

Rincon, L. (2021). *The Paradox of Universality: Preferences for Universal Basic Income in Finland and Spain* (Unpublished doctoral dissertation). Universitat de Barcelona.

Rincon, L. (2022). A Robin Hood for All: A Conjoint Experiment on Support for Basic Income. *Journal of European Public Policy*. https://doi.org/10.1080/13501763.2021.2007983 [onlinefirst]

Rincon, L., Vlandas, T., & Hiilamo, H. (2022). What's Not to Like? Benefit Design, Funding Structure and Support for Universal Basic Income. *Journal of European Social Policy, 32*(4), 467–483.

Robeyns, I. (2000). Hush Money or Emancipation Fee? A Gender Analysis of Basic Income. In R. van der Veen & L. Groot (Eds.), *Basic Income on the Agenda. Policy Objectives and Political Chances* (pp. 121–136). Amsterdam University Press.

Roosma, F. (2022). A Struggle for Framing and Interpretation: The Impact of the 'Basic Income Experiments' on Social Policy Reform in the Netherlands. *European Journal of Social Security, 24*(3), 192–212.

Roosma, F., & van Oorschot, W. (2020). Public Opinion on Basic Income: Mapping European Support for a Radical Alternative for Welfare Provision. *Journal of European Social Policy, 30*(2), 190–205.

Roosma, F., van Oorschot, W., & Gelissen, J. (2016). The Achilles' Heel of Welfare State Legitimacy: Perceptions of Overuse and Underuse of Social Benefits in Europe. *Journal of European Public Policy, 23*(2), 177–196.

Rossetti, F., Roosma, F., Laenen, T., & Abts, K. (2020). An Unconditional Basic Income? How Dutch Citizens Justify Their Opinions About a Basic Income and Work Conditionality. *Journal of International and Comparative Social Policy, 36*(3), 284–300.

Rothstein, B. (1998). *Just Institutions Matter. The Moral and Political Logic of the Universal Welfare State*. Cambridge University Press.

Rowlington, K., Sood, A., & Trinh, T. (2021). Public Attitudes to a Wealth Tax: The Importance of 'Capacity to Pay.' *Fiscal Studies, 42*(3/4), 431–455.

Rueda, D. (2007). *Social Democracy Inside Out: Partisanship and Labor Market Policy in Advanced Industrialized Democracies*. Oxford University Press.

Sanzo, L., & Pinilla, R. (2004). A Household Basic Income. In K. Widerquist, J. A. Noguera, Y. Vanderborght, & J. De Wispelaere (Eds.), *Basic Income: An Anthology of Contemporary Research*. Wiley Blackwell.

Schakel, W., Burgoon, B., & Hakhverdian, A. (2020). Real but Unequal Representation in Welfare State Reform. *Politics & Society, 48*(1), 131–163.

Scharpf, F. W. (2000). Basic Income and Social Europe. In R. van der Veen & L. Groot (Eds.), *Basic Income on the Agenda. Policy Objectives and Political Chances* (pp. 155–160). Amsterdam University Press.

Schneider, A., & Ingram, H. (1997). Social Construction of Target Populations: Implications for Politics and Policy. *American Political Science Review, 87*(2), 334–347.

Schwander, H., & Vlandas, T. (2020). The Left and Universal Basic Income: The Role of Ideology in Individual Support. *Journal of International and Comparative Social Policy, 36*(3), 237–268.

Seong Yoo, Y., Choi, G., & Yu, I. (2021a). *What Do People Think of Universal Basic Income? Findings of UBI Opinion Poll 2021: Part I* (GRI Issue & Analysis No. 455). Gyeonggi Research Institute.

Seong Yoo, Y., Choi, G., & Yu, I. (2021b). *What Do Koreans Expect of Basic Income? Findings of UBI Opinion Poll 2021: Part II* (GRI Issue & Analysis No. 456). Gyeonggi Research Institute.

Seong Yoo, Y., & Jooyoung, M. (2021). *The Public Perception Survey on Basic Income*. Gyeonggi Research Institute.

Shafarman, S. (2004). Mobilizing Support for Basic Income. In G. Standing (Ed.), *Promoting Income Security as a Right: Europe and North America* (pp. 195–206). Anthem Press.

Shelton, B. A. (2006). Gender and Unpaid Work. In J. Saltzman Chafetz (Ed.), *Handbook of the Sociology of Gender* (pp. 375–390). Springer.

Simanainen, M., & Kangas, O. (2020). Speaking to Those Who Know It Best: Does Participation in an Experiment Explain Citizens' Attitudes to Basic Income? *Journal of International and Comparative Social Policy, 36*(3), 269–283.

Simon, H. A. (2001). UBI and the Flat Tax. In P. Van Parijs (Ed.), *What's Wrong with a Free Lunch?* Beacon Press.

Skocpol, T. (1991). Targeting Within Universalism: Politically Viable Policies to Combat Poverty in the United States. In C. Jencks & P. Peterson (Eds.), *The Urban Underclass* (pp. 411–436). Brookings Institution.

Spies-Butcher, B., Philips, B., & Henderson, T. (2020). Between Universalism and Targeting: Exploring Policy Pathways for an Australian Basic Income. *The Economic and Labour Relations Review, 31*(4), 502–523.

Stadelmann-Steffen, I., & Dermont, C. (2020). Citizens' Opinions About Basic Income Proposals Compared—A Conjoint Analysis of Finland and Switzerland. *Journal of Social Policy, 49*(2), 383–403.

Stambolieva, M. (2019). *Welfare State Transformation in the Yugoslav Successor States: From Social to Unequal*. Routledge.

Stam, K. (2015). *The Moral Duty to Work: A Cross-National and Longitudinal Study of the Causes and Consequences of Work Ethic Values in Contemporary Society* (Unpublished doctoral dissertation). Ridderprint.

Standing, G. (2020). *Battling Eight Giants: Basic Income Now*. I.B. Taurus.

Statistics Belgium. (2022). *Employment and Unemployment*. https://statbel.fgov.be/en/themes/work-training/labour-market/employment-and-unemployment

Steensland, B. (2008). *The Failed Welfare Revolution. America's Struggle over Guaranteed Income Policy*. Princeton University Press.

Svallfors, S. (2012). *Contested Welfare States. Welfare Attitudes in Europe and Beyond*. Stanford University Press.

Takamatsu, R., & Tachibanaki, T. (2014). What Needs to Be Considered When Introducing a New Welfare System: Who Supports Basic Income in Japan? In Y. Vanderborght & T. Yamamori (Eds.), *Basic Income in Japan. Prospects for a Radical Idea in a Transforming Welfare State* (pp. 197–218). Palgrave Macmillan.

Tavits, M., & Letki, N. (2009). When Left Is Right: Party Ideology and Policy in Post-Communist Europe. *American Political Science Review, 103*(4), 555–569.

Taylor-Gooby, P., & Leruth, B. (2018). *Attitudes, Aspirations and Welfare: Social Policy Directions in Uncertain Times*. Palgrave Macmillan.

Thomas, C. C., Walton, G. M., Reinhart, E. C., & Markus, H. R. (2023). Mitigating Welfare-Related Prejudice and Partisanship Among U.S. Conservatives with Moral Reframing of a Universal Basic Income Policy. *Journal of Experimental Social Psychology, 105*. https://doi.org/10.1016/j.jesp.2022.104424 [online only]

Tobin, J. (1966). The Case for an Income Guarantee. *The Public Interest, 4*, 31–41.

Torry, M. (2016). *The Feasibility of Citizen's Income*. Palgrave Macmillan.

Torry, M. (Ed.). (2019). *The Palgrave International Handbook of Basic Income*. Palgrave Macmillan.

Torry, M. (2021). *Basic Income: A History*. Edward Elgar Publishing.

Tourangeau, R., Edwards, B., Johnson, T., Wolter, K., & Bates, N. (Eds.). (2014). *Hard-to-Survey Populations*. Cambridge University Press.

Vanderborght, Y. (2004). *Universal Basic Income in Belgium and the Netherlands: Implementation Through the Backdoor?* (EUI Working Paper SPS, No. 2004/4). European University Institute.

Vanderborght, Y. (2006). Why Trade Unions Oppose Basic Income. *Basic Income Studies, 1*(1). https://doi.org/10.2202/1932-0183.1002 [online only]

van der Veen, R. (2019). Basic Income Experiments in the Netherlands? *Basic Income Studies, 14*(1). https://doi.org/10.1515/bis-2018-0023 [online only]

Van Hootegem, A., & Laenen, T. (2022). A Wave of Support? A Natural Experiment on How the COVID-19 Pandemic Affected the Popularity of a Basic Income. *Acta Politica*. https://doi.org/10.1057/s41269-022-00260-9 [online first]

van Oorschot, W. (2000). Who Should Get What, and Why? On Deservingness Criteria and the Conditionality of Solidarity Among the Public. *Policy & Politics, 28*(1), 33–48.

van Oorschot, W. (2006). Making the Difference in Social Europe: Deservingness Perceptions among Citizens of European Welfare States. *Journal of European Public Policy, 16*(1), 23–42.

van Oorschot, W. (2008). Solidarity Towards Immigrants in European Welfare States. *International Journal of Social Welfare, 17*(1), 3–14.

van Oorschot, W., Laenen, T., Roosma, F., & Meuleman, B. (2022). Recent Advances in Understanding Welfare Attitudes in Europe. In K. Nelson, R. Nieuwenhuis, & M. Yerkes (Eds.), *Social Policy in Changing European Societies, Research Agendas for the 21st Century* (pp. 202–217). Edward Elgar Publishing.

van Oorschot, W., & Meuleman, B. (2012). Welfare Performance and Welfare Support. In S. Svallfors (Ed.), *Contested Welfare States: Welfare Attitudes in Europe and Beyond* (pp. 25–57). Stanford University Press.

van Oorschot, W., Reeskens, T., & Meuleman, B. (2012). Popular Perceptions of Welfare State Consequences: A Multilevel, Cross-National Analysis of 25 European Countries. *Journal of European Social Policy, 22*(2), 181–197.

Van Parijs, P. (2004). Basic Income: A Simple and Powerful Idea for the Twenty-First Century. *Politics & Society, 32*(1), 7–39.

Van Parijs, P., & Vanderborght, Y. (2001). From Euro-Stipendium to Euro-Dividend. *Journal of European Social Policy, 11*(4), 342–346.

Van Parijs, P., & Vanderborght, Y. (2017). *A Radical Proposal for a Free Society and a Sane Economy*. Harvard University Press.

Van Trier, W. (2018, January 3–5). *Scheme for a State Bonus and the Early Roots of the Basic Income Idea in the UK*. Paper Presented at the HES Sponsored Session "Basic Income: The Past and the Present", AEA-ASSA Conference, Philadelphia.

Vlandas, T. (2021). The Political Economy of Individual-Level Support for the Basic Income in Europe. *Journal of European Social Policy, 31*(1), 62–77.

Weisstanner, D. (2022). COVID-19 and Welfare State Support: The Case of Universal Basic Income. *Policy & Society, 41*(1), 96–110.

Widerquist, K. (2018). *A Critical Analysis of Basic Income Experiments for Researchers, Policymakers, and Citizens*. Palgrave Macmillan.

Widerquist, K., & Howard, M. W. (Eds.). (2012). *Alaska's Permanent Fund Dividend. Examining Its Suitability as a Model*. Palgrave Macmillan.

Widerquist, K., Noguera, J. A., Vanderborght, Y., & De Wispelaere, J. (Eds.). (2013). *Basic Income: An Anthology of Contemporary Research*. Wiley Blackwell.

Widerquist, K., & Sheahan, A. (2012). The United States: The Basic Income Guarantee—Past Experience, Current Proposals. In M. C. Murray & C. Pateman (Eds.), *Basic Income Worldwide. Horizons of Reform* (pp. 11–30). Palgrave Macmillan.

Wilensky, H. (1975). *The Welfare State and Equality: Structural and Ideological Roots of Public Expenditure*. University of California Press.

Wlezien, C., & Soroka, S. N. (2012). Political Institutions and the Opinion-Policy Link. *West European Politics, 35*(6), 1407–1432.

Wright, R. E., & Przegalinska, A. (2022). *Debating Universal Basic Income. Pros, Cons, and Alternatives*. Palgrave Macmillan.

Yang, J., Mohan, G., & Fukushi, K. (2020). An Analysis of the Factors Influencing Public Attitudes Toward Implementing Basic Income (BI) from an Individual Perspective: A Case Study of Hokuriku Region, Japan. *Societies, 10*(3). https://doi.org/10.3390/soc10030052 [online only]

Yeung, E. S. (2022). Can Conservatives Be Persuaded? Framing Effects on Support for Universal Basic Income in the US. *Political Behavior*. https://doi.org/10.1007/s11109-022-09824-z [online first]

Zaller, J. R. (1992). *The Nature and Origins of Mass Opinion*. Cambridge University Press.

Zimmermann, K., Boljka, U., Rakar, T., & Filipovic Hrast, M. (2020). The Social Legitimacy of the Universal Basic Income From a Social Justice Perspective: A Comparative Analysis of Germany and Slovenia. *Journal of International and Comparative Social Policy, 36*(3), 301–331.

Index

© The Editor(s) (if applicable) and The Author(s), under exclusive license to Springer Nature Switzerland AG 2023

T. Laenen, *The Popularity of Basic Income*, Exploring the Basic Income Guarantee, https://doi.org/10.1007/978-3-031-29352-8

The manufacturer's authorised representative in the EU is Springer Nature Customer Service Centre GmbH, Europaplatz 3, 69115 Heidelberg, Germany. If you have any concerns regarding our products, please contact ProductSafety@springernature.com

Printed and bound by CPI Group (UK) Ltd, Croydon, CR0 4YY
01/10/2026
02225894-0016